ADVANCE PRAISE FOR
EVERYTHING IS AN AFTERTHOUGHT
THE LIFE AND WRITINGS OF PAUL NELSON

"Paul was one of my first and most ardent supporters when I played at Max's Kansas City. He was one of the great early voices of rock criticism."

—**BRUCE SPRINGSTEEN**
singer-songwriter

"If it wasn't for Kevin Avery, the life and work of one of the world's first and greatest rock writers might otherwise have remained scattered in time and space. Written and compiled with intelligence, meticulousness, and passion, *Everything Is an Afterthought* is simultaneously a moving biography, a classic criticism anthology, an earnest expression of fandom, and, most importantly, an overdue addition to the canon of essential rock books."

—**NEIL STRAUSS**
author of *The Game* and
Everyone Loves You When You're Dead

"Paul Nelson's life was a fierce quiet drama of devotion to culture, with a run of triumphs along the way to a slow-motion tragedy. This book restores the triumphs of his writing to a conversation that may not have known, or remembered, what it was missing. That alone would make this book essential; the biographical research, the unpublished pieces, and the photographs make it a human saga as well, as heartbreaking as the novel or film Nelson never managed to write. The whole thing proceeds out of Kevin Avery's own quiet devotion, for which I can hardly express my gratitude."

—**JONATHAN LETHEM**
author of *Chronic City*
and *Motherless Brooklyn*

"Paul was his own kind of subterranean—disappearing around corners on the surface, thinking his way through the catacombs beneath it. He cultivated his obsessions over decades, until he could pass on the glow they gave off for him to other people. He left behind more than one ghost, and many of them are in this book."

—**GREIL MARCUS**
author of *Like a Rolling Stone:
Bob Dylan at the Crossroads*

"This is a rich and mysterious book. Kevin Avery has glimpsed Nelson's soul, and the image he presents is fascinating and deeply human. Avery's respect (and affection) for Nelson is evident, but the details he presents of this elusive man's life are effectively clear-eyed. We sense the joy in Nelson's creative gift and equally shiver in the shadows of his dark side.

"Yet, shimmering through it all are Nelson's words. No one wrote about music the way he did. You can feel the rhythm in every phrase. His writing moves like an effortlessly constructed wave carrying insight, understanding, and thought that is always profoundly satisfying and original."

—TOM DICILLO
writer-director of *When You're Strange:
A Film About the Doors*

"This book beautifully balances Paul Nelson's life and work, the struggling man and the gifted craftsman. Its Nelson is equal parts Hammett and Bartleby, a connoisseur and a Coke-head, possessed of wisdom and uniquely self-destructive. That Paul's actual writing makes up half the book takes nothing away from Kevin Avery's scrupulous reporting and remarkable empathy with his subject. I don't know if the story of my friend and mentor, colleague and neighbor will break your heart. But that's exactly what it did to mine, and in a way that leaves me grateful."

—DAVE MARSH
author and SiriusXM radio show host

"Paul was a classic personality of his times. Radically talented, seriously flawed, loved by many of us, forgotten by too many of us, Kevin Avery brings him to life in his sympathetic biography and his fine selection of Paul's writing."

—JON LANDAU
critic and producer

"In this riveting, original and comprehensive biography, Avery not only captures the essence of one of the first and finest chroniclers of rock and roll history, but he gives us insight into the oddly mysterious character that so many called 'friend.' Paul Nelson was as odd as he was honest, as eccentric as he was salt-of-the-earth, as outspoken as he was introverted—a brilliant journalist who walked away from it all and left us wanting. Thank you, Kevin Avery, for your masterful portrait of this important man, and for bringing back to life his work, without which no history of rock and roll would be complete."

—CRYSTAL ZEVON
author of *I'll Sleep When I'm Dead:
The Dirty Life and Times of Warren Zevon*

"Kevin Avery has done something heroic here. Avery has rescued the work and the passion, the life and the meaning of the great Paul Nelson. Nelson was a deep and beautiful writer, mysterious and painstaking and brilliant. Thanks to Avery and *Everything Is an Afterthought*, Paul Nelson's work finally has a home. This wonderful writing is here for the faithful, and now forever available for new fans who'll never forget him."

—**CAMERON CROWE**
writer-director of
Almost Famous and *Jerry Maguire*

"Like the very greatest critics, Paul Nelson took whatever he wrote about far too personally. He was a dynamo of hyper-responsiveness, his tastes forever in motion and never at rest. This book is a chance to tap into his mind and energize our own minds in the process. Just make sure to read it at full volume."

—**WALTER KIRN**
author of *Up in the Air*
and *Thumbsucker*

"F. Scott Fitzgerald said, 'Show me a hero and I'll write you a tragedy.' Once upon a time, Paul Nelson was my hero and in many ways his life was a tragedy. But nobody ever wrote about the music that matters with such poetic intensity, such delirious commitment as Paul did. He opened my eyes, ears and imagination to the holy trinity of Music, Books & Films. *Everything Is an Afterthought* is a finely written and well-deserved legacy … Thanks, Kevin Avery."

—**ELLIOTT MURPHY**
singer-songwriter

"Here is the gospel according to Paul Nelson. Finally, that unholy ghost in Rock-kritics' Trinity—with Lester the father, Nick Kent the bastard son—has received his due. Amen to Avery."

—**CLINTON HEYLIN**
author of *Dylan Behind the Shades*

"*Everything Is an Afterthought* is remarkable. A biography, literary excavation, history of rock 'n' roll—New York wing. Kevin Avery summons all appropriate demons for a party of the first quality. Everyone is present and speaking, as if for the first time. All your heroes, all everyone's heroes. If you care about the culture of the Sixties and the years that followed, you must read this book."

—**FREDERICK BARTHELME**
novelist and short story writer

EVERYTHING IS AN AFTERTHOUGHT

Also by Kevin Avery:

Conversations with Clint:
Paul Nelson's Lost Interviews with Clint Eastwood
1979–1983

EVERYTHING IS AN AFTERTHOUGHT

The Life and Writings of

PAUL NELSON

Kevin Avery

FANTAGRAPHICS BOOKS

Fantagraphics Books
7563 Lake City Way NE
Seattle, Washington 98115

Editor: Gary Groth
Designer: Jeff Wong
Associate Publisher: Eric Reynolds
Publishers: Gary Groth and Kim Thompson

EVERYTHING IS AN AFTERTHOUGHT
The Life and Writings of Paul Nelson

To receive a free full-color catalog of comics, graphic novels, prose novels, artist monographs, and other fine works of artistry, call 1-800-657-1100, or visit www.fantagraphics.com.
You may order books at our web site or by phone.

Distributed in the U.S. by W.W. Norton and Company, Inc. (800-233-4830)
Distributed in Canada by Canadian Manda Group (fax 888-563-8327)
Distributed in the U.K. by Turnaround Distribution (44 (0)20 8829-3002)
Distributed to comic stores by Diamond Comics Distributors (800-452-6642 x215)

ISBN: 978-1-60699-475-7

First Fantagraphics Books printing: November, 2011

For Paul

TABLE OF CONTENTS

Unless otherwise indicated, Paul Nelson's work is reprinted herein as originally published.
† indicates that the work is reprinted as written from the original manuscript.
‡ indicates that the work is previously unpublished.

- FOREWORD -
BY
NICK TOSCHES

It seemed we were always amid shadows when we were together, he and I. Beautiful bright afternoons, dark nights, indoors, outdoors. Somehow it always felt like it was him and me and shadows.

I remember walking out of my front door one day. I hadn't seen him in years. There he was sitting on a stoop directly across the street. This was on Commerce Street, in the Village. I walked over, sat beside him, and it was as if those years that had passed had never passed. The same familiar Paul, lean and languid, in his newsboy cap and dark shades, the smoke from that non-filter brown Nat Sherman of his drifting toward nothingness. He looked, as always, as the quiet guy amid the dim of the somewhat unfathomable noir tale that was his life. If you didn't know him, you might say he looked suspicious. If you knew him, you would laugh at that notion.

I asked him what he was up to. Just waiting to go to work, he said. He had a job at Evergreen Video, a store a few blocks away on Carmine Street. When I had first met him, maybe fifteen or more years before, he was a big deal at Mercury Records. He was no different then than he was now. One job, another job, what did it matter? That's why they called it "the job."

My friend Richard Meltzer and I had very little money back when Paul was at Mercury, and he took us about once a week to a good lunch at an Italian restaurant uptown, and then at his office gave us all the free records we wanted or could carry. Records for listening, records for selling. He always ate the same thing at the same restaurant. I remember what he ate more than I remember the name of the restaurant. Veal piccata. And he always drank Coke with it. He always drank Coke, period. I never saw him take a drink of liquor, or even a beer for that matter. There was some sort of memorial service for Lester Bangs in the spring of 1982. It was on Fourteenth Street. We were looking to get out of there, and we ended up walking back to my place. He opened the refrigerator to get a Coke and seemed shocked that I didn't have any. It may have been his most pronounced reaction to anything I witnessed him encounter.

The only thing that had changed, between that executive office uptown and the video store downtown, was that he was now broke. He had just taken care of his mother in her dying days, and he had returned from her death without the last of what he had. I was pretty bad-off myself at the time, but I lent him some money. Two hundred, something like that. He seemed to sense that I myself needed it almost as much as he did; and somehow he did manage to pay me back exactly when he said he would. To me, he was that kind of guy.

I took to visiting and hanging out with him at the video store. He always worked nights. God knows what we talked about. Everything. That's what we talked about: everything. Yes, everything and nothing. Which, in the end, is what it all comes down to. And I always felt better after we talked.

One time he ended up in the hospital. Bellevue, where they have to accept everybody, regardless of circumstance. I don't recall what he was in there for. Probably some undiagnosable malaise of the shadows. Probably for being Paul Nelson. I went up there to see him on a weekend afternoon, bringing him some Nat Shermans and Coke. As I was searching for his ward, the sky through the windows darkened, turned almost black as night, thunder boomed, lightning flashed, and there came a storm to end all storms. It was like something out of a bad horror picture. I remember all these characters, wraiths and big lost fat black daddy-cool-breezes alike, wandering the halls, mumbling, talking trash to unknown spirits, trying to grub smokes from me. It *was* a bad horror picture.

Finally I found Paul, placid in his bed. We spent a good while together, the darkness and thunder and lightning a perfect background, especially for what we ended up talking about: the 1947 movie *Nightmare Alley*. I think it was Paul on that stormy, eerie afternoon who first told me about the novel on which it was based, and about William Lindsay Gresham, who wrote it and ended up killing himself in a Times Square hotel room. It was an afternoon I'll never forget. Paul said he had an old book, *Tough Guy Writers of the Thirties*, that had something about Gresham in it, and that he'd find it and lay it on me when he got out. And he did find it and give it to me when he got out. As I said, he was that kind of guy. I've got that book beside me right now as I write this. I look at it, and I see Paul and I feel all the inarticulable feelings I have for him now as I had for him in life. He was one of a kind.

He was also a remarkable writer, with one of the most singularly subtle eloquent voices of his time. And he never wrote about anything he didn't know to the full of its depths. But whatever the opposite of prolific is, that was Paul. To say that he wrote slowly and with profound care is an understatement. I remember when I heard that he was reviewing my book *Hellfire* for *Rolling Stone*. How great this was, I felt. How bad this was, I felt. For I believed that no matter how wonderful and perceptive his review would be, he would ultimately never finish writing it.

I was wrong. He did finish it. And all that rare subtle eloquence of his took a deep breath at one point, and he said plainly, like an exhalation of that Sherman smoke of his, that the book was "quite simply the best rock and roll biography ever written." To me, coming from him, that meant a lot.

He had about him at times a certain melancholy. And it's hard to remember him without feeling a certain melancholy. But, far more meaningful and far more powerful, was the sense of taciturn strength he emanated. No matter how bad a deal this world dealt him, as it often did, he remained unvanquished.

That day when I encountered him on the stoop, he mused a bit in that quiet voice of his about how he was ever going to get out of the straits he was in, I asked him if any possibilities had come to him. With the slightest of smiles, a smile as grave as it was light, he said: "Outlawry."

I knew the word, of course, but I had never heard anybody actually say it. Then again, I had never known anybody else like Paul Nelson. Outlawry. It was something—not the word, but what it meant—that he had been practicing all his life, perhaps without knowing it. In a way, it was the very thew and sinew of his life.

Not many of us really knew him, either personally—and I consider having known him as such to be a gift—or through his writing, which has been far too under-known, under-recognized, and under-remembered.

No, he was not prolific, and no, he was certainly never prolix, not in speaking, not in writing. But this was a blessing of sorts. The words he did deliver were and are as remarkably fine as what he stood for and what he was.

EVERYTHING IS AN AFTERTHOUGHT

The older you get, the more you live with ghosts. Some of them haunt you, some of them comfort you. Paul is one of the latter.

I have no glib writerly line with which to end what I've said here. Glib last lines are for glib last-liners. So I'll say only that there is something noble in what Kevin Avery has undertaken in this book—to bring Paul Nelson and his writing closer to us and make them more known to us, both the writer and the writing, as they most surely deserve to be.

- INTRODUCTION -

In his critiques of various artists, Paul Nelson may at times come across as too obsessed, too much of a fan. If the truth be known, he lives his life by rock & roll's most important virtue: friendship.

I used to envy Nelson because he could call so many of my heroes his friends. But I was wrong. It's them I envy for having a friend as fine as Paul Nelson.

—KEVIN AVERY,
April 30, 1981,
a letter to *Rolling Stone*[1]

Straight from his pen to my heart—his words connected with me in a way few other writers' did. Beginning in the Seventies, as a teenager, I heard what he'd heard, felt what he'd felt. Pointing me towards music that was new, he introduced me to the old. I'd learn that in his later life he'd sometimes lament that he hadn't taken a teaching path, yet that's what he'd been doing all along. He helped me understand and verbalize why I felt the way I did about rock & roll: that it was a belief system

1 "Zevon Resurrected" by Kevin Avery from *Rolling Stone*, April 30, 1981. © Rolling Stone LLC 1981. All rights reserved. Reprinted by permission.

founded in the kind of "you're supposed to do something about it" ethos embodied by Bogart and Sam Spade. Reflecting the hardboiled sensibility of the detective writing he so admired, his clean, sharp prose illuminated the shadows. Forever concerned with friendship and loyalty, it seemed as if, when something mattered to him, he wanted it to matter to me, the reader, too.

He taught me that all good romantics destroy everything they touch and that the worst thing in life is that everyone has his reasons. I somehow knew that these two maxims explained why, in the early Eighties, his byline became more and more scarce, finally vanishing altogether.

The decades passed, but I never forgot Paul Nelson.

In February of 2006, after having moved a couple of months before from Salt Lake City to Brooklyn and bringing with me clippings of everything of his I'd ever read, I wrote him a letter—as much an unabashed fan letter as it was a business proposition—and suggested that we work together to collect his best works into book form. I never received a response—not directly anyway.

Five months later the phone rang. Michael Seidenberg introduced himself and said he was calling to tell me that his good friend Paul Nelson had passed away. That Paul had been dead a week before somebody discovered his body in his apartment, on the Fourth of July. Eviction looming, and his short-term memory so bad that he had to leave notes to remind himself to go out for food, he'd simply shut down and stopped eating.

INCIDENT REPORT

019 PCT 153 EAST 67 STREET NEW YORK, NY 10021   DATE: 7 / 4 / 06
Telephone: 212-452-0600/01/02/03

ACCIDENT#_____   COMPLAINT#_____   AIDED#_____

LOCATION OF
OCCURRENCE: 4 0 0   E 7 4 ST

DATE OF OCCURRENCE: 7 / 4 06

TYPE OF INCIDENT/CLASSIFICATION OF OFFENSE:_____

REPORTING OFFICER: JAN EC   SHIELD# #6068

019 PCT 153 EAST 67 STREET NEW YORK, NY 10021
Telephone: 212-452-0600/01/02/03

With all these sad details swirling around in my head like dried leaves on a dreary autumn day, I heard Seidenberg say that Paul had been touched by my letter.

"Paul really felt that he was forgotten. When you sent the letter, he was very excited about that. A number of times he would say to me, 'Let's call that guy. Let's have him here.' I was just waiting for him to be a little clearer-headed. Because some days he'd be more alert, but then he'd have patches of bad times. The thing was, he was always clear about the past."

On July 4, the temperature was almost ninety degrees for the third day in a row on Manhattan's Upper East Side. The police received a call from someone at 400 East Seventy-Fourth Street regarding a strange smell seeping from the top corner apartment.

> DECEASED WAS FOUND SUPINE ON MATTRESS IN BEDROOM OF APT. EMS PRONOUNCED INDIVIDUAL DOA AT 1930 HRS. DECEASED LIVED ALONE IN APT FOR SEVERAL YEARS. NO MEDICATIONS FOUND AT APT. BODY REMOVED TO MORGUE.... UNIDENTIFIED....

The NYPD complaint report failed to mention those features that would automatically register with his friends upon the mere mention of his name: the flat cap (placed one last time upon the shelf just inside the door), the dark glasses, the little brown Nat Sherman Cigarettellos, and his penchant for ordering two Cokes with every meal. The most important fact omitted, however, was that the body in Apartment 21 belonged to a writer as brilliant as he was forgotten, whose almost entire sum of work was lost to out-of-print back issues of a variety of magazines and newspapers, many of which had gone the way of his prose, a kind of critical writing, as beautiful as it was exacting, no longer practiced.

The police may not have known to whom the body on the mattress on the floor belonged, but if they had ever read his heartfelt and harrowing account of singer-songwriter Warren Zevon's struggle with alcoholism, they would've never forgotten it.

The following January, forty-two-year-old Mark Nelson, a lawyer who had seen his father only a handful of times since childhood, flew in from Dallas to collect Paul Nelson's belongings and cremains. Because nobody had been allowed to identify the body, the medical examiner had kept the apartment sealed until DNA testing was completed. Over five months passed until the ME finally issued a death certificate. Even in death the notoriously slow-writing Paul Nelson had managed to drag out a deadline.

Mark called to say that I should come over to his dad's apartment, that there was something I should see. After climbing the eighty or so steps to the sixth-story walk-up, I stepped into the apartment and was engulfed by years' worth of clutter. Thousands of books and CDs and videotapes occupied every level space. I got the feeling that everything Paul Nelson had ever loved or forgotten—or loved *and* forgotten—was contained in these three rooms. Names and numbers were scribbled on the walls in Magic Marker. There was a plastic clamshell case in which he kept his money and his important papers. Post-it Notes splattered every surface with reminder after reminder of his favorite grocery items—Tropicana apple juice, ice, cigs, cookies, and a variety of cough suppressants: Ricola Honey Herb ("pretty good") and Orange ("not this CVS stuff"), and Robitussin Honey Lemon and Menthol

Mark Nelson enters Paul's apartment on January 28, 2007, after the medical examiner unseals it. Photo by Kevin Avery.

cough suppressant ("the best")—and notes like *I need some money. I got $15.00 total. I need some meals* and *I got $2. I'm hungry. Thirsty.* Among them Mark pointed out at least a half dozen instances where his father had written, in various combinations, my name, address, and phone number. *The book guy*, one tiny strip of paper read. *Get his phone number. Meet him.*

"**A** lot of people have celebrated Lester Bangs's writing already," singer-songwriter Elliott Murphy says, "and for me Paul Nelson was in the same league at the total opposite end of the spectrum. He wrote about rock & roll with a sense of romanticism and seriousness and very interesting connections to all other art forms, particularly American literature."

Writer Mikal Gilmore says, "In all the years that I've been caring about this world of rock & roll—and also the world of rock & roll criticism, history, and writing, which in many ways has meant as much to me as the music and that I've gotten as much from—there is nobody that I felt more enriched by, moved by, informed by, educated by than Paul. In the end, he certainly means as much to me as Dylan."

In 1987, in his introduction to *Psychotic Reactions and Carburetor Dung*, Greil Marcus wrote of fellow critic Lester Bangs:

> Perhaps what this book demands from a reader is a willingness to accept that the best writer in America could write almost nothing but record reviews.

Though I might quibble, it wouldn't be to place Paul Nelson upon a similar mantel. To paraphrase what he wrote about his beloved New York Dolls: I do not claim he was the best, but Paul Nelson is still my favorite writer, although I will understand if you do not like him. I will understand, but deep down, I will not want to know you.

Surrounded for fourteen years by old cinema, which he loved even more than music, Evergreen Video served as Paul Nelson's sanctuary from writing about music, which, for all its demands on his psyche, proved more a passion than a love, something to be wrangled rather than embraced. In 1976, he had written of Bob Dylan, the Rolling Stones, and Jackson Browne: "I couldn't live without their music"; but by the Nineties, Ralph Stanley, Chet Baker, and Johnny Cash had all but supplanted them.

He also retreated from ten, twenty, thirty, forty years' worth of friends, whose calls he seldom if ever returned. It was more likely that they encountered him on the street, which, with his leather bag full of favorite bluegrass CDs slung over his shoulder, he navigated with the same unhurried pace that he applied to his writing. For most of his friends, however, he just faded away.

Robert Christgau, his editor at *The Village Voice* in the early Seventies, recalls their last meeting in 2005: "I saw him on the street in the wintertime near St. Mark's Bookshop. He told me that he was listening to bluegrass— maybe it was Ralph Stanley—and that was all he could listen to. He'd gone back to where he'd started. We talked for five minutes. He looked like a bum." He corrects himself. "No, it wasn't that, it was that he was missing *teeth*. That's always a sign that someone is not in very good shape. His voice was very quiet, the way it tended to be, but more so. And I was made slightly uncomfortable by the *holes*—holes where teeth should have been.

"Not a person I felt I wanted to be close to, nor did I feel that he wanted me to be close to him. From what I understand, in those last years you really had to make an effort, and I certainly wasn't going to do that. It was a completely cordial five-minute conversation, but then we said goodbye."

"Even with that," screenwriter Jay Cocks says of his old friend Paul Nelson's "dental tribulations," "he had tremendous élan. It was the hat and the shades and the Nat Shermans that really did it. But there was not a sliver or a measurable ounce of bullshit in Paul. Not a moment. There was no moment of falsity, there was no moment of dishonesty in his life or his writing. He may have been looking for refuge all the time from whatever *deep* demons he had, but he never came on as being anyone or anything other than what he was. He was remarkable."

In the East Village on the evening of Thursday, September 7, 2006, a little over two months after Paul Nelson's body had been found, I attended a memorial service at St. Mark's Church in-the-Bowery, the second oldest church in Manhattan. Critic Kurt Loder, the elder presence at MTV, presided over the ceremony. The small Parish Hall was packed with a great many of Paul's old friends, as well as yesterday and today's rock critic establishment. Bill Flanagan, executive vice president at VH1, remarked, "It's actually amazing that so many people who could not agree on anything could all agree on loving Paul."

Photographer David Gahr was an old friend. "He's got about 200 people that loved him. The rest of the people don't know he exists and never did."

It was difficult for many members of the Evergreen Video staff, who'd worked with Paul for so many of his final years, to connect the man being described from the lectern—an influential figure from the Sixties and Seventies—with the endearing curmudgeon they'd known. They felt somewhat shortchanged, as if, because the setting was a video rental store, Paul hadn't touched their lives, too.

Critic Dave Marsh spoke first, clutching a battered first edition of *Red Harvest* that Paul had given him. "On the way down here, I got to reading it and the spine fell apart. I thought maybe there'd be something of Paul in the book, but other than the precision of the writing I couldn't really think what it was.

"I can remember him walking into my office at *Rolling Stone* one afternoon to declare that he had found the next Jackson Browne—this guy named Townes Van Zandt. I said, 'Really? Is he that good?' He said, 'Yeah. You kind of have to get past the voice.'"

"You never read even the smallest capsule record review by Paul," Ken Tucker, *Entertainment Weekly's* editor-at-large, says "without knowing immediately that he had listened to that music over and over, had given it the full benefit of his concentration, and had attempted to figure out the artist's best intentions and to come to some conclusion as to whether he or she had achieved them." He fondly recalls a late-night viewing in Paul's apartment of Sam Peckinpah's *The Killer Elite*. "And when it was all over, Paul broke the silence by saying, 'Yeah, boy, Gig Young. There's a guy who got a raw deal out of life.'"

Crystal Zevon began by noting that the day marked the third anniversary of her ex-husband Warren Zevon's death. "Paul was in our lives for the highlights. He took us to Santa Barbara to meet Ross Macdonald. Two days later, he was around for the birth of our daughter Ariel. He came to Boston to celebrate with us when we called to tell him that 'Werewolves of London' was a hit. And later he came to Santa Barbara when Warren tried to get sober.

"When Warren was diagnosed with cancer, he asked me to write his biography after he was gone. My first thought, true, was that I had to find Paul Nelson. But no one could ever tell me exactly how to find him. As I started working on the Warren Zevon book, I tried harder and people promised to give him my messages, but he never called."

Lenny Kaye, rock critic-turned-rocker, took the podium with his guitar and sang, as a nod to Paul's love of Chet Baker, "My Funny Valentine."

Sarah Lazin, founder of Rolling Stone Press, recalled that "At one point I actually had a contract in hand for a biography of Warren Zevon by Paul Nelson. We almost had it signed, and then he decided not to do it, and I don't know why."

New York Dolls front man David Johansen delivered a eulogy that was at once funny and reverent and profane. "I've been asked to say a few kind words about Paul Nelson. Really all I could come up with was: Jon Pankake was worse." Pankake had been Paul's best friend back in Minnesota. After the nervous laughter subsided, Johansen added, "I'm kidding, I don't know Jon Pankake. Tough crowd.

"I met Paul at Mercer Art Center. And right away, you know, I understood what kind of guy he was, because I had been hanging around the East Village for a couple of years and I knew the *type*. Not that he wasn't unique, but there was a certain type of person who was really an *appreciator* of music. A lot of people in life go around and think of things that they can complain about. I think Paul's whole life was just kind of *whipping past* the stuff he didn't dig until he found something he dug and then he grabbed onto it. He picked the best way to live."

Voice quavering, Mark Nelson said, "I want to start out by saying a few things about Paul that I don't think anybody knows except for his sister Linda and her family, who are also here tonight. Some of this will center around cheeseburgers, I think." He talked about his father's disdain for vegetables. "He used to basically sit there as long as it would take him to sit until his family finally gave up—he was more stubborn than they were—and then he'd go out to the drive-in and order a hamburger. And that's where he met my mother—his ex-wife. She worked at a drive-in, complete with the roller skates and the head bob. He married his high school sweetheart and the homecoming queen—my mother—and I can say with a hundred percent authority that she still loves him to this day."

Writer Kit Rachlis came from the opposite coast to tell how Paul introduced him to Los Angeles. "My theory is that he loved Los Angeles

With Ross Macdonald (left) and Warren Zevon (right) at the Coral Casino Beach Club in Santa Barbara, July 31, 1976. Photo by Crystal Zevon.

because he had lived there so long in his imagination, including Ross Macdonald's and Raymond Chandler's." He recalled how, after they spent five days interviewing Kenneth Millar (Macdonald's real name) in Santa Barbara, Paul and he took a Trailways bus to Hollywood. "We went to Musso & Frank. He, of course, ordered two Cokes. We then spent the rest of the night looking for where Lew Archer and Philip Marlowe's offices had to be. It turned out Lew Archer's place was now a Denny's, which just crushed Paul. He looked up at me and said, 'How could you not like this place?' And that's the way I feel about it when I read Paul's writing.

"There is something about the quality of Paul's prose. I do think—and I'm risking offending many people in this room—that he was one of the few greatest stylists that rock & roll criticism ever produced. There's a purity and a precision and a compassion for the language that he used. You read that stuff and it takes you to a kind of world that, for Paul, was an ideal world."

Michael Seidenberg came up and said: "He was not clinically depressed. Paul was depressed at the end because he wasn't feeling well, he was losing

At Mercury Records in the early Seventies.

his apartment, life was just not working out so well. But he never wasn't Paul and never was not in control of his own life. And as far as his end and how he died, I think that Paul always made his own decisions. He made the decision to leave *Sing Out!* magazine, he made the decision to leave *Rolling Stone*, and he made a decision to leave life. He just stopped."

Critic Anthony DeCurtis had a decidedly different view of how Paul chose to spend his final years (i.e., working in a video store). "The power in Paul's writing came from his sense in the belief of what music can accomplish in people's life and what it could mean. For him to be *that* good, and do writing that's *that* important and *that* significant and be *that* prominent and end up in *that* place, that was harsh, it was really harsh."

INTRODUCTION

Afterwards, Warren Zevon's "Lawyers, Guns and Money" took over the PA system and the crowd made its way out to the courtyard and the awaiting night. David Johansen found Michael Seidenberg and hugged him for what he'd said. Seidenberg found Anthony DeCurtis and told him, "I think all you guys just get nervous that this can happen to you."

Barbara "Bobbi" London approached Mark Nelson and slipped a note into his hand, saying that she can probably answer some questions for him. Paul had left his wife—and Mark—for her back in the Sixties.

Gahr: "Since I don't hear well, it bored the piss out of me. I didn't understand a word." But the significance of the event wasn't lost on him. In words worthy of Peckinpah, he said, "Paul rode with me a long way. We were very close, but it's the kind of close that didn't take place with words. He knew who I was and I was sure aware of who he was, and that's all you needed. I figured if Paul wanted my company, he would've sought me out. And he didn't. I tried.

"But I tell you, life is very difficult. Many things to take care of."

If Paul had been asked to speak that night, he probably would have applied his own aesthetic rule of thumb to the life being considered: "Anything that you can explain 100 percent isn't worth bothering to explain at all."

About Elliott Murphy, Paul Nelson wrote:

> If we are all, to some extent, a compilation of those whom we most admire, Murphy takes it a huge step further; he *needs* heroes, desires dreams, for personal and artistic sustenance. He wears his idols—most of them, significantly, dead ("The past is all that lasts," he has written elsewhere)—proudly on his sleeve: James Dean, Greta Garbo, Scott Fitzgerald, Ezra Pound, Ernest Hemingway, Lord Byron, Jimi Hendrix, Brian Jones, and Lou Reed.... Haunted by their singular accomplishments and trapped by their collective unrealized expectations, none so different from his own, the artist discovers a common ground in the painful struggle to both answer and retain the romantic's archetypal dilemma: How does one deal with the loss of important illusions when those illusions are clearly the key to one's own survival?[2]

2 "Elliott Murphy—*Lost Generation*" by Paul Nelson from *Rolling Stone*, July 17, 1975. © Rolling Stone LLC 1975. All rights reserved. Reprinted by permission. Reprinted from the original manuscript, which first appeared in *Rolling Stone* as an edited version.

Nobody wore his idols (many of the same ones attributed to Murphy) on his sleeve more proudly than Paul. Is it possible that, living without the nourishment of those whom he had once called heroes, he had in effect surrendered his own illusions? Without them, what remained? Had he, like Gatsby, "paid too high a price for living too long with a single dream," and, if so, what was that dream?

"I think the day he stopped writing is the day he stopped growing," Dave Marsh speculates.

If that's the case and he abandoned his typewriter prematurely, the best part of the story remains in what he *did* write, his extraordinary words revealing as much about the man himself as the subjects he wrote about. The rest of what follows, my words, like Nick Carraway's about Gatsby, that elegant object of his own admiration, merely point the way back to Paul Nelson, into whose life I arrived too late, but who came into mine none too soon.

—KEVIN AVERY,
Brooklyn, New York,
February 11, 2011

- BOOK ONE -

INVITATION TO A CLOSED ROOM:
THE LIFE OF PAUL NELSON

His writing was flinty, elliptical, and romantic, an unusual combination. He was drawn to loners and the excluded. There was something seductively hermetic about his work, an invitation to a closed room.

—GREIL MARCUS

1

With mother Clara and father Clifford Nelson circa 1938.

BORN January 21, 1936, in the Red River Valley corner of Minnesota, Paul Clifford Nelson grew fond of telling people, "It was forty-five below the day I was born. I thought the whole world might be forty-five below. Who knew?" Clara and Clifford Nelson, his Warren-born and raised, second-generation Swedish-immigrant parents, had married five months before. Paul's presence at the wedding was never openly discussed.

Clifford, who was almost twelve years older than Clara, was a savvy and successful businessman who'd quickly gone from pumping gas to operating the whole service station. He'd lost almost everything in the stock market crash, then gained it all back. A couple of years before Paul was born, Clifford, with his brother Eddie and sister Hilda, took over the local Ford-Mercury dealership and built it into one of Minnesota's largest agencies. Warren, a community with a slowly dwindling population of about 1,500 citizens, mostly of Swedish and Norwegian descent, was largely rural. Clifford also acquired a JI Case franchise, selling farming equipment, and owned a 2,000-acre farm of his own, where the hired help raised mostly wheat and barley.

The Nelsons lived in town. Warren, where the major landmark was the drugstore, had no record stores or bookstores, and, until the addition of a drive-in years later, only one movie theater. Young Paul's introduction to cinema, which was against the family's Evangelical Mission Covenant religion, came when his father took him to see Paul Muni in *Commandos Strike at Dawn*. "My mother was much more religious than my father," Paul remembered. "She frowned on movies as being evil." She also frowned on dances, playing

3

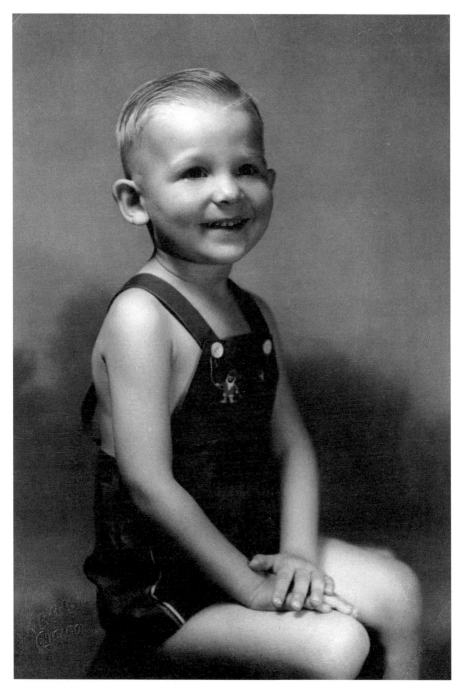

Circa 1940.

cards, and drinking. In time, she would frown on Paul's girlfriend Roberta, who was Catholic.

Though Clara was stricter than Clifford and had no problem telling Paul what to do, Linda Nelson Barna, Paul's younger sister by nine years, says, "I think he just did what he wanted to do. My dad was more easygoing, always kind of quiet and smiley. He wouldn't say anything no matter what you did." Though Paul appreciated the leeway, he would confide in Kenneth Millar in 1976: "I went through a time when I wasn't sure that my father was actually my father. I had the idea that someone else in town was."

Music played a part in young Paul's life. "My aunt played piano. I remember hymns very fondly as the first music I ever heard." There were also a dozen or so 78s in the household. "I couldn't read but I would learn by the scratches on the label what they sounded like."

Paul claimed that, other than his father's subscriptions to *Time* and *Newsweek* (where Paul flipped directly to the book and movie reviews), the only reading matter at home was the Bible. He said that whenever he'd ask his parents for books or records for his birthday or Christmas, "they'd always say, 'Oh, don't you want a pair of socks or a shirt or something? Books are such a colossal waste of time.' That was the prevalent attitude, so it was totally anti-anything to do with art. As it was, I think I bounced the other way by overreacting to that probably. It pushed me towards art, as a form of rebellion, I suppose.

"Even in school I always read all the stuff that wasn't on the reading list. Something in me just wouldn't let me read what was required. It never became fun until I could do it without any A as a goal or 'pass' as a goal. I didn't start reading seriously till I was out of school. I could read what I wanted to, not what I was supposed to." Reading Nathanael West and Graham Greene and seeing "those sentences so perfect" made him want to try his own hand at writing.

"The first good book I read was *The Third Man*, and it wasn't even really that good a book. I simply read it because I'd seen the movie. I remember I had to order that book from 300 miles away to get it. It was a whole production number and quite a thrill when it came in the mail. You didn't have to depend on what paperbacks just happened to turn up at your drugstore, which wasn't much. Or the thirty or forty books in the town library. Actually, the corner drugstore was a better library than the library was." Paul boasted of having read every book in the Warren Public Library at least once to supplement the "*Reader's Digest*-abridged version of literature" that the Minnesota Department of Education had provided him.

Paul also sent away for *From Here to Eternity*. The day after it arrived, he couldn't find the book when he came home from school. "My mother had burned it up because she'd paged through it and seen that there were dirty scenes in it," he told singer-songwriter Rod Stewart. "I was so fucking mad."

With sister Linda and mother Clara circa 1947.

"The only good teacher I had in high school was a journalism teacher. She was the whole experience. I learned more in that class than I did in anything else. Changed my life all the way around. Her name was Mary Lou Sullivan.[1] I wanted to be a writer, not necessarily a journalist. I wrote short stories in high school and worked for the local paper. I covered sports events

1 "He liked her a lot," Paul's ex-wife Doris Hoper said, "he may have had a crush on her. She was very good-looking."

6

for the high school teams. Crap work. I never liked journalism per se. I wasn't surprised that I could do it, I never had any problem with it." In July of 1953, *The Warren Sheaf* published what was probably Paul's first byline; in a column called "Fair Chatter," he wrote: "Seems like the Marshall County Fair gets a little bigger, a little better, and a little different each year."

Elliott Murphy: "He had an incredible collection of comic books. One day he came home from high school and his mother had burned them all. He always told me, 'If I still had them today, I wouldn't have to work.' It sounded like he never forgave her for that. I just could imagine: sixteen years old or whatever—and I'm sure Paul didn't have an easy time with adolescence—and coming back home and his mother telling him that Jesus told her to burn his comic books."

Paul was one year older than Doris Marjorie Gehrls, a sophomore at Warren High School, when they met in 1952 and started going steady. "Some weekends we went to movies," Doris Gehrls Hoper remembered in 2006. "Three on Saturday and a couple on Friday nights, and maybe some more on Sunday."

When he got old enough, Paul would "borrow" used cars from his dad's lot and drive to nearby Crookston and Thief River Falls, or across the border to Grand Forks, North Dakota, all of which were only thirty miles away. Farther away lay Winnipeg, where Paul liked to go for fish and chips. Canada was the only foreign country Paul ever visited. "I always used to love it because you could look at English books there and English records," he said. About one of these jaunts, Paul wrote:

> When I was ten or eleven, I was caught for stealing two singles in Grand Forks, North Dakota. Because I was a minor and it was my first offense, I was released in my father's custody. The experience was embarrassing and stupid, but in the end, it was worth it. I got to keep the records. One was by Hank Williams as Luke the Drifter. The other was Chet Baker's "My Funny Valentine."[2]

Jay Cocks: "See, he just picks the best. Even if he's going to be put in the pokey, he still picks the best."

For Warren, television reception was no closer than 350-mile-away Minneapolis, and Paul didn't see his first TV transmission, in a department store window, until he was seventeen or eighteen. "He said that everyone

---

2 "Chet Baker Gets Lost in Time" by Paul Nelson, *Musician*, October 1990.† One of several instances wherein Paul misremembered his age. "My Funny Valentine" by Chet Baker with the Gerry Mulligan Quartet was released in 1952 when Paul was sixteen.

Circa 1948.

owned one," Michael Seidenberg says, "but they just didn't broadcast there. Every night people would turn the TV on, waiting. Waiting for some flicker of an image to finally get broadcast to where they lived."

"Bob Dylan got TV reception," Nick Tosches says, "Paul Nelson didn't."

In 1954, Paul graduated second in his class and received a scholarship to St. Olaf, a small, liberal arts college in Northfield, Minnesota. That summer, however, he boarded a Greyhound and headed east. "I had about a hundred dollars, period, for two weeks. I just stayed at the Y and walked around the city twenty-four hours a day practically. I slept on Forty-Second Street sometimes and in the all-night movies. It was wonderful. I just embraced culture like it was Marilyn Monroe."

> Maybe you had to have been there, but I've always felt that the Fifties—that much-maligned decade rightly chastised for its blandness, repression, and worse—was also, paradoxically, America's last golden era. Framed on one side by Depression communalism and post-World War II optimism spiked with noir and on the other by the sensational Sixties before they exploded into apocalypse now, the Fifties tendered nearly everyone a humane lifestyle complete with an undercurrent of dimly unaware, thwarted, and mostly unwanted innocence: i.e., something to rebel against—personally, socially, politically, whatever. From this potent brew came a strange band of vulnerable romantic icons whose solitary allure and smoky touch are still very much with us and will probably withstand time's every test—larger-than-life, good-bad, twang-of-the-void one-namers from the country's heartland: Clift and Brando from Nebraska, Dean from Indiana, Elvis from Mississippi, Marilyn from sunny California and, on the cusp of the Sixties, Dylan from Minnesota. I'm not sure that any other decade could have produced such intense introspection, sweet rebellion, and naïve, confused cynicism. Or such an air of utter aloneness.[3]

3 *Ibid.*

EVERYTHING IS AN AFTERTHOUGHT

Despite his upbringing—or more likely because of it—Paul was not religious. "Which is not to say that he was an atheist," writer William MacAdams says.

Paul felt that he was the logical result of his Swedish immigrant ancestors who, the way he saw it, would've been right at home in an Ingmar Bergman film. "I can understand all that fear and trembling from the movies because my parents were very much like that. I'm not sorry that I grew up that way. I learned a lot probably by having to think for myself at a very young age."

The Evangelical Mission Covenant of America was founded in Chicago by Swedish immigrants in 1885.

Paul: "They believed in some sort of emotional salvation. You were saved and everybody from every other church was damned. People actually spoke in tongues at times in church. I remember being scared to death at four and five by somebody just screaming, 'You're going to hell! You're going to hell unless you come up and say you're saved!'

"The minister used to come over all the time. My father never really joined the church, he was like an honorary member, but my mother was a member. There was constant pressure on my father and me to join. I think he did capitulate eventually, but all through my junior high school and senior high school I just couldn't accept this, that one day I would know that I was saved and that suddenly I would have the shining truth and all my friends wouldn't.

"Dances were a sin. I used to go to the high school dances and dance, but I was the only kid in our church that did. I was brought up to consider movies a sin, which probably explains why I like movies. I just did it and they didn't say anything to me. What was sillier, our next-door neighbor was the guy who owned the theater and my parents were friends with him. I was considered a pariah in the church because as soon as I was old enough I hoisted my nine cents up to the ticket window of the theater to get in."

MacAdams: "I think that he probably rejected whatever that Swedish fundamentalist group was more on aesthetic grounds than any other grounds."

"They used to have traveling ministers. It was much like this movie *Marjoe*," Paul said, "with tabernacles where people actually fell on the floor. The entire emphasis was just sheer terror, just scare everybody literally to the edge of death and then save them practically. Which always seemed to me an odd thing for a religion to do, based on this gestapo-ism of terror."

Many years later, Paul told writer John Morthland how as a young boy he'd witnessed the congregation stone a teenage couple that had been caught making out. "That sort of haunted me ever since," Morthland says, "and I'm sure it did him to his death."

Paul told Kenneth Millar another story that haunted him: "I remember in a town next to mine when I was a child there was a runaway boy in his teens who had done something minor at school and was afraid of punishment. He hid out in a church for literally three years and stole food from the pantry and had lost half of his mind by the time they found him. No one knew he existed there."

Paul would come to regret not traveling more, or learning a practical trade he could fall back on, before diving directly into academe. At St. Olaf, "Everybody knew twenty times more than I knew. I think I learned more in my first week in college than I ever did in eighteen years. I didn't even know what classical music was till I was eighteen years old. I came from the total sticks, and I felt like I was I running about eighteen leagues behind the rest of the people. I mean, when I got to college they were all talking about people that I never even heard of. They were common knowledge. I didn't know what the fuck they were talking about. I didn't know who William Faulkner was or any of these people. Where had I been for eighteen years? It was terrifying."

Paul's grades at St. Olaf ranged from an A+ to an incomplete with no in-between. It wholly depended on the subject being taught and whether he liked the teacher. Torn between where he could learn the most, be it the short trip to the classroom or hitchhiking into the city to enjoy what it had to offer, St. Olaf made the decision for him—bolstered additionally by his refusal to attend ROTC—and invited him not to return after his first year and a half. He transferred to the University of Minnesota and spent the next six years in Minneapolis. That same year, Doris, maintaining a long-distance relationship with Paul from the University of North Dakota in Grand Forks, moved to Minneapolis, too.

Looming large in Paul's mind throughout was the draft. "I would've done anything to stay out of the Army, I think," he told Warren Zevon. "I was determined to psych out of that no matter what, and I did." It wasn't so much the war that troubled him but the thought of "all the marching and orders." On the initial psychological test, he answered the questions in such a way that, he hoped, would construct an undesirable pattern in his personality. "I listed all the left-wing folk people I knew from the magazines I subscribed to, hoping that they would ring a bell. Then I had to go and see a shrink. I sort of sat and trembled and kept saying, 'Well, I really wouldn't mind being in, but I think I'd fuck everything up because I can't get along with people at all.' But I didn't know until weeks later, until they sent the classification through the mail, so every day I would come home and shudder at the mailbox."

With Doris Gehrls at the Nelsons' house, 1957, two years before they wed.

In the spring of 1957, Paul's neighbor in his rooming house was Jon Pankake. Paul would sometimes pass the time playing APBA, a baseball board game that incorporated real-life statistics. Pankake, who had played the game in high school and recognized the roll of the dice through the paper-thin walls, came over and introduced himself. The two became close friends for several years.

Paul and Pankake discovered their love of folk music at the same time when, along with Doris, they drove to Ames, Iowa, to attend a Pete Seeger concert at Iowa State. Pankake says, "It just seemed more American, more direct, less contrived. It seemed like something that we could possibly do, which you never get from pop music, which is always so contrived and elevated." Paul was there when Pankake purchased his first pawn-shop guitar. Paul took lessons from Schmitt Music, a downtown instrument dealer, where his teacher was folklorist Gene Bluestein, then a grad student at the U of M.

Musician and writer Tony Glover says, "Jon was a banjo player. Paul played a little guitar, not much. Basic chords and stuff. They knew some people over in the folk scene around the university. There was a group of academic kind of people, they had a folk song society, and they would send off to the Library of Congress where you could get tapes of old string band music for seventeen bucks an hour."

In 1959, Paul and Pankake made the acquaintance of local musician Bobby Zimmerman, a fellow student on his way to becoming Bob Dylan. Later, after Zimmerman dropped out and Paul and Pankake started publishing *The Little Sandy Review*, a homegrown folk journal devoted to publishing criticism about serious folk music, he came to them and proposed that they help promote his concerts. Uninterested, they instead introduced him to some rare recordings. In return, he committed an act of larceny in the name of art.

"Dylan came around," Paul said. "He was starting out, he was still Bobby Zimmerman then. He was singing in coffeehouses and doing Odetta and Harry Belafonte songs. He wasn't writing at that point. But he came over—and we had gotten some Jack Elliott records from England and some Woody Guthrie stuff—and we played him his first Guthrie and Jack Elliott. I *know* we played him his first Jack Elliott for sure because there were no American Jack Elliott records. We had to import stuff.

Circa 1959 in Minneapolis.

"And he stole a bunch of them from my friend. He came along and he took about twenty or thirty of them, and he had impeccable taste. He took the best. I saw his notebooks, and he would go through one record and he would always pick the right song from that record to cover. He had an unerring sense of what was the right stuff.

"So we tracked him down all over, and there were like six other people looking for him, too, for various indiscretions apparently. It wound up a truly

Minneapolis Daily Herald *clippings, 1962.*

comic scene. My friend is quite tall, six-five, and rather burly, but not at all violent. But he had a bowling pin in his hand and he was sort of threatening Dylan with it, getting his records back. He wasn't actually going to hit Dylan, but he was doing his John Wayne act. And Dylan was a little afraid for the first five minutes because it looked pretty menacing—you know, a big guy with a bowling pin. Jon Pankake was the guy's name.[4] He went through his John Wayne speech and Dylan was a little worried. Another guy got all the records out and everything, and Jon went through the John Wayne speech again, the same speech more or less, and Dylan sort of realized, 'Well, he's not going to really hit me.' It sort of played for an hour into the theater of the absurd where Jon would tirelessly go through this speech, but it was getting pretty threadbare. It became a comedy, just like a Harold Pinter play, repeating

4 The six-foot-two-inch Pankake says, "It was a table leg. I worked at the time at a university garbage dump, and one of the old tables had a handy looking leg so I took it."

An advertisement from the pages of The Little Sandy Review, *1963.*

itself in this loop. And then Dylan sort of smiled at me at the end and said, 'It's been kind of a bad night.'"

"It's a key moment in history," *Rolling Stone* publisher Jann Wenner says. "I mean, anybody who had their hands on that key where Bob found Woody was standing at the crossroads. I think Paul was very proud of that, but I imagine at a point he got tired of that being his claim to fame, wishing people would think to talk to him about something else."

Paul's debut as a critic in the mainstream media took place in 1962 when the *Minneapolis Daily Herald* published more than a dozen of his reviews of books, film, plays, TV shows, and art exhibits.

"Paul did not have a musical gift," Pankake says. "I didn't either, but I kept at it anyway." Regardless, that didn't prevent Paul from producing *Blues, Rags and Hollers*, the first album by Koerner, Ray & Glover, a folk-blues trio whose members—"Spider" John Koerner, Dave "Snaker" Ray, and Tony "Little Sun"

Koerner, Ray & Glover make the cover of the last LSR *to be published in Minneapolis, 1963. From left to right, "Spider" John Koerner, Tony "Little Sun" Glover, and Dave "Snaker" Ray. Cover photo by Paul Nelson.*

Glover—had met at the University of Minnesota. Paul also managed to score the band a record deal with Elektra, despite some things he'd written. Jac Holzman, the label's founder, says, "Paul's *Little Sandy Review* skewered Elektra for folk releases they didn't feel were sufficiently 'ethnic,' but I loved reading his reviews and we began a lively correspondence." In 1963, the relationship turned professional. "Paul sent me the first album of his friends Koerner, Ray & Glover, and within a few days I was on my way to Minneapolis to sign them. KR&G were seminal artists for me, and pointed Elektra in the direction of white blues."

For the group's second album, *Lots More Blues, Rags and Hollers*, "Paul Rothchild was ostensibly the producer," Glover says. "He was behind the board and all that. But as far as 'Was that a good take or can we do better?' Paul was the guy that we would look to more than Paul Rothchild."

Before 1963 was out, Paul had graduated with a BA from the University of Minnesota. "It took me a little longer than it should have, largely because I kept branching off into various interests and I wound up taking so many of the required courses my last semester rather than the first semester. I was taking a lot of graduate courses when I was a sophomore by special permission. I wound up with enough credits for majors in two subjects—English and art—although it really wasn't planned. It was a very free-form thing, going where the interests were," and it determined a pattern he'd follow for the rest of his professional and personal life.

As Paul closed one door, another one opened. Standing there was Irwin Silber, cofounder and editor of the preeminent folk publication of the day, *Sing Out!* Paul and Pankake had met Silber the year before when the two friends went to New York for a few days on vacation.

"When I graduated from the University of Minnesota, it was in the middle of the folk boom. *Sing Out!* had quadrupled its circulation because of this and they needed a managing editor. There was only one other folk magazine practically, and Silber asked me if I wanted to do it. I just wanted to get to New York. I was going to go to New York anyway, and I thought, Well, why not take this?" Doris, who was six months pregnant, agreed.

Paul corresponded with his old friend Jon Pankake for a while after the move, and once, when he returned to Minneapolis in 1967 on his way to somewhere else, he spent a night at Pankake and his wife Marcia's residence. "Paul and I went out and shot baskets in the neighborhood basketball court and talked movies." After he left, the letters soon stopped. Pankake wasn't surprised; nor was he surprised that Paul equally lost touch with his own family. "I think he was never that high on his family. His dad was a Sinclair Lewis, small-town businessman who always wanted Paul to come back and take over the Ford agency after he had done his nonsense at school. And Paul, of course, regarded that as a fate worse than death."

Circa 1964 in New York City. Photo by David Gahr. Used by permission.

Jon Pankake credits Paul Nelson with coming up with the idea for *The Little Sandy Review*, which they began publishing semi-whenever in 1960. At first, though, they couldn't decide whether to make it a film journal or a music journal. "We flipped a coin to see if it was going to be about movies or folk music," Pankake says. "Folk music won—or lost, as the case may be."

Paul: "I worked at probably the best record store in Minneapolis and Tony Glover used to come in there. Mel-O-Dee Records. And I was working for Coda Distributors, which distributed Folkways Records. I was this guy back in the shipping department. Folkways would send review copies and nobody else in the place wanted them, so they gave them to me for nothing."

The diminutive, four-by-seven *Little Sandy* was elegant in its inexpensiveness. Paul always maintained that "We started it for somewhat altruistic reasons but also because we were students in college and couldn't afford to buy the records. I thought, Well, jeez, if we review these records they'll send them to us free. So we just figured, Well, we won't make any money, but we'll get the records." According to Pankake it never worked that way. "At first, Paul bought our records at cost from the Minneapolis record store where he worked. Later on, Folkways, Prestige, and a couple of other small folky labels sold us records at wholesale. We were proud that preview freebies were not on the table so that we could maintain our air of independence."

Paul told Bruce Hornsby: "Sometimes we thought, Well, they'll balk at having to send two copies—one for me and one for the other guy—but they did. God, one of my biggest thrills was seeing this seven-record Atlantic set, the Lomax series on Atlantic. I remember seeing they'd sent it out special airmail and it had cost them twenty-two dollars to send two copies of the Lomax set."

Mel-O-Dee also had a Gestetner, which Paul called "a glorified mimeograph machine. You could print photos badly, but you could print them." For the cover of the first issue they used a photo of Dizzy Gillespie at Town Hall that Paul had taken on his first trip to New York. "It wasn't folk at all, but it was the only picture of somebody famous that we had."

Paul and Pankake also account differently for the origin of *The Little Sandy*'s name. Pankake says, "It was a mixture of different things. There had been a critical magazine called *The Little Review* some years before that we'd heard of, and then there's the Little Sandy River—I think it's in Kentucky or Tennessee. So we put those together." But Paul grew fond of telling people, "It was based strictly on the fact that every sorority girl in all the classes we took were always called Sandi. That's what it was. It was always Sandi with an *i* and we changed it to a *y*."

One thing Paul and Pankake did agree on, however: though the two's writings in the magazine were almost always bylined "By Paul Nelson and Jon Pankake" or simply "Editors," the pieces were often written individually. "We each wrote reviews and usually typed them onto the ditto master ourselves," Pankake says. "Very little editing of anything went on, as is all too evident in the printed copy."

"Sometimes we did sections of it," Paul said, "sometimes one of us would write the whole thing."

Pankake: "We, of course, thoroughly discussed every record, and so the review, while written by one of us, actually reflects a synthesis of our joint thinking, and so the joint attribution is appropriate. We were very much on the same wavelength and there was never an 'I love it/you hate it' disagreement."

They also employed pseudonyms to make it seem less like a two-man show. The writing staff doubled when Tony Glover inquired why they weren't covering blues. Paul asked him to start doing it, and Glover in turn recruited his friend Barret Hansen (better known in later years as Dr. Demento) to contribute pieces about early blues.

Pankake: "*The Little Sandy* really came out of the Harry Smith Anthology, as I recall. Paul found that and brought it home and we listened to it. We were so struck with that music, that's when we dumped Pete Seeger and everyone else." It solidified their interest in traditional, authentic folk.[5]

Warren Leming, of the band Wilderness Road, discovered *The Little Sandy Review* while in high school. "The *Little Sandy* was really, on a journalistic level, the precursor of the underground newspaper. Paul had all of his soldiers in place, because he was a film noir guy, more than a bit of a film buff—he wrote very, very, very cogent stuff about the evolution of American film—and he tied in the literary tradition, people like Raymond Chandler and whatnot. You add Guthrie to that mix and then you add the *Anthology of American Folk Music* and all, and what you wind up culminating with or within is somebody like Dylan.

"Paul and Jon represented the American underground tradition, which was just beginning to surface. And of course it led to some remarkable music. It led to the post-beatnik/hippie world, it led to a lot of idealism, a lot of civil rights work. It led to some extraordinary things. But it was one of those journals that really set things moving in a way that nobody could have foreseen. They weren't supported, there were no subventions, no universities were supporting them, and yet these guys were doing the work that led to the sea change, for a time, in American consciousness."

The Little Sandy Review continued for three more issues—28, 29, and 30—after Paul, now listed on the masthead as the New York Editor, headed east in 1963. Pankake says, "The last issues were more professionally printed. Paul had contacts in New York and it was printed there. It had Dave Gahr photographs and so on. It was starting to look pretty good, but Paul was having less and less time to spend on it because of his other work, and I was having less and less time to work on it here."

"We had three subscribers for the first issue," Paul said. "It got up to 1,000 before it ended."

Pankake: "In Minneapolis when I was involved with subscriptions, the mailing list, kept on three-by-five cards, was about 300. After moving to NYC Paul assumed all responsibility for subs, printing, and mailing, so I have no way to question his numbers."

In 1964, Pankake sold *The Little Sandy Review* to Barret Hansen. "I bought the magazine for one dollar and published two issues, then sold it to someone else for one dollar." Hansen shifted the focus of the journal from folk to rock, much to the dismay of Mike Seeger, founding member of the New Lost City Ramblers, who penned a painful letter objecting to the change.

Pankake: "In 1968 I started graduate school at the University of Minnesota, so that sort of sealed our diversion: Paul went into rock & roll and I went into

5 Folklorist, filmmaker, and magician Harry Smith compiled the six-album *Anthology of American Folk Music*, which was released by Folkways Records in 1952.

THE LITTLE SANDY REVIEW

THE FOLK RECORD MAGAZINE   MAIN OFFICES: BOX 581, WOODSIDE, NEW YORK 11377

Editors: Paul Nelson, Jon Pankake, Barry Hansen/Photography Editor: David Gahr/Associates: Doris Nelson, Marcia Pankake

Minneapolis Branch Office: Jon Pankake, Box 1109, Minneapolis 40, Minnesota 55440

Los Angeles Branch Office: Barry Hansen, 11017 Strathmore Drive, Los Angeles, California 90024

Photography Editor: David Gahr, 132 West 15th Street, New York, New York

The Little Sandy Review *letterhead (top and bottom), 1964.*

academia. I think that some of the last letters that I wrote to him were about how excited I was about the American history project that I was working on. I think he was not interested in it. He was getting really excited about the rock scene and the New York Dolls and all that stuff. We drifted apart."

"**I** think we had written something about topical songs in *Little Sandy* saying basically we just didn't like them much," Paul told Jeff Rosen, Bob Dylan's manager, during the interview session for *No Direction Home*, Martin Scorsese's film about Dylan. "Some of his weren't very good, some of them were great. We agreed with the politics and everything, but it was sort of like sticking a slogan on the *Mona Lisa*'s forehead. To us, it was kind of embarrassing to come right out and say you're against child abuse or somebody dropping the bomb. It seemed pretty obvious, basically, and most of the songs weren't very good."

On July 17, 1963, Dylan invited Paul and Jon Pankake to a concert at the home of Dave Whitaker, who was something of a mentor to Dylan, in the Dinkytown area alongside the U of M campus. Paul went in alone.

"It was like going into the enemy camp. I mean, there were like twenty of his friends around who loved topical songs, and he played a bunch of new stuff, old stuff, and it was like, 'How did you like that one?' After 'Who Killed Davey Moore?' Dylan would say, 'Well, how did you like that one?' and I would have to say, 'Not very much, Bob.' It wasn't a great situation to be in."

After Dylan played "Only a Pawn in Their Game," Paul said, "The thing is, I don't necessarily like it because of its subject matter. I like it because it's a good song, as well." With "Boots of Spanish Leather," he was less complimentary: "It was all right. I didn't think it was the greatest thing I've ever heard, frankly."

21

"I've got lots of respect for *The Little Sandy Review*," Dylan said, but he lectured Paul on his and Pankake's wrongheadedness when it came to bad reviews, saying to leave Harry Belafonte and Judy Collins alone. "You should dig Joan Baez. If you knew her, you wouldn't put her down."

"He was really feeling his oats that night and he was talking to us brilliantly," Paul told Rosen, "just really brilliantly, and I was feeling really out of my element. But I felt I owed it to him to show up and defend what was written in *Little Sandy* and I kind of wanted to get to know him better a little bit also. I think we came out of it pretty well. The argument sort of ran all night ...

"The political situation in New York was, to get your songs published in magazines, you had to write topical songs. My argument was 'Jeez, Bob, you're so much better than this. Why would you want to go down this blind alley and write this stuff all your career when you could do anything?'"

"I've surely got to hand it to you," Dylan told Paul that night. "It takes a lot of courage, or it takes a lot of something, to stay and just write a magazine like that. You know what I mean? Because I could never do it."

A few months later, Dylan wasn't writing topically anymore.

"He was the champion of topical songs that night because of the audience for one thing," Paul said. "I'm sure he just routed me completely in the arguments, but at the same time he said some awfully nice things about me that night also. There was something—some form of friendship between us."

On February 28, 1964, Doris gave birth to Mark Christopher Nelson. The next year, in April, Doris remained in New York with the baby while Paul returned to Minnesota to visit his father in the hospital. While he was there, Clifford, who'd suffered coronary thrombosis, passed away. Paul stayed for the funeral. It would be his last trip to Warren. "He didn't even come back for his mother's funeral," Doris said.

The Paul Nelson that most people remember was six-one and frail as a rail, but when he first arrived in New York he weighed in at 233 pounds. "I'm not naturally thin," he said almost twenty years later. "Unless I run or keep in shape and watch what I eat, I do go up." He lost the weight by only eating once each day at four o'clock in the afternoon. When illustrator Jeff Wong befriended him in the late Eighties and early Nineties, Paul was still only eating one meal a day: a hamburger and two Cokes at one of his favorite restaurants, Jackson Hole (though by then it was probably because one meal a day was all he could afford).

Paul took pride in having made the leap from one of the smallest towns in the U.S. to the largest. Jon Pankake says, "Paul always wanted to go to

Mark and Doris in New York, December 1964.

New York. It was *the* place to be. I remember when he was an undergraduate, Paul showed me a short story he'd written for an English class. He'd had the hero walk through Central Park on his way from Times Square to the Village, and the teacher had pointed out that this wasn't the right geography. But Paul imaginatively was already in New York, even though he'd never been there."

Mike Gormley, one-time Mercury Records head of publicity, says, "For a guy from Minnesota, he was a real New York guy. He fit right in."

"I'd go to the movies three times a week and every time I saw New York that's where I'd want to go," Paul told poet-singer-songwriter Leonard Cohen in 1991. "At that time there was a great romance with New York, but that's evaporated in the last decade."

"Now it's a marriage," Cohen chuckled.

"It's a bad marriage," Paul said. But it didn't start out that way.

In New York he perfected a first-person style of writing, later popularized by others as "New Journalism," that located himself within the story. "I'm certainly guilty of writing autobiography and disguising it as criticism somewhat, or at least combining it with criticism." He told Cohen: "If criticism or articles can be autobiographical, they were always autobiographical in the sense that I wrote about people's albums who reflected what I was feeling at the time. They were sort of autobiographical by 'oral transfusion.' I found my life in those songs. When I was writing about your songs, I was probably writing about me as much as I was about you."

What Nick Carraway was to *The Great Gatsby* and Lew Archer was to Ross Macdonald's detective novels, Paul Nelson was to the subjects he wrote about. But it was a reluctant, tight-lipped participation. "In his writing, it was a kind of a Gary Cooper/Gregory Peck quality," Bill Flanagan says.

Anthony DeCurtis: "It's introducing biographical elements to advance another kind of point. That redeems it. It makes it more valuable because you go, 'Well, okay, not only is this guy making this point about this music, but he's also describing this aspect of his life.' It seems more generous. Rather than the music and everything else trailing after the life, rather than the music providing a platform for a kind of exhibitionism, it was more a case of bringing in your biography as an effort to kind of make yourself more vulnerable and more open to your readers so that they could feel the impact of what you were feeling."

Flanagan: "He had an almost unique ability to put himself into the story in a way that did not seem egotistical. It didn't seem like he was either being obsequious or he was trying to put himself on the same level as the artist, which are the two traps that people fall into when they write and put themselves in the story. It seemed like he was there for a reason, he was there to advance the story, to give you more insight into the artist and the artist's situation. You always felt like he was also holding back a lot more than he let on. The supreme example being the Zevon story, where you realize that Paul was part of the intervention, that he was *that* close to Zevon. But it never in any way felt self-aggrandizing, like Paul was letting you know, 'Man, I'm really down with the artist.'"

Paul's writing remains so alive for writer Jonathan Lethem that he still speaks about his old friend in the present tense. "He has that gift of absolutely personal vernacular style that's also completely erudite, that wears its knowledge very easily. And then he has that drive to make you know what he feels or thinks about something—that almost synesthesia of critical vocabulary, where he has to find the unexpected verb or adjective that will just make you feel that you're listening through his ears or looking through his eyes."

Paul recommended that author David McGee read a paperback anthology called *The Hardboiled Detective: Stories from Black Mask Magazine, 1920–1951.*

Paul holding Mark circa 1967.

"It turned out that, after I found out about his fondness for that type of fiction, he wrote a lot like those guys. It was very straightforward, unadorned, it wasn't flashy prose, but it had a real energy and a heat to it, real cool heat."

"It was the best kind of writing," Nick Tosches says. "That's what makes me think he could've really written great books. It's as simple as that. It's as simple as him expressing what he felt, being able to articulate those feelings—a natural eloquence—and not trying to dress it up or adorn it with writerly ornamentation. That's what made him special. Not trying to be special is what made him special as a writer—and probably as a guy, too."

Writer and editor Fred Schruers: "The writing was full of hope and what people might aspire to, and about the connections people would make and that music would make. But of course it became clear ultimately what he was looking for in the music were some answers and some consolations that regular ol' life wasn't supplying."

The day the baby came was something straight out of Bergman for me. My moods these last three weeks have been shifting like so many roller coasters anyway, and that day saw the highest and lowest at once, often doing battle with each other. Doris went to the hospital about nine o'clock in the morning and had the baby about six that night. The only waiting area for fathers was right outside the labor room; there were at least a dozen expectant mothers in labor just a few feet away through a very thin door, and I could hear the screaming and moaning very clearly the whole day, never knowing whether or not it was Doris, or if she were even in there. A real horror show, let me tell you.... All day, I thought of nothing but death, death, death (I was sure I was never going to see Doris again), and, when the baby finally came, the news of birth meant nothing at all to me; all that seemed important was that there had been no death. And then soon, Doris came out on a stretcher, looking like a poor wounded animal, and it was all over. Never, never again....

Most babies I've seen have been pudgy and round, but Mark looks just like Gary Cooper. Lean, lanky, and not an ounce of fat on him. He has long arms and legs and may make the perfect Western hero. Maybe John Ford will live long enough to break him in right.[6]

"I met my wife-to-be when she was a sophomore in high school. If you went steady with someone, the community expected you to get married. I just didn't know any better. I didn't know who I was, she didn't know who she was. We did the expected, and we were not *un*happy. It turned out we weren't at all compatible. She wanted to go back and live in Minnesota, back in the hometown, but there was nothing there for me. After quite a few years, I could feel myself exploding inside."

After Paul fell in love with Bobbi London, he decided to leave Doris. But that also meant leaving Mark, which was "just murder," he told Leonard Cohen. "It was at a period when I was freelance writing, so I was able to see Mark a lot and take him around the city with me because I didn't have to go to work regularly. So we were very, very close. When the split came down, I will never forget the look on his face when I told him we were not going to

---

6 *Lists: One Year's Worth of a Mythological Autobiographical Journal of a Life Seen through Popular Culture Transmogrified* by Paul Nelson.† This unfinished, unpublished work from the mid-Sixties borrowed from Paul's published articles, mixing them with passages from his journals and letters.

be living together anymore. His lower lip just trembled and he got this terror in his eyes. And I thought, Oh my god. This is like taking a bullet that's going to be there forever—and it *is* there forever. I think that was probably my single most horrifying moment: watching his face disintegrate."

Mark began acting out in preschool. "They made him leave the class. He was only three and a half. We went to counseling. Maybe this was totally the wrong decision, but their decision was it would be much easier for my son if I *didn't* stay in touch with him. I didn't know what to do. But I went along with it, possibly out of personal cowardice because it was just killing me to see him. Possibly because I thought it *was* right—the contact with him seemed to be disturbing him. Maybe a clean break would be the best."

Family and friends back in Warren were shocked. "They were such a great couple and he was so happy with her," Linda Barna says. "He would do anything for her. I remember her saying if they'd even walk past a store and she'd say, 'Oh, isn't that nice?' the next day he'd come home with it or something. He just couldn't have done enough for her, he was so crazy about her. I never would've thought that would've happened."

"It did me in for three years." Paul, who never had a problem walking away, said, "I resolved that I never want to leave anybody again—I'd rather be left."

Doris said, "He didn't even respond to the divorce summons or complaint." Seven years passed before they finalized the divorce. In 1973, Paul suggested that she and Mark meet him in Winnipeg, 125 miles north of Warren. He didn't want to go home. "People didn't get divorced there. That's one reason we met in the neutral ground of Winnipeg, because I was the villain of the piece. Because I broke the marriage up." He hadn't seen either of them since she returned to Warren in 1968, a few months before Mark turned five.

In the early Seventies, Paul regularly visited Jay Cocks and his wife, the actress Verna Bloom. "We used to see a lot of Paul. Our son Sam, whom he knew when he was a very little kid, used to call him 'Hobo Paul' because he looked like a hobo. Paul would tell about Woody Guthrie and give him a couple Woody Guthrie records and stuff. He was really lovely with Sam.

"I'd known Paul for a long time, and he knew how desperately Verna and I wanted to have a child and how hard we tried. When it finally happened he was very happy for us. But it also made him reflect on a certain side of his life that very few people knew about.

"Just bringing his son up seemed to speak volumes. I got the sense that, having brought it up, he was telling you something about himself that was so private and painful that just the plain fact of it was all he could bear to say."

Kit Rachlis says: "On one hand, Paul was extraordinarily honest and complete masked at the same time."

May 1968 in New York.

"He made it quite obvious that he did not want to discuss it, so we did not discuss it," Betsy Volck says. She and Paul lived together in the Seventies. "I'm an Episcopalian and we just basically avoid bringing up personal topics. So that's ingrained in me, I have no problem with that."

Writer-editor-turned-producer-manager Jon Landau says, "I can tell you that of the thousands of hours I probably spent talking with him, I did not have the slightest idea that he had a son. I don't think any of us from that time knew. It wasn't that he was secretive, it's just that Paul, who was such a control freak in a world of control freaks, was a guy you talked to about songs, artists, music, books, movies, so on and so forth. That was his element, that was what he was comfortable with."

"But again, in the same way that he would not name the various women in his life, he didn't name his son," Mikal Gilmore says. "The son was 'the son' when he talked to me. When he would talk about the son there was some

With Mark in May 1968, a few months
before the boy returned to Minnesota with Doris.

regret there, but he also felt at that time that it had been too long and he had to live with that regret."

Bobbi London: "He often cried, literally cried, over it. I kept saying, 'You've got to get in touch with him, you have to see him, you have to be in his life.' But they moved back to Minnesota, and he would never go to Minnesota. He felt that he was not welcome in Warren and his whole family probably hated him. But my feeling there is he probably hated his mother."

Paul talked about Doris and Mark with Crystal Zevon. "He always spoke well of them and always said that she was better off without him. I think he really felt that." He also discussed how he might introduce himself back into his son's life. "By the end of the conversation, he would back off several light years. He felt extremely regretful, guilty. He would always come back to 'What would I have to give to him? What would I have to offer him? I'm not a father.

And why should I disrupt his life?' He didn't feel like he was capable, but also wasn't willing to make the commitment that he had felt would be necessary to be married and a father. I think it's part of why he withdrew. I think it's part of what that solitary persona was about."

But whenever the opportunity arose to play the role of the proud father, Paul seized it. In 1977, when the Rolling Stones' Keith Richards described his kids' fascination with dinosaurs and how it turned them into "little professors," Paul said: "Mine would have these books that he would memorize when he was two years old. If I was feeling like, Oh God, I don't want to read all this and I'd skip some of it, he would recite the places that I'd skipped. He knew right off." He recalled Sinclair Oil's green brontosaurus logo and how Mark would keep an eye out for the company's trucks. "He could spot one six blocks away and say, 'Dinosaur!'"

"**H**e rose quickly at *Sing Out!*," David Gahr remembered in 2006, "which was a great magazine at one time. It's garbage now. It's slick, it's color, and it's pablum. But years ago, when Paul and Julius Lester ran the magazine, it was at its height."

Mike Seeger: "To me he was the best editor of that magazine. He made it into a good magazine—as good as he could, considering the people he had around him."

Paul had been managing editor for a little over a year and a half when, on Sunday, July 25, 1965, Bob Dylan plugged in his guitar at the Newport Folk Festival. The experience changed Paul's life—"I went electric pretty much when Dylan did"—and music as we knew it. Bobbi London was in the photographers' pit beside him. Gahr was there, too. "Dylan played his first set," London says, "and then came the second half of it and the sea parted."

At Newport, Paul ran into an old friend, Jac Holzman. "Paul and I couldn't believe the boos and hisses from the fearful crowd, because we loved it. I never saw him smile as widely as that night. We both knew to an absolute certainty that the walls of the city were going to fall and wanted so much to be part of the exciting unknown about to happen."

Paul shot a dozen rolls of film. Gahr shot ten times that.

Kit Rachlis heard a story that, once the Dylan performance was over, Paul turned to Gahr and said that there was no point in staying, they'd seen everything they needed to see. Nothing was going to be better than that.

"The folk press was very small, but I was a reasonable cog in it." Anticipating a rift between *Sing Out!*'s target audience of topical, traditionalistic folksters

With Tony Glover at Newport in '65. Photo courtesy of Tony Glover.

and burgeoning rock & roll, Paul resigned as managing editor with an article that concluded:

> It was a sad parting of the ways for many, myself included. I choose Dylan, I choose art. I will stand behind Dylan and his "new" songs, and I'll bet my critical reputation (such as it may be) that I'm right.[7]

Although Paul always maintained that he had to sneak his pro-Dylan article into the magazine, countering editor Irwin Silber's anti-Dylan one, Silber, who passed away in 2010, went on record saying that Paul's piece wouldn't have been published without his approval. "Nobody would be able to sneak anything into that magazine without Irwin knowing about it," Bobbi London says. "It did not go to bed without him reading the whole thing."

Paul: "Dylan loved that article. I think I was the only folk guy who defended him. He sent me tickets for years to concerts after that article."

Though the article didn't appear until the November issue, Paul had tendered his resignation on July 29 (four days after the Dylan concert) and

7 "Another Review," *Sing Out!*, Volume 15, Number 5, November 1965. Reprinted by permission.

Bob Dylan at Newport, July 25, 1965. Photo by Paul Nelson.

worked for the magazine until October. He left behind a steady salary of $131.75 a week after taxes.

Differences of opinion between Paul and Silber were nothing new. "*Sing Out!* was a very political magazine and I was sort of the aesthete. I was interested in the style and I was interested in the art of it. It seemed to me that we were preaching to the converted too often." For Paul, the best part of his job had been laying out the publication pages, pasting them up using rubber cement.

An amped-up Dylan wasn't the sole reason for Paul's departure. According to musician Dave Lightbourne: "What Paul told me was that working at Folkways/*Sing Out!* was insufferable. Everybody there was pretty much an old line Leftist with more political fantasies than artistic values directing their efforts." Right before Newport, Paul had told folklorist Richard A. Reuss, who was working at the magazine for the summer, that he felt he was getting fired: "Paul says that he and Irwin just don't hit it off anymore like they did when they first started, and Irwin has become more and more dissatisfied with Paul."[8]

Paul didn't care for the organization's business practices either. Years later he told actor-director Clint Eastwood how, even after the magazine denounced Dylan's rock & roll, they continued using him to promote their benefits. "They used his name for two years afterwards in concerts, knowing he wouldn't be there. I said, 'How can you guys do this? You're supposed to be so idealistic and everything and here you are using the guy's name. You know the audience is going to get ripped off.' They said, 'Well, he *ought* to be there. He *ought* to feel like we do.' I said, 'Jesus, in any revolution you guys would have to be the first ones to go.'"

> Things are so dismal and Antonioni-like around here these days that I have all I can do to force myself to work on anything I'm supposed to. For every day of the past two weeks, I've had to battle with myself every morning to come to work and not to call in sick for two or three days. I guess it's one of those dreary stretches when the whole world is made out of shit and there you are, up to your neck in it and slowly sinking.[9]

Though Paul's defense of Dylan in the November 1965 *Sing Out!* doubled as his own resignation letter, in that same issue Silber penned a nevertheless friendly farewell:

> A familiar name will be missing from the *Sing Out!* editorial box next issue. Paul Nelson, our managing editor, is putting

8 *Folk Scene Diary Summer 1965 by* Richard A. Reuss.
9 *Lists: One Year's Worth of a Mythological Autobiographical Journal of a Life Seen through Popular Culture Transmogrified* by Paul Nelson.†

his last issue of *Sing Out!* to bed—and when he's done tucking us in, he'll be on his way to a new career as a screenwriter. Lest any of our readers get the wrong idea, our man Paul is not Hollywood-bound, but will be a part of a new company working out of New York. As some of you know, the silver screen has always been Paul Nelson's first love, and all of us here wish him the best in making his mark in this medium.

In the course of his two years at *Sing Out!*, Paul Nelson has made an important contribution to the growing vitality of this magazine. A man of independent thought, he has expressed his views freely as a writer, and done his utmost as an editor to give all points of view to the reader. His sensitive eye has helped make *Sing Out!* a more interesting place to be. His love of folk music and his respect for artistic integrity have been a valuable standard for all who have read these pages. These valuable contributions will not be lost, however, for Paul will continue to write articles, reviews, and provocative prose for *Sing Out!*, even from "way out there."[10]

In his notes from the time, listing various works in progress, Paul wrote: "I am currently completing an original screenplay for Jac and will, of course, continue to work in films as often as I can. I hope to do many more scripts and eventually progress to directing my own films as well." According to Reuss:

> Paul told me that he met a friend of his at this past Newport festival who offered him a job writing scripts for films which Paul can do when and where he wants. The guy offered Paul $4,000 to write a script on anything he wants, also a piece of the company. They shook hands over the deal, and Paul is only waiting for a contract before pulling out of *Sing Out!*[11]

"He should have been involved in making movies," rock & roll renaissance man Danny Fields agrees, "but that's such a communal thing, and he was such a solitary person."

Jac Holzman: "As for the screenplay, it was my way of giving Paul money in the hopes he would rise to the opportunity and turn out something wonderful that could be produced. The subject matter was to be entirely of his choosing. He felt down at the time and I just wanted to support him and show that someone believed in him and was willing to encourage his effort." He recollects

10 "Editorial," *Sing Out!*, Volume 15, Number 5, November 1965. Reprinted by permission.
11 *Folk Scene Diary Summer 1965 by* Richard A. Reuss.

that he paid Paul $500 a month for six months. "My expectation was that he would be paid substantially more if it was viable."

In the meantime, in the months after Newport, Paul attended two more Dylan appearances: at Forest Hills and Carnegie Hall. The music was presented in acoustic and electric sets. "I felt there was a little bit less animosity," Paul told Jeff Rosen. "At that point, he was sort of winning them over.

"Bob had invited me to some party after that because he loved what I wrote at Newport. It was somebody's house somewhere on the East Side. I remember we talked a little bit and he said, 'Well, what did you think?' and I said, 'I liked it. I liked the acoustic part as well, but I must say I waited for you to get to "Like a Rolling Stone" because that's the song I want to hear you do. It seems like that's just a very special song.' And he said, 'Yeah. You know, I wait for that moment, too. I get to sing it.' That was nice."

> Dylan has really shown me that there isn't a critic in the world that knows, really knows, anything about what the artist is trying to do, and therefore, none of them, you and I included, is really worth a damn.... You need more than negativity in this world to pull you through. I'm getting the completely wacky rationale of If-I-Dig-It,-It's-Good;-If-Not,-So-What? It's not doing anybody any harm; and there are more important things to consider.... Only pieces which discuss, try to understand, probe the artistic methods, etc., with something else besides Criticism in their hearts have any real value. I really think Dylan taught me this. He also taught me not to chicken out, not to be afraid to take a chance. Believe me, it would have been the easiest thing in the world to rationalize my way out of this script job—and the job itself scares me to death sometimes!—but I figured, and rightly, I think, that to get anywhere, you've got to take the chance, make the jump, and not consider whether you know enough or not. Worry about that later. If you make the leap first, you're out in mid-air: you've got to come through out there. If you consider first, you'll never make that leap—and you'll never know. So from now on, I jump. Jump first and worry later. Take the chance that I'll land on my feet. If I do, great. If I don't, I'm no worse off than before.[12]

Paul never delivered a screenplay to Holzman. Despite his creative and ethical differences with Silber, Paul left *Sing Out!* on good enough terms to

---

12 Letter to Jon and Marcia Pankake, October 20, 1965.

continue contributing to the magazine for a few more years. Focusing more often than not on the "New Music" better known as rock & roll, he eventually devoted a regular column, "Pop*oeuvres*," to the subject.

> While no one in their right mind is going to deny that the New Music has been influenced to a great degree by Negro rock-and-roll and rhythm-and-blues, it is too easy to overestimate their importance on its final worth. The question is, can one really correlate the Mississippi Delta and Chicago's South Side to the triumph of Bob Dylan's *Highway 61 Revisited* or the Beatles' *Rubber Soul*? Only indirectly if at all, I think, and certainly no more (and perhaps a good deal less) than other correlations which would include women, experiences, ways of dealing with everyday craziness on any street in any city, abstract painting and poetry, modern dance, comic books, genre movies, the works of John Barth, J.P. Donleavy, Thomas Pynchon, Joseph Heller, Jack Kerouac, Ken Kesey, Bertolt Brecht, Susan Sontag, Marshall McLuhan, Charlie Chaplin, Jean-Luc Godard, François Truffaut, Brigitte Bardot, Humphrey Bogart, Jean-Paul Belmondo, et al.[13]

Over the next few years, Paul wrote about rock & roll for an assortment of publications, including *The New York Times*, *The Village Voice*, *Penthouse*, and *Hullabaloo*, which he also edited for a year and a half after it changed its name to *Circus* (Paul's never-ending thirteen-part interview with the Who's Peter Townshend spanned both incarnations of the magazine). Paul had only written one piece (about the Band) for the still San Francisco-based *Rolling Stone* when, in the February 15, 1969, issue, publisher Jann Wenner placed a small notice far back in the same issue:

> Paul Nelson, formerly the editor of *Little Sandy Review*, *Sing Out!*, and other musical publications, has been appointed as the editorial representative of *Rolling Stone* in New York City. Mr. Nelson is the first person to represent *Rolling Stone* in a full-time capacity in New York, and he is the only person employed by *Rolling Stone* to conduct editorial business in New York. So don't let anyone else fool you. Beware of imitations, Mr. Nelson is the man.[14]

13 "The Extensions of Rock," *Sing Out!*, September 1966. Reprinted by permission.
14 "2 New Yorkers" from *Rolling Stone*, February 15, 1969. © Rolling Stone LLC 1969. All rights reserved. Reprinted by permission.

The next month, Paul wrote the infamously unflattering "Janis: The Judy Garland of Rock and Roll?" Myra Friedman, Joplin's publicist, said, "It was pretty much a disaster, but it wasn't his fault. The issue was her. He later told me that he had never in his life heard anybody, let alone a big star, talk like that, begging for support. I mean, all he did was report it and turn it in and feel terrible."

"I wanted to do a favorable story," Paul said, "and she told me so much more and was so negative about herself and her quarrels with the band. There was no degree of self-understanding or self-protection. I just thought, My God, this woman is going to get eaten up alive by this business. You cannot go around saying things like that to people in this business. Because if you tell them to the wrong person, they're going to turn a double-barreled

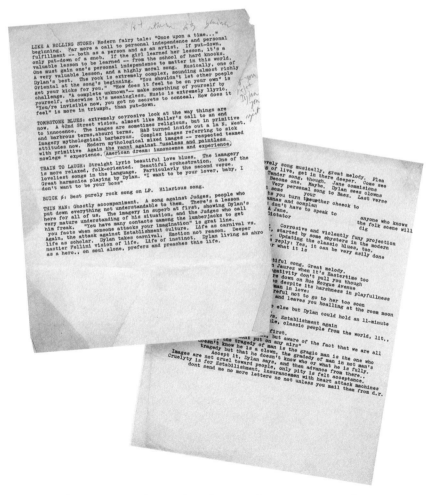

Paul's notes regarding Bob Dylan's Highway 61 Revisited, *1965.*

shotgun on you and just wipe you out. I really became very much afraid for her after that interview."[15]

A few months later with only ten articles to his name, Paul surrendered his position of East Coast eminence at *Rolling Stone* and, for a while, stopped writing altogether. "I was just totally broke and sort of written out as a critic. I just wrote so much that I sort of burned out for a few years." Instead, he went to work for Mercury Records: "Five good years, five bad years. The same five years: 1970–1975."

"**T**his was the first woman I ever really loved," Paul told Leonard Cohen. "She was an artist without an art[16]. She was very smart. She had an artistic mind but she didn't write or paint. She was a singer. She's on a Folkways record in a chorus doing Balkan songs."

He'd met Bobbi London in the office of Oak Publications, which published *Sing Out!* and was aligned with Folkways Records. Paul wasn't attracted to her because she was a folksinger in a group called the Pennywhistlers. Only after they'd been together for a couple of years did she find out that Paul's interest had been piqued when a coworker told him that London slept with men for books. "He found that irresistible. He was different than anybody I'd ever met. Paul was very sweet. But it was his writing that really attracted me to him."

At first London kept her distance. She and Paul occasionally dined together, but he was still living in Queens with Doris and Mark in a two-bedroom apartment on Queens Boulevard. London says, "I wasn't looking to split up a family. I thought children should have fathers in their lives." But Paul persisted in wooing her—and, in case the rumor was true, giving her books. She'd been part of Paul's electrified experience at Newport. "We stayed in a funny little hotel that had staircases that went nowhere."

In November of 1966, Paul left Doris and Mark and moved in with London, first in the East Village (where the Hells Angels became next-door neighbors), later in Brooklyn. "If no one else had come along, I don't know whether or not he would've made the move. But he felt he didn't have anything besides Mark left in that family." They were together until the spring of 1971 when, to Paul's dismay, London left.

"Mostly because Paul was *absent*. He was not really emotionally complete." She suspected that reason lay with his upbringing back in frozen Minnesota.

---

15 In the 2003 film *Masked and Anonymous*, rock journalist Jeff Bridges echoes Paul's concern when he prompts Bob Dylan's character, "Remember Janis Joplin, huh? The Judy Garland of rock & roll?"
16 Paul lifted this line from the 1950 film version of Gerald Kersh's *Night and the City*.

"It was something like Evangelical Mission Covenant, which was something that this New York Jew didn't know of at all. I always felt that there was something really serious about his childhood. He was so incomplete and absent in so many ways that I just felt that something knocked him down, you know. He wasn't a complete person.

"You know, Paul's interests really were in three areas: music, books, and movies. He really didn't have much to say about anything else. If we were in a social situation, I would almost feel like I was socializing for two. He would take everything in, but he just wouldn't say anything. His writing, it took so much. I'm not sure that he had room for anything else.

"Our relationship progressed from really sweet to a real good friendship. It's part of why I knew it was time for me to leave. I was too young to be in that kind of relationship. Yet I knew he really, really loved me—and I loved him." Mindful of how he might react, she underwent four months of therapy to help prepare for the day she broke the news. When she did, there was no discernible reaction. "There's no doubt in my mind that it hurt him. The only emotion that I ever saw Paul exhibit really was emotion over Mark."

Paul was leaving town for a few days on business. When he returned, London was gone. She left their Eastern Parkway residence as intact as possible. "I wanted everything to look the same except that my books, my records, my stuff—the guitar that he bought me that I still have—and I wouldn't be there anymore."

Leonard Cohen wanted to know what caused the breakup. Paul said, "It was possibly so intense for the three years maybe we burned it out, I don't know. It wasn't burned out on my side. It was more romantic than any romantic movie I have ever seen, it was more idealized than anything I could have ever imagined. I felt so strongly about it that I'd walked out on the

Circa 1970.

39

marriage. We spent every twenty-four hours together. We would do everything together, and we both wanted it that way. Ironically, I was the freest I'd ever felt. The last six months, she was becoming more and more distant, and so we weren't together as much.

"I keep thinking about it and thinking about it. I filled notebook after notebook with it. I read these things back and I find that sometimes I've rewritten it in my memory and it didn't go down exactly as I remember it going down. So I have to read the diaries again because I've made up my own version in my memory. But I read those and I think about it and I still don't know the reason, I just don't.

"I don't think I'll ever understand and I probably won't ever get over it, although it doesn't kill me now. It *did* kill me for five years at least after it. She calls every once in a while to keep in touch. I've long since given up hope that it would ever start again. For a long time I did think it was possible. I thought, Well, Jesus, it's happened once, this is the first time it's happened to me, it'll happen to me again, you know, on the same level. But it never did. I've lived with women since, been in love with women since, but not to that extent."

"I don't think you have too many of those," Cohen said. "I don't think you could stand too many of those."

Bobbi London: "I think he locked up permanently after we split up. I really think that a key was turned."

Among New York literati, Paul Nelson is known for drinking two Cokes with every meal and not eating a single green vegetable since Dylan went electric.
—*Rolling Stone* author bio[17]

Perhaps as much as the cap, dark glasses, and the expensive but longer-lasting Nat Shermans (which he never inhaled), for many of Paul's friends the mere mention of his name evokes restaurant memories of Paul invariably ordering two Cokes, something from a very short internal menu of permissible entrées, and "nothing green." Regardless of the main dish (each one denoting a different era: veal piccata at La Strada in the Sixties and Seventies, hamburgers at Jackson Hole in the Eighties and Nineties, then barbecue at Dallas BBQ in his final years) he without fail pushed the vegetables aside. Paul frequented these restaurants with such regularity that, upon his arrival—always at the same time—the servers automatically set his table with twin colas when he sat down.

17 "We Are All on Tour: Are You Prepared for the Pretender—Jackson Browne?" from *Rolling Stone*, December 16, 1976. © Rolling Stone LLC 1976. All rights reserved. Reprinted by permission.

40

*With Rod Stewart, on tour with the Faces in the Carolinas or Virginia, circa 1971.
Photo by David Gahr. Used by permission.*

When Bobbi London lived with Paul, she finally succeeded in getting him to eat eggs by scrambling them and serving them on a hamburger bun. For years that was the only way he'd eat eggs. "What he was unfamiliar with he didn't want to know about. He wasn't adventurous—except in his imagination. There he just flew."

At Paul's memorial service, New York Dolls lead singer David Johansen recalled what it was like dining with Paul in the Seventies: "He would order two Cokes and he's smoking the Shermans, and every day he would eat veal piccata—and nothing that came with it. After about five or six times, I realized this fuckin' guy's like Schopenhauer: the same fuckin' meal every day."

Also missing from his menu were some of the Sixties and Seventies' more notorious offerings. "Here's a guy who only smoked cigarettes," Bobbi London says. "He didn't drink coffee, he didn't drink tea, he never took a drink. He would have Coke when he woke up in the morning. And yet everybody he hung out with—drinking, doing drugs, just enjoying the era fully, myself included—he was, you know, an observer."

Still, a few casual acquaintances made the assumption that drugs were the reason for Paul's sometimes ghostly appearance and withdrawn affect. Even close friends like David Breithaupt, who knew Paul in the Eighties and Nineties, couldn't help but sometimes wonder, what with the cigarette burns on Paul's clothing. "He was almost like a jazz musician that was on the nod."

"He did look like a user," Dave Marsh says, "but he wasn't one."

41

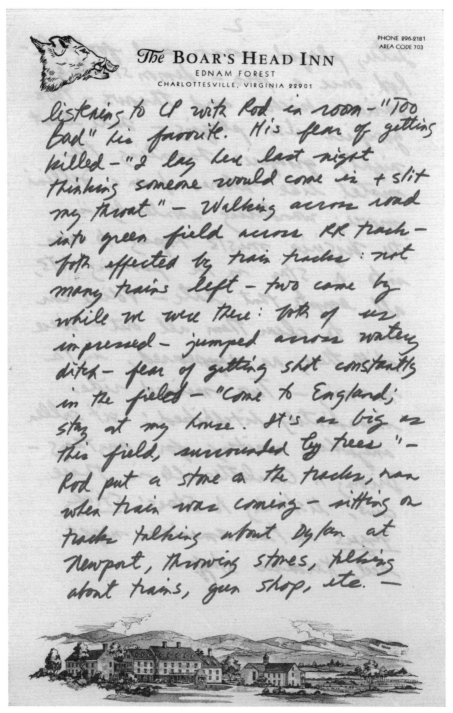

PHONE 296-2181
AREA CODE 703

The **BOAR'S HEAD INN**
EDNAM FOREST
CHARLOTTESVILLE, VIRGINIA 22901

listening to LP with Rod in room – "Too
Bad" his favorite. His fear of getting
killed – "I lay here last night
thinking someone would come in + slit
my throat " – Walking across road
into green field across RR track –
folk effected by train tracks : not
many trains left – two came by
while we were there : both of us
impressed – jumped across watery
ditch – fear of getting shot constantly
in the fields – "Come to England;
stay at my house. It's as big as
this field, surrounded by trees " –
Rod put a stone on the tracks, ran
when train was coming – sitting on
tracks talking about Dylan at
Newport, throwing stones, talking
about trains, gun shop, etc. –

Charlottesville, Virginia, hotel note, written while on tour with the Faces circa 1971.
"… Rod asked me to watch some of the concerts from backstage so I could

2

later, played soccer and football-
Rod once a pro — demonstrating
various kicks and throws — Two
groupies also playing — late last
night, groupies haunting the
motel like whores from a Fellini
movie; wandering aimlessly in
the Virginia mists hoping to run
into a star in the parking lots,
all empty that late — Police car
come to clean them all out — Were
still there, or reappeared, in the
morning — Two missed rides,
immediately hitchhiked; sit sullen
anywhere waiting for anything —
Driving to Charlottesville in three
cars, listening to Stones' _Sticky
Fingers_ in the American night:
real Kerouac stuff —

*get a performer's-eye view of what it was like to have all of those people
staring at you, coming for you. All of those eyes, taking direct aim."*

With Mike Seeger and Charlie Fach at Mercury Records in 1972 or '73.

Breithaupt: "He was so—I guess the expression would be *laid-back*—I wondered if he was on medication sometimes."

Marsh: "It's a weird way to describe him, from my point of view. He's one of the most intense people I knew. What he was, he was taciturn. He was very much sort of what I like to imagine Dashiell Hammett might have been like. He didn't run his mouth all the time."[18]

When music writer Bud Scoppa invited Paul up to Boston to see the Tubes perform in the fall of 1975, "I tried to get him to snort some blow. He didn't do a very good job of it. I'm sort of glad it came out of his nose. I don't think he would've been able to handle it."

A couple of years later when Paul was on tour with Rod Stewart, Stewart and bandmate Jim Cregan encouraged him to partake in their snort fest. "For once in your life," Stewart urged. "Come on, Paul." Paul declined again and again, insisting unconvincingly, "I've had it many times in my life."

Warren Zevon couldn't understand why someone *wouldn't* want to take drugs to, among other things, make his worries go away. "I'm not really sure why not," Paul told him. "I think I sort of fear loss of control. I don't know quite why. I don't feel good if I start to lose control. I get worried *that* way."

Years later, when Paul interviewed Leonard Cohen just before sunset on a Friday, Cohen invited Paul to join him in the lighting of the Shabbat candle. After

18 Paul had a caricature of Hammett in his apartment, a gift from Jay Cocks.

singing the blessing over the flame as part of the Havdalah ceremony, he offered Paul a glass of wine, then instantly remembered, "Oh, you don't drink, eh?"

"I wish I did," Paul said.

Cohen encouraged him to take the glass anyway: "Here, don't drink it, just lift it up."

"I can't tell the difference between one wine and another."

"If you don't like it, you don't like it," Cohen told him.

"God help me, I like the taste of Coca-Cola better than anything."

Music executive and manager Danny Goldberg felt that Paul was an odd choice for a record company publicist. "He was incapable of being insincere. His taste was so important to him. He was not someone who would exaggerate or hyper-bullshit, which are things that you have to do a little bit of in doing PR. He was the same guy, his opinions about things were the same no matter what, regardless of whether he was getting paid or not." He remembers that Paul was more apt to rave about the latest Leonard Cohen album than the newest Mercury release.

Yet for five years he worked at Mercury Records, first in publicity, then in A&R, where he was responsible for scouting and developing talent and where he badgered and battled his higher-ups until they relented and signed a ragtag band of lovable miscreants named the New York Dolls.

Bud Scoppa: "He was a rock critic posing as a publicist. It was sort of like a guerrilla tactic."

"It was an accepted mode back then," Robert Christgau says, "the company hippie. Danny Fields was the classic guy who did that, but there were many." After their first lunch together, Paul took Christgau back up to his office and played him Tom T. Hall, turning him into a lifelong supporter of Hall's music. "Not that he needed me, but I helped his career. I made Hall visible in places that he wasn't visible. Paul did that.

"I think for somebody like me, he was an extremely effective publicist. There wasn't this enormous entertainment news industry that there is now. I'm sure he would be terrible with those people. But in a world where most rock critics, at one level or another, were kind of arty people who did what the fuck they wanted, yeah, he was a very good publicist. He couldn't probably get you into *Life* magazine or on television—that wasn't what he did. But he did that other thing quite well, because people respected him and because he did try to sell the stuff he liked and he sold it well."

Nick Tosches: "He had a pretty nice setup for a guy who was never a businessman. At one point—it was at either the Sherry Netherlands or the Pierre

With Blue Ash in Youngstown, Ohio, February 1973. Left to right: Frank Secich, Jim Kendzor, Bill Bartolin, Paul Nelson, and David Evans. Photo by Geoff Jones.

With Geoff Jones in Youngstown, Ohio, February 1973. Photo by Frank Secich.

Hotel—Rod Stewart threw this private party in his suite and told Paul to bring anyone he wanted. So we all went up there. It was like whatever Paul was supposed to be doing at that record company, he was doing the opposite—and Rod Stewart at that time really liked what he was doing. Rod loved the fact that Paul wasn't trying to set up any interviews for him. It was just eat, drink, and be merry."

"I think it's hard to imagine today," Elliott Murphy says, "the power of the critics and the way the music business took them seriously. Because it was really still the time where the music was leading the industry, not the industry leading the music like it is today. These were mysterious people to the music business. You know, who were these guys who knew everything about every record and had these collections and these bootlegs? Who were they, these Jon Landaus and Paul Nelsons and Lester Bangses? So they really took them seriously. They thought they knew something they didn't know. And they did."

Frank Secich, Blue Ash's bassist, tells the story how someone from Ohio happened to be in Paul's office at Mercury and, spying the group's demo atop one of the numerous stacks on his desk, encouraged Paul to give it a listen. He liked what he heard. That same evening, Paul and Bud Scoppa, who succeeded Paul in publicity, went to dinner at La Strada where they overheard three girls from Jamestown, New York, at an adjoining table talking about what a great band Blue Ash was. Figuring it was fate, Paul made his way to Ohio to see the band perform live. Their manager, Geoff Jones, picked him up at the airport.

Secich: "We were playing at a place called the Apartment in Youngstown, which was our home base. We did our set and we went back to the dressing room. Five minutes go by. Ten minutes go by. Paul doesn't show up—he's not there. Geoff says, 'Well, he probably didn't like you guys, then.'" Secich eventually found Paul holding court with two Cokes at the bar and asked him what he'd thought. "He's quiet for about five seconds and then says, 'Well, I think you're one of the best bands in the United States, and I'm going to sign you up to Mercury. I've just been trying to plan it all out.'"

The four weeks of recording sessions lasted from mid-February through mid-March of 1973, Paul flying over to Youngstown on Monday and returning home on Friday. In addition to cautioning the band never to sequence two songs in the same key next to each other on an album, he gave them a bootlegged tape of an obscure Dylan number called "Dusty Old Fairgrounds" and encouraged them to cover it. Mercury tried to obtain the necessary release from Dylan's publishing company, but they didn't recognize the song and had to forward a copy to Dylan, who confirmed that he had indeed written it.

Secich: "When our album came out in June 1973 we flew to Chicago to play at the Aragon Ballroom with the Stooges. It was also set up that we would spend a day at Mercury's headquarters and meet the execs and everyone who worked there. They had a whole day planned for us and we split up in focus groups. Our last session was with VP Lou Simon. Lou had tons of charts and graphs and proceeded to give a talk about distribution, rack-jobbers, one-stops, and on and on. About halfway through (we were having a hard time following it) he just looked at me and said, 'You guys haven't understood one word I've said, have you?' He then looked at Paul and said, 'How about you, Paul?' Paul slowly pulled the lit Sherman from his lips, shook his head and said, 'You lost me about ten minutes ago, Lou.' We all just busted up laughing. Even Lou did. So then Lou said, 'How about if we just play records the rest of the time?' and we did."

Ron Oberman, who hired Paul, says that just as John Hammond's signing of Bob Dylan was christened "Hammond's folly" at Columbia, at Mercury the New York Dolls became known as "Paul's folly."

With David Johansen of the New York Dolls and Christian Rodriguez (aka Frenchy), the band's valet. Backstage at the Whisky a Go Go in Los Angeles, September 1973. Photo by Bob Gruen.

At a Modern Lovers concert circa 1973. Photo by Danny Fields.

Paul the fan said, "I had the feeling when I saw the Dolls that I was lucky enough to be in the one spot in the world where the best band was playing. There wasn't any other music I'd rather have heard, and I held that feeling through hundreds of shows. I knew they were going to have to be a big success or I would lose my job—and I did."

Bud Scoppa says, "You don't think of Paul as a gutsy guy or a confrontational guy, but he did believe in his taste. It was fueled by passion and belief."

Elliott Murphy: "I think in a way he overestimated the interest of the American public in these things, but it was still an ideal worth fighting for. Paul had a firm belief that if the music he liked was exposed to the public, then they would like it, too. I think he was justified in those beliefs."

Paul always maintained that his demise at Mercury was due to the Dolls ("That's why they fired me," he told Rod Stewart, "I'm sure of it"), but whether he jumped or was pushed remains something of a mystery.

Betsy Volck: "He got sacked or he quit, and I'm sure it was over the Dolls. But I don't remember the epiphany when he wasn't working over there. I think they respected Paul, but he was odd and they didn't know what to do with him."

Nick Tosches: "At one point they were going to fire him, and Rod Stewart was a big deal. The story I heard was that Rod Stewart said, 'You fire him, I'm going to leave the label.'"

"If you put his tenure there under the template of A&R performance," Scoppa says, "I imagine they didn't renew his contract because he didn't have anything to show for it. He didn't sign anything that generated revenues for the label."

Paul said, "I didn't do it for any other reason than I really loved the band. This was a once in a lifetime shot to get this band. Screw the job, screw everything. I knew that if they didn't make it—I had made such a bad lot of it and caused rifts within the company—that I was gone. My career as an

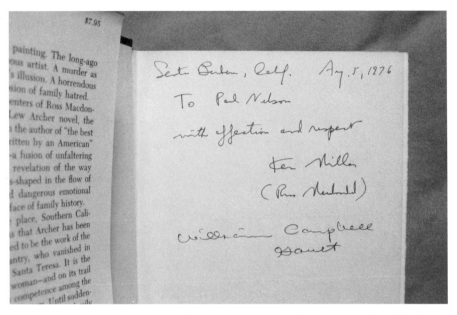

Paul's inscribed first edition of The Blue Hammer *by Ross Macdonald, also signed by William Campbell Gault, the book's dedicatee.*

But a few of the cassette interviews Paul conducted to supplement his almost forty hours of taped interviews with Ross Macdonald in 1976.
Photos by Jeff Wong.

A&R man was irretrievably tied to the New York Dolls, and I didn't care. I wouldn't have had it any other way. Even if I knew that it wasn't going to work out and the band would be no more after two albums, I would've done it anyway. You can't take those years away."

Frank Secich visited Paul's apartment in 1973. "He just had like a bed, a television, and a stereo. And in the living room part, no furniture. It was just completely bare.

"It struck me as funny because he would always wear this football jersey— he had a purple one and a white one—and he always wore blue jeans. And when I opened his closet, he had twelve of each one of those shirts and fourteen or fifteen pairs of the same blue jeans."

Bud Scoppa: "When you went into his apartment, you could see the compulsive nature of his personality. He would have particular kinds of shirts and Levis, I guess Frye boots, and his closet was just incredibly well-organized with these plastic hangers and then the shirts, which were identical button-shirts, and they were all organized by color."

"I remember mostly bookshelves," Greil Marcus says, "just meticulously arranged with, all over in various places, a book pulled out and displayed cover forward. In other words, the bookshelf was like a knickknack shelf as well as a bookshelf. It was a display case, and there were a number of books that were on little stands, like you used to put a framed photograph on it. I was there with a couple of other people, and I remember somebody saying, 'Paul, why do you have these books here like they're art objects or something?' I understood perfectly because I have a fetishistic tendency, too, towards books and records and stuff like that. These were things of magic. They were there both because they were beautiful to him and he liked to look at them, but also because they signified his oneness with the books that he loved. It was a kind of a mystical connection. Any collector would understand that: that's a thing that he or she loved. It was just a matter of making that patently physical. I just thought that was wonderful."

Writer Tom Carson: "He did have that hermit side all along. You walked into his old apartment on Lexington Avenue and you *knew* this was someone's *lair*. It was not a place where you could just bring in a huge company of guests—it was one man's lair. All of his first editions of Chandler and Hammett and Ross Macdonald and all of his prized records. And you could just tell: that's where he was happiest and he was happiest alone, surrounded by all the talismans that meant the most to him."

Marcus: "I had never seen Paul without his cap on, and I had no idea he was completely bald. So here I was in his apartment and here's this guy I've never seen before, and I just thought that was shocking—either at my own naïveté or his being effective in his disguise. What was really true was that it was only in his retreat or his shrine for the things that he loved, his apartment, that he could reveal himself without any embarrassment or shame."

There is a certain type of movie nut who sits front row center, leans forward and lets the film wash over him like the rush of wind past his ears, *feels* what is going on up there, his face aglow from the light of the screen. There is no distancing here, no attempt to push back for perspective.

It is the same with loudness, the sheer volume of the New Music: no distancing, no perspective, only that caught on the run, the imp of meaning, the wisp of nuance, the new cool drawing one right into its tactile heart, its shifting surfaces of sound.[19]

"Music was my second love. Movies were my first love," Paul told journalist Steven Ward. "I wanted to come to New York to be a movie critic, but that was hard. But it was easy as hell to be a rock critic in those days."

In fact, while Paul credited Dylan with dragging him into the world of rock & roll, the movies also played a part in that abduction with the release of the film *A Hard Day's Night*. "The Beatles sort of existed for me on the radio, but until I saw Richard Lester's movie I didn't get it. Whereas the kids knew it all the time, that they had something, it took a movie to get them into the grownups' mind. All of a sudden they could go to *A Hard Day's Night* and say, 'Wow, they are pretty good,' and *then* they could go back to the records."

Written-out and earning a steady income at Mercury, Paul enjoyed the luxury of being able to write only when he wanted, contributing to various publications, including *The Village Voice*, *Chicago Daily News*, *The Real Paper*, and *Fusion*. For *Rolling Stone*, in addition to a smattering of record reviews, he wrote a string of impressive, in-depth pieces about films (*Dirty Harry, Fat City, The Getaway, Marjoe, What's Up, Doc?*) for editor Jon Landau. "It was all seamless, you know: music, film, books—it's just the people that he identified with and who had that certain kind of personal vision that spoke to him. I think the aesthetic and the point of perspective that he brought to it was similar, whether it was one or the other. He was a multimedia man."

19 "Living Stones" [published as "Bolts of Lightning"] by Paul Nelson, *Hullabaloo*, May 1967. Reprinted by permission.†

A small part of Paul's video collection. Photo by Kevin Avery.

In the second half of the Seventies, Jay Cocks and Paul would go in together and buy blank videotapes in bulk to support their movie-taping habit. "The commonality with Paul, besides the music, was movies. You didn't come across that many people who had seen *Jules and Jim* a dozen times. It would be like coming across a lot of people who play Robert Johnson records for a weekend straight. There weren't that many, but, boy, when you met them you were half-married already. That's the way it was with movies, especially with film noir, and John Ford, Hawks, Walsh, Wellman, all these great people that Paul adored. He was as passionate about movies, as knowledgeable about movies, and felt them as deeply and responded as truly to them as he did to 'Desperados Under the Eaves' or *The Pretender.*"

Landau remembers Paul's review of Peter Bogdanovich's screwball comedy homage *What's Up, Doc?* "It was almost an impossibility to edit because the thing was mapped out so jigsaw puzzle-like. You literally would have trouble changing a word. Anyway, I made some changes. Normally, anything I changed I always went back to the author for approval. Being primarily a writer, I was very sensitive to that. But for some reason, I changed a *the* to an *a* or something. Paul wasn't mad, he was just so despondent. He said, 'Ah, the review just doesn't make any sense.' It destroyed the thing for him. He wasn't built to be edited."

Paul had started writing about movies back at the University of Minnesota with Jon Pankake. "We would see most of the movies that came into town and after reading people's reviews—we had a terrible reviewer in the local paper whose reviews were just awful and missed the point every time—we started writing, just for the fun of it, reviews of the movies we'd seen. Then we'd show them to each other and nod. It was just writing for the fun of writing, and writing out of the spirit of discovery.

"We were discovering directors, that how good a movie was depended on who directed it. We kept finding these names Howard Hawks and John Ford, and we both liked John Wayne Westerns; but we realized when John Wayne was in a John Ford movie, like *The Searchers*, this was way, way different from his other movies.

"We found out at that time that there was this school of French movie criticism called the *auteur theory*. Basically, the auteur theory was that the person who was really the author of the movie can get depth and consistency into his movies that someone who's just doing a job for a studio can't. I think one of the writers we discovered that through was Peter Bogdanovich, who wrote articles for *Film Culture*, which was kind of a *Little Sandy Review* of movies."[20]

Arguably, Paul's favorite film critic was Andrew Sarris, whose book *The American Cinema: Directors and Directions 1929–1968* was instrumental in introducing the auteur theory to the United States. "He really had a high regard for Sarris," Bud Scoppa says. "This book was like the Bible. He loved the organization of it, too: the 'Lightly Likable,' 'The Far Side of Paradise,' 'Pantheon Directors,' the ratings, the levels of greatness. It was that array thing, just like his closet." Undoubtedly, one of Paul's favorite sections was "Expressive Esoterica," where some of his favorite directors, like Don Siegel and Budd Boetticher, resided. "These are the unsung directors with difficult styles or unfashionable genres or both," Sarris wrote. "Their deeper virtues are often obscured by irritating idiosyncrasies on the surface, but they are generally redeemed by their seriousness and grace."

Though they wrote about different disciplines, Sarris was a huge influence on Paul's work. In his critique of Dylan's *Highway 61 Revisited* for *Sing Out!*, Paul acknowledged a conversation that he'd had with Sarris, whose "ideas on director Josef von Sternberg had a partial influence on portions of this review"

---

20 Paul also was an admirer of Bogdanovich's films. Jonathan Lethem remembers watching *The Last Picture Show* with Paul, as well as *St. Jack* and *They All Laughed*, "which was another outré movie that was a very big passion for him." Paul kept three extra VHS copies of the 1981 romance-detective pastiche on hand just in case something went wrong with his original copy.

(but the magazine deleted the nod). And when Paul wrote about the first Ramones album, he mirrored what Sarris had written about Samuel Fuller in *The American Cinema*.

Jac Holzman says that at one point he and Paul met with Sarris over dinner and proposed launching a magazine together. "Paul always wanted to do something with film and never was able to do it. I would've been willing to finance it if Paul had a chance to edit it. Nothing actually ever came of it."

Andrew Sarris fondly remembers Paul. "We must've met at some screening or something, and I was very, very taken. A very acute intellect. I had a tremendous respect for him, even though I wasn't in his field, so to speak."

Critic Richard Meltzer recalls when Paul contributed to *Changes*, a newspaper published by Sue Graham Mingus (fourth wife and widow of jazz great Charles Mingus). "He wrote a piece about how great beach movies—surf movies—were. He liked the fact that Sarris kind of singlehandedly made the world safe for Westerns again, and so he picked some genres where he clearly would be the one trailblazing and said that all these Frankie Avalon/Annette Funicello movies were just pure joy. How can you knock 'em?"

> I finally got to see *Bikini Beach*, the first of this series I've caught. I'm really sorry I missed the first two *Beach* pictures, and, if they ever come around again, I certainly won't make the same mistake twice. If they were anything like this one, the series must be the closest thing to pure cinema being turned out anywhere in the world, France included. No attempt at a narrative, no attempt at expressiveness, no attempt at establishing a moral order—simply two hours of entertaining and amusing images and sounds, a sort of color symphony of silliness and the bizarre.[21]

William MacAdams: "He really wasn't interested in anything except for American culture. His interest and knowledge in foreign films was strictly from the 1960s, which was the high point of when foreign films were shown on American screens. There were lots of foreign directors—Antonioni, for example—he didn't like. He liked Godard, he wasn't that crazy about Truffaut, and Fellini he really liked."

Paul in particular liked Godard's *Made in U.S.A.* In the film, ostensibly inspired by *The Big Sleep*, the characters' names were largely lifted from cinematic, political, and literary figures (Donald Siegel, Richard Widmark, Richard Nixon, Robert MacNamara, et al.), and the protagonist, played by Anna

21 *Lists: One Year's Worth of a Mythological Autobiographical Journal of a Life Seen through Popular Culture Transmogrified* by Paul Nelson.†

Karina, was named Paula Nelson. "Paul was convinced Godard had named her after him," according to MacAdams, "which is very possibly true since almost all the characters were named after real people. (The two other writers, Goodis and Céline, plus Paul make for a truly bizarre trio!) Paul wondered how Godard could know of him: *The Little Sandy Review*? Pieces in *Sing Out!*? Doesn't seem likely, Godard never waxing Godardian about American folk music or rock & roll (yes, there is the awful Rolling Stones picture, but that was a political film). So if Paula were Paul, where and how did Godard make his acquaintance?"

When it came to movies, Paul's taste often was at odds with the critical darlings. "He liked the dark horses," Jonathan Lethem says, "the ones that everyone had rejected, like *Heaven's Gate*" (he liked the soundtrack to Michael Cimino's film so much, and was so sure the record would be discontinued, that he bought three copies). Conversely, he hated Cimino's *The Deer Hunter* but loved the largely dismissed Clint Eastwood-Jeff Bridges buddy-heist hybrid *Thunderbolt and Lightfoot*. He thought Woody Allen was "The joke of the age," "The most overrated director in the history of cinema," and wanted to know "If he's this reclusive genius, what's he doing at Elaine's every night?" He wasn't a fan of Kubrick's films, but he loved *The Way We Were* and went to see it six times. He adored Kim Novak and never felt she got the respect she deserved.

Paul enthused about David Cronenberg's *The Brood* to John Morthland. "I said, 'Wow, that sounds really cool,' and he said, 'Well, I've got it right here.' Of course, I'd never seen a video before, and he had a whole wall of them. He popped it in and we watched that movie."

"He had this endless collection of obsessively hand-lettered videotapes," Lethem says, "this entire body of great Hollywood films that he'd been taping off late-night television (complete with all these obsolete, hilarious commercials)."

Michael Seidenberg: "Videotapes. Thousands. And every time he'd lend some to someone, he'd have index cards. You had to sign the index card." His wife Nicky Roe says, "He had little red numbers on each one and then the title and then the card reference."

Lethem: "He was such an expert on Orson Welles and on John Ford and Howard Hawks and took us on such a great journey with his knowledge. He always would know, 'Well, there are two versions of *Red River*. One is the good one and you have to make sure you see that one.'[22] We would watch these obscure Orson Welles films like *Mr. Arkadin* and he would know the production circumstances. Of course, now in the Criterion Collection era, it's easy to be an expert on that stuff, but he had totally mastered it when it was like being a detective. He was following his clues and gathering up this information."

---

22 Paul preferred the "book version," which utilized handwritten entries from a cowhide-bound journal to tell the story, to Hawks's director's cut, which was seven and a half minutes shorter and relied instead on narration by Walter Brennan.

"He could appreciate a corny sci-fi B-movie as well as a classic Orson Welles like *Chimes at Midnight*," David Breithaupt says. "He could tie everything together in his own way and see some redemption in most things."

"There's rarely a movie so bad that I will truly dislike it," Paul said. "There's something endearing about some of the bad ones."

At Paul's memorial service, writer Michael Azerrad read a list of thirty of Paul's favorite films and their directors, based largely on his viewing habits at Evergreen:

The Asphalt Jungle, John Huston, 1950
The Big Heat, Fritz Lang, 1953
The Big Sleep, Howard Hawks, 1946
Blade Runner, Ridley Scott, 1982
Bullets Over Broadway, Woody Allen, 1994
Chimes at Midnight, Orson Welles, 1965
Crossfire, Edward Dmytryk, 1947
Gizmo!, Howard Smith, 1977
High and Low, Akira Kurosawa, 1963
In a Lonely Place, Nicholas Ray, 1950
The Killers, Donald Siegel, 1964
Letter from an Unknown Woman, Max Ophüls, 1948
Lola Montès, Max Ophüls, 1955
Madame de ..., Max Ophüls, 1955
My Darling Clementine, John Ford, 1946
The Naked Gun: From the Files of Police Squad!, David Zucker, 1988
The Naked Gun 2 1/2: The Smell of Fear, David Zucker, 1991
The Naked Gun 33 1/3: The Final Insult, Peter Segal, 1994
Once Upon a Time in the West, Sergio Leone, 1968
Opening Night, John Cassavetes, 1977
Out of the Past, Jacques Tourneur, 1947
Peeping Tom, Michael Powell, 1960
Raging Bull, Martin Scorsese, 1980
The Searchers, John Ford, 1956
Sunset Boulevard, Billy Wilder, 1950.
Sweet Smell of Success, Alexander Mackendrick, 1957
The Unforgiven, John Huston, 1960
Vertigo, Alfred Hitchcock, 1958
The Wild Bunch, Sam Peckinpah, 1969
The Yakuza, Sydney Pollack, 1974

With Martin Scorsese on Christmas Day circa 1978.
Photo courtesy of Jay Cocks and Verna Bloom.

In the mid-Eighties, William MacAdams had asked Paul to list his ten favorite films of all-time. "There are eleven pictures because Paul couldn't decide on which Coppola to include. The list is not hierarchical."

Touch of Evil, Orson Welles, 1958
The Searchers, John Ford, 1956
Once Upon a Time in the West, Sergio Leone, 1968
The Outlaw Josey Wales, Clint Eastwood, 1976
Mean Streets, Martin Scorsese, 1973
Contempt, Jean-Luc Godard, 1963
Vertigo, Alfred Hitchcock, 1958
Letter from an Unknown Woman, Max Ophüls, 1948
The Wild Bunch, Sam Peckinpah, 1969

Apocalypse Now, Francis Ford Coppola, 1979
The Godfather: Part II, Francis Ford Coppola, 1974

Cut free from the gainful employment that Mercury had provided, Paul returned to freelancing. In 1976, he contributed four essays to *The Rolling Stone Illustrated History of Rock & Roll*, including a legendary one on Dylan that remains as definitive as it is affectionately noirish. Greil Marcus worked with editor Jim Wilson on the book. "Jim and I were the people who were hounding Paul for his stuff. I got to know him much better in terms of being a hermit, in being someone who would shut himself off."

That same year, Paul contracted to write *John Lennon: A Biography in Words & Pictures*, one of a series of six books about notable rock & rollers of the day. It was especially embarrassing to the publisher, Sire Books/Chappell Music Company, when he failed to deliver the manuscript, as the book with Paul's byline had already been advertised on the backs of the other five volumes.

Before the year was out, Paul landed a gig as record-review editor at *Circus* magazine, which he'd edited back in the Sixties. He quickly made the section his own, which is why any given page might include reviews of not only Arlo Guthrie, Judy Collins, and Danish rock band Gasolin', but also classic film composer Bernard Herrmann:

> Although the late Bernard Herrmann's soundtrack recording for Brian De Palma's magnificent *Obsession* probably stretches the critical confines of this column, it certainly deserves mention here if only because this score was among his last and best. That Herrmann, a composer who worked closely with Alfred Hitchcock and Orson Welles (among others), contributed a great deal to the art of the film as well as to film music is unarguable. Neither *Psycho* nor *Obsession* would work quite like they do were it not for his pulse-pounding music. Bernard Herrmann's work was compelling, unnerving, absolutely haunting, and ultimately important. He will be missed.[23]

Wesley Strick, now a screenwriter, reviewed records for him. "Paul's section was totally independent from the magazine. *Circus* was a great magazine, but

---

23 *"Obsession—The Original Soundtrack Recording*—Music Composed and Conducted by Bernard Herrmann—National Philharmonic Orchestra" by Paul Nelson, *Circus*, December 14, 1976. Reprinted by permission.

there was something kind of low-rent about it. It had none of the credibility of *Rolling Stone* or even of *Crawdaddy!*, for that matter. It was like a teenybopper magazine." But it provided Paul with an income for the next two years.

A routine: Once every thirty days, for almost as long as I can remember, I transfer last month's albums from a teetering pile by the phonograph to a more orderly place of reference just to the left of my typewriter. From there, a process of selection begins.

The most obvious junk—LPs in which I have no interest or do not like—goes into a black carrying case, soon to be exchanged for filthy lucre. The remaining items are divided into three idiosyncratic categories: Don't Miss, Don't Avoid, and Don't Bother.[24]

"I get so many records," Paul said, "but I go through most of them and, after one listen, that's that. But I find a good one and it doesn't come off the turntable for six months. I'll play three records all year."

Paul met Jay Cocks, then film and music critic for *Time* magazine, in the mid-Seventies. "Paul was one who deserves the word *critic*; the rest of us were reviewers. Up until that time, writing about music was pretty technical. You had to know about musical form and structure. With rock & roll, there were all these people who had ways of wanting to express themselves about rock & roll but couldn't play an instrument—or wouldn't or didn't want to—and they started to write about it. They started to write about how the music made them feel and where the music sent them. Well, this was a totally unorthodox way of writing about music. It had something to do with the way that rock & roll could engage you on some kind of almost preconscious level. But there were very few people who could refine that emotion and follow it right into the heart, right where it led them. There were not very many people who would let the music lead them all the way. Paul was one of the people."

Kit Rachlis: "He helped create a form and a language that we now take for granted. He linked rock & roll to the great genres of American pop culture: the Western, noir, screwball comedy, and, most especially, the detective novel."

"My sense was that he went through the world looking around himself without seeming to," Greil Marcus says. "I think he really did inhabit the world as a kind of detective, someone who always had the world under surveillance.

24 "Paul Nelson Reviews" by Paul Nelson, *GO Magazine*, April 1970.

With Jay Cocks in the early Seventies.

He was always watching, he was always suspicious. I don't mean in a paranoid sense at all, I mean in a sense of curiosity."

Jon Landau remembers when Paul, during his Mercury years, brought a young David Bowie up to Massachusetts on a radio tour. But he knew Paul's writing from many years before when he'd subscribed to *The Little Sandy Review*. "Paul was in a class by himself. I think that although he was a lyric-oriented listener, his insights were so penetrating and his interpretations were of such great interest. He was very sensitive to the music, but it's just not where his expertise was. In his writing, he didn't dwell on the musicianship quality of people. He was in defiance against any kind of hierarchy of musical quality. That wasn't his take on things."

Chris Connelly, who went on to become a contributor to ABC News and ESPN, graduated from manning the switchboard at *Rolling Stone* to writing record reviews: "He could really like a Jackson Browne record and he could write so brilliantly about that Sex Pistols record, and mean it. Not everybody could work both sides of the room like that."

Robert Christgau: "I think it says a great deal for Paul that he loved Jackson Browne and the New York Dolls at the same time."

Singer-songwriter Bruce Springsteen's early career was bolstered by some key articles and reviews written by Paul. "I haven't seen writing like this about my stuff really very much since then," Springsteen says. "Obviously, there are still good writers out there, but the general approach is very different today. I think the power of rock criticism in the Seventies would be unrecognizable perhaps to rock writers today in some ways. It was a very powerful forum for guys like me at the time who had a couple of records out and no commercial success. In Paul's writing particularly there was a mixture: you always felt the fan's enthusiasm yet it was tempered by the incredible intelligence—just the immersion in not just what you were doing but who you *were* and where everything was growing from."

Paul sports a new lid in the early Seventies.

Cocks: "Even when he was describing his own turmoil or the turmoil of the people who made the music there was a gentleness and compassion in everything that he did. I think it was unique in rock writing, that kind of compassion.

"He totally disarmed me early in our relationship once by saying to me, 'You know, I really don't get black music.' Which is, of course, like a tremendous heresy in *any* kind of music writing, never mind rock & roll. It wasn't as if he was excusing himself or explaining himself—just defining himself, just setting out that parameter. You really got the notion that he would like to be able to respond to black music but there was so much that moved him anyway that it really wasn't that important."

Jonathan Lethem: "It was almost like an autism. If he didn't hear it, it was inaudible."

Christgau: "Paul was not attracted to African-American artists. For me, finally, that's the core, as far as I'm concerned. When I got to *The Voice*, it was very important for me to cover that music, and I was very proactive about it. Paul just wasn't. He liked what he liked—and that wasn't it. He had the things that touched him, that went into whatever core of suffering was obviously buried in his personality, and that's where it stood."

"It wasn't ever the box score with Paul," Cocks says. "It goes back to what I was saying before: he was not a reviewer. Any creative person could spend a minute with this guy and know that he was not an ally necessarily—not a guy who was going to give you a pass on something he didn't like, not a guy who wasn't going to ask a tough question—but that he was a *kindred spirit*. You would look at him—and this was Paul's thing about creative people, I think—and you got a sense almost immediately, not only in the way he acted and how he spoke, but what he asked and how he followed up what he asked with a tremendous sympathy that ran concurrent with an absolutely insistent honesty. He was not like a guy who was giving you a grade. He was a guy who was opening himself to you because you had opened yourself to him. When he listened to *The Pretender* or when he listened to Warren's first album or *The Wild, the Innocent & the E Street Shuffle*, his reaction wasn't 'It's great, you can dance to it' (I don't think you'd ever want to see Paul dance anyway), but it was more like, 'I understand where this came from and I live in the same place. I may not be able to express it the same way, but I recognize it.' It's this 'Hey, I know you. You're working the same territory I am. You understand that hidden place where the creativity comes from.'"

"His knowledge was so vast and he was so articulate," Bud Scoppa says, "that artists really embraced the opportunity to spend time with him."

Landau: "I was not a big fan of *The Wild Bunch* at the time (I have since come to have a different view of it), but it was one of our favorite rolling debates because he adored that picture. I always remembered him expounding on it in perfectly analytic terms—just the way he would write it—and sort of pointing to the most intimate and small detail to confirm his interpretation of the picture and what he was saying. Things like this, he couldn't have cared more about them if he had made the movie himself. He identified with them so strongly that he would just sort of take possession of them."

Cocks says, "You might say that one of Paul's fallibilities is that he invested so much of himself in what he was writing about that he started seeing things that were in *him* rather than the work."

When Paul wrote about a work of art, he had no agenda beyond understanding it. Perhaps befitting of his Midwestern upbringing, his writing is tellingly devoid of sex, politics, and religion. "He was the least political person I knew," Dave Marsh says. "But he did tell me that the only time he ever voted for president was in '64 when he wrote in Jac Holzman's name" ("And Norman Mailer for vice president," Paul claimed, "to write the story"). As he explained to singer-songwriter Suzanne Vega: "In a realistic way, if we assess the facts, I don't think one person's vote has ever decided any election. I used to vote but I don't anymore. Every time I did I got jury duty. As much as I love to read, I did not love sitting on a bench eight hours a day reading for two weeks. I just rationalized it to myself that my vote would never have counted in a single election in history to break a tie."

In the Seventies, Paul, Dave Marsh, Kit Rachlis, Jay Cocks, and Jon Landau comprised a core group of rock critics who used to hang around together. "I miss reading him," Marsh says, "but I really miss *him*. He was a wise person, and you never have enough of those in your life."

Late in 1976, Billy Altman attended a Lou Reed concert at the Palladium with Paul, Lester Bangs, and some other music writers. Reed performed before a backdrop of forty-eight black-and-white TV sets bombarding random images. "It was one of these phases where he was about as nasty as he could possibly be onstage. He was really vitriolic. We were sitting really close up in front, and the show ended and we all started to get up. Paul was not moving. He just sat there. He always wore his dark glasses, so we were actually afraid that something had happened to him. Lester and I and the whole bunch were waiting. 'Paul, are you okay?' And he just looked up and said, 'I feel like I'm shell-shocked.' He couldn't believe what he'd just seen: how horrible it was and how oppressive it was."

Publicist Susan Blond would see Paul at various hangouts around the city. "He sounded the opposite of New York. Ethereal—it didn't sound to me like he was from this planet. He talked a little slower, he considered words a little bit more, he wasn't a fast-talking guy." When he used the words *at all*, they came out as '*tall*.

Singer-songwriter David Forman: "He always seemed so quiet and reticent, but when we talked on the phone, especially late at night, he'd go on and on and on."

"If the phone rang at three or four in the morning," writer Charles M. Young says, "I knew it was either the Butthole Surfers or Paul."

Blond: "So then I heard this weird thing about him: that he slept with a gun next to him on his pillow or something. So that made him even more intriguing, although I never brought that up to him. All the characters at that time, we all were quirky."

Fred Schruers: "You might turn around at 11:37 PM and you'd see him at the Ritz trying to stay out of everybody's radar. The inevitable Sherman would be hoisted and he'd be watching the band. He seemed kind of invulnerable to noise. As smart and delicate as his sensibility was, he had an appetite for noise and an appetite for destruction—for destructive noise."

I just wanted to get the story the way I wanted it. And if it did not get there—where I wanted it to go—I did not turn it in. I didn't hack it out. If I didn't like it, I did not want it published. I wrote them for me. I was not really thinking about anyone reading them. I admit that I was a slow writer and I missed some deadlines, but I must have made a lot of deadlines, too, or you would not be writing this story about me.[25]

"Whether you agreed with Paul or not," John Morthland says, "you knew every word he wrote was just what he meant, that he'd been over it time after time until he had exactly what he meant by it."

Stephen Holden, critic for *The New York Times*, says: "I've got to say, Paul had the most extraordinary sense of integrity of any writer I've ever met. He was a purist—just a 100 percent purist in his commitment to get to the bottom of whatever he felt and find the essence of it and tell the truth, no matter who it would hurt."

Paul said, "It can take me a week to get the opening paragraph sometimes. People will look at it and say, 'Well, it's the same as the last one,' and I say, 'No, there's a semicolon here.' It makes all the difference. I can't even write a letter without rewriting it six times."

Jann Wenner remembers him in his office at *Rolling Stone*: "You'd go down there and he'd be sitting at his typewriter, and there was just no shaking that pace. He just operated at one speed."

It always began with yellow legal pads. "He'd use up pads and pads until he finally had every word in order," Bobbi London says, "exactly what he wanted to say, and then he would proceed to type."

"When I do get to the typewriter," Paul said, "it feels so good because then I know it's done with. It's as good as I can get it in longhand. Once I get it on the typewriter page it feels like I don't have to look at it anymore."

Ken Tucker: "As I got to know him a bit better, I would go over to his apartment and see stacks and stacks—these pieces of paper, things that he was writing—I would realize they were drafts of record reviews that he was writing out in longhand. It was a huge effort for him to write so effortlessly."

Anthony DeCurtis: "Paul was the sort of writer where the sweat didn't show. If you just read through the stuff you might even miss how good it was. It was

---

25 "What Ever Happened to Rock Critic Paul Nelson?" by Steven Ward, RockCritics.com, March 2000.

designed to be easy for you. It was like, 'The reader doesn't have to do the work, I'll do the work.'"

London: "If he made one mistake on a page, instead of correcting it that page would be ripped out of the typewriter and he would type it again."

Bud Scoppa says, "He had to get every word precisely right. It had to look beautiful as a manuscript. Combining that with his compulsiveness, his anal-retentiveness or whatever you want to call it, that made every piece an ordeal."

Chris Connelly: "You know, there are two types of people in the typewriter world: there were the people who were incredibly OCD about their words and there were people who were really OCD about how the words looked on a typed piece of paper. Paul was both."

Of equal concern was how his work made the journey to the printed page, and his manuscripts were rife with handwritten instructions to the copyeditor. Because he wanted his Chet Baker article for *Musician* to approximate the effect that Baker's music had on him, he scrawled across the first page of his perfect manuscript: PLEASE DON'T CHANGE THE PUNCTUATION—*NO SEMICOLONS*—BECAUSE IT REALLY IS RIGHT. THANKS. There was no place in Baker's music or Paul's writing for the semicolon.[26]

"Obviously," Greil Marcus says, "no writing's ever perfect and he understood that. But the artifact was important to him. People who love art or who love writing tend to fetishize certain aspects of it. Paul was a great fetishist that way. A fetishist of battered, lurid covers of detective stories, or of his own manuscripts."

The kind of paper he typed on mattered, too: "A coral color, little gray squiggles in it," London says. "He loved that paper. He'd buy reams and reams of it. Paul never took drugs of any kind or drank alcohol, but I did. I remember looking at the paper once when I was on a trip, and I was looking at the type and I saw rainbows around it, and I said, 'Now I know why he loves this. Now I get it.' He went into a real funk when they discontinued it, till he found another one that he would be able to use and like. But never as much as that orange paper."

"It takes *enormous* effort to write critical prose," Kenneth Millar said.

"It's not easy to be a good reviewer," Paul agreed. "I don't know that I'm a good one, but I think I'm better now than I was. It seems like it's going slower and slower, and harder and harder."

"And getting better and better," Millar said.

---

26 Later in his career, Paul grew to despise the semicolon. Saying that he'd rewrite an entire paragraph to circumvent its use, he admitted to Suzanne Vega, "It's totally illogical. The semicolon is used by all the best writers. I just won't." He was, however, an ardent believer in the emdash.

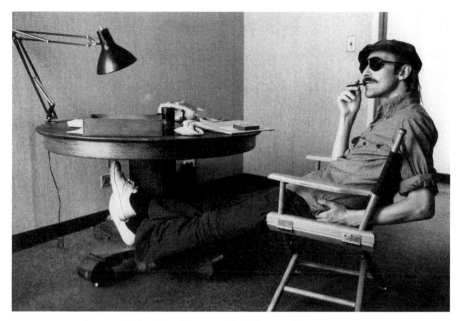

Circa 1978. Photo by David Gahr. Used by permission.

Paul Nelson, who's been reviewing records since Dylan went electric, is a thin, mysterious figure who rarely makes a deadline.

—*Rolling Stone* author bio[27]

In 1978, *Rolling Stone* music editor and one-time *Little Sandy Review* reader Peter Herbst asked Paul to succeed Dave Marsh as the magazine's record-review editor. "Paul was a fine writer, he was astute, he had a graceful style, but my primary interest was in the catholicity of his taste. Despite his folky background, he liked hard rock, he liked punk rock. I felt he wouldn't be prejudiced in any way towards any genre. In addition, he was a mature person. He was a little older, he'd been through a lot of things. I felt that he stood a chance of handling that environment, which was a very difficult environment. Jann was volatile, passionate, very smart, very opinionated, and knew what he wanted—except that thing that he wanted changed every week. Sometimes he could articulate it, sometimes he couldn't. Paul was one of those people who didn't get rattled. I mean, he'd get unnerved by things, but he didn't lose his cool. So I felt Paul stood a chance of working well with Jann." And Paul had worked with him before, albeit from 3,000 miles away, back in 1969, and had freelanced for the magazine ever since.

27 "The Songs that Still Remain: Our Favorite Records of the Past Ten Years" from *Rolling Stone*, December 15, 1977. © Rolling Stone LLC. All rights reserved. Reprinted by permission.

Herbst wasn't concerned that he'd sometimes had to poke and prod Paul to make his deadlines. "I guess I felt that once he was in a position of authority he would respond, and he did. The fact that people have trouble completing their own stories doesn't have anything to do with whether they can get a section in on time. In fact, it's kind of liberating. He always got his section in on time."

Paul told Steven Ward: "When I went back to *Rolling Stone* the second time, Jann offered me extra money to be a feature writer and the record-review editor. I picked just the record-review editor job because I was incapable of writing about someone that I did not like. So he paid me per piece I wrote. Either I had to love them or hate them. He let me pick the articles I wrote." He authored several lengthy, landmark pieces championing artists whose themes coincided with his own, whose work "consumed and transformed" him and sometimes caused his hands to shake.

Jann Wenner: "Every now and then he'd do a long, slow feature, take his time. That was the work that was suited for him. He had a day job and he had his night job; and the night job he loved, and the day job paid for that. We never pressured him really to produce stuff."

"I first read the byline *Paul Nelson* on December 25, 1966," Charles M. Young says. "Somebody gave me the two albums by Dave 'Snaker' Ray for Christmas: *Snaker's Here* and *Fine Soft Land*. Paul, of course, produced these albums and wrote these thrilling liner notes about the necessity of inspiration when you played the blues. Pure competence was not enough— it had to be inspired, which was really the point of Paul's life, his entire life.

"I remember playing those albums one night just because I wanted to listen to them, and I was just kind of idly rereading this stuff that I'd reread a thousand times since junior high, and it was like, Holy fuck, this is by Paul Nelson, whose office is next to mine!"[28]

Ken Tucker remembers dropping by *Rolling Stone* once to drop off a review and finding Paul sitting on the floor because his chair was filled with books and papers and albums, which came into his office at a much faster rate than they ever left. "In every way he was in his own world," critic Jim Farber says. "You'd go in his office, and it was this complete riot of detritus and material."

Young: "We were both introverts, so it took us a while to discover each other. But I knew he was a kindred spirit because his office quickly became even messier than mine, which was spectacular. We spent a lot of time

---

28 In the Sixties and Seventies, Paul's artful and perceptive liner notes graced many of the albums of artists whose work he admired. Billy Altman says, "Having grown up in a household where my sister, who's five years older than me, was into the folk movement in the mid-1960s, it seemed like every Elektra record that she brought home had liner notes on the back written by Paul Nelson."

discussing the edict from the owner of the magazine that had come down telling us to clean up our desks."

Paul Scanlon was a managing editor at *Rolling Stone* in the Seventies. "His office seemed almost womb-like. He was really, really comfortable in there and he never left, it seemed, not even to go to the john. If we wanted to say something to him, we'd all go into Paul's office. He'd receive us. I swear to God, I don't think I ever saw him leave the office."

Author Parke Puterbaugh says, "The fire marshal came in and inspected the premises and declared that Paul's office had to be cleaned out or there were going to be fines and citations. It was such a wreck. And here's this very organized man, who fussed over every comma and word."

Occasionally Paul found himself in the uncomfortable position of having to edit something Wenner had written. Herbst says, "He would sometimes review a record if he took an interest in it—meaning that it was somebody he knew and liked—and then Paul would have to work with him on the review. Jann was a credible writer, but he didn't write for a living and Paul would have to, in his very delicate Midwestern way, ease Jann into syntactical perfection and weed out some of the stuff that people might snicker at."

Paul had only been at his post six months when Wenner flexed his publisher muscle and wrote his own review recanting Paul's tempered assessment of the Rolling Stones' *Some Girls*.[29] Also taking exception with a recent concert review of the Stones by Dave Marsh and Greil Marcus's less than laudatory take on Dylan's *Street-Legal*, Wenner acknowledged that he was challenging the opinions of three writers who "are among the top five or six critics in the world," but wrote that the reviews had been "exceptionally negative and, in many ways, seemed based on weird hostility and bitterness."

Stephen Holden: "Jann would insist on positive reviews for his personal friends, including Boz Scaggs and Art Garfunkel, in particular, and Jimmy Webb. They got lots of coverage and they always got positive reviews."

"Jann was very fond of Art Garfunkel," Herbst says. "If he had an album coming out, he would want it to be the lede review.[30] Paul would say, 'Well, I don't know if that's really a good idea, Jann.' Art Garfunkel's a great guy and a charming fellow and a wonderful singer, but Paul was interested in how *Rolling Stone* was perceived by the purists who made up its base. Jann, I think, is sensitive to the base—and the shifting base—of *Rolling Stone*

29 Paul had originally assigned the piece to Ariel Swartley. A week or two before her wedding to Kit Rachlis, however, she'd concluded that there was no way she could make her deadline and get married and go on her honeymoon. As his wedding gift, Paul volunteered to review the album for her, saying, "Well, that's one excuse you won't be using again."
30 In publishing parlance, to avoid any possible confusion, *lede* is an intentional misspelling of *lead*, dating from when the metallic element lead was used in typesetting.

over the last forty years certainly better than anybody else. But Paul believed in this stuff. There was no calculation—Paul was totally idealistic about rock & roll. He believed in its transformative power, I think because he was transformed himself. I think that it was a difficult job for him, but one that he really loved."

Paul told Kenneth Millar that Wenner's close friend Paul Simon hadn't at all appreciated the snidely literate opening passage in Paul's lede review of *Still Crazy After All These Years* and, without going into detail, said it had "rather devastating results, I'm afraid."

> Although his aim may be higher, Paul Simon has always been more a wistful classicist than an adventurous romantic: He wouldn't dream of taking the Kierkegaardian leap to faith without first making a reservation at the best hotel on the other side.[31]

David McGee: "Jann always had his standards about the lede review being an important record, and that changed. That was one of the bones of contention between him and Paul at the end: Jann wanted the record reviews to reflect what people were buying, and Paul wanted them to reflect records that were moving the art forward, that said something about the state of the art, and it didn't have to have any relevance to the charts. A lot of them were punk records—and Jann hated punk. That was the beginning of the end for them."

"I find myself such a supreme romantic that it worries me a lot of times," Paul told Kenneth Millar. "People who get locked into romantic images are not only limited, it seems to me, but running along a sort of monorail that reduces their greatest strengths and their greatest weaknesses. In the end it's rather a tough haul, I think. On the one hand, I really admire people who are wallowing in this, and on the other hand I realize that it usually winds up doing them in or narrowing their vision down to an often useless point."

Debra Rae Cohen, now an assistant professor at the University of South Carolina, wrote for Paul at *Rolling Stone*. "Paul could be very, very gentle and very intimate in a way that largely had to do with silences. He was unbelievably romantic, but he was a romantic in terms that seemed to come out of the literature he read, not out of any kind of connection with real-world women. But he tried

---

31 "Pinin' Simon: Still Slick After All These Years" by Paul Nelson from *Rolling Stone*, December 4, 1975. © Rolling Stone LLC 1975. All rights reserved. Reprinted by permission. Reprinted from the original manuscript, which first appeared in *Rolling Stone* as an edited version.

hard, many times, to make that connection. In that way, he was very much like Lester, and that's one of the reasons that neither of them, I think, *ever* realized the romantic ideals that they had."

"He was always kind of lovelorn," Bud Scoppa says. "There were a couple of girls that he, I guess, considered his girlfriends for a while. There was this young blonde girl named Beth. It seemed like an unlikely pairing."

Paul had met her at a music festival in the early Seventies. She'd come by bus to Woodstock in 1969 when she was nineteen from a town in Tennessee with a population of less than 100. Not only did she own every Rolling Stones album available, she held dear the old hillbilly cylinders that her parents played every Saturday night on their antique phonograph.

When it didn't work out and she returned home, Paul filled the flyleaves of his hardcover copy of Hemingway's *The Nick Adams Stories* with felt-tipped feelings both bitter and forlorn.

> The Beth in Boston, the Beth that said we'd live together, that was the real Beth, the Beth that was willing to be courted. Disregard me, but all the experience in the world isn't going to do you a damn bit of good now because you lack all of the basic equipment. You can't give, take, answer a simple question, and until you face that, you're going to learn nothing, fail at everything, because you're going to run every time something important comes up, screening your basic failings with rationalizations that it's really something else, *anything else*, but your basic fear to be courted that caused the failure. Use us, if it has to be that way, just to learn (I hope it's more than that), and you may get someplace, and will at least have had a try, a *real* try, too. The other way, you'll just grow old, wondering why you never got anyplace, never really connected with anyone, and why nobody seems to understand what you are talking about, or care.

Betsy Volck joined Mercury Records as a press agent in 1973. She and Paul were thrown together when she had a fire in her building and moved into his apartment, which he was subletting from Janet Maslin and Jon Landau. Volck bought Paul a writing desk. "He would start around eleven o'clock and he would just write all night. Although I loved him madly and dearly, we were just opposites in every way. Paul was just, God bless him, one of God's finest people. Just one of the nicest people who ever walked on the earth. Never gossiped about people, never said nasty things about people. So we were polar opposites. Better friends than boyfriend-girlfriend."

*With Betsy Volck at the Bottom Line
in the mid-Seventies. Photo courtesy of Betsy Volck.*

*With (left to right) Betsy Volck, Kit Rachlis,
Ariel Swartley, and Carola Dibbell at Ken Tucker's wedding in 1978.
Photo courtesy of Bachrach Portrait Photography.*

"She was straight out of *The Thin Man*," Robert Christgau says. "She was a wisecracking broad, a fairly tough cookie."

William MacAdams: "I liked Betsy and all, but it was obvious that that was certainly not love on Paul's part. I think it was loneliness more than anything else."

At the end of 1976, Paul ran into Rob Patterson, who'd written for him at *Circus*. Patterson told him how much he liked his review of a recent Graham Parker and the Rumour concert. "He talked about it almost like it was a prize fight. I was just really blown away by how he used that metaphor to try and capture what Parker and the band were trying to do musically and how Parker was battling against the music industry zeitgeist that had kind of preceded everything to that time."

> Graham Parker, third on the bill at the Palladium Friday night, came onstage like he'd just seen Sylvester Stallone in *Rocky* and was about to give us a harder-hitting rock & roll/ rhythm-and-blues version of that endearing tale in which the pure-at-heart Little Guy (you and me, babe) makes his stand and gains far more than reality would ever give him, in a stunning, if unbelievable, moral victory over the so-called Champ (that two-timing bastard). Hell, for Stallone everything falls into place—money, love, his whole life. I'd walk a moonlight mile for that kind of satisfaction.[32]

Patterson told him that he'd really captured what Graham Parker was all about. Paul responded that he'd actually written the review about his and Betsy's breakup.

In the end, she left him with the writing desk and their two cats. "I was a rock & roll chick at that point. I wanted more excitement. I obviously was not giving him what he needed and I was more than a bit younger than he."[33]

Billy Altman: "When they broke up, I know he seemed kind of lost for a while on some levels."

32 "Graham Parker Pours It All Out" by Paul Nelson, *The Village Voice*, December 20, 1976. © Mark C. Nelson 1976. All rights reserved. Reprinted by permission. Parker landed on Mercury Records in the U.S., but ended up sharing some of Paul's misgivings about the company. The artist celebrated his departure from the label by cutting a single in 1979 called "Mercury Poisoning."
33 "Apparently he was kind of sensitive about his age," David McGee says. "He would never let on how old he was." When Paul interviewed himself for his 1972 review of *Bob Dylan's Greatest Hits, Volume II*, he wrote: "You're thirty, I'm thirty, Dylan's thirty," when in fact Paul was about to turn thirty-six. Volck says, "I know when we started dating, he shaved quite a few years off his age." On the copyright page of his and William MacAdams's book, *701 Toughest Movie Trivia Questions of All Time*, Paul's year of birth is shown as 1938 instead of 1936. When Steven Ward interviewed him in 2000, he refused to say how old he was. In 2006, when Paul took a look at his own birth certificate, he was surprised to discover that he'd turned seventy.

Elliott Murphy: "I remember him telling me that when Jann Wenner used to push albums on him that he didn't like, it was like being forced to eat rotten food or something."

"The first three years I was there," Paul said, "I won, I'd say, about two-thirds of my fights with him. If I could argue with him in a reasonable manner and not get angry, I would usually win. The last two years I didn't win any fights. I mean, just none."

Murphy: "The story Paul told me was that Jann called him into his office to say he was going to start the star system with the reviews. Paul said, 'Excuse me,' and walked out of the room and never came back." Paul wondered what they would do—give five stars to *Gatsby* and three to *The Sun Also Rises*? And what about *On the Road*? Four and a half?

"That was the death of rock criticism right there," Dave Marsh says, "and that may have something to do with why Paul stopped writing record reviews. I don't think it explains why he didn't finish the Clint Eastwood piece, though."

Charles M. Young: "You don't listen to music for a grade, you listen to music for its own sake. The point of a review: you describe what's there and then you convey your enthusiasm or distaste after in some way having an accurate description in there of what the album is, to be fair to the artist, and then you say 'it works' or 'it doesn't work.'"

While Paul ultimately didn't prevail in thwarting the star system, Wenner says he did delay it. "I finally, of course, did have my way, but I think he was an early refusenik and finally had his voice heard."

Terry McDonell joined *Rolling Stone* as managing editor in 1980. "To the end that change is good, I was the agent of that change, I think. The situation at the magazine was that Jann Wenner was very involved in the movie business at that time and spending a lot of time in California. The bottom had more or less fallen out of the music business. There was not as much interesting stuff going on as there had been three or four years earlier, or three or four years after that when MTV came and everything changed. The tradition of the *long* record review that hits all the bumpers and tells you a lot of other things, that was over. We just weren't going to do that anymore. They all say that it was all about Jann—'Jann is the devil'—but that is very much an oversimplification. I wanted a broader reach for the magazine, and you couldn't do that when you had two to three thousand-word record reviews. So I wanted more—and therefore shorter ones. Paul thought, I believe, that this was not necessarily a mistake, but that he just didn't want to do it. So we were never really at odds about anything, except what he was going to do himself.

"You know what else we did—this was endlessly debated and thought to be yet another one of the crashing mistakes—was we started putting movie stars on the cover. I didn't give a shit. Quite frankly, Jack Nicholson was a lot more interesting than the Cars, I thought."

With Warren Zevon and Jaime Rivman in the Zevons' Boston hotel room in 1978 during the Excitable Boy *tour. Photo by Crystal Zevon.*

"**P**aul's appeal to women was always very interesting to me," Dave Marsh says. "He was inordinately his own man. He was about as flexible as an iron beam—on certain issues. He was intensely lonely, and that's sexy. It's certainly appealing. The other thing is he was incredibly smart, he was really funny, and he was nice to people. Misanthrope that he could be, he never stopped being a Midwestern gentleman."

Paul started dating twenty-five-year-old Jaime Rivman, a *Rolling Stone* photo editor and a resplendent redhead, while he was still living with Betsy Volck. "We spent every day together," Jaime Rivman Mitsch says today of their three-year romance. "We used to go out to lunch. I remember we had dinner one time with Scorsese. It was before he married her, but he was dating

Isabella Rossellini. It was fun. It was just the four of us." The two of them also hung out with Warren and Crystal Zevon. Mitsch says that while she knew Paul was living with Volck and Paul knew she knew, the situation was never discussed. When she left *Rolling Stone* to work with Tommy Mottola, she left Paul, too. "I started to feel really guilty that he was living with somebody. I met my husband, and I stopped seeing Paul."

As the years went by and Paul's contemporaries and protégés parlayed their talents into something more substantial and stable, Paul fell by the wayside professionally. "That was the same thing with women," says William MacAdams, "he just couldn't sell himself. He was really a wonderful guy, but how do you communicate that? He was so shy, he was so romantic. First dates, it was like the 1950s again. He would send the girl a bouquet of flowers before he would meet her that night for their first date."

Stephen Holden says that "Paul was the loneliest person in the world. It was rather terrifying to watch how he created these *fantasies*—God, these fantasies—very, very quickly, and no one could ever take that."

Somewhere in the mid-Eighties, Mikal Gilmore found himself commiserating with Paul about their respective romantic slumps. "At one point in one of those conversations, he said something along the line that he had lost so much hope or so much faith that he couldn't imagine ever having that kind of relationship ever again or loving somebody again. That stayed with me, it bothered me. I think I questioned him on that because I certainly was not at a point where, as bad as I felt about things, I could say that I would never risk anything again. But Paul said he had reached that point."

Kurt Loder first wrote for Paul at *Circus*. "I remember he was really hot up on some girl who worked at *Rolling Stone*. She was very sweet and he got involved with her. Immediately it was like 'I'm going to get married' or something. He just jumped into it wholeheartedly."

Daisann McLane was the youngest music writer who wrote for Paul at *Rolling Stone*. "I used to interpret his distance romantically, I believed he acted the way he did because he had a poet's melancholy. As if he were so into the musicians he loved, like Neil Young and Dylan, that he'd absorbed their pain, intensity, and fondness for crypticism. But I was young and inexperienced—Paul's behavior was probably clinical depression."

Gilmore: "I think there was some kind of experience or process that went on in Paul's romantic life that was part of why his shutting down happened. I think sometimes for people this stuff kind of accrues and every loss or defeat becomes like a tunnel through the past, where all the other losses resonate and compound. So the current loss deepens the past losses and the past losses deepen the current losses until at some point it becomes unbearable."

Paul first met Jackson Browne in 1971 or 1972, shortly after the release of his debut LP. During their friendship, Paul wrote about him and his work several times and at length. The last time was in 1980 for a *Rolling Stone* cover story about *Hold Out*, Browne's sixth album. The record, by the songwriter's own admission, fell short of his previous efforts, but that didn't prevent Paul from treating it as if it were more than it really was. Consequently, "Jackson Browne on Love, Marriage and the Girl in His Songs," a clumsy Q&A that didn't go much deeper than its title, also fell short of Paul's previous treatments of the artist.

Chris Connelly: "Paul loved very hard musically, and it means that Paul wasn't always right in the choices that he made. Paul fell and fell hard. You wouldn't really grade him or assess his legacy on the basis of him as a pure critic the way you would Marsh or one of those guys. Deborah Jowitt, the dance critic for *The Village Voice*, was once asked, 'How could you review that dance concert? Your lover was in it.' And she said, 'I like to review every concert as if my lover were in it.' I think Paul a lot of times wrote about music that way."

Only in his introduction to the interview did Paul's writing approach his earlier writings about the artist:

> Why Browne is special is probably a personal thing, but I've always suspected that those of us who admire his admittedly autobiographical art usually find in it more about our own lives—not Jackson's—than we'd care to convey. In the Sixties, Bob Dylan had an uncanny ability to define a decade and its denizens. Throughout the Seventies and into the Eighties— for me, at least—Jackson Browne has taken over this job and done it better than anyone else....
>
> Since we'd done stories together in the past (for *The Pretender* and *Running on Empty*), both of us knew what to expect. I knew he'd do his damnedest to avoid explaining what his new songs meant, and he knew I'd attempt to drag it out of him. The give-and-take was pretty funny at times.[34]

At other times it wasn't. While the subsequent Q&A bears out that Browne had no desire to cater to Paul's theories about what *Hold Out* or its individual songs were really about (probably because he knew that Paul was attempting to

34 "Jackson Browne: The *Rolling Stone* Interview: Jackson Browne on Love, Marriage, and the Girl in His Songs" by Paul Nelson from *Rolling Stone*, August 7, 1980. © Rolling Stone LLC 1980. All rights reserved. Reprinted by permission.

*With Jackson Browne in Bud Scoppa's Greenwich Village apartment, late 1971
or early 1972. Photo by Bud Scoppa.*

invest too much importance in an album that just wouldn't support such scrutiny),
the original audio tapes reveal that at one point Browne became downright
surly, saying he didn't want to offer his interpretations of his own songs because
it might then limit somebody else's. "I really don't think it's a good idea, I honestly
don't. If there were ways of alluding to these things and suggesting what I mean
without sounding like I'm teaching a course on the meaning of my songs—"

"I think by saying that, that you're defusing all that you're afraid to say
about them."

"I'm not afraid to say anything about them. I feel I've said them in the songs."

"I don't see anything so wrong for—"

"Explaining what I said? The reason you believe that's okay is because that's
your job. I really think that it's the work of a writer, particularly a record reviewer,
to *illuminate*, and I find that in most cases writers tend to illuminate nothing
and pass judgment on the work in general."

Browne today says, "There was something that happened before that that
might have made me a little guarded with him—or with everybody. It was after
a show, where I was always very euphoric and full of the music and full of
enthusiasm. A time like that. But it was a very cocaine-fueled euphoria, as well."
In 1976, towards the end of the all-night bus ride that Paul describes in "We
Are All on Tour," Browne had delivered a spirited harangue on the state of rock
criticism. Citing a particular writer and his work, Browne told Paul, "I suppose

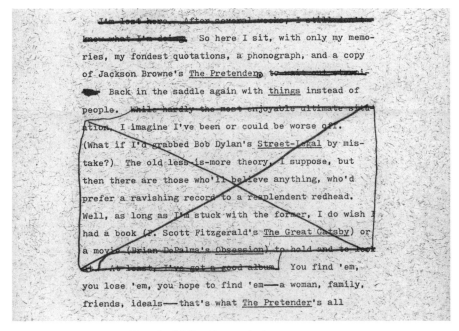

Detail of "The Pretender" manuscript.

I have contempt for those reviewers who are not talented enough. They don't have confidence and conviction in what they say, and they must say things in such a forceful manner as to convince themselves and hopefully convince their readers. I suppose it's my simply making a judgment about their talent. I guess I'm just saying, Well, they don't fucking know what they're talking about. They have a deadline to meet, they have to have an opinion, and so they think too much. They don't feel. They don't intuitively know. Whereas other people who are a little more free and take themselves less seriously understand that it's merely their opinion, but at least they're confident about their own opinion."

Browne believes that Paul repeated what he'd confided in him to the writer in question, "who had, by the way, been very complimentary of me at times. Right around that time that guy just got totally turned off."

Something else had happened that contributed to the tone of the 1980 interview. The year before, Paul had convinced Browne to let him write his biography. But then he reviewed the new J.D. Souther album for *Rolling Stone*.

> If narcissism paid two bucks an hour, J.D. Souther would be a billionaire. Writing songs for Linda Ronstadt, the Eagles, et al., he probably is anyway. But take a quick look and a careful listen to his third record, *You're Only Lonely*, and you'll realize that this very spoiled and unfunny valentine

wears his heart on his sleeve only so he can see it reflected in the mirror. Like Patti Smith, he's his own greatest fan, just doing us a favor by existing.

It's too bad, because Souther's not untalented. His debut album, *John David Souther* (1972), was sadly underrated, one of the finest of the year, and has held up very well. It's full of good songs and genuine emotions. The second LP, *Black Rose* (1976), is best remembered for the most hilarious and/or pathetic advertising pitch ever: "The Scent of Genius." On *You're Only Lonely*, the artist's pretentiousness and self-satisfaction sink him like a stone.

These days, J.D. Souther is mostly a parody of the sensitive California singer-songwriter. He's calendar art, the aural equivalent of a Kodak color slide: leaves turning in the autumn as photographed by Felicia Filigree of Vassar. He's so lazy that too often his songs have trouble holding even the most clichéd poses, because their creator can't be bothered to supply the necessary conviction, much less any at all. "If you don't want my love / Well, there's nothing I can do," he mewls, sounding like he's mildly annoyed because his Perrier is getting warm. The vain singing in tunes like "The Last in Love" is embarrassing enough, but when Souther actually tries to rock & roll on side two, it's time to put this record away and stop. Right now.[35]

The review didn't go unnoticed by Souther's good friend Browne or his other West Coast compadres, as evidenced by a letter to the editor that appeared in *Rolling Stone* two months later:

Paul Nelson's blade seems to be getting too big for him to carry. He's so busy being cute and is such an obviously biased little prick, he invalidates his own reviews. We even got the word out here that one of his underlings did the review of J.D. Souther's album first, but Mr. Nelson didn't think it enough of a "chop job" so he did it himself.

It is clear that the music—good or bad—is of no consequence to him. He just doesn't like John David Souther. That's sad and strange (not to mention unprofessional), because he doesn't even know the man. More's the pity, because if

---

35 "J.D. Souther—*You're Only Lonely*" by Paul Nelson from *Rolling Stone*, December 13, 1979. © Rolling Stone LLC 1979. All rights reserved. Reprinted by permission.

Nelson could listen with an objective ear, he might realize that Souther is practically the only American artist who is carrying on the musical traditions of Tex-Mex and Rockabilly. The press keeps right on blathering about the British Rockabilly scene as if it's just been discovered. Souther has been doing it for years—and with credentials. He grew up in the Texas Panhandle—Buddy Holly's backyard.

The fortunate thing for all of us is that Mr. Nelson's opinion makes very little difference, if any at all. He should go try to write the Great American Novel or something, because he surely must get awfully weary carrying that big hatchet around all the time.

—DON HENLEY
Los Angeles, Malibu, Aspen[36]

There was no love lost between Paul and Henley. "As much as he loved Warren and as much as he loved Jackson," Jon Landau says, "that's how little respect he had for most of the other California-based writers, especially the Eagles. Zevon was the road to heaven and the Eagles were the road to hell."

Ken Tucker: "I think part of that was that certainly the Eagles represented something to him that he didn't like, that kind of slick, corporate rock. But I also think that it was at a time when the Eagles were at their most morally reprehensible: all the coke and rumors of underage girls in the hotel room."

"Very bad company," concluded Lew Archer about certain decadent people in *The Moving Target*. "As bad as there is in Los Angeles, and that's as bad as there is."

Although Ross Macdonald's private detective wasn't really talking about the affluent and popular Eagles, in the frosty eyes of many he might well have been. Because, while the Eagles have won their share of praise and prizes, they have also been vilified from beginning ("Take It Easy," cowritten by Jackson Browne) to end ("Life in the Fast Lane," "Wasted Time") and are often characterized as cocaine cowboys, ersatz macho harlequins, artistes manqués, and hedonistic, misogynous, Warren Beatty/New Hollywood schmucks. If something were indeed rotten in the state of California (and it is), it's almost as likely this band as the city they so narcissistically represent—yet, despite my distrust of the Eagles and my

36 "Eagles II" from *Rolling Stone*, February 7, 1980. © Rolling Stone LLC 1980. All rights reserved. Reprinted by permission.

keen endorsement of honest hatred in a worthwhile cause (there are those who just shouldn't be forgiven), I do think they have been handed at least a partial bum rap. While the Eagles may never display much of Lew Archer's fine moral consciousness, there is proof enough on their albums that they aren't Sammy Glick either.[37]

Paul told Crystal Zevon that "The Eagles seem like the biggest spoiled brats in the entire world," and with that in mind he responded to Henley's letter:

> As usual, Don Henley's information is incorrect. No one but me wrote a review of J.D. Souther's *You're Only Lonely*. In fact, if space hadn't opened up in the particular issue in which the review ran, I would have killed my own piece because the record was—at best—of borderline interest. I don't dislike Souther: as Henley says, I've never met him. I've seen him onstage and found his whole act extremely narcissistic (maybe Eagles don't notice that). And Don Henley's claim that J.D. Souther "is practically the only American artist who is carrying on the musical traditions of Tex-Mex and Rockabilly" is the biggest laugh I've had all year. Let Henley's career as a critic begin and end with that statement—it's so fabulously stupid (and wrong) that he'll never top it.[38]

During his 1980 interview with Browne, who cited the Eagles as his favorite band, Paul showed a bit more diplomacy: "Most people, whether I like their music or I don't like their music—agree with them, disagree with them personally—I can get some sort of a grip on who they are by their songs or their words or something. But Henley just baffles me. And his reaction to critics just baffles me. I don't get it. I mean, apparently he just wants to punch anybody from *Rolling Stone* out—unless I'm being given misinformation."

"I think you are," Browne deadpanned before bursting into laughter. "But don't go over there."

Ineluctably, talk returned to J.D. Souther, the album he'd worked on for two years, and Paul's review. "It was as if he had wasted his time making this record. It was as if his first record, which you liked, was made last week, and

---

37 "The Eagles Fly from a Penthouse Aerie" by Paul Nelson, *The Village Voice*, February 7, 1977. © Mark C. Nelson 1977. All rights reserved. Reprinted by permission.
38 "Correspondence, Love Letters & Advice" from *Rolling Stone*, February 7, 1980. © Rolling Stone LLC 1980. All rights reserved. Reprinted by permission.

this week he didn't do so well. Now, I don't think that's the job of the reviewer—if you don't mind my telling you your job this once. I think often reviewers are given assignments and they write about something and they might not care for the thing. They may be actually pissed off that they have to write about it, and that anger gets handed over to the artist."

"If I don't like John David's album, I don't see anything wrong with my saying that I don't like it. Because I know his work."

"By the end of the review," Browne said, "I still didn't know why you didn't like it."

"Because I thought it was real narcissistic," Paul said.

"You know," Browne snapped his fingers, "that can be said just like that. I disagree. But I think it could be said without cultural references like *Perrier* and the amount of money one might have made."

"I wanted to shake him up," Paul shot back. "Which I told you in advance when we talked, that I thought—"

"No, you didn't tell me in advance. You told me after you'd written it and before I had read it."

After he'd read it, Browne had called Paul and demanded to know how he could've written such a thing. Towards the end of the call, Paul asked if they were still going to do the book together. "I wasn't calling him to cancel doing that," Browne says, "but I wound up saying, 'Well, I don't see how we can do a book now.' I couldn't go and do a book with the journalist that had savaged my friend."

For those artists whose work offended him (Paul McCartney and Wings, Patti Smith, and Billy Joel are among the most famous examples), and even sometimes those whose work he admired (most notably, Bob Dylan and Rod Stewart) Paul's pen more than once turned into a sword. "That's how he spewed," Bobbi London says. "His emotions were all on the written page."

Regarding the proposed Browne biography, Paul's version of what happened varied—sometimes within the same conversation. Talking with music critic Jim DeRogatis about the *Rod Stewart* book, he said, "I wanted to do a book on somebody else—Jackson Browne—and they were insisting that it be Rod Stewart"; but a little later when asked why he didn't write more books, Paul replied, "I wanted to do Jackson Browne, but this other guy got in there." The other writer, Rich Wiseman, indeed published a biography of Browne—without his subject's cooperation. "It was very shallow and badly researched," Browne says. "Had Paul done the book, it would have been a great fucking book."

He wishes he'd handled the situation differently. "Maybe I should've said we'd postpone it. I didn't mean to break off my friendship with Paul, but in effect it's what happened when that all went down. I didn't think that that's what I was doing. I didn't say, 'Never darken my door' or anything."

All because of 285 words that Paul had written about J.D. Souther.

"Musicians," Browne says, "they try everything they can to do something of value. It's not out of some cynical, nefarious plan to sneak by you and do something bad that you will think is good."

And critics?

"I can see that, regardless of any liberties or any divergence of opinion about things, they write about music for the highest of reasons. Especially Paul. Paul was one of those guys that really was sort of an idealist about it. You could see how that would turn into acrimony in the case of somebody they just didn't like or get. I think he must've felt *called* to draw some sort of line between the stuff that he liked and didn't like."

"Here's the thing," Chris Connelly says, "we constantly—including us little whippersnappers writing in the music section—held the artists we wrote about to an amazingly high standard in terms of credibility and not selling out and being true to their message. We didn't want them to do advertisements, we didn't want them to do bad collaborations, we scolded them when they did bad music. We demanded complete emotional openness from the artists we wrote about, and we were the most cynical, ironic, conceal-your-true-feelings people imaginable. That Paul could live in both of those worlds—or try to—was something. He was the only one among us who was really living up to that standard."

There were several reasons why Paul missed the May 1, 1980, deadline for the book he and Lester Bangs were writing about Rod Stewart, and the fact that he was in Minnesota was only one of them. He'd come not to visit family or friends but to move a young woman named Laura Fissinger, a self-described lifelong clinical depressive, back to New York to live with him and get married. It was the first time they'd met face-to-face.

Fissinger had been writing locally in the Minneapolis-Saint Paul area for four years when, in the fall of 1978, she decided to make the leap to the next level. "I called the New York offices of *Rolling Stone* for fourteen months straight, once a week—Paul Nelson's office—because I was going to write nationally or die trying." She also sent him letters with her clippings, but he never responded. Then one Friday in early 1980, Paul picked up the phone.

Stephen Holden: "Oh God, when he fell for her, he just envisioned 'you and me against the world' in that really scary way. And she was so innocent. It was like the emotional equivalent of kidnapping someone and locking them up, you know. I just thought, Oh Jesus, she's not going to be able to take this for long."

For Paul, the long-distance relationship rapidly turned from professional to personal, while for Fissinger it remained both. They spoke through the night and wrote love letters. Paul composed poems.

> a confessional writer, ah yes—
> truth of the matter is
> my partner's the real zhivago
> the real poet
> one who can make me tremble
> with or without words.
>
> cradled in chrysanthemums
> she uses pencil as pool cue
> running a rack of phrases
> banking line after line, three-cushion true
> straight into my astonished heart
> like a row of exquisite diamond bullets
> no one will ever be able to remove.
> they bring tears, such tears:
> tears of life, as fresh and healing
> as jackson browne's redemptive arthurian waters.
>
> laura says: "when you see me
> i want you to fall on your fuckin' knees."
> with spirit and spunk
> and a small amount of fear, she laughs.
> hey, heartbeat, i think to myself
> if you only knew
> (which, of course, you do)
> you knocked me off my feet eons ago
> yet i've never stood taller
> and i'll never feel surer or prouder
> than when, with gold or silver ring
> i'm on my knees once again before you
> offering summer and winter
> spring and fall
> the plaza on an orange autumn day
> a midnight run down park avenue in a white
>   Manhattan snowswell
> every light in the quiet city smiling at us
>   on our edenic romp

calm summer dawns in central park, hand in hand
spring celebrations and frolics for our everyday
    anniversaries.

god, laura, i've always had this thing about airports.
the last ten years
i've gotten off hundreds of planes
in perhaps a third that many cities
almost always alone
no one waiting
except maybe jackson's roadie
rod's flunky
clint's publicist
at times warren:
somebody but nobody really.
often I've had a sense of adventure
(the lone rider of santa fe
stalking another city—
that kind of fantasy)
but mostly i've felt invisible, incomplete
standing there hailing a solitary taxi
that rolls like a ghostly billiard ball
across the dark city streets
toward the same anonymous hotel room.
once there, find a movie
find a bookstore
or just walk until dawn
smoking cigarettes
soaking it all in
making life's little notes
on some raggedy piece of paper:
the master of minutiae
playing his mood solo to the streetlights
until the next interview
the next airplane
the next city.

no self-pity there
but not a hell of a lot of happiness either:
you were always missing
and what good's a romantic hero

without his romantic heroine?
what good's a giver
without a taker?
love is more giving than taking, I suppose
but when you're in love
there's really no difference between the two.
you don't even bother to separate them
because it's not important.
all that counts is being together
growing together
breathing each other's breath
kissing, touching.
you and I, a tangle of souls
building and sharing our secret wonder world
while coexisting
in a reasonable way
with all those public people
who aren't as lucky as we.

i'm convinced tickets to heaven come only in pairs
and it could be we got the last one
so living our life that way
seems not only natural but inevitable.
at the airport, I walk in and there you are: my other
    half.
you walk in and there i am: your other half.
awesome, incredible and comfortable as an old shoe.
it's a gift.[39]

After a few months of long-distance courtship, Paul returned to Minnesota for the first time in more than a dozen years. "He never went up to Warren, never tried to see Doris," Fissinger says, "never tried to see anybody. He was at my side the whole time. I couldn't understand why he didn't go see his boy while he was in Minnesota. When I asked why, there was this vacant place he'd go to, a look of shutdown. It would simply be like there was nothing more to say on the subject."

Two friends he did reach out to while in Minnesota (albeit long-distance to California) were Jackson Browne and Warren Zevon. "He phoned them from my place and said, 'I'm in love. I've got to get my girl back to New York.

39 "the laura poems" by Paul Nelson, 1980.‡

87

She's not working. She's kind of having anxiety problems, and I'm having trouble working. Can you front us some money?'"

Paul, who ran several miles daily, gave Fissinger his 1979 New York City Marathon medal. "That was big," she says. "That was like getting pinned." They were in love. "He loved with the ferocity that he wrote those most passionate reviews. That's something that knocked you off your chair, to be on the receiving end of that intensity. It's not as observant, oddly enough. He understood Dylan better than he understood me. But he wasn't going to marry Dylan. He was going to marry me."

Arriving in New York penniless, the twenty-seven-year-old Fissinger discovered that the Paul she'd known in print and on the phone was drastically different from the one who lived over a coffee shop on Lexington Avenue. "I just assumed if you have a job at *Rolling Stone* you clean your house. Cockroaches *everywhere*, mice *everywhere*, piles of paper. He often, when he didn't know what to do, would simply lie down. And when he was too discouraged to sit up, he would lie down. When he was sick of lying down, he would lie down some more until he got over it. I saw him horizontal more than I care to remember.

"The OCD was out of control. His cap was marinated in sweat and body oil and dirt." She upset Paul when she washed it. "I was breaking his pattern and it made him angry because it felt like a rejection. He was so deeply ill by the time I got to him."

They seldom left the apartment. Fissinger met few of Paul's friends. They'd watch the beginning of *Touch of Evil*, with its famous three-and-a-half-minute tracking shot, over and over. "He was going to school me in cinema because I was ignorant as a stone. He was happy to be my total teacher. But when it came to pragmatics, it was I who would say, 'How are we going to do this? I've told you a bunch of times I have no money. And no prospects.'"

Paul objected to Fissinger's attempts to clean the apartment. "It was like togetherness for him had to do with both of us not functioning. That was romance." He couldn't write, and he didn't want her to leave him. She couldn't understand how he'd read her so wrong: "I was never unclear with Paul about the career. I was driven, and he knew it."

By the time she arrived, Paul was already in trouble with the *Rod Stewart* book. "He didn't want to do anything but hang with me, and I kept saying, 'Paul, how are we going to live? Jackson and Warren aren't going to pony up more money for us to live.'"

Jackson Browne: "At some point she called me, and I don't know whether they were in a big argument or fight, but she said, 'I'm sorry, I don't really know you, but I know that you're friends.' I felt that she was trying to reach out to one of his friends, you know: 'Somebody tell me what's happening.'"

Manuscript for "the laura poems," 1980.

She says there was also a "Big jealousy problem. Jealous of television shows I liked, jealous of artists I listened to, jealous of the typewriter. So I'd sit there and I'd type. I'd write. 'You're not going to work, fine, I'll work.'"

Three months after she arrived in New York, it was over: the passion, the fighting, the making up.

"He took me to the train station. I told him he didn't have to, but he dragged himself there, shaking visibly." She remembers his hands. "They were so beautiful. I would spend just a really long time tracing his fingers, which were delicate and long, but were not unmasculine. Like a basketball player's. And that hand was just trembling when he was putting me on the train."

Paul and Fissinger remained in tenuous contact after her return to Minnesota. One of the last times they spoke was the night of December 8, 1980. "It was one of the most awful nights of my life, and the fact that Paul would even talk to me was so wonderful." The ex-lovers commiserated over that night's shooting of John Lennon, which troubled Paul on more than one level. "He hated the new album, *Double Fantasy*. Hated it. He was about to file his review, and then John died. And this was his reaction: 'How can I say I hate this album when John just died?' He was really in agony about that." He pulled his own review and assigned the LP to Tom Carson, whose own regretful piece was also ultimately withdrawn.

Asked how Paul edited, Debra Rae Cohen replies, "Through three feet of smoke.

"He had a peculiar kind of pretention-puncturing drawl; he would sit back and repeat one of your sentences and look at you quizzically. So much so that you would fall over yourself to agree with him. Paul wouldn't attack you in the way that Bob Christgau would sometimes attack you in the hope that you'd be roused to attack him in return, but he would repeat your own words in such a way as to make it clear that what you were saying might not necessarily, in the idea, be absolutely bullshit, but that the way you had said it was unworthy of you."

"If I could wave a magic wand," Charles M. Young says, "I would have Paul Nelson edit everything that I ever wrote. He was a perfect editor. If there was something new and original, or if I was using some weird quirk to get into the music, Paul loved it. If he made any changes, he'd run it by you. Otherwise, he'd just print it like you wrote it. He wanted the unmediated reaction. He didn't want it to be the statement of *Rolling Stone* about this, he was not a homogenizer."

In his various editing roles, Paul mentored scores of junior writers, including Rob Patterson. "It was a thing with some of us young critics. Sitting there and emulating Paul, drinking Cokes and smoking Nat Shermans." Even Debra Rae Cohen started smoking the Cigarettellos.

"I just turned into a smaller version of him for that time," Bud Scoppa says. "Shermans. Frye boots. The veal piccata.

"The primary thing that inspired me in the context of knowing him and talking to him every day was reading the stuff." He recalls how Paul loved using the word *mythopoeic*. "I wanted to be able to do that. I wanted to be able to illuminate deep down inside something. That was what inspired me and still inspires me."

"I think when I discovered the word *mythic* I figured out what it was all about," Paul told singer-songwriter Greg Copeland. "I guess I tend to have a mythic attitude toward things or see things in mythic terms."

Robert Christgau: "He had a way of forcing you to see the myth and the 'mythic-ness' of the artists he liked."

"You didn't want to disappoint him by being late," Fred Schruers says. "He exerted a gentle control. You wanted to do well for him because he expected you to and he wanted you to. He could say, 'Just connect,' and you knew what that meant somehow, as brief as that instruction was."

Ken Tucker: "He always made you feel like, yes, there was time for whatever you wanted to talk about. Over the years, I'd always think more and more how remarkable it was how generous he was at a time when he was probably feeling tremendous pressure. It was part of that code that he lived by, all that sort of hardboiled romanticism that he took from people like Chandler and Ross Macdonald. He had a certain esprit de corps to him, but he was a much more gentle soul than so many of the kind of Lew Archer-Philip Marlowe heroes that he emulated."

"He was very painstaking," Connelly says. "I really think of him as the last non-computer-based editor. You'd get the copy back and he would've tightened everything up. You would have these little pencil marks all over your copy that made it funnier, tighter and better, and more acute."

Debra Rae Cohen: "I think in some ways Paul was the perfect editor for those of us who came out of a literary background. In fact, in some ways I think he encouraged tendencies that we later had to train ourselves out of—not as writers, but as rock & roll critics. Because he did care so much about lyrics. Unlike Bob Christgau, he didn't always push us enough to move beyond lyrics, make us push ourselves to write about the *music*. Now, that was something that *he* himself could do. He could really convey the pleasure of the music in a way that didn't involve musical terminology or musical training. But that's a very hard thing to do."

Susan Murcko, who edited Paul's work at *Rolling Stone*: "From my perspective as a copyeditor, I know when he was typing up reviews that he had edited or things he was writing himself, he had this very rigid format: he had to alternate the use of *record*, *album*, and *LP*, and he would spend a lot of time figuring out which way they should be alternated. He was very adamant about that."

"For a copyeditor there (and there were about four of us, I think), you could spend half an hour arguing over a comma with him," Parke Puterbaugh says. "He quickly decided he wanted to work with me because we had pretty congruent sensibilities. For a number of years, every two weeks we'd have one of these sessions and that's how it would go on, until two in the morning or something. Some of my favorite memories of working at *Rolling Stone* are of sitting up with him and tunneling through these reviews, bit by bit, and piece by piece. Then we'd finish up in the wee hours, and he'd put on his tennis shoes and go for a seventeen-mile run in Central Park."

David Forman was among the friends Paul invited to join him when he began long-distance running in the early Seventies. "It was the first and last time for me, and I don't think I'd have done it for anyone else on earth. I managed about seven-eighths of a mile—not bad. He was a good runner with huge alabaster ostrich legs. You'd never have imagined it from his scrawny chest."

Bobbi London says, "He was never athletic in any way, though he loved baseball and he loved the Twins. And then when he started running, it was amazing."

"I don't know the impetus for that other than that we lived within proximity of Central Park," Betsy Volck says.

"The health isn't the primary reason," Paul told Clint Eastwood. "To me, it's a substitute psychologist."

Rock & roll writers in the Seventies and Eighties weren't a particularly athletic lot, but several of the younger writers leapt at the opportunity to socialize with Paul on foot. Wesley Strick was already something of a runner himself. "The funny thing is that Paul was like twenty years older than me, but he could jog forever. And also he smoked, so I was sure that between my twenty-year advantage on him and the chain-smoking that I could at the very least keep up with him. But he would always go for one more lap around the reservoir. The truth is, he could run easily three laps, which I think is a mile-and-a-half a lap, and just talk—long monologues—about the Ramones or whomever he was obsessed with. I was usually in agony by the third lap with a terrible cramp. But I didn't want to let on because then I thought he would stop and have pity for me and then this great thing would stop, which was being able to hang out with Paul."

By the turn of the decade, Paul was regularly running the New York City Marathon, which starts in Staten Island and winds its way through the other four boroughs before reaching the finish line in Central Park. "You can't fake a marathon, that's the nice thing about it. You really have to be there and be in shape. You can't fake 26.2 miles. You can run it and finish it in five hours and walk through half of it, but I don't really want to do that. I want to run the whole thing and feel semi-competitive. I'd like to break my PR. I did 3:36 the first time and finished top third, which is pretty good for a first effort. I finished like 4,000th out of 16,000 or something like that." Training for five months before each marathon, he said that it felt like an empty day if he hadn't run ten to twelve miles.

A few months before the 1980 marathon, Paul told Eastwood: "I feel good, I've done three twenty-two-milers and I've been doing seventy miles a week. I've run close to a thousand miles this summer."

"About time for an oil change," Eastwood said.

The following year, when writer Deborah Frost began training for the Marathon, she was surprised to discover that so was her editor. "He would only run after dark, with the cigarette in the mouth, with the little hat on, and he'd wear these shorts. He was in the midst of having this big writer's block. He would always talk about Jackson Browne and Zevon, he would go on about them like they were his great heroes. He used to talk about Neil Young, too. These were his frames of references. He loved to quote them and talk about them."

Jann Wenner, one of Paul's more unlikely running mates, remembers Paul puffing on a Nat Sherman while showing him how to stretch. "He wanted to get me into running, so I went along and we did the reservoir a couple of times." Paul liked to tell how Wenner ignored his advice to take it slow and just took off running.

Michael Seidenberg: "Jann, this little, very kempt guy and Paul, this really tall, unkempt guy, running around the reservoir together. It just had to be quite an image."

In the early Eighties, another obsession having literally run its course, Paul stopped running. "I don't live by the park anymore," he told Bruce Hornsby.[40]

I n November of 1981, Paul ran Parke Puterbaugh's snarky tandem review of the two new releases on Cleveland International Records by Meat Loaf and Steinman. "Both LPs race along like a flash flood," Puterbaugh concluded, "their excesses sending them over the banks of listenability and out to sea. Or out to lunch, as the case may be." Within a week, Steve Popovich, the label's founder, sent a note to Jann Wenner letting him know that he wasn't amused. (As a VP at CBS, Popovich had worked with Boz Scaggs, whose 1969 album was produced by Wenner.) Wenner, agreeing that the review was "malicious" and "unnecessarily nasty," wrote a letter to Popovich promising that this "critically reprehensible" practice would never happen again. Soon after, he instituted a compulsory formula for reviewing records at *Rolling Stone*:

> 1) Lede Review: There will be only one per issue,
>   not to exceed three columns of type in length....
> 2) Order of Reviews: The lede review will be
>   followed by reviews in this order:
>   First: All four star albums;
>   Second: Major artists (top 15 chart position or
>   having a long history of highly acclaimed work;
>   so-called "superstars";

40 Though Paul's running days were over, he did carry a different healthy habit well into the Nineties: taking Vitamin C. Clint Eastwood had told Paul that, because he smoked so much, he should take the supplements. According to his friend Andrew Leigh, Paul would keep enormous bottles of the supplement in supply: "C was like burgers, fries, and Coke to him—every day and that's that."

Third: In order of stars.
This order cannot be altered."
3) Lengths: The standard length of every review will
conform to the following length, without
deviation: 32 lines....
4) Style, Tone, and Content:
a) Reviews are to deal with musical content of the
recording.
b) Image, personalities, literary references, jacket
art, etc., are acceptable points of discussion
only insofar as they directly bear on the
musical content.
c) Personal insults, including gratuitous negative
references to other artists whose work is not
included on the record being reviewed, are not
allowed.
d) Every review must contain one sentence
directly advising the reader whether or why he/
she would like the LP, in whole or part, or not
and wish to listen to/purchase it.

Reading the memo today, Wenner shakes his head. "This is ridiculous. It's like trying to codify common sense. Paul was *sui generis*, he was going to do it his way and his way was to write long things. I wanted to get more reviews in and shorten up some of what I felt was self-indulgent stuff. This is an attempt to reason with Paul and get him to understand parameters which he perfectly well understood but wasn't at all prepared to abide by. It was really to be respectful of the audience and not give them back word-for-word their tastes. It was never 'follow their tastes,' it was just 'follow their interests,' for God's sake, and follow the way people really consume records, really read about them. I mean, these guys were getting deep into trying to be more literary than the rest and writing long essays using the records as stepping off points. To write a long essay would be impressive to Robert Christgau or Lester, but really it didn't have much relevance to the reader."

Paul Scanlon: "It's service copy, really."

"That's what the records section is," Wenner agrees. "We were already allowing some of the talented ones—and they were all talented—to be very indulgent and use the space. Paul, in particular, had to write whatever he *wanted* in there. It was his section. He was running his little literary rock critics salon there. The whole thing mirrored his personality, his take on things, but it was appropriate in that time. He had the desire and the ability to encourage and nurture this group of very talented but quirky people."

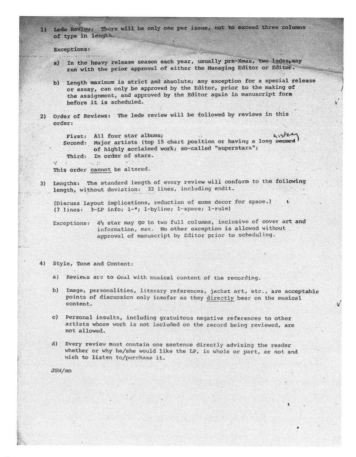

Paul's copy of the memo addressing editorial requirements for reviews.

David McGee: "I think Jann saw the short-attention span generation coming on. Long, rambling thousand-word discourses were fading at that point. I think Paul thought that that's one thing that wouldn't happen and it really hurt him that that day was gone."

Flying in the face of Wenner's directive, in 1981 Paul encouraged and published Mikal Gilmore's 2,700-word post-punk twofer: a consideration of the latest Public Image Ltd. album and Joy Division's entire body of work. "What I'd heard was Paul had to slip it in when Jann was on vacation," Gilmore says, "and then when Jann came back he wasn't happy about it. There was some kind of exchange that Paul passed along to me, where Paul had asked him if he thought it had been too long and Jann said, 'If it had been in the classifieds it would've been too long.'"

Wenner: "Sometimes I wasn't paying attention or I didn't care that much. But at a point it just becomes egregious. I mean, when you pick up the section and it's three pages on one record and you barely touch on it. It wasn't of those times anymore. The culture was different. He was old-time. He was a very old-fashioned kind of guy."

Jay Cocks: "Every time the rock press would say here was the next big thing, they *were* the next big thing—maybe because they were already the next big thing when they were thus anointed by the rock press. But when the rock press got ahead of something, or they got on to something that didn't catch fire in a popular way, then things got weird. Our criticism began to seem elitist. It was the early Seventies, it was the end of the Beatles, it was the L.A. music (which critics didn't like and consumers *loved*), and then came punk (which critics loved and the marketplace *hated*)—critics seemed to start to get out of step with taste. I think maybe that bothered Jann, and so that bothered Paul. And I don't think Paul could compromise."

"My cubicle was right outside Jann's office," Puterbaugh says. "The music industry was in a period of transition then. The punk and new wave stuff was happening. Paul picked up on that and embraced it really quickly. Championed it. Jann, on the other hand, wasn't so sure about it all. I think Jann wasn't convinced this stuff had lasting significance or was anything more than an uprising and a flash in the pan."

"The good news and the exciting part was that he was able to get away with it for a few years," Jim Farber says, "that he was really able to run an autonomous record-review section within a magazine that was becoming increasingly corporate."

Chris Connelly: "There was revolution in the air. Paul was trying to lead us all—if not over the cliff, then to the very edge of it. Paul marched in his direction and the rest of us kept doing our thing."

Paul told Bruce Hornsby: "Actually, I quit *Rolling Stone* because it was just getting too much to deal with Jann, who was like a coke maniac, an alcoholic. You'd hand him a story and he'd say, 'Cut it by two-thirds,' without reading it. He was really out of control." For Paul, Wenner was "a fame and power guy" who'd lost sight of how important music was to the culture and who was refocusing on celebrity instead of substance.

For all of his disagreements with Paul, Wenner remembers him fondly. "That visage, those dark glasses, and a cigarette dangling out of his mouth. His sleepy, kind of tired, world-weary voice, it was very quiet and kind of droned. In that way, he was just this great character. Not effusive, not flamboyant. Flamboyant-less in his insistence on his own sense of what was right and what was good and what was bad. He just would hold his line—that was that. How could you not respect or admire somebody like that?

"He finally quit on his own, right? I probably wasn't going to fire him ever." By the time Paul left, however, the atmosphere between the two men was so poisoned that he might as well have been fired.

In his Rolling Stone *office, 1979. Photo by Lawrence White.*

Holden says, "I really do think in a funny way Paul respected Jann. I just think he knew that Jann was crazy from all the chemicals and stuff like that, and an egomaniac. But I think he respected Jann because Jann had the same obsessive qualities and involvement that he did."

Paul composed a letter that at once stated his case and made demands that he knew wouldn't be met and would result in his resignation. "I just figured, all these restrictions, he just wants me out of here. He wants somebody who'll just do it. But it turned out that wasn't what he had in mind. He was quite stunned when I left."

Farber: "Not only was he the last person, I think, at the magazine who was speaking from his own voice, but each of his writers was speaking with his own voice. Later it just became the voice of *Rolling Stone*." One immediately noticeable change was that the critics' names were relocated from above the review to below it. "It was a way of saying, 'This is the *Rolling Stone* review, not this writer's opinion.'"

"And rather than impose that on other rock writers, he quit," Charles M. Young says. "Rather than edit other people in a way that he himself did not want to be edited, he would not do it."

"He didn't want it to end," McGee says. "He really believed in what *Rolling Stone* was doing and the power that *Rolling Stone* had and its history and that that meant something. I think he really tried to work it out with Jann. But ultimately it's Jann's book and he had a vision for where he wanted *Rolling Stone* to go and the way he thought readers were changing in their approach to reviews."

Singer-songwriter Steve Forbert, for whom Paul's critical knife cut both ways, says, "He put a lot of himself into these reviews. He liked it pretty real. You find with a lot of this stuff that it ain't just about the love of the music and it's not just about the writing. You know, things were changing, changing, changing, and you have to be the sort of person with the inclination and the ability to get in there and play that political game. It doesn't hurt to be a good schmoozer. But as times get tougher and it gets more competitive to make a living writing about rock—which isn't as interesting as it used to be—you could be in a pickle. That would be a real problem for someone who isn't kidding."

McGee: "Paul really agonized over it. It was a long, two- or three-week ordeal leading up to that resignation letter. I think I was the only one who saw it before it went to Jann. The last week or so he was in Jann's office three or four times a day, as I recall. He was really trying to work it out—and maybe Jann was trying to work it out, too. Jann didn't have a chip on his shoulder about Paul Nelson."

Rereading Paul's letter of resignation today, Wenner is especially affected by Paul's farewell lines:

> I'm afraid you have a big decision to make. I'm sorry, old friend, but I'm not going to back down on this.

Thursday, February 25

Dear Jann:

After giving careful consideration to your most recent guideline for the record section——and after thinking about what the last seven months have been like for all of us in the music department—— I must respectfully make the following demands, all of which are nonnegotiable. I want:

(1) A $5,000.00 bonus check by two o'clock tomorrow afternoon to make up for my not receiving any substantial raise in salary for far too long a time.

(2) An immediate raise, which must be reflected in my next pay-check, to $40,000.00 a year.

(3) Total editorial control of the record section (other than the usual work with Parke Puterbaugh, my copy editor). All guide-lines from you——past and present——are out the window. I'll be making the decisions about ledes, word lengths, style, content, writers, the star system, etc., and I promise to do so in a responsible and professional manner. Members of the music depart-ment will consult with and assist me in this. No policemen.

(4) No hassles from you about anything.

If you feel you can't comply with all of the above demands, then I must ask you to fire me immediately and give me a check for the full amount of my severance and vacation pay (more than four years' worth). There are those here who feel that I haven't a chance of collecting severance and vacation pay from you (let alone unemploy-ment compensation) if you should choose not to accept my demands. These people are greatly concerned about how you're going to handle this. I don't think they have to worry, though, because I believe you're an honest man and will prove them wrong.

I'm afraid you have a big decision to make. I'm sorry, old friend, but I'm not going to back down on this.

Best,

Paul

PAUL NELSON

Copies to: Terry McDonell, David Rosenthal, Jim Henke, Kurt Loder, Chris Connelly, Parke Puterbaugh, Susan Murcko, Maryanne Vollers, Alan Weitz, Lynn Hazelwood.

Paul's Rolling Stone *resignation letter, 1982.*

"That's just a sad fuckin' last letter. I mean, what do you say? Here's a guy saying, 'I'm in pain. If I can't do it my way, I just don't want to do it. I understand that you want to do it your way, but my way is the only way I know how to do things.' It certainly is friendly enough. He's really saying, 'I'll give you every reason to fire me. I'm handing my body to you. Please chop the head off.'"

Tom Carson told Scott Woods and Steven Ward at RockCritics.com: "He was so mild that you'd never think someone like this would go to the mat with Wenner, especially since there had been times, I think, when Paul had had very little money and this was obviously a berth worth protecting. But he did it over and over again, when some piece of mine or somebody else's had pissed off the great Jann, usually by being too complimentary about punk. I think he would have really loved to be in a John Ford or Howard Hawks Western, and instead he was stuck in this sort of grim Anthony Mann one where nobody's motives are pure but you do what you can. So Paul did what he could."

Paul was gone, his office vacated. "Somebody else had to clean it up," McGee says. "I do remember somebody in there boxing up the records." Among what was left behind, the Deems Taylor Award presented to Paul by ASCAP in 1979 "in recognition of the excellence of his articles" published in *Rolling Stone* (for "Rod Stewart Under Siege" in particular). The plaque eventually found its way back to him.

Wenner: "Paul was probably the last of that string of editors of the *Rolling Stone* reviews section who were big auteur kind of guys in their own right. He had that authority and that level of gravitas that these other guys, Landau and Greil, had had before him. He was the last of that tradition. I guess that era of the independent fiefdom came to an end with Paul."

It was a big battle for me. I was the *Rolling Stone* record-review editor at that point and I edited the record section in a very loaded way—pro Clash/Sex Pistols/what I liked. And it didn't work out. People did not buy those records to the extent they bought the other records, and the bands weren't there anymore pretty soon. And rock got rather uninteresting.

The Clash and the Sex Pistols, that to me was the great battleground of rock as to which side would win this. Would it be the Dolls/Sex Pistols/Clash or would it be the other side—which I wasn't interested in *at all*—the side that was selling more records and was more acceptable? The wrong side won as far as I was concerned, and my heart just went out of the whole scene at that point.

I found myself losing interest in it. For the first time it felt like, Oh God, I've got to listen to all these records now because I have to decide which ones to get reviewed and not because I really liked them anymore. I just didn't like most of the stuff. It seemed like the average rocker coming up—and this is a terrible generalization, but I'm going to make it anyway—they were much more business-oriented than they were passionate, music-oriented. The whole thing went sour for me. I didn't find any bands that had that fire that I responded to. Not many anyway. Some. I just lost interest in the field. The Dolls were the first warriors in that field.[41]

He told Warren Zevon in 1979: "If rock once stood for some sort of a rebellion against whatever you had, like Brando said, really it now stands for complete conformity, it seems to me—outside of ten, twelve artists: Jackson, Bruce, Clash, you, Neil Young. The Doobie Brothers don't strike me as even thinking about anything besides commodity. Power pop has proven to be the most dismal line of Campbell Soup cans in existence. Punk rock soon became power pop and became exactly what it was that it started out to be against supposedly. The difference between fifty new power pop bands is so negligible, it seems to me that it's the Beatles played a little harder, basically."

Chris Connelly: "I think you could argue that the music and the audience's relationship to music was what had really changed. That was the end of kind of the singer-songwriter era. You had Dylan, then you had Springsteen, and the other guys hadn't really lived up. Paul was looking for the next guy, which is why Paul was writing about Forbert that way. Paul invested enormous hope in guys who sounded like they could get it done, and nobody could get it done.

"But Paul was right when it counted."

On a 1977 phone call with Ray Davies of the Kinks, Paul had still been hopeful. "Rock & roll is one of the few art forms that nobody knows what it's going to be like when all the artists are forty because it's an art form that's growing old *with* the artists. So there's no logical reason why people couldn't be doing it when they're fifty, but no one's ever done it that way because no one's been fifty yet who's doing it."

"Bands like Culture Club," Tom Carson says, "Paul didn't have a great deal of use for that kind of pop no matter how well-crafted it was. He wanted music that resonated emotionally—and that resonated in adult terms. I think coming

41 Paul Nelson to Marty Thau, 1994.

out of folk music, the side of rock & roll that Paul had the least familiarity with and appreciation for was that it was music for teenagers. So he liked folk music because it was music for grownups and he liked rock & roll because, thanks to Bob Dylan, it *became* music for grownups. For Paul, I would guess Dylan was vastly more important than the Beatles, and again that set him apart from a lot of us."

Regarding Paul's ultimate dismissal of rock & roll and immersion in bluegrass, David McGee says, "I really relate to that as an older music writer because I have nothing to say about these young rock groups, these twentysomething kids or teenagers. They're writing for their generation— it has nothing to do with my values or the way I live my life. These kids are downloading single songs, they're not downloading albums that make a statement."

Jay Cocks: "You don't want to be the old crotchety jerk waving his critical cane in the air going, 'You young whippersnappers don't know what's going on!' So you feel, I'm out of it, and I think he may have felt that, too. He'd already written about great people like Jackson and Warren when they were starting out. You can't keep writing about them unless there's some *sea change* in what they're doing. You keep reaching out for different kinds of music."

Jonathan Lethem: "I always gathered that putting pen to paper was never particularly easy for him, but he had such a vital relationship to the music in the Sixties and into the Seventies that mattered to him. Getting that right, I always felt, was what had given him his reason for being and kept him working. I just think that musicians he liked weren't working in a way that he liked as much anymore."

McGee: "For those of us who grew up in the generation and learned to take on all the themes and develop them and really look insightfully and incisively into a record and treat it as much a literary event as a musical event for some artists, there's not a lot of places for us to write anymore. Maybe no place."

Punk was the last "New Music" Paul embraced. "He absolutely loathed rap and hip-hop," William MacAdams says. "Hate it," Paul told Bruce Hornsby. "I can't stand it. It's valid artistically and all that, but no, not for me." In 1991, he summed it up best to Leonard Cohen with "I'm very conscious of how many years really are left. I just find that I only want to listen to certain things, with some sort of essence, that mean something."

Although Paul's resignation letter was dated Thursday, February 25, 1982, he wrote a handful of pieces for *Rolling Stone* over the next year. "Jim Henke, who became the music editor, went to enormous efforts to try to get Paul's writing into the magazine," Chris Connelly says. "He sent him to the Rickie Lee Jones concert and asked him to write something. Anytime Paul showed the slightest enthusiasm for something, Jim really did whatever he could to get Paul to write, to kind of lure Paul into writing—because he knew it would be a big win for the magazine and because he genuinely cared about Paul, too." Paul also kept in contact with Jann Wenner and pitched him an idea for a regular column called *Modern Times*.

> Dear Jann:
>
> Here are just a few ideas for the column we've been talking about—an arts column that would include coverage of music, movies, video, books, etc. Subjects and approaches would be varied: think pieces, profiles, a profile combined with a review, sneak previews (where possible) of important new works, satire, rediscoveries, reviews of special live performances, etc. Often, I'd like to mix things up a bit: Marty Scorsese on the rock & roll he listens to while editing his films, Bruce Springsteen on John Ford, Thomas McGuane on his new novel as well as how it feels to write rock & roll songs for Warren Zevon's new album—stuff like that. Also: various directors, novelists, musicians, et al., with various lists: e.g., their twenty-five most wanted, as-yet-commercially-unavailable video cassettes. Jackson Browne on producing his high-school friend Greg Copeland's upcoming album. Why *The Godfather Saga* video cassette isn't what Paramount claims it is. I'd like to check in, from time to time, with those artists I consider special: Neil Young, Jackson Browne, Robert Stone, Clint Eastwood, Marty Scorsese, Brian De Palma, James Crumley, Michael Herr, et al. Also: every few issues or so, some rather telling vignettes on the music biz—"The True Story of Rock & Roll, Part 1," etc. Plus much more stuff.
>
> I'm very excited about doing the column and hope we can work out a satisfactory money arrangement. I've checked around some, and the prices are higher than I thought—Greil Marcus, for instance, gets more than a thousand dollars a column for *California*.
>
> In addition to the column, I'd promise you substantial pieces on Clint Eastwood and Ross Macdonald within the year, plus some record reviews. (For the Zevon feature, I got $2,750.00.)
>
> Let's talk soon.
>
> Best,
> Paul Nelson

"I thought it was a great idea," Terry McDonell says. "He wanted to do it, Jann didn't want to do it."

Dear Jann:

Here are just a few ideas for the column we've been talking about
---an arts column that would include coverage of music, movies,
video, books, etc. Subjects and approaches would be varied: think
pieces, profiles, a profile combined with a review, sneak previews
(where possible) of important new works, satire, rediscoveries, reviews of special live performances, etc. Often, I'd like to mix
things up a bit: Marty Scorsese on the rock & roll he listens to
while editing his films, Bruce Springsteen on John Ford, Thomas
McGuane on his new novel as well as how it feels to write rock &
roll songs for Warren Zevon's new album---stuff like that. Also,
various directors, novelists, musicians, et al., with various
lists: e.g., their twenty-five most-wanted, as-yet-commercially-
unavailable video cassettes. Jackson Browne on producing his
high-school friend Greg Copeland's upcoming album. Why The Godfather
Saga video cassette isn't what Paramount claims it is. I'd like to
check in, from time to time, with those artists I consider special:
Neil Young, Jackson Browne, Robert Stone, Clint Eastwood, Marty
Scorsese, Brian DePalma, James Crumley, Michael Herr, et al. Also:
every few issues or so, some rather telling vignettes on the music
biz---"The True Story of Rock & Roll, Part 1," etc. Plus much more
stuff.
I'm very excited about doing the column and hope we can work out a
satisfactory money arrangement. I've checked around some, and the
prices are higher than I thought---Greil Marcus, for instance, gets
more than a thousand dollars a column for California.
In addition to the column, I'd promise you substantial pieces on
Clint Eastwood and Ross Macdonald within the year, plus some record
reviews. (For the Warren Zevon feature, I got $2,750.00.)
Let's talk soon.
Best,

Paul Nelson

Paul figured his magazine-writing days were behind him anyway (though he still thought there was hope for his three-year-overdue *Rolling Stone* cover story on Clint Eastwood), and intended to dive headfirst into two book projects—biographies of Neil Young and Ross Macdonald.

Karen Moline edited the *Rod Stewart* book. "Paul definitely wanted to be part of that bigger world. Magazines are ephemeral. You can spend six months doing a cover story for *Rolling Stone*, but two weeks later there's another issue out and you're done. A book is a much more longer-lasting testament to your talents."

"But then my whole life sort of fell apart," Paul said.

Lester Bangs died from an accidental overdose on the night of April 30, 1982. The two were the unlikeliest of friends, but Paul loved him. "I remember playing Jackson Browne for Lester and converting him," he told Jim DeRogatis. "I said, 'Lester, it's all about love and loss and all this stuff—why don't you want to hear it? Some of this is just about as heartrending as it gets.'" Paul convinced the hard-rocking Bangs to listen. "Then I played a Neil Young song about salmon spawning upstream, this big romantic thing, and he just thought that was the greatest song in the world. It was ludicrous, but moving."[42]

Thinking that his *Modern Times* column at *Rolling Stone* was a go, Paul delivered a manuscript beneath a handwritten cover letter to Terry McDonell that began: "When Lester Bangs died, I *had* to do the first column on him. I think you can understand." When Paul's piece, "It Seemed like Forever," ran, however, it was as a stand-alone obituary using only his subheading ("Lester Bangs: 1948–1982") with some of his more personal remembrances gone.

> At his best, he could go one-on-one with any New Journalist you'd care to name. That he wasn't more widely recognized as an important American writer is tragic but not surprising: he wrote about rock & roll, still a subject not taken seriously by most of the literati; he wrote about rock & roll with all the beauty, wildness, and clangor of the music itself; and, finally, he had a sense of humor. That's three strikes against him right there....
>
> Needless to say, I loved the man, his writing, what he stood for. While we were different in a lot of ways, I felt especially close to him and always figured that he and I, among all our rock-critic friends, were somehow the least grown up: we weren't married, we hadn't much family, and we invariably led the league in falling in love hard, fast, and disastrously. (I am *not* plying the old rock-was-his-life, writing-was-his-life cliché here. If someone said that about me, I'd probably throw up and I'm sure Lester would, too. *Life* was his life.) When I was having a terrible time trying to do a solo on *Rod Stewart*, he saved me from a fate worse than deadline by signing on as a coauthor and turning out pounds of copy to my ounces. One weekend, he wrote eighty-eight pages (many of them spiked with meaningful digression, one of his favorite strategies) while I managed but five. Yet when *Rod Stewart* was published, Bangs insisted that my byline appear ahead of his.
>
> Ah, Lester, I know I haven't done you any sort of justice. I was in a store today and heard Jackson Browne's "The Load-Out/Stay" on the radio, and it hit me like "For a Dancer" and "Sleep's Dark and Silent Gate" (remember

---

42 The song was Young's "Will to Love."

when I played those for you?) and I started to cry and I had to leave.[43] I wish you could have come over last night and watched Sam Fuller's *The Big Red One* on HBO. Says one young soldier who's survived half of World War II: "After a while, we began to think of the replacements as walking dead men who had the temporary use of their arms and legs." That's the kind of joke you'd have appreciated.[44]

That summer, sounding all but defeated by the year thus far, Paul conducted a telephone interview with Greg Copeland, whose largely and unjustly ignored debut album *Revenge Will Come* had been produced by Jackson Browne. Two hours into the call, Paul disclosed that he only had a "tentative connection" to the magazine from which Copeland knew his work. "I'm going to do this piece for *Stone*, but they're not giving me much more than 800 to 900 words. But I'm also going to review the record for *The Boston Phoenix*, so we'll get two shots at it. I wish I had four or five thousand words because it would make a lot more sense."

Though Paul offered Copeland a detailed song-by-song analysis of his album, he never wrote either piece. And before the call was over, it became more about him than Copeland.

"To me, *Rolling Stone* is just a fucking tragedy," he said. "I don't think it's a music paper at all anymore, I think it's more of a joke." Copeland kept trying to buck up Paul's spirits, suggesting other magazines that might welcome his writing. Paul said he wanted to write books instead. "There isn't that much in music that I have a burning desire to even write about, to tell you the truth. I did want to talk to you and get to know you because your record's my favorite record of the year."

Copeland thanked him. "I think it's wonderful that you want to step past magazines."

"I more or less left *Rolling Stone* without enough money in the bank to last two months, so I don't know what's going to happen."

"This is your moment."

"Yes, I hope. It had better be." Paul bemoaned the fact that book publishing had gone the way of the movie business in that each one was looking for the next blockbuster, and that required selling out.

"I'll bet you've got something in you," Copeland said, "that you would

---

43 In the final manuscript, Paul crossed out "God damn it, I'm crying again."
44 "It Seemed Like Forever" [published as "Lester Bangs: 1948–1982"] by Paul Nelson from *Rolling Stone*, June 10, 1982. © Rolling Stone LLC 1982. All rights reserved. Reprinted by permission. Reprinted from the original manuscript, which first appeared in *Rolling Stone* as an edited version.

not consider being compromised, that five million people would think was just dandy."

"I don't know. I hope so. I find it scary, though."

"Most good stuff is scary."

"I don't write easily. I'm of the Warren Zevon torture school of writing. I love it when it's over, but I hate doing it. I wish I was a photographer, where you've either got it when you push the shutter or you don't. You don't have to sit and look at it for ten hours or twelve hours or thirty days or whatever. Writing ain't like that, I'm afraid."

"I must confess," Copeland said, "that's one of the things that I like about it: it satisfies all that work ethic in me because it *is* so difficult."

"God, it's harder than digging ditches, I'll tell you that. The romanticized view of the writer is not very true. Not very true at all. Sometimes I wish I was like 'Bartleby the Scrivener,' where I just worked away at an office and didn't have to think. Not seriously, but there are times."

"You'd hate yourself if you did that."

"I know, I know."

Jay Cocks: "Without trespassing on the creativity of the artist, Paul would write about this music as if he had written it. When he couldn't do that, as with Suzanne Vega—and I don't mean to hold her off as an example, because he was very fond of her personally—when he felt something was good but it couldn't get his whole heart, it was then that he'd clench up. So he was damned if he did and damned if he didn't. If he loved someone too much, he couldn't get it all down, and that drove him crazy—whether it was Clint or Warren or Jackson or Ross Macdonald. Or, if he didn't love them enough, that would drive him crazy in the opposite direction. So either one tied him up in knots."

Ironically, Paul discussed the problem with Suzanne Vega. "There have been times when I've had a lot of trouble writing, an awful lot of trouble."

"Do you know, is it confidence?" she asked.

"Yeah, to some degree. To some degree it's fear. I don't ever really do pieces unless I really want to. Other times I would just have *too much* to say. Also, I just have this thing about it having to be better than the last one. You know, it just has to be really perfect, perfect, perfect before I would turn it in."

Debra Rae Cohen: "I think that part of what caused greater and greater problems for Paul is that he started thinking about his writing more and more seriously. He ended up making the mistake that a lot of us make, which is that he wanted to write about the things he cared about most deeply—and it's exactly those things that are most resistant to our ability to express ourselves as perfectly as we want to.

"His habits were solitary, his habits were self-protective. His mode of composition was lapidary and self-critical to the point of *actual* paralysis. I think that perhaps if his personal instincts had been different, if he had been the kind of person who was able to recognize that he needed to jolt himself out of that kind of survival mode by engaging with other people, he might not have been as prone to that kind of intense writer's block, intense work frustration."

"He was a perfectionist in the best sense of that word," Charles M. Young says. "Ultimately, he didn't want anything to get between him and the art that he loved. Especially other human beings."

Phillip Blumberg, who was a VP at ABC Motion Pictures, met Paul socially several times over the years. "The thing about Paul that is so interesting and makes it so tragic is that there were so many people who were loyal to him, who were worried about him. I think towards the end he'd pulled back from them, and they may have pulled back from him in some way that everybody felt too guilty to cop to. That is not infrequent with somebody who's drowning like that, particularly when their friends are writers. There's nothing more frightening to another writer than a writer with writer's block."

"**I**n all the years I knew him, whenever I would be with him and he would interact with people, it wouldn't matter whether it was somebody who was really green like me or whether he was talking to Warren Zevon, everybody was exactly the same," Ken Tucker says. "He never deferred to somebody he thought was a great artist and he never talked down to anybody because they were lower on the writers' chain than him. He was just completely democratic in all of the ways he dealt with people, which is just incredibly unusual in anyone, and even more so in somebody who was so extremely talented and modest about his own gift."

It was the same when it came to money. He may have secretly coveted Zevon's actress girlfriend, but not the singer-songwriter's home in the Hollywood Hills. He valued Clint Eastwood's friendship more than his riches and power. And, when Jay Cocks made the leap from successful critic to successful screenwriter, Paul was happy for him. "He loved to hear the stories about the frustrations and the struggles, and he genuinely was pleased at the fact that I got this stuff going with Marty. He was a great source of comfort when I got screwed out of *The Last Temptation of Christ* credit and he was as proud as a noncompetitive older brother could be when *The Age of Innocence* finally worked out. He loved Marty, he loved Marty's movies, loved spending time with Marty—but he was not a competitive guy, except deep inside with himself. He was competitive with wanting to get the best out of himself. That was his struggle. I think he was delighted for the people who could hit it big and still stay true, whether it was Bruce, or Rod Stewart—the early Rod Stewart—or Jackson with *The Pretender*."

The need to earn a living wasn't just something that took time away from watching movies, listening to music, reading books, and, to a point, writing. "There's nothing much one can do about it," Paul told Greg Copeland, "the very fact that you have to think about money in this society and that it means so much. You spend so much of your time just worrying about the next buck and not wanting to really sell out to get it."

Even after he'd been on salary for a year at *Rolling Stone*, things were shaky financially. "I remember when I was working through college I was making fifty bucks a week and I had more than enough money for rent, food, going to the movies, buying a new record or a book. God, now I'm making $25,000, which is not great but it's not bad either. In this city, you have to almost make that to be one level above poor. I've got $600 in the bank. I'm already in a situation where I'm in a fourth-floor walk-up, small, one bedroom, and I can't afford to move. I'd love to—it's getting too small for me. I'm by myself, I'm not married and I don't have kids, and I can barely make it. I'm not lavish. I mean, I buy a lot of running shoes and stuff like that. I don't go to '21' and I don't spend a lot of money on clothes."

When Crystal Zevon asked Paul to come to Los Angeles for Warren's intervention, she also loaned him $1,500. "He was buying time to write his screenplay, but then he wouldn't finish anything."

As much as Paul needed money, when film critic Richard Schickel asked him to write a 2,000-word article about director Nicholas Ray for a British magazine, he declined on principle. According to Paul, "He said, 'I don't really know anything about Nick Ray.' I thought, Jesus, this guy's been a film reviewer for *Time* magazine for twelve years or something like that and he doesn't know anything at all about Nicholas Ray? In talking to him, I realized he didn't have the foggiest idea of any of Nick Ray's films."

Anthony DeCurtis says, "Even when you're watching him being interviewed in *No Direction Home*, he knew who he was and he knew what he had done. This is entirely speculative, but you kind of get the sense that he found it a little beneath him maybe to be hustling for stuff or to do things that were not up to the kinds of things he had done in the past, and that something got poisoned about the whole endeavor—about writing, about the kind of music that he was drawn to. I mean, look, everybody struggles with how commercial do you have to be, what kind of writing do you have to do to make a buck. That's been going on since forever. But I think that when you completely opt out of that game and essentially run yourself into the ground, that can't be explained away as 'Okay, you're kind of an eccentric.' I just don't buy it."

After Paul left *Rolling Stone*, the writing stopped coming out and the income stopped coming in. He began selling his books and records. That was when bookseller Ralph Sipper, who used to sell books to Paul, would reverse roles and buy some of the books back. "Not only back to me, but to other rare book dealers. I think he accepted the fact that in some cases he lost money, but he was very serene, philosophical about that. Pragmatic."

When the books and records ran out, Paul started asking friends for help. "He seemed pretty broke," Ron Oberman says, "and he asked if I could loan him some money. A few hundred bucks here, a hundred bucks there, which I gladly sent him. I never asked for it back." None of them did—except for Warren Zevon.

William MacAdams remembers when Paul reached out to Bob Dylan. "Paul in desperation called him up and borrowed money from him. Small sums, like $3,000, $5,000, something like that."

"We would go get him some money," Kurt Loder says of himself and David Fricke, "or take him out to get something to eat. Just because he had done so much for us, it was not a problem. 'You need some money? Here.' We did that a couple of times. It was very sad. You're watching somebody going down slow and you don't know what to do about it. There was just nothing you could do."

Jon Landau: "He needed some money, which I lent him. Two thousand dollars or something. I didn't care if I ever got it back or not. Two years later, he called me and seemed to be virtually crying. He said he just wasn't going to be able to pay this money back, which I had long since forgotten. I said, 'Paul, it's fine.' 'Well, it's not fine with me.' He just beat himself up mercilessly about this."

Several of Paul's other friends received similar phone calls.

Mikal Gilmore says, "At one point Susan Murcko called me and told me Paul was in trouble and that he needed to pay some back taxes. She was talking to people about whether they would help, and I told her I would. I didn't hear anything more from her on that."

"When I knew Paul he never ever borrowed money from anyone," Betsy Volck says. "It would never have occurred to him. He was very generous. When we were courting I quickly learned not to admire something in a shop window because he would buy it for me. Apart from the goddamn Nat Shermans and the running shoes he had no habits that would cost any money. When we ate out or went out it was usually a justifiable expense and billed to the record company, either on his tab or mine.

"I do know that he never paid income tax. Not because of any political motives—Paul was amazingly apolitical—but because he simply never did and I think the longer he didn't pay the more difficult it became to make the move to pay. Perhaps the feds caught up with him. Certainly his income decreased when his writing dried up."

Tom Carson: "I remember once back in the Seventies, I was talking to Kit [Rachlis] about Paul—a mutual admiration society. Kit said very expansively, 'You know, if I were a millionaire I'd give Paul $50,000 a year just to sit in a room and write detective novels.' A week or so later I repeated it to Paul, and Paul just got the most wonderful smile on his face and said, 'Any chance he'd pay me twenty-five grand just to sit in a room?'"

By the time Paul came to Michael Seidenberg's Brazen Head Books on the Upper East Side, he didn't have any first editions left. "He'd already sold off his really, really good stuff and then he came to me to buy the rest. So I did." But Seidenberg came up thirty-five dollars short and asked Paul to come back another day for the balance. When he did, "He looked at my shop and he saw it was empty—like it was the first time he came in. We talked about the book business and he said, 'You know, why don't you keep that thirty-five bucks and put it towards an ad?' For me, from that point on, I would have done anything for him."

Brazen Head was also a place for people to meet and talk, and for a while Paul became a regular. He became well-known for his reading binges. "Say, if he was reading a Vietnam novel," David Breithaupt says, "he wouldn't read just one—he'd read every Vietnam novel he could get his hands on. He would exhaust the genre." It was the same way when Seidenberg turned him on to science fiction author Philip K. Dick.

Jay Cocks: "I had a lot of Philip K. Dick books that I gave him so he could feed the fire and then, when the fire died, he could get a little money and sell them off."

"He was obsessively buying every paperback he could find," Jeff Wong remembers. "At one point he lent me one of the books, *The Transmigration of Timothy Archer*, which was a hardcover. I remember the binding was split. I offered to archivally mend it and he said, 'Don't repair it.' He wanted it just as it was for whatever reason. He had some sort of fondness for it being the way it was."

As a young writer, Jonathan Lethem was part of the Brazen Head bunch. Breithaupt says, "I remember Paul was very much a mentor to Jonathan, helping Jonathan with one of his stories, going over it line by line, practically."

Paul served as the inspiration for the aesthetically obsessed Perkus Tooth, one of the main characters in Lethem's 2009 novel *Chronic City*.

Lethem: "It seemed in a way that he couldn't think about any other writer at the time he was collecting all of Dick's first editions and arguing so much with me and Michael about the virtues of different books. It is as though Dick was the only writer. And, at the time that I was spending so much time with him in the middle of the Eighties, Chet Baker was kind of the only musician. I would sometimes get him to talk about Dylan or about some of the other things he cared about and he was always very generous, but it felt as though his present attention couldn't make room for these other things."

After Lethem moved to California, he attempted to stay in touch with Paul, but it was difficult. The distance wasn't a contributing factor—Paul's friends in New York were experiencing the same widening gulf. As Paul became less and less interested about the music he had once loved, it was as if he had less to say about everything. "It's like the aperture was getting smaller in some ways," Lethem says. "What distinguishes that early writing from what he did later is he stopped seeming to be curious about his own dislikes."

Crystal Zevon recalls the first time she met Paul, in 1976. "Paul came to the show at the Bottom Line and a day or two later he came up to our hotel room to interview Warren. It was two o'clock and we were just getting ready to order room-service breakfast when Paul arrived. I asked what he'd like and he tried to decline. But I insisted. Finally, he acquiesced and ordered cornflakes with orange juice in place of milk, and two Cokes. I remember Warren watching Paul as he spooned OJ-soaked cornflakes into his mouth between sips of Coke and drags off his Sherman cigarettes. Finally Warren looked at me and said, 'I think this guy's weird enough to be our friend.' Paul smiled shyly and a friendship was born."

"He thought the world of Warren," Betsy Volck says. "I remember he had to go out to L.A. for an intervention and he was really quite horrified by that. Understandably so."

Greil Marcus: "Paul talked about that with great optimism and pride, that he had been able to take part in something that's really going to make the difference, that was really going to save somebody from both self-destruction and the destruction of maybe other people."

"He had many reservations," Crystal Zevon says. "He was very frightened by it." But he had also seen how Zevon treated her when he drank too much. "Warren was a pretty violent drunk. Paul would stand up for me in a quiet way.

.44 caliber friends: Warren Zevon with a Smith & Wesson and
Paul with a Ruger Blackhawk. In Zevon's Hollywood Hills home, 1979 or '80.
Photo by George Gruel.

He would say, 'I think you might want to reconsider the way that you're treating Crystal, the mother of your child.' I think he was very much a calming influence.

"After Warren and I split up, Paul was one of the people who really remained a loyal, steadfast friend to both of us during that difficult period."

Down the road, Paul's participation in the intervention contributed to the ongoing discord between Zevon and his wife and, ultimately, to bad feelings between Zevon and himself. "I paid for Paul's ticket to come out for the intervention, and Warren was furious about that. He found out because he looked at a credit card bill or something, and that infuriated him. He felt if Paul was really a friend he should have paid for his own ticket. He probably *would have*, but I offered to pay because I knew he didn't have money and we did. You know, I was really grateful that he was coming, but to Warren that was the

Paul and Warren take aim while James Dean looks on, 1979 or '80.
Photo by George Gruel.

kind of thing that was a point of honor. He let that one go because he blamed
me. But later, when Paul had borrowed money and wasn't able to repay it ..."

Three years later, though, when Clint Eastwood asked how Zevon was
doing, Paul said, "He hates me now. He's just crazy again. I don't think he's
drinking but I think he might be drugging. He hates me for a totally absurd
reason. I wrote a negative review of a friend of his and got everybody upset—the
California music scene—except him and he understood. 'It's your opinion,' you
know? And now suddenly, years later, he hates me for that reason, which is
obviously bullshit.

"Everybody who was at the intervention and helped him, he's cut us all off
totally. I feel sorry for him. He's pretty alone. He refused to take my phone
number even. I'm afraid he's falling apart, but he won't even talk to me, so I
can't find out. I made fifteen approaches and he doesn't seem interested, so
that's about all I can do. It's up to him, the next move."

Zevon still wasn't speaking with Paul in the mid-Eighties when Jim Farber
interviewed the artist in California. "He said to me at one point that he thought
that some things that Paul Nelson had written about his songs were better
than the songs themselves. It so struck me that a performer would say this
about a critic."

After Zevon was diagnosed with inoperable mesothelioma in 2002, he asked
Danny Goldberg, then the head of Artemis Records, Zevon's label, to give his
phone number to three old friends. One of them was Paul.

Crystal Zevon was in touch with her ex-husband almost daily through most of the last year of his life. "He didn't want to talk to many people, but Paul was someone he did want to talk to. Warren and I talked about Paul. He had a lot of regret that he had let that friendship slide. Paul didn't ever call him, however."

In Paul's final round of interviews with Clint Eastwood in late 1983, when talk turned to the actor-director's *Play Misty for Me* and its tale of twisted, obsessive love, Paul said, "I lived that whole story out this year." He told how he'd received a letter from a woman who'd been especially enamored with his Zevon cover story. "She said she was dying of something and would like to meet me. It was a really intelligent, beautiful four-page letter. She lived in Philadelphia. I thought, Well, jeez, I'm pretty lonesome. I mean, maybe this will be something."

"Sure," Eastwood understood.

William MacAdams: "This woman, whose name I don't remember, had written Paul what was in essence a fan letter at *Rolling Stone*. She was familiar with his articles, apparently intelligent, educated, cultured—all this according to Paul."

"I went down there," Paul said, "and I could tell five minutes later that I was in *Nightmare Alley*. She wanted to marry me. It had to be right now. The romance started *instantly*"—he snapped his fingers—"and it was going to be perfect." He lasted the day before fleeing back to New York. "She was bats, she was nuts."

"Awful lot of that happens," Eastwood said.

MacAdams: "When Paul got back after the weekend in Philadelphia with her he was disappointed, at least partially because he wasn't that attracted to her physically, more so because he had really built up this connection in his mind, talking with her for many hours on many occasions on the phone."

Paul told Eastwood that she kept calling for a month. "Day and night the phone would ring—but she wouldn't listen to reason. 'Look, we don't even know each other. It's like never playing football before and you're expected to be the quarterback in the Super Bowl romantically. Let's get to know each other, you know? I'm not saying no, I'm not saying yes, but let's be friends for a while and talk. I don't want to move to Philadelphia and marry you. I don't even know you. You don't even know me.'" The downstairs neighbors mentioned to Paul that there'd been someone suspicious hanging around. "There were a couple nights when I went up the stairs, I didn't know if she'd been on top with a gun or not. I mean, she was crazy enough to do it."

"It's scary," Eastwood said.

"It *was* scary. This was real emotional blackmail. She sort of intimated that, if I didn't do this, she would go back into her disease and die, or that she would kill herself. Jesus Christ, why did I ever go down there?"

MacAdams: "What he didn't tell Eastwood is that he borrowed money from her (not that weekend but not long after). How much he never mentioned, and I never asked. When he never repaid any of it, she did begin phoning and phoning, Paul avoiding her, not taking her calls—though to my knowledge she never came to New York to stalk him as the lunatic does in *Play Misty*."

Over twenty years later, on the morning of January 1, 2004, a woman identifying herself as Dr. Barbara Horwitz began posting to alt.music.zevon, a newsgroup devoted to Warren Zevon:

> This morning, waking with too much WZ on my mind, I remembered the days when I used to date Paul Nelson, old critic for "Rolling Stone" but also the man who did the incredible Zevon alcoholism and intervention feature in the very early '80s. He was himself a genius and a tragic figure in a "minor key" and brought so much baggage that we couldn't have worked in a hundred years but that is not saying we didn't try. Made the NYC to Phila. run a dozen times....
>
> [L]ast I knew of Paul, he was working with his first love, at a NYC video store, Year 2000. He wanted a nobrainer job with movies all around him, his first love....
>
> He shared our love of Ken Millar, and I hear he prefers bluegrass now, and never writes anything else about rock 'n' roll, and never will.

Horwitz presented herself online as attractive, forty-three years old, an immunologist, a resident of Lower Bucks County, Pennsylvania, and a breeder of snakes and champion dogs, among other exotic pets. Her posts about life with Paul spilled over into the first week of the new year.

> It was something that was a prolonged bout of sadness, as he was so involved in the lives of others, mostly Warren and Neil Young, and fighting with Jann Wenner, and looking for his 18 year old son from a long LONG dead marriage....
>
> He's a man who never gave himself a chance. BA U of Minnesota by the way, College of Journalism of course.

> Paul, who was getting a nice piece of money from "Rolling Stone," lived in an apartment that was divey in the Lew Archer sense, which was over a Chinese Take-Out restaurant, and had a door leading to the long flight of stairs, right next to the restaurant's door. So a lot of people looking for egg foo young or whatever

ended up banging on Paul's door and, disappointed with what they found, had to "go to ground" again.

The Chinese food aroma permeated his apartment day and night but he just wouldn't move, though he did not like Chinese food, would have preferred hamburgers.

That gives the best feel of him.

Am I gagging this list with history?

As the Son of Sam said, if I am, "Stop me before I kill again."

Zevon newsgroup member Lucy Pfeffa posted the link to Steven Ward's "What Ever Happened to Rock Critic Paul Nelson?" and noted: "Dr. H, since what little you know of the current Mr. Nelson contained in your post is also in the following article, I'm assuming you've read it."

Well, Lucy, it ain't nothing but the stone truth. Sadly I did not take photographs.

Nor read this article (although I have now, and thanks).

Was the Chinese restaurant bit in there too? And his lost son and his degree? I didn't notice.

After other members posted their memories of the Zevon alcoholism article ("If a person writes something that so many people remember after all those years, whatever else he does the rest of his life is fine"), Horwitz returned to say that she'd checked an online telephone directory, found two Paul Nelsons listed in Manhattan, but decided, "Sometimes well enough is too much."

A few months later, after crediting Paul for turning her on to Ross Macdonald, Horwitz noted another newsgroup member's preference for the New York Dolls:

Paul Nelson is what, in "Godfather I," they'd have called "a true Sicilian." Remember when, asked if Sollozzo was willing to risk everything, gamble it all, on a principle, the response was a question, "Do you mean, is he a Sicilian?" That's one reason he no longer writes about rock 'n' roll, although the primary reason is that his first love is and even then was video, and he listens to a lot of bluegrass, and writes the beginnings of novels....

The Dolls had some outrageous tee shirts to go with those first two outrageous albums and I had one and used it, believe it or not, as a tourniquet. Then I couldn't get the blood out afterward. It did not appreciably detract from the motif of the shirt but my mother felt, and for once rightly, that there were limits.

In September, after a spell away from the keyboard, Horwitz resurfaced with an epic, purportedly jetlagged post claiming she'd just returned from the scene of the Beslan school massacre.

> It was like working in a MASH unit times twenty. I was cutting bones with saws. The severed limbs we threw in buckets. We were all covered with blood. The floor was slippery with blood. No one rested for 36 hours, the casualties kept coming, carried in and laid on cots, no separating the living from the dead in advance. There was no preparing for this.

"Can somebody please show me a news report saying U.S. doctors went to Russia to help with this?" one member asked. Even Howard Roseman, who initially "stuck with her because she was a devoted e-mail correspondent, well-read, and, frankly, a shameless flatterer," says, "People wondered how an AIDS physician managed to find the time to bang out thousands of words per day on a non-medical newsgroup, not to mention the voluminous e-mail correspondence she maintained."

Other details of the good doctor's life soon came into question: that she ran the biggest AIDS hospice in Philadelphia; that she'd contracted anthrax when the U.S. Postal Service brought her in to assist in the investigation of the anthrax attacks; that she was a former beauty contest runner-up; that she dated Warren Zevon for years and refused several of his marriage proposals; and that she'd helped Stephen King with the finer epidemiological points in his revised version of *The Stand*.

Roseman: "By the time I stopped my e-mail correspondence with Barbara, she was apparently living with Stephen and Tabitha King full time in their mansion in Maine." His own relationship with her ended when he confronted her about some of the inconsistencies in her stories. "She went ballistic. Not only was she a fantasist, but she developed a seething hatred for anyone—which turned out to be everyone—who dared question her accounts."

Once outed, Dr. Barbara Horwitz's name vanished from cyberspace until 2005 when word spread through the newsgroup grapevine that she'd died from lung cancer that had spread to her liver.

Roseman: "Her death was announced in an e-mail sent out by her lawyer to a few people. When some of these people called her house, they spoke to her dog groomer who lived on the property with her and was totally unaware of her online life." The groomer revealed that her name was apparently the only true part of her story. She was actually sixty-three years old at the time of her death, a retired school teacher, and a heavy smoker with a chronic condition that had left her housebound.

Roseman says, "What I heard from her was that Paul was the love of her life. Even though they almost certainly never met, he definitely made a strong impression on her." However, of all the fantastic tales she'd spun, the one about Paul might've been true. While virtually all the details she'd posted about him could have been gleaned from either his Zevon article or from Steven Ward's Q&A, neither made mention of a son (who indeed would have been eighteen at the time of their alleged meeting) or a failed marriage. She did get a couple of points wrong—Paul didn't reside above a Chinese restaurant but rather the Lenox Hill Diner, and his degree from U of M ("I started in journalism," he told Ward, "but quit after one class because I decided that Mary Lou Sullivan already taught me everything I needed to know about journalism")—but, if you allow for twenty years and a terminal illness, it's not difficult to believe that Barbara Horwitz was Paul's pen pal from Philadelphia.

"**M**y mom and I weren't really very close," Paul said. "When she died there was not only this sorrow but the incredible feeling of 'My God, I have no sources left'—that the two people who had brought me into the world had no connection with me anymore. I never expected to feel that and that it would be that powerful. You really can't go home again. In a way, I wasn't supposed to be alone that much. It was an incredibly primal feeling and so overpowering.

"When my mother died I just found myself praying, and I hadn't prayed in years." The only solace Paul found was in Leonard Cohen's "If It Be Your Will" and Bob Dylan's "Every Grain of Sand." He played them over and over.

David Breithaupt: "The only piece of personal history he did talk about was taking care of his mother when she was dying of cancer, because he said he had to sell a lot of his books to help finance her medical treatment. And that only came up because I helped him move probably ten times during that decade, from one illegal sublet to another. He'd say, 'Well, if I had the books that I had to sell for my mother's treatment, we'd really be in trouble.'"

Dave Marsh: "Paul was very wrapped up with her life for a while, which I could tell made him uncomfortable. Totally understandable. You know, those of us who live a thousand miles away from our families do so for a reason."

"Paul started to get desperate after *Rolling Stone*," Jay Cocks says. "He was desperate financially, he was desperate *in* and about his writing. If you

Paul's signed copy of Archer in Hollywood, *bearing his ownership signature.*
Photo by Jeff Wong.

lose that kind of soft-landing spot—plus one of the persons who's so important in your life is going—you can really get unhinged easily. Plus your very limited resources are being tapped by this person. You're probably feeling guilty about worrying about it."

"I had no idea he was paying for it," Betsy Volck says. "I thought he was simply being a dutiful son and ferrying her back and forth to her appointments."

While visiting Paul's sister Linda in Pennsylvania early in 1983, Clara, almost seventy-three, had come down with shingles. When she went to the doctor, she also pointed out a lump in her neck that had been getting bigger. It was diagnosed as lymphoma. The lump was removed and Clara remained at Linda's for the next nine months while receiving chemotherapy at Sloan-Kettering in New York. Every three weeks, Linda's husband Nick Barna drove Clara into the city. Paul would meet up with them and, while his mother received her treatments, he and Nick went to Jackson Hole for cheeseburgers. So it went for the rest of the year.

Once the chemo was finished, in January of 1984, daily doses of radiation for one month followed. Since driving Clara two hours each way every day was impractical, Paul found his mother a small apartment close to the hospital. For the next month, he checked on her three times a day and accompanied her to and from her treatments.

Finished with the radiation therapy, Clara stayed with Linda and Nick before finally returning home to Warren, Minnesota, in April. Approximately one year had transpired from diagnosis to cure.

But that was not how Paul remembered it.

"Just spending two and a half, two and a quarter years seeing people dying—little kids dying, teenage girls dying—I'd just go home and stare at the wall and sank into clinical depression. I was unable to write a word, was basically unable to go to Los Angeles because I couldn't leave New York. So I blew the Neil Young book, I just eventually canceled it. I just cracked up, basically. All the time I was not in the hospital with my mother, I was just sort of sitting there like a vegetable. I really couldn't concentrate enough to read anything much. I tried to finish this one article on Clint Eastwood and I managed to get a page and a half written. I couldn't tell whether one sentence had any connection to the next sentence. People read it later and said, 'Hey, it's great,' but I couldn't tell.

"I remember entering into such a state of mental panic that I was asking myself as I was going into it, Am I going to come out of it? When? And will I be the same when I come out of it? I really did not know the answers to those questions.

"Every day I would be terrified to go to my mailbox because there'd be another bill in it for something. Electric, phone, rent—everything was running miles behind. I didn't know what I was going to do. A couple of friends helped me out and paid my back rent. I lived from friend to friend. If somebody was leaving town for a month, I'd stay at their apartment. I wound up living on the floor over on Avenue B in somebody's apartment for six, seven months. There were weeks when I had no idea where I was going to spend the next week, and I just realized how close to homelessness you can come. If one of these persons doesn't come through, you're sleeping in Central Park. That's the truth of it. I've been very close to that," Paul told Leonard Cohen in 1991. "I still am not too far away from that.

"I didn't have a home for two, two and a half years. There was just a succession of apartments with only books and records and a bed on the floor and a table. I was just sort of living by my wits and taking up friends' floors." He managed to scrape together $300. "I had just gotten the money up for half the rent for this Long Island City apartment with an old friend of mine who'd come back to New York and had as little money as I did—and my mother died. I thought, Jesus, what do I do? I can get off this floor on Avenue B, with the mice and the rats and get into my own place again—at least half my own place—or I can go to my mother's funeral. And I said, 'Mother, please understand. I've got to get out of here. I'm not going to go to the funeral.'"

Linda Barna: "I don't know why he said he had to sell things to take care of her when she was sick. I mean, he did as far as he went and got her every day at the room and took her to the appointment, but as far as money I don't think he had to do anything like that. She had money and she had insurance and she paid for that room in New York. She was very much the type who paid her own bills and she had the money to do it. She wouldn't have wanted him to. If anything, she would have probably given him a little money to help him out as she was always trying to give money."

Deborah Frost: "I didn't even realize there was a sister. The way he presented it was that he was the sole dependent, that the mother depended on him."

William MacAdams: "He would say, oh, he just couldn't write because he had to spend all of his time with his mother, but that was an excuse. Because his mother wasn't there constantly. In the period where she was in town having cancer treatments and he would spend morning till night with her, yeah, okay, he didn't really have any time. That doesn't explain why he just couldn't write anymore."

Paul always ended the story the same way: "I think it was a case where the cure was equal to the disease. My mother got cured of cancer and died two months later. She died apparently of a stroke, watching the TV with a smile on her face and the remote in her hand."

In reality, Clara survived another year and a half after returning to Warren before dying from a heart attack in front of the television one September night in 1985. Her estate was equally shared between Paul and Linda, who called her brother to tell him that their mother had died. Paul said that he wouldn't be coming to Minnesota because he didn't have anything appropriate to wear to the funeral.

"**S**o I called him up and just said, 'Hey, this is Mark. I want to come out and see you. What do you think?' He was really real open about it and real excited about the idea." In 1985, Mark Nelson, a junior in college, with the emotional and financial support of his mother flew to New York to spend three weeks with Paul over the Christmas holiday. Paul hadn't seen Mark since he was nine in Winnipeg. Doris, who remarried in 1978, was surprised that Paul hadn't made any effort to keep in touch with his son. "Those four years that we were there in New York, he was a pretty doting father. It was his loss."

Mark's early memories of Paul were few but vivid: baseball games, going to the zoo and out to Far Rockaway for clams, and climbing on the rocks in Central Park. "I was very fortunate that my mom was a pretty special lady, so I got over any resentment that I would've felt a long time ago. I appreciated Paul for who he was—and he was a pretty great guy."

It wasn't until Mark was already aboard the plane that it occurred to him that neither one of them had any idea what the other looked like. "I figured,

With Mark Nelson at Christmastime 1985.

Well, okay, I'll look for the most uncomfortable-looking person I can find and figure that's got to be him. And sure enough, it was."

"I was *absolutely terrified*," Paul told Leonard Cohen. "I met him at the airport in Jersey, just scared to death. You know, what is he going to say? Does he hate me? He didn't. We had a good time together. It was not father and son so much as an interesting young person. We got along as friends more than blood."

It was a tough time for Paul. He couldn't write, his mother had passed away a few months before, and, earlier in the year, Coca-Cola had announced the advent of "New Coke." Mark arrived to find Paul's apartment something of a stockpile. "It was wall-to-wall cases of 'Old Coke.'"

Michael Seidenberg says, "When Coke was changing their formula, he went into a fury. A nervous reaction. He went out and bought every six-pack and filled his apartment with six-packs of Coke because he was scared what the formula was going to be like. And, of course, the whole world agreed with him: the new formula was bad." Public acceptance was so poor that, less than three months after its debut, "New Coke" was pulled from the shelves and the old formula reinstated.

Paul proudly took Mark around and introduced him to his friends. When Mark returned home, Paul couldn't stop talking about him.

Paul and Mark got together every five or six years after that, and twice in 2004. The last time was just before Mark's wedding, when he and his fiancée both happened to be in New York on business. "The three of us met one night in a hotel bar. After a couple hours she left, and Paul and I stayed up all night and talked.

"Over the course of the years, when we did see each other we would usually have a real good time, good conversations, and then sort of agree to keep in touch. I'd leave a call or two and they would always go unreturned. It was hard to get through the movies and the books and that sort of stuff. There was obviously so much going on inside, based on what was coming out on paper. So we dropped that charade afterwards and just said, 'Until the next time, we'll see ya.'"

Steve Feltes, who owned Evergreen Video, compares it to gambling. "There are those kind of people who have *that* kind of addiction, and having an addiction to the arts, I guess, is similar."

Paul was well aware of the problem. "My major reactions are to books and movies and records. I really want to find a person to react to, not a thing."

Jon Pankake says Paul was always "Inward. His inner life was always much greater than his outer life was. He had great imagination and great powers of expanding on it. He would easily become obsessed with things in a way that I never did. When I first met Paul, the Jimmy Dean movies were out then. Paul was obsessed with James Dean to the extent that he somehow had managed to get the life-sized cutout of Dean from *Giant* and he had it in his room. He also had a red nylon zip-up jacket like Dean wore in *Rebel Without a Cause.*"

Paul told Kenneth Millar: "It became fashionable for a time, it seems to me, to become a rebel without a cause whether you actually had a cause or not. I think I fell prey to some of that. It almost made it fashionable at that time to be mixed up. He was so powerful and such a romantic actor that everybody wanted to go out and get as screwed up as they possibly could, it seemed to me, because that's what Dean did on the screen, therefore it must be good. It just doesn't work out on the screen like it does in real life. I found it did that to me. I seemed to be going out of my way *to* get mixed up rather than the other way around. Half of it was sort of creative and the other half was destructive, but I couldn't always tell the difference."

"You couldn't tell the difference because there is no difference," Millar said. "The creative and the destructive do go hand in hand."

Pankake: "When he got into something, he was into it all the way and it really consumed his inner life. I'm sure it was the same way with rock & roll. When he took it inside himself, it must have been quite an obsession. I know it coincided with the breakup of his marriage, and there just wasn't room inside him for all of that at the same time."

The last time Paul spoke with Bob Dylan was a phone conversation in 1984. Dylan was apparently having troubles of his own. Concert promoter Bill Graham was fighting Dylan's desire to tour South America, Columbia wasn't happy with the song selection on his upcoming record, and the singer was befuddled by concert audience reactions to his songs (they seemingly preferred substandard performances of his own tunes to his heartfelt covers of traditional songs). "Here's a guy who can't get his booking agent to do the tour he wants," Paul said, "his record company doesn't want his record, and he's the greatest figure in rock & roll. How strange. I just have the feeling he didn't know *who* was listening to him or *why* they were listening to him or *if* they were listening to him. He sounded about as confused as I did at the time."

"I didn't want to think for a while." It was a phrase that Paul had kept handy ever since leaving *Rolling Stone* and one he would intone through the rest of the decade. He embarked on a variety of odd jobs, including part-time proofreader at *Time*, a gig no doubt secured thanks to Jay Cocks, a regular contributor to the magazine. Jeff Wong recalls that "Paul, at one point, through Cocks, did some work for Scorsese. He used to go over to Scorsese's place and catalogue his videos for him." For a while Clara's inheritance money was still coming in from the family farms and property that had been sold. "I know he used to always wait for this check to come in," Wong says. "At one point, it ran out."

In 1985, Paul landed for three years as a copyeditor at *The Jewish Week*. "What the fuck was he doing there?" Charles M. Young still wants to know.

"That was at least a regular income," Michael Seidenberg says. The job paid $24,500 a year—about $5,000 less than Paul had been making when he left *Rolling Stone*. "And it wasn't like it was *mind*-consuming, it was just *time*-consuming."

In 1988, *The Jewish Week* cited "computerization and restructuring of the editorial department" and sent Paul out the door with a letter of recommendation in hand:

> In truth, Paul's being laid off was not an easy decision to take. He is an excellent employee and an equally excellent human being. Unfortunately, someone had to be let go and he was low man on the totem pole.
>
> Paul received two weeks' notice in lieu of severance....

Jon Pankake: "That article about him that I read where he said he wanted to do something where he wouldn't have to ever think again was pretty much the tipoff that he'd reached the end somehow and didn't want to write anymore."

Kit Rachlis says, "It was clear to several of us that Paul was in really bad shape and that he was selling books to make ends meet. Dave Marsh and Jay Cocks and I got together and decided that we would have our own version of an intervention. Jay was very close to Paul in those days and I think was lending Paul money and helping out for a long, long time afterwards. We met at Jay's house, the three of us basically saying to Paul, 'We're really concerned. You're going to lose your apartment. You're going to mount up $900 a month for a two-room apartment,' which was an outrageous sum of money in 1986. 'And here's the deal: we will lend you the money'—we put together four or five thousand dollars between the three of us—'to help you get over this hump. No expectation that you'll ever pay us back. But you need to find a cheaper apartment.'" Rachlis even convinced Stephen Holden, who was moving out of his rent-controlled apartment on East Eighty-Third Street, to sublet it to Paul for $115 a month.

"The rent was very cheap because I'd been there for many years," Stephen Holden says. "It was a very cozy little place, a fifth-floor walk-up with three rooms. I knew that the chances of his not being caught were very, very slim, but he was desperate. He moved in with his cat. It lasted maybe for two months or so before the landlord caught me, as I knew would happen." Holden never saw Paul again. "We lost touch because I just didn't want to be part of the drama anymore, frankly. He stuck me with a lot of cable TV bills and stuff like that. He had no money. He did that to lots of other people, too. It wasn't swindling on his part, it was just that he was poor and just did it. I wasn't mad at him. He was trouble."

Rachlis: "The other part of the deal was that Paul had to see a therapist, which Paul had done off and on over the years. And Paul agreed."

The self-proclaimed "reclusive, gloomy Swede from northern Minnesota" had first undergone therapy after the breakup with Doris. Now, almost fifteen years later, when Clara fell ill and Paul found himself inordinately depressed and stricken with complex, terrifying dreams from which he'd awaken into a different nightmare, he reached out for the same psychologist and told him up front that he couldn't afford to pay him. He told Paul not to worry about money.

Paul also feared that he might be coming down with Alzheimer's. "I could not remember people's names. I couldn't remember the names of books, movies, anything like that. I found that when I was with people I could barely talk. I was just like a kid trying to stammer a sentence out."

It scared the hell out of him. He'd seen what Alzheimer's had done to Kenneth Millar.

P aul ran into Bobbi London and told her that he had to give up his apartment but didn't know what he was going to do with all his belongings. She suggested that he store them, including a drawered platform bed, in her spacious loft.

"Bobbi was so enamored of the bed," he told Leonard Cohen, "and I had so little money, that I said, 'Do you want to buy the bed?'" He sold it to her for $200. "Then she got married shortly after that and they were sleeping on my bed. God, the irony of it—they're sleeping on my fucking bed. The goddamn wedding bed was mine."

P aul met Jeff Wong when the owner of Murder Ink, a bookstore devoted to crime and detective fiction, brought the two Ross Macdonald fans together. "He became very reclusive. We used to talk very frequently and long into the night. Sometimes he had trouble paying his bills and his phone would get disconnected for a period of time, and it'd be tough to stay in touch. I would hear through second- or third-hand sources what he was up to."

Paul's sister Linda Barna, says, "I'd call him once in a while at the store if we were coming in, but I didn't want to bother him there while he was working. He didn't make any effort to keep in touch with people, but yet I think he really cared."

Debra Rae Cohen says that back when Paul attended parties and concerts it was an easy way for him to socialize without really having to be social. When that stopped, he withdrew even more. "I can't even figure out the proportion of phone messages to calls returned. It had to be twenty to one. I mean, you had to either catch him at the right moment or he had to be in a particular mood where he would actually open a door to you—both literally and figuratively."

Fred Schruers: "If you hadn't prepared him for your visit, your chances of someone answering the door were pretty slim."

Steve Feltes remembers the day in 1988 when the elevator broke down. At the time, Evergreen Video was located fourteen floors up in the garment district, but that didn't keep some of his more dedicated customers from climbing the stairs. One of them was Paul.

Another time, Feltes was waiting on him when the name clicked. Might he be the same Paul Nelson who'd edited *The Little Sandy Review*? Not only had Feltes been a subscriber, he was a fellow Minnesotan who'd run film societies at the University of Minnesota. He'd even known "Spider" John Koerner and Dave "Snaker" Ray, whose girlfriend he'd dated. He used to see Tony Glover around Dinkytown.

When Feltes split up with his wife in March of 1990, Paul invited him to stay with him for three months in his Long Island City apartment. "I remember walking up the stairs, and in the living room there was this cloud of smoke that hung a foot or two off the ground, just permanently there. In the front of the place was a sunroom—almost all windows, very light and airy—and Paul didn't use that area at all," so that was where Feltes moved in. "The good sized L-shaped living room led into a kitchen and a very little (no more than eight-by-ten-foot) bedroom. It might even have been smaller. Paul had blocked off the windows and painted the room black, painted the window black—blacked off the windows in the kitchen, too—so he could sleep during the day. He really lived in the little room. His refrigerator had about eight or ten six-packs of Reese's Peanut Butter Cups and three or four six-packs of Coca-Cola and nothing else. I don't think he had salt." Paul had turned the kitchen sink into a kind of sunken bookshelf.

Feltes says that Paul's bathroom floor was lined along the wall with twenty or so almost empty one-quart bottles of shampoo. "Paul had this thing about running out of things," a trait that would extend to his work habits. "He couldn't stand having only ten each of nickels and dimes in the cash register. No matter how many times I told him that if we started the day with zero nickels or dimes that we would end the day with plenty of nickels and dimes, Paul would fill the nickel and dime section with one or two rolls. You just lived with it."

In 1991, Feltes moved his shop closer to the street, a second-story location on West Houston Street, and opened up for night business for the first time. "Paul was my night clerk, which worked for him as his day didn't begin until five PM. This was one of the big dropouts of New York City at least in the last twenty years. He just wanted a job where he could talk to people about something that he liked, which was movies. Because we sort of specialized in old movies and foreign films, it was right up his alley, although he was not such a big fan of foreign films as he was old American films. Film noir." One of Paul's favorite customers was the actress Winona Ryder (a Minnesota native who would later star in Jay and Marty's *The Age of Innocence*). When the shop acquired a cat named Noir, Paul had indeed found a second home.

It took a while before Paul's younger coworkers discovered the backstory of the old guy who worked the night-shift and who showed up without fail as the last bell in the nearby church chimed. He told them that he no longer liked popular culture, had no passion for the music, and wasn't going to support it or condone it—or waste his talent—by writing about it. Several of them, especially David Aaron, Matthew Yeager, and Reggie Lewis, occasionally brought in new music to try to pique Paul's interest, but to no avail.

"He basically slammed the door behind him," Aaron says. Old friends would call the store (and Michael Seidenberg's apartment, too), but Paul wouldn't return their calls. Just as he'd closed the door on his family and friends in Minnesota, on folk music and *Sing Out!*, on rock & roll and *Rolling Stone*, after he settled in at Evergreen he shut the door on whomever was left. "Eventually people just gave up."

Paula Farmer says that a typical shift at Evergreen with Paul was based around what movie to watch. "The rest of us, we could kind of compromise. With Paul there was no compromise. For me, I just learned what his repertoire was and there were things that we did agree on."

Warren Leming wants to know: "Why should somebody who is as significant a figure as Paul, in terms of the writing and the thinking that he did about American culture and American music and American literature, wind up clerking in a video store? Everybody has to ask themselves that question at some point if they're going to understand Paul."

Nick Tosches, who began dropping by Evergreen, didn't think Paul had changed since his Mercury days. "He evolved, but he was always the same guy. Only the walls were different. He never got swayed by anything anywhere. Even in that context, in that video store, he was like a throwback to the Eighties when people who worked in the stores had their own ideas and would recommend things. He was a throwback, a beautiful throwback. It was almost like he materialized here from beyond those foothills where there was no TV reception."

John Morthland: "He was the same old Paul in a lot of ways, but he had no sort of attachment to a lot of the things that he had once been attached to when I knew him well. He seemed in good spirits. He seemed a little distracted or distant. Not really distant from me, but from the world. It seemed like his whole life was there in that store sort of. He told me if I wrote to him to write him at the store because he was subletting some place on the East Side and he couldn't get mail there."

Charles M. Young says, "I'd stop by and we'd talk about the old days a little bit. He still had his sense of humor, he was surrounded by the stuff that he loved, and he didn't have to be edited. He loved that."

Aaron: "It didn't happen very often that people came in that he knew from his past, but when they did he would always say, 'Well, that was nice.'"

Michael Azerrad only lived two blocks away from Evergreen. "I walked in, and here was this guy with straggly hair and missing some teeth. He didn't appear to be in good shape, and I just felt like maybe this was not where he wanted to be. But the fact is, the more I got to know him, he was exactly where he wanted to be." He recalls one visit in particular: "I was just standing looking at the rack for about half an hour, just sort of trying to find something to look at. All of a sudden, Paul just materialized next to me like, you know, the Cheshire Cat. He sidled up to me and he said, 'You might as well give up. You've seen all the good ones.'"

"He hid there in that old store," David Gahr said. "It was perfect for him."

Reggie Lewis says that, as with everything else, Paul had a set routine after work. "As soon as he would leave Evergreen, he would go right to Tower Records and look through the bins for some bluegrass, try to make some Ralph Stanley finds, whatever he could, and from there he would go to BBQ's." Uptown at Dallas BBQ, Paul had ordered the same thing and come in at the same time for so long, his meal would be waiting for him when he'd arrive.

Jeff Wong: "I remember when Evergreen was still on Houston Street, before they moved to Carmine, there was this woman who used to come into the store. I forget her name now. She was a redhead and he had developed this crush on her. I guess he was working up the nerve to ask her out and I think he eventually did, but she kind of just politely turned him down. But he was just talking on and on about her for quite a while."

"I think there was more than one," Steve Feltes says.

Paul stayed in treatment up until the psychologist, who'd put him on Valium, retired in 1990. "He just saw me free the whole time. He really saved me."

So did the encouragement of the few friends he'd allowed to remain in his life, especially Jay Cocks. Paul said, "Jay was a big help, championing, 'Don't give it up.'" But it was a Christmas gift from Cocks—a CD player—that made the biggest difference. Before that, all Paul had was a tape deck, a few cassettes, and a broken turntable. "I still knew enough people at the record companies where I could get some free stuff." For the first time in years, the music of Bob Dylan, Leonard Cohen, Bruce Springsteen, and Warren Zevon was back in his life. He replaced some of his favorite old records with CDs, but mostly he began amassing, for the rest of his life, an extensive collection of bluegrass.

"I think having Jay give me the CD player and beginning to listen to music again had a wonderful effect. I remember being aware month to month that I could make sentences better when I talked to people and I could make decisions better. I could go buy the paper without deliberating all afternoon whether I would or wouldn't go downstairs to buy it."

He even added a Procol Harum greatest hits CD to his library so that he could have 1967's "A Whiter Shade of Pale" nearby. For him and Bobbi London, it had been their song.

"God knows, there was a certain similarity, wasn't there, between Chet and Paul?" Stephen Holden says. "Chet was an enigmatic man of mystery and either a tortured soul or a narcissist so total that he was not engaged with the world except to get his drugs. But there was something so Paul-like about Chet Baker's singing and playing. So hermetically sealed."

"He was never snobbish or high-handed or pretentious about his tastes," Jonathan Lethem says, "but he was always absolute about it. For him, if the magic wasn't there, end of conversation. But when he detected the true spirit, his persistence and patience in locating every possible manifestation was incredible. The time he spent, for instance, figuring out that there were these disparate, occasional, great Chet Baker tracks scattered through the live recordings of the Seventies and the early Eighties that no one else would've ever troubled to find. It's easy to love the two or three great vocal records from the Fifties—"Let's Get Lost" and so on—but he had become a scholar. Just out of the ferocity of his need to find every great moment, he was compiling an extraordinary list of Chet Baker concerts and recordings. He always knew where there was this one good vocal take of something that he'd done in concert a dozen times but only nailed it once." Paul had boxfuls of cassettes of Baker recordings to start him on his way—including seven and a half hours of nothing but Baker vocals that he carried around with him in his bag.

"He was thinking a lot about a Chet Baker biography," Lethem says. "He got as far as having a proposal and pitching it, and in fact had an offer from a publisher, but he felt he wasn't offered enough to do the research that would've been necessary. There was so much travel in Europe that it would have involved and the advance he was offered didn't begin to cover the process he was projecting. Who knows, if there'd been another $20,000 in that advance, how his life might've been different."

Paul's 1990 article, "Chet Baker Gets Lost in Time," hinted at the book that might've been:

> Later, I saw him a lot in both Minneapolis and New York, and he'd nod at me occasionally at Stryker's on West Eighty-Sixth Street when he played there regularly in the mid-

Seventies. He'd just walk in the front door a little later than the last minute and go straight to the stage, where the other musicians would be already. Considering his problems, he looked amazingly good, his long hair slicked back over his collar like a brown crow's-wing, the eyes sharp but shy, the ears sticking out slightly, giving only the faintest impression of the sexy hick as well as the bop hipster but really looking more like Woody Gatsby from East Egg, Oklahoma. The audience response was as if the hero of Hitchcock's *Vertigo* or Leonard Cohen's "The Stranger Song" had arrived and said: "I'm unarmed, except for my sensibility, and even that seems like a blank sometimes."

Onstage, Chet always sat in a chair. Straight and erect, somewhat stiff, the trumpet's golden bell resting squarely on his right knee, he looked unnaturally quiet and alone in repose, as though he spent sixteen hours a day that way, sandpapering the cigarette smoke and darning that dream: a vulnerable, aging Mafioso, stylishly seedy, the face older and rounder than it first appeared, the body tightly composed in the severe right angles of a Walker Evans photograph. His voice was Southwestern soft and polite, but there was a surprising directness in his speech.[45]

"I think Chet Baker was one of his last great musical obsessions," Jay Cocks says. "The thing with June Christy and all the other female jazz singers, which we kind of shared, we got into that because punk and grunge and all that stuff had kind of taken over, and we were getting older and we didn't tune into that. We'd been through that before, we'd seen all that, it seemed old to us. It wasn't speaking to us and we were looking for some other fresh feel. We found it with jazz vocals, and we shared a lot of that."

"I'm beginning to love these songs with such passion," Paul told Leonard Cohen. "They get to me. They seem real. There's still a lot of rock I like, but I'm just turning away from a lot of it. In the space of going through all the bad times, I've had to sell a lot of my record collection, a lot of the books and everything. Thinking about rebuying it, there's not a lot I'd like to replace. I liked it at the time—I wouldn't listen to it today, I really wouldn't."

Cocks: "Rock is so intense, it's so confrontational—it just grabs you. It doesn't leave room to be reflective, and there comes a time in your life when you don't need stuff like that in your face all the time. You start listening to

---

45 "Chet Baker Gets Lost in Time" by Paul Nelson, *Musician*, October 1990.†

Mr. Sinatra, June Christy, Billie Holiday (the greatest of all). You listen to the resonance of these old songs and these old lyrics and you go, 'Wow, that's really something,' and you begin to appreciate the continuance. When you hear the later stuff, you begin to understand where the earlier stuff comes from, and you begin to see connections between Johnny Rotten, Warren Zevon, and Johnny Mercer that you never thought of before. It's all part of the fabric."

"I was watching somebody on TV a couple of years ago," Paul told Cohen. "Some rock & roller came out in the most ludicrous get-up I have ever seen on anybody. I just thought, God, something is wrong. Anybody wearing *that*—how can I take it seriously? And what he was saying was just as ludicrous as his outfit. I just thought, Gee, I've become my parents."

"Well," Cohen said, "that's what happens with the Arthur Rimbaud. We're not really interested in what a twenty-year-old says about his love affair. I'm interested in hearing what an eighty-three- or eighty-four-year-old says about his love affair."

Several of Paul's best friends moved to the West Coast to follow better opportunities. When Kit Rachlis became editor-in-chief at *LA Weekly*, he told Tom Carson, who was also on staff at that time, that he was considering offering the paper's music editorship to Paul. "In practical terms," Carson says, "Kit knew it would have been a terrible idea. L.A. wasn't Paul's scene. I don't know the details, but Paul had stopped being able to produce for a while by then. But Kit cherished Paul so much, he couldn't help being tempted. I think the reason he called me in was, first up, he *wanted* to hear someone say, 'No, it's a terrible idea.' But he also wanted someone who valued Paul the same way he did to understand what he was going through."

Rachlis came up with an alternative. He proposed to Paul that he come to Los Angeles and spend one week interviewing Lucinda Williams, the next week interviewing Leonard Cohen, and then write profiles of each for *LA Weekly*. "We didn't pay to fly people out from New York, but I figured I could figure out how to cheat this." Paul spent the first week with Rachlis and Ariel Swartley, then moved into a motel. "Fred Schruers, a huge fan of Paul's, said, 'Look, I know you guys can't afford this, but I really want Paul to write. Let me pay for the motel.'" Rachlis repaid Schruers by employing a "dirty little secret of editors": "I assigned Fred a piece, then killed it three weeks later and gave him a kill fee that covered Fred's motel expenses for Paul."

Paul liked Los Angeles. There was something about it that always reminded him of the Midwest. While he was there, from February to March of 1991, an old friend and associate from his Mercury days spotted him at a bus stop and took him to Musso & Frank for something to eat. "I don't think he was in good money shape," Denny Rosencrantz says. Before he bid Paul farewell, he handed him some cash.

Paul's interview with singer-songwriter Lucinda Williams started off well with the discovery of some mutual acquaintances (she'd met Tony Glover and Dave Ray and, many years before, recorded a demo at CBS for Paul's old boss at Mercury, Ron Oberman) and shared musical passions (a huge Chet Baker fan, the more she heard about Paul's compilation of Baker vocal performances, the more she wanted a copy). She also admired the article he'd written about Suzanne Vega. But things soured when, already tired and cranky and in the midst of packing to move back to Austin, Texas, Williams caught on that this wasn't going to be the usual hour or two chat about the new record but rather three days of intensive questioning. "How much more could you possibly—" she began. *"God!"*

"I really want to do a good, long, detailed, Suzanne Vega-type story," Paul said. "You'll be less tired next time. I could play you some Chet Baker stuff."

"I've got to get a copy of that tape."

"Yeah, well, you have to talk. I don't like to do it half-assed. I take it real seriously. It's not just something to hack out. My name's on it, I want it to be good."

Reaching a temporary truce, Williams invited Paul to dinner and took him on a drive around Burbank—past several different restaurants. "She went right by this first hamburger place—after asking what I like to eat. She said, 'I know you want to eat there, but we won't. I have to draw the line somewhere.' We looked for this place where we could get both a burger *and* what she wanted, but we couldn't find it, so we went to this Mexican thing. She got a kick out of my usual appetite, my Minnesota meat and potatoes style. I wound up ordering fried chicken with French fries and skipping all the Mexican parts."

Paul summed Williams up this way: "She just has this bullshit detector, a sort of correctional way about her—maybe it could be annoying at times— but it's rather sort of sweet."

They were supposed to get together again the next morning at 11:30, but, after numerous phone calls back and forth, the meeting was pushed back to ten o'clock that night. Paul asked Williams if she could pick him up.

"So I get a call from her manager, who's in New Jersey—she's twenty minutes away—telling me that she doesn't understand why she has to come

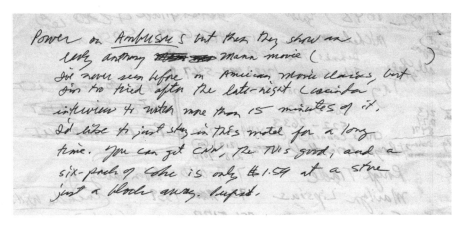

Los Angeles motel note, February 1991.

get me—which *is* a drag and everything, but why can't *she* just say that instead of having her manager call me from New Jersey?"

Whatever sweetness Paul detected had dissipated as he attempted to interview her at home while she was packing. "She's in a *really* ticked off mood and just starts wailing about: 'I don't even know if I want to do this interview! I hate the *Weekly*! I hate that paper! I don't know why I should care about this article!' Just whiny and awful like a two-year-old. Just really nasty. Not so much at me—at the *Weekly*—but it's not what you want to walk into, which was even much worse than she was over the telephone. I really felt like just walking out the door and saying, 'Screw it.'

"I think half of her felt guilty that she didn't come and get me. A big Labrador puppy kept crawling over me and biting my hand and jumping up in my face. Without any real hope at all, I read off the first question and she sort of gets this sweet smile and amazingly enough once we started to talk it was a good interview. It was better than the first day's. I just ignored hints that she was getting tired and kept rolling until it became apparent she wasn't going to go any further. I called a cab again. She offered to take me back, but it wasn't a serious offer. If I would've said yes, God knows what she would've done tomorrow."

Williams was an hour and a half late for their last meeting, backstage at the Palomino Club, but she was in good spirits—even when she'd hint, "Are we almost done? Come on, Paul." Things took an even more surprising turn for the better when he asked about her musical influences and she cited a 1964 Elektra LP, *The Blues Project*, which included cuts by John Koerner, Dave Ray, and, under the moniker "Bob Landy," Bob Dylan.

"Do you know who wrote the notes for *The Blues Project*?" Paul asked leadingly.

"You wrote the notes for that? God, I can't believe it, and here we are talking. I ate that album up."

When she cited Leonard Cohen as another key figure, Paul said, "I talked to Cohen briefly today and I said I was interviewing you. He said to say hello."

"Really?" her voice cracked. "He knew who I was? *Really?*"

As night slid into the next morning, Williams opened up. As several of her friends came backstage to bid her good night, she proudly introduced them to Paul and mentioned his *Sing Out!* and *Little Sandy Review* credits.

Later, back in his room, Paul pushed the record button and lit up a cigarette: "On that note, we were done. That was a really fabulous night. Just great. This is the Lucinda I wanted to see and hadn't seen until this point. Instead of short answers there'd be long answers. It was all terrific, introspective stuff, which I didn't expect. It's just a great relief for it to be over. It's going to be a pretty terrific story, I think."

"I've always sort of felt a kinship to your music," Paul told Leonard Cohen at the outset of their first meeting. Indeed, the two men's similarities extended beyond their penchant for doomsday-dark romanticism: unlike many of Paul's musical idols, they were roughly the same age (Paul was a year and four months younger); Paul was born sixty miles shy of the U.S.-Canadian border in a climate as wintrily unforgiving as Cohen's Westmount, Quebec; both had cared for their cancer-stricken mothers; and, unbeknownst to either at the time, for half of 1965 they'd both resided at the same address, 222 West Twenty-Third Street in Manhattan, for $23.75 a week. When Paul wasn't living with Doris and Mark on Queens Boulevard in Woodside, Queens, he stayed in Room 928 at the Chelsea Hotel. "My marriage was going," he said. "I took a room at the Chelsea in a way to just get out of the house."

After meeting first at The Chariot, a coffee shop on La Brea and Wilshire, they adjourned to Cohen's nearby home (not far from Lew Archer's fictional pre-divorce two-bedroom stucco cottage in West Hollywood). Compelled to further introduce himself, Paul said, "I guess I was an early champion. I wrote a lot of early reviews."

"I know you did," Cohen said. "There weren't very many people—outside yourself, incidentally—who were giving me very favorable attention."

Over three days, with Paul running more than ten and a half hours of tape, the two men bummed countless cigarettes off one another while discussing every aspect of Cohen's life and career. Throughout, Cohen was the most gracious host, from ferrying Paul to and from his hotel to occasionally reciting a poem or the lyrics to a new song. He asked Paul to suggest a possible title for his then unrecorded "Anthem." When Paul expressed an interest in Buddhism and the calm and order it had brought to Cohen's life (while remaining an observant Jew), Cohen described it in depth and got down on the floor to demonstrate the lotus position (just as, many years before, Clint Eastwood had hit the deck to show Paul a favorite and effective exercise routine). "You only begin this kind of practice because of suffering," Cohen cautioned. "It's too rigorous for people who are just checking it out."

Leonard Cohen interview cassettes.

Cohen also understood what it's like to wrestle with the word. When talk turned to writing, Paul said, "I can't compare my work even remotely with yours."

"Every man's work is his work," Cohen said.

"It's the thing that I like doing the most and I don't really have a life other than that. I only feel good when I am doing it, basically. And whether anybody reads it—it probably won't ever be collected anywhere, it'll just lay around in old magazines—it still matters to me."

Paul also felt comfortable enough to go into great detail about his breakdown after the death of his mother. Cohen, returning the trust, talked about his own depression and told Paul several things about himself that he asked be kept off the record—ultimately an unnecessary request.

```
Songs of Love and Hate
Leonard Cohen
Columbia C 30103


      Leonard Cohen, who are you?  Are you
(C 30103)?  Is that enough?  Sinner or saint,
lion or Christian, is there really any dif-
ference?  Like Meursault and his Arab, has it
crossed your mind "that one might fire, or
not fire—and it would come to absolutely the
same thing."?  The trees may be burning in
your promised land, but there's still the mu-
sic on Clinton Street all through the eve-
ning, and the crayon in the hand of last
year's man
```

life and
withing is
1st love

Bright
crayon, 1
/1873

*Dylan seemed to rage to chyan, or to be
a clown, in finally to ignore, you seem
to count it like a sky long to treat
it with tender love, almost to wistfully
miss it.*

*Needlest say, not people havent even come
to grips with not coming to grips with
Leonard Cohen*

Early draft of a Leonard Cohen review, 1971.

At the end of the day one, back in his hotel room, Paul began his recorded notes with "Oh, what a great guy he is. Wow. Looks like Dustin Hoffman sort of when he smiles. A really wonderful, open smile. Battered good looks.

"Afterwards, we drive back and stop at the Burger King on Highland. He buys me a cheeseburger, fries, and a Coke, and sort of starts interviewing *me*. We talked about Styron's book on mental breakdown. He seemed very sympathetic.

"Much to my surprise, talking about writing, I said I'm the only writer I know without a computer or even a typewriter that works, and he offered to help me get one and get a job out here. One thing he said that was terrific, talking about the rents and how much he loves it out here, he said, 'All I need is a table and a room, a room and a table. I live the same where I am anywhere.'

"It just went spectacularly well, and I kept telling myself, Is this the breakthrough interview I really wanted?"

A week or so later, after Paul had returned to New York, Leonard Cohen was speaking with a critic who happened to be a friend of Paul's. Cohen wondered aloud if Paul would ever write the article.

Kit Rachlis gave Paul a month or two before calling to see how the articles were coming. He left several messages, but heard nothing back. Late one night, the phone rang. "It was Jay Cocks saying, 'Kit, I'm calling for Paul. He is mortified, but he's not going to be able to write those pieces and he wanted me to let you know.' I said, 'Jay, it's okay. Tell Paul he can call me. It's not going to affect our friendship.'

"And I never heard from Paul again."

"The picture that comes to mind when I think of Paul's last visit to us in L.A. is brown and sad," Ariel Swartley says, "colored by the smoke of his endless Shermans and tinged with his obvious despairing lethargy. There's nothing more I can add. Just sorrow."

Paul hadn't owned a functioning typewriter in years. Steve Feltes says, "A friend of Paul's, I think in California, was shipping Paul a Kaypro," one of the first personal computers on the market. "Paul was so excited about that and every day was coming in: 'Did UPS make a delivery?' Finally it arrives. I told Paul that I'd had a Kaypro and knew my way around it, and I'd show him how, too. I'm sure he opened it and looked inside, but he just put it away on his shelf and I never heard him talk about it anymore."

"I gave him a couple of computers," Jay Cocks says. "Anything to get him writing." One of them was still sitting on the shelf in Paul's apartment when he died.

Paul's writing enjoyed a three-year resurgence beginning in 1990 when *Musician* editor Bill Flanagan, encouraged by Charles M. Young and Jay Cocks, invited Paul to start contributing to the magazine. His work hadn't seen print since 1983 when, in the same issue of *Rolling Stone*, he penned Ross Macdonald's obituary and panned Rod Stewart's *Body Wishes*. Paul himself had planted the seed for his return one night in 1988 when he spotted Suzanne Vega backstage at Carnegie Hall after a Leonard Cohen concert. He only knew her from her hit song "Luka," but he thought she looked interesting and decided then and there that, if he ever wrote again, he'd like to write about her. Two years later, when Flanagan suggested that he write about her new release, *Days of Open Hand*, the timing couldn't have been better. Paul was almost broke.

As he wrote the piece, he kept eyeing the spot on the bookshelf where he kept his dwindling cash. "As I was finishing the story it was down to forty dollars and that was it."

Suzanne Vega: "My publicist Susan Blond had told me that it was a very special interview because he didn't do interviews much anymore and that he was interested in doing this one. He had certain conditions that he wanted met—it wasn't just a simple, in-and-out, half-an-hour slot, the way it was usually done. I remember that we had two days planned for it, and he wanted a certain amount of Coca-Cola and a certain amount of freedom that we didn't give to the other journalists." There was only one problem.

"He didn't like Suzanne Vega's music," Jay Cocks says. "He was not that thrilled with her stuff and got less thrilled the more he got into it." To Paul's frustration and Vega's amusement, his interpretations of her songs were almost invariably wrong.

Vega says, "I liked him and so therefore I ended up revealing maybe more to him than I would to somebody else." Paul liked her, too, and told her that this was his "comeback story." Playing with her cat, he told her that "I had two of them, I had them for twelve years and they both died within three weeks. Oh, was that terrible. Cats are so wonderful." And though he didn't disclose it, they had something else in common beyond cats that became the thrust of his article: Vega had discovered at the age of nine that the man she thought was her father really was not, and it wasn't until she was well into adulthood—like Mark Nelson—that she got to know her biological father.

After "Suzanne Vega: On the Couch" was published, she sent Paul a Chet Baker import she'd picked up for him in Japan and a note saying how much she'd enjoyed what he'd written. It had made her cry. "It was really nice to hear that," Paul said, "particularly since I hadn't written a piece for seven years."

Writing two other pieces that year for *Musician* (the Chet Baker one and a review of Bob Dylan's *Under the Red Sky*—the last thing he'd write about Dylan), Paul ventured to Virginia to interview Bruce Hornsby. The resultant article found him once again tapping touchstones both personal and pop culturish.

> Just a couple of blocks away from the surreal, Walt Disney-meets-David Lynch Colonial Williamsburg section of the otherwise appealing Williamsburg, Virginia, the reporter, musing mawkishly about the pull that small towns have always had for him, decides to order an archetypal American meal—cheeseburger, fries, Coke, and apple pie—as a salute to the fact that both he and the artist he's waiting to meet were rurally born, reared, and marked. It is not an empty gesture. A foolish one maybe, but these places get to you. Judging by his music, Bruce Hornsby would understand both the sentiment and the cynicism.
>
> Set smack in the heart of the Tidewater/Southside region, Williamsburg—minus the silver dagger of the almighty dollar that its aberrant colonial area holds at every tourist's throat—seems as fine and resonant as a sleepy summer day. Stately and reasonably sanitary rivers flow through abundant woodlands into nearby Chesapeake Bay, which watermen have worked for centuries. If Frank Capra had directed *Twin Peaks* in the 1940s or '50s, I wonder, would he have let Laura Palmer die?
>
> When the six-foot-four, thirty-five-year-old Hornsby—wearing jeans and a T-shirt and looking not much different from the sports-crazed high school basketballer that he was—bounds into the restaurant and interrupts this maudlin movie reverie, two not-altogether disparate images jump into my head: Warren Zevon's "excitable boy" zinging through the Southland and (this is the one that really sticks) Jimmy Stewart's likability, prankishness, and quiet but untrimmed intensity as George Bailey in Capra's *It's a Wonderful Life*, a movie about a man's love-hate feelings toward Bedford Falls, a small town that, no matter how desperately he tries, he never manages to leave.[46]

Hornsby: "My main memory of Paul is that he had a very funny and contrarian negative reaction to the Colonial Williamsburg area of my town. He stayed at the Williamsburg Lodge, if I remember, so he was right in the

---

46 "The Virginian: Bruce Hornsby Finds His Way Home" by Paul Nelson, *Musician*, January 1991.†

heart of the Colonial restored area and it gave him the creeps." Hornsby good-naturedly suffered Paul's occasional cantankerousness. "I just feel like we had a connection right away personally and it was a real easy rapport between us. I consider myself to be fortunate—and anybody else like me should feel the same way—to have known him and crossed paths with him and had him write about me."

On the second day of the interview a photographer arrived. Snapping shots of Hornsby and commenting on his well-stocked library, he brought up Herman Melville. Paul said: "He took a job as a clerk because he just wanted a mindless job that he could exist on and then he wouldn't have to use his mind. He would write and he wouldn't have to expend any energy. 'Bartleby the Scrivener' is sort of about that."

"I did have some doubts about writing again," Paul admitted, "because I thought, I don't want to go back and have to catch up with six years of music when I'm going to hate ninety-nine percent of it. I thought, Well, don't do that. Just go after the one percent you like. So I don't even pretend to be a rock & roll scholar or anything." He said it thrilled him not to care anymore who was currently enjoying their allotted fifteen minutes of fame.

Paul jumped at the opportunity to write about Willie Nile and his 1991 album *Places I Have Never Been* because, back in the early Seventies, Nile had sent him a demo at Mercury. Paul had liked what he heard and encouraged Nile to keep writing and singing. Over the next few decades, the two men's paths occasionally crossed in Greenwich Village.

The last time was on Bleecker Street. "He had on his hat and his glasses and some hair on his face," Nile says. "He had the walk about him of a seer and a seeker. He said he was in good spirits, working away, writing. I know what it is to be adrift in a sea of words and pages, and you could tell he was. Sometimes you're lost, sometimes you're found. But it was an honorable search.

"Listen, life can be tough. You can get lost in the woods sometimes. There's no judgment to be passed on that. You want the best for someone like Paul. You want them to be happy and be financially set and secure and to be able to write. Sometimes the winds that blow and the storms that brew internally and externally in the world can knock you aside. He was a gentle guy."

Danny Goldberg used to see Paul around the Village, too. "He just seemed fragile and vulnerable and sensitive, like a lamb in the jungle. Certain creative people you feel that about, and he was one of them."

"I like *Can You Fly* so much that I'm almost afraid to write about it," Paul wrote in 1992 about Freedy Johnston's second album, calling it "the best record I've heard in years.… To put it bluntly, Freedy Johnston is the one newcomer in ages who's made me feel good about the future of rock & roll."[47]

"Because of his enthusiasm," Bill Flanagan says, "he had just written four times as much as he was supposed to write. But it was really good, so we decided to blow it up and make it a feature, although no one had heard of Freedy Johnston." Paul's article made such a good case for the singer-songwriter that an executive at Elektra Records told Flanagan that the article played a part in their subsequent signing of Johnston to the label.

At the age of fifty-six, Paul had published his last long-form piece about rock & roll.

Leonard Cohen had offered Paul some advice: "When you're dealing with disorder in your own mind, it's agreeable to have at least your surroundings well-ordered." Paul agreed, but he could barely keep a place of his own—and the city he'd once loved had turned "truly terrifying" and "horrible." He was in Manhattan late one wintry night when, on his way home to Long Island City, Queens, he descended into the subway. "I got halfway down the steps and just saw bodies. I was so stunned. I would guess 250 to 300 people sleeping in this one subway station. You could barely get to the tollbooth—you had to step over and around them—and you could barely get down the steps to the train. I felt like this must be what Calcutta was like—and this was just one stop.

"You don't stay sane on the street," Paul said, "you don't. You walk around that city and there are people lying on the sidewalk. You cannot avoid it unless you don't leave your apartment. You're going to be touched by it. It's so pervasive. It's just taken for granted that there are going to be six people lying on the sidewalk when you walk out that night or forty people are going to ask you for money. You just become immune to it and you become unhuman."

When Michael Seidenberg's brother's apartment became available for around $500 a month, Paul moved in. "Once Paul went to my brother's apartment, people say he disappeared. But he was just living under another name, in a way. He wasn't hiding."

---

47 "Freedy Johnston Learns to Fly" by Paul Nelson, *Musician*, August 1992.†

Jay Cocks visited the apartment with Verna Bloom. "That's the kind of place that guys who took the bus into town because they were being chased went. All it needed was a blinking red neon sign, that joint. That was hard. Scary. Tough-going."

Another illegal sublet, Paul didn't care that his name wouldn't be in the phonebook or that the one on the mailbox would be someone else's (in fact, he preferred it that way). Nor did he know that this was where he would live out the rest of his life.

I really like this book. You can learn from it, because both Nelson and Fuller know a lot about movies and write well about them, and you can have a lot of fun with it, because these guys put such a neat and intelligent spin on their thousands of intriguing facts. While reading *You Must Remember This!*, I was reminded of so many good movies that I wanted to see again. You might say it made my day. Now what movie is *that* from?

—CLINT EASTWOOD, actor-director[48]

Paul's videotape collection and library of cinema books had come in handy in the early Eighties when his friend William MacAdams (who also wrote under the name Steven Fuller) suggested that they write a movie quiz book together. Bearing various titles, from *Movie Catechisms* to *Who Was That Masked Man?* to *Everything But Trivial Movie Quiz Book*, in 1984 Pinnacle Books bought it with the proviso that they change the title to *You Must Remember This!* Pinnacle subsequently went out of business before the book could be published.

"We thought the book was dead, which it was for some years," MacAdams says, "then a friend of mine wanted to try her hand at agenting and very quickly sold it. We had to do an update. The work itself not taking long—motivating Paul, though, was excruciating." In 1993, MacAdams, now living in Indiana, updated his material while Paul worked on his parts of the book from New York. "It was a little bit top-heavy on Scorsese and Eastwood questions," MacAdams says.

When Pinnacle went out of business, they'd failed to return the twenty or thirty photographs used in the book's photo quiz. MacAdams asked Paul several times to visit a photo archive in Chelsea and pick up the inexpensive

---

48 From Paul Nelson and Steven Fuller's book proposal for *You Must Remember This!*

replacements, but Paul kept putting it off. MacAdams finally made a trip to New York to collect the photos himself, spending the nights at Paul's apartment on a pallet on the living room floor. When MacAdams went to the photo archive, Paul tagged along.

A few nights later, MacAdams returned very late to the apartment to find that Paul had placed all of his updated material on the pallet and gone to bed. "Whether he had just done them all that day, I have no idea," MacAdams says. Paul was running late for work when he emerged from his room the next day. "He just came out and said, 'You've got to leave.' I said, 'Well, okay, tomorrow.' He said, 'No, you've got to be out today.' We'd never had an argument in all the years we knew each other, and I'm mystified to this day. And that was the last time I saw him."

In 1995, Citadel Press published *701 Toughest Movie Trivia Questions of All Time*. It was another publisher-imposed title.

One Thursday Paul was walking along East Seventy-Eighth Street near Second Avenue, not far from home, when a cappella singing wafting through an open apartment window caught his attention. One floor up, David Forman was rehearsing with his doo-wop group, Little Isidore & the Inquisitors.

"I look out the window and there's Paul Nelson standing underneath my window." Forman called for Paul to stay put and ran downstairs and outside to see how he was faring. They hadn't seen each other in at least a decade. Forman immediately gathered from Paul's shrug and his overall appearance that things weren't well. "All the guys in my group were standing around and, of course, I didn't want to get into anything. I saw what his dental scene was. It was brutal. He wanted to say everything was fine, but he couldn't because it wasn't. Oh, it was so fuckin' sad." He asked Paul if he would write some publicity for Little Isidore, but neither of them ever followed up on the offer. "I always felt bad about it, too. I always felt, Fuck, this guy helped me so much. I could've helped him. It's a nagging feeling and it doesn't go away easily: that feeling that maybe 150 bucks might've helped on a Thursday."

Fred Schruers: "I was walking with a friend through the Village after I hadn't seen Paul in a couple of years, and here came Paul. You could see he hadn't been going to the dentist a lot. He was wearing that hat. I stopped him and he said, 'Thanks for stopping me. People usually don't.'"

Paul walked from his apartment late every afternoon to Lexington Avenue and caught the 6 train on the first leg of his journey to the West Village, where Steve Feltes had relocated Evergreen Video on Carmine Street. Several times a week, a familiar face boarded at the Grand Central stop: Bobbi London, on her way home from her job at the Alzheimer's Association. As her day ended, Paul's began. "He used to sit in the same seat all the time at the end of the car," she says. "I'd look over, there he is. And he'd look over, and there I am. So I'd go over and we'd sit and talk until we got to Bleecker Street."

"Sounds like Lubitsch to me," Jay Cocks says.

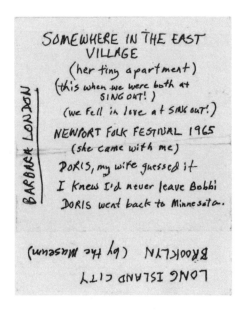

"I lost track of him for a bit," Cocks says about the time when Paul had his gallbladder removed, "and then I heard he'd been in the public assistance ward at Bellevue Hospital. He talked about that and said it was really an incredible scene—there were rats running around on the bed. He was living, I would guess, on or below the poverty line."

Writing regularly for *People* magazine in 1997, Billy Altman was flipping through the latest issue when a familiar name caught his eye. "Alongside me on the page was a little review of Townes Van Zandt by Paul. I'm probably as proud of being able to sit on that page next to him as anything else I've done in thirty years or so of writing."

It had been four years since Paul's last appearance in *Musician*, and once again Bill Flanagan played a part in getting him back into print. Flanagan put Paul in touch with George Kalogerakis, an editor at *People* for about a year. "In the second six months or so, one of the things I was in charge of was the record-review section. I was trying to open it up a bit to not the obvious releases. For a while I got away with that."

Kalogerakis invited Paul up to his office—"He sat on this little sofa, looking refreshingly out of place"—and sent him home with a stack of recently released CDs. Paul decided that he'd like to write about the Burns Sisters' *In This World*, *Keepers* by Guy Clark, John Prine's *Live on Tour*, and *The Highway Kind* by Townes Van Zandt.

"It felt great to infiltrate that magazine with those reviews by that writer on those musicians," Kalogerakis says. And while only the Clark and Van Zandt pieces made it to print (becoming, respectively, Paul's last published works), he says, "Had it been up to me, all four would've run."

Some of Paul's old friends were dismayed to discover him working at Evergreen. "I never felt with Paul like he cared about anybody else's opinion particularly," Bill Flanagan says. "He wanted to have a spot for his books and his records and a chance to see his movies. That's why I always felt working in the video store was fine. Some people thought it was a terrible thing. Well, you know, it probably pays better than writing record reviews. It pays as well. It's more steady and it's more stable. If it was kind of like a more comfortable working retirement for him—to sit around watching French films and Clint Eastwood movies and talking with the cats at the video store and going out and listening to Chet Baker records—I don't see why that's any different from somebody who spends their life working as a brain surgeon and then takes the time and plays golf."

Anthony DeCurtis was the *Rolling Stone* record-review editor in 1990 when he assigned a Waterboys album to Paul to review. It was the only piece Paul wrote for him and the last one he wrote for the magazine. "If somebody wants to work in a video store or take a retail job of some kind, there's nothing wrong with that—except if you happen to be one of the best writers in the country. Then that's a problem. People make a lot of decisions that don't involve them losing their teeth. I understand why people kind of want to put the best face on this, but I think that there was a problem there. I think that was somebody committing a long, slow suicide."

Flanagan says, "I don't think that the fact that somebody has a talent means that he has an obligation to keep forever doing that trick for people. I think that kind of makes creative people into court jesters in a way."

"I wish I knew why," Bud Scoppa says, "if there was a fundamental self-doubt or self-torture that eventually got hold of him. He was always wired sort of tight. In the Seventies, he was embracing a lot of popular art and that seemed to keep him going. When he let go of that, it became apparent that the fire had gone out of him or something."

DeCurtis says, "I would say that the same reason he jettisoned the music is the same reason that he stopped writing. You know, those records never changed. The same qualities that he discovered in them are still there to be further mined."

Michael Seidenberg: "His life didn't end when he stopped writing music criticism. I don't think he saw it as some kind of a calling, that he had some obligation to do anything in any way other than to be truthful. I think people mistake, because he had this connection to the truth, that he had this connection to rock criticism. No, he was just true in everything, and that's what he did for a while."

"It's terrifying to people how a life can unravel," Phillip Blumberg says. "I think as he got older, something that he could sort of jury-rig—at least in the writing part of his career—it came undone. I think he was too ashamed to let anybody help him, and he was deeply ashamed by his own needfulness and by his helplessness."

It wasn't just that Paul had lost interest in rock & roll and writing about it, he also left behind his dream of writing a series of detective novels and assorted other books that dated back to the Sixties.

> A book with three main characters—one, a retired police inspector and *National Enquirer*-type who still yearns for the smack of action; two, a perverse killer who chooses never to speak and works eight hours a day as a photographer's developer and printmaker, seeing all day long nothing but images of babies and weddings; and three, a movie-mad, ineffectual young man who has lost his wife and children (and reality as well) by falling in love with the screen image of a movie starlet he has never met....

> An absurd novel of the American South. Again concerned with mystiques and mythologies, this time not of movies,

murder, and violence, but of baseball, heroism, the Negro question, et al....

A Hollywood novel....

I would like to try a short and experimental novel in which the action and all the characters revolve like sick wheels around the New York subway system, particularly the vast, loony underground of Times Square, a sort of undersea world of its own late at night. Nothing in this novel would ever get out of all those tunnels and trains.

A book similar to Agee's and Evans's *Let Us Now Praise Famous Men*, this time on the small towns of America, particularly the Midwest, where I grew up. I've done some work on this, taken some photographs, and thought about it a great deal.... I worship at the altar of the FSA photographers, and am an excellent photographer myself.[49]

The books of Paul Nelson.

In 1976, Paul told Kenneth Millar another idea he had for a book: "At one point in his life Pat Garrett was a private detective. It was a few years after he killed Billy the Kid. He retired for a short time as a sheriff and became a private detective, and he worked on a rather legendary New Mexico murder case which several detectives had worked upon but never solved. And he didn't

---

49 "Notes on Projected Novels" by Paul Nelson, circa 1966.‡

solve it either, and he went back to being a sheriff. It seems to me that's a good book: Pat Garrett as a private detective. I don't know what the details of the case are, but I'm going to find out."[50]

He either lost interest in these projects or, as it sometimes happens with writing, they lost interest in him.

Jay Cocks: "We're talking about a critic in a way that you talk about a writer of fiction or a musician. Whatever that disposition is inside of us that makes us reflect on the work rather than create the work, if Paul had ever been at a crossroads early in his life where he saw 'I Can Do It' or 'I Can Talk About It' and he chose to talk about it instead of do it, I wonder, if he'd gone down the 'I Can Do It' road, what that would have been like for him. And for us."

"I think it's important to separate the incredible quality of the work that Paul did from whatever it was that drove his Bartleby-like withdrawal," Anthony DeCurtis says. "I mean, it seems to me that writers write. I still think there's a lot of kind of writing that somebody like Paul could have done and that I certainly wish he had done. I think he would've been happier if he'd been able to do it."

"But that kind of assumes that being a rock critic is a glorious vocation," Bill Flanagan says. "I'm not sure that Paul saw it that way. Listen, a lot of these jobs that people invented and fell into in the high tide of the counter culture didn't have any 401(k)s planned. This goes for the musicians as well as the people tangential to musicians. In that sense, being a rock critic is kind of like being a drum roadie. It might be something that's really fun and plus you make a little dough and sleep late and get to shows for free when you're twenty-two. But when you're sixty-two, it might seem like a dubious career path."

Jann Wenner: "I also got the feeling that when he left *Rolling Stone* he was kind of at the end of—not his rope—but he was at the end of that road. I mean, where was he going to go with this from here? I think he was exhausted."

"For me," Flanagan says, "my feeling was that Paul wasn't looking at the world that way. He wasn't thinking about, Can I have a big success? In terms of success and influence within his medium, well, he *had it*—to the biggest

---

50 Paul was fascinated with the Billy the Kid/Pat Garrett legend. Numerous times in his journals (1974 to 1976) he wrote about how Billy embodied youth, freedom, and individuality, whereas Pat epitomized the Establishment, responsibility, and bowing under the weight of life. Mark Nelson at one time considered inscribing *He remained Billy* on Paul's headstone.

degree anybody could have it. He was probably the best music writer of his generation. Maybe of several generations. In a way, there was no higher to go on that pole anyway."

Michael Azerrad was editor-in-chief for eMusic, the music download service, when he visited Paul at Evergreen. "I felt an incredible, humbling sense of gratitude. Paul had helped set up a system in which I could make a pretty decent living doing exactly what I do. What I want to do.

"I now worked at a place where I could find people like Paul work, and I offered him some work writing about his last musical love, which was bluegrass. And he declined. He really needed the money—we were paying really well—and he just said no. I asked him why. I was very frustrated and let down. He said he simply couldn't do it justice."

Charles M. Young: "I know why he didn't want to write about bluegrass. It was the same reason I don't want to write about Mozart. I want something that's pure, that's not associated with any traumatic edit or any fucking thing else. I like the Eagles music, but I can't listen to it without thinking of Don Henley being mad at me for writing about his diarrhea. If I wrote an essay about Mozart for the Arts & Leisure section, for example, and they put me through *The New York Times* editing process, I wouldn't be able to listen to it again for the rest of my fucking life without thinking about the editing process at *The New York Times*, which is devastating. You don't have one editor there, you have seven of them. I'm sure Azerrad would have run Paul's article just like he wrote it, but Paul wanted to keep bluegrass pure for himself. He wanted to be able to listen to it without any of the fuckery of rock journalism messing up this music that he loved. It's always dangerous to write about music that you love, because you're going to get fucked with. Your love will be fucked with. And that's what drove Paul out."

Mikal Gilmore: "I spent the year of 1999 in Manhattan and I was coming out of a music show with a friend, a woman, who's a book agent. It was probably about one, one-thirty in the morning and I ran into Paul. I saw him crossing the street in front of me down in the Village. I was really pleased and excited to see him and I asked what he was doing. It was not a long conversation. Paul would sometimes have this way of talking to you where he didn't look at you, he would look to your side or something. I was kind of used to that, but I was more aware of it this time. I did ask him how I could get in touch with him and he said he didn't have a phone. I gave him my phone number where I was. I never heard from him. I also remember telling the woman that I was with that he was this remarkable writer and that he was somebody that she should seek out for a book because he certainly had the talent and the material. But that was it, that was the last time I saw him."

At Evergreen, Paul enjoyed introducing his coworker Reggie Lewis, an aspiring writer who went on to become a public school teacher, to the works of Graham Greene, Nathanael West, Raymond Chandler, and, of course, F. Scott Fitzgerald and Ross Macdonald. "At times I almost felt like I was under his tutelage," Lewis says, "like a little writing workshop. We'd get into it at length discussing voice, tone, shading, contrast, language, and how that translates into film. He was very much into detail and subtlety. That's why it was always funny when it would be broken up by customers asking for the latest commercial films. That would just rankle him, he would get so upset at times he would go off on these little rants. They would ask him about movies, and he was like, 'I don't watch that!'"

Steve Feltes suspects that Paul was annoyed by the sad fact that his impeccable taste in films didn't come as easily to other people as it did to him.

David Aaron: "He pissed off a lot of people. He was not into customer service."

Lewis recalls a regular customer named Ed. "Ed would come in, a sort of heavyset gentleman, and would annoy Paul to no end because all he wanted to do was talk about starlets. The kind of guy who looked really lonely and just wanted to have someone to talk to. But when he disappeared, Paul hadn't realized how fond he was of the guy. You could just tell, it was like married couples, there was an attachment."

There were other customers, too, who appreciated Paul's knowledge of cinema laced with his crusty worldview. Some of them even baked him bread, while others brought him the kind of shirts he liked to wear. Paula Farmer says, "For weeks I would see them sitting in the back, still in the plastic."

She admits, "Certainly at the store he was difficult to work with when he wasn't pulling his weight or when he was complaining all the time. He'd get real close and complain about the customers—with them there. But Paul was such a character and if he liked you, he liked you and you knew it. There was something rewarding about being accepted by Paul, the patriarch of the store."

Late in 1996, Paul took a liking to another one of the Evergreen youngsters, a New York University film student grad named Jason Ruscio. "He became almost like a Yoda figure to me in my late twenties," Ruscio says. "I owe a great deal of my cultural knowledge to him. Why he befriended me is a bit of a mystery." Ruscio came from a long line of "gloomy Finns. I think I knew how to deal with emotionally reclusive personalities. So he trusted me."

Despite the fact that Ruscio's short film *Eclipse*, about a boy who loses his mother during World War II, had premiered at the Telluride Film Festival and recently won a Student Academy Award, Paul was reluctant to see it. "If he didn't like it he thought it might affect our friendship." Paul was swayed, however, when Ruscio mentioned that Norman Mailer had come up after a screening to say how much he loved the film. After attending a screening at NYU, Paul told Ruscio, "That was the best short film I've ever seen. I was so afraid I wasn't going to like it."

Ruscio had grown up in the Eighties listening to Iron Maiden and Judas Priest, and he had several friends whose rock bands (Weezer, No Doubt, Foo Fighters) were finally taking off. "I was introducing Paul to a lot of these new rock stars and, of course, he wasn't very impressed. He'd been there, done that." "My God," Paul said one day, "you've got to stop playing this stupid pop rock. Let me play this Dylan record for you." "It just changed my whole perspective on music."

Ruscio immediately shared his new discovery with his friend Matt Sharp, bassist for Weezer. "I said, 'Listen, this might fuck up your whole lifelong agenda,' but he was just blown away. He inherited that completely and tried to be a little more acoustic with his music. I attribute that to Paul."

The record Paul had played was a live recording of "Visions of Johanna." "It was very somber and just got under my skin in a way that I turned Weezer and these modern rockers on to it and they became Dylan fans."

Ruscio lived around the corner from Evergreen, on Cornelia Street. "We'd see each other almost nightly and talk and come back to my place and maybe watch a movie or listen to music. He'd come over all the time and have pasta with me and my girlfriend Petra Wright, who became my wife and lead actress. We all became very close."

In 1998, Ruscio told Paul he was moving to Los Angeles to pursue his film career. Paul was heartbroken. "You're the only friend I have left," he told Ruscio. "I don't know what I'm going to do."

Paul seemed more depressed than usual when musician Dave Lightbourne dropped into the shop to say hello towards the end of 2001. "He was bummed about 9/11 is what it was all about. It was about walking to and from work every day past the 'missing' posters. It's now eleven o'clock at night and there's not a person on Park Avenue, and there isn't a tree or a spike in the fence that doesn't have somebody's name and picture on it. He said there was no way around it, there was no route you could take to avoid having to put up with this."

Although their bylines had appeared on the same pages many times through the years, Paul never met Ed Ward until 2002. "I was doing a story on my old pal, rock eccentric Andy Zwerling. Andy was quite close with Paul and was amazed that, although we'd corresponded, we'd never met. So he set up a meeting and I picked Paul up after work. We sat in Washington Square Park and talked for the better part of an hour, and the whole conversation was so depressing that I was almost sorry it had happened. He wasn't in very good shape at all. Realizing where he'd ended up after all the things he'd done, it was really disturbing. Seeing someone who had a head start on me reduced to working in a video-rental store in his old age didn't paint a very nice picture for my own future."

Bill Flanagan didn't live far from Evergreen and often saw Paul on Bleecker Street or at the video store, either behind the counter or sitting on the bench out front having a smoke. He decided that a bunch of Paul's friends, including Jeff Rosen and Willie Nile, should take Paul out to dinner. He called Paul and convinced him to join them at a restaurant close to Evergreen. "The thing I remember is," Flanagan says, "we must've been there for three and a half hours and Paul didn't eat because they didn't have hamburgers. The rest of us ate and Paul had a glass of water." Afterwards, Flanagan and Rosen commiserated about what a bust the night had been. "But the next time I ran into Paul, in a week or two, he said, 'Oh, I had a great time. We really need to get together and do that again.'"

Steve Feltes took good care of his senior employee. When Paul's threadbare flat cap started falling apart and Paul couldn't be convinced to replace it on his own—not knowing where he'd go or what he'd ask for once he got there—Feltes went to a hat store and bought him a new one. When Paul's eyesight worsened and he started misfiling things in the store, Feltes encouraged him to get new eyeglasses and bring back the receipt so he could reimburse him. Paul never went. It wasn't so much that he was a creature of habit as he'd become the habit himself. There were no hat shops or eyeglass stores in his world.

Paul had turned sixty-five in 2001. Steve Feltes spent the next three years trying to convince him to take the steps necessary to apply for Social Security, and it took another year and a half after that for Paul to complete the process. There was a growing inability on Paul's part to deal with even those things that were part of his routine. "Everything seemed to be too much for him," Feltes says. "He wouldn't go down to Motor Vehicles to get an ID. His sense of ID was, 'Here's a ten-year-old Tower Records video-rental card: it's got my name on it: I know who I am: this is me.'" He also needed a copy of his birth certificate.

Identifying himself as an "ex-Warrenite," he scribbled a lengthy and surprisingly heartfelt letter to his hometown county recorder and requested a copy. "From what I understand I'm eligible for certain government benefits just for getting old," he began in what turned into a three-page walk down memory lane. "I remember so much about Warren." He wrote about Clara and Clifford, Linda, Doris, Mark, his schoolmates, and driving to the nearby big towns. He made Warren sound not like someplace from which he'd fled but someplace to which he wouldn't mind returning.

> What else do I remember? Kelly Peterson, my mother's brother. He was some kind of an inventor. He made some kind of a metal submarine and sat in it for about an hour

PAGE NUMBER	DATE		
	/ /		
PROJECT			

Dear County Clerk,

I hope I'm sending this to the right person. I'm an ex-Warrenite, born there Jan. 21st, 1936, father Clifford Nelson, mother Clara Nelson. One sister Linda, now Mrs. Nicholas Barna ~~a lawyer~~ Her husband is a lawyer, Nicholas Barna, Honesdale, Pennsylvania 18431. From what I understand I'm eligible for certain government benefits just for getting old. Social Security, et cetera. It seems I'm required a birth certificate. Enclosed a Xerox of ~~that~~ and several other pieces of identification. My middle ~~name~~ is Clifford.

my Social Security card

I graduated high school 2nd in my class. 1st was my best friend Jimmy Nybakken. 1954 we both got a scholarship to St. Olaf College, Northfield, Minnesota. I later went on to the University of Minnesota, then moved to New York with my ~~wife~~ wife Doris (Gehrls — I'm not sure of the spelling), also from Warren, and we had a son, Mark Christopher, now a lawyer in Houston, Texas. ~~Doris~~ Doris is remarried and living there too.

CAMBRIDGE

under the Snake River. I remember winning some kind of a golf tournament while in high school. We had sand greens…. But I'll stop boring you. It's been nice to remember.

P.S. I'm still a Minnesotan

The Marshall County Recorder was so taken with Paul's letter that she passed it on to *The Warren Sheaf*, where Paul's first articles had appeared,

PAGE NUMBER	DATE			
PROJECT		/	/	

②

I've had various jobs in journalism (SING OUT! magazine, ROLLING STONE, CIRCUS) and as an editor and also worked in the record business (Mercury Records in publicity and also as an A+R man).

I remember so much about Warren. My father and his brother Eddie owned Nelson Motor Co. and had several farms. Robert and Warren and Janet were Eddie's children. I remember The Warren Sheaf, run by the Mattsons. I worked for them in high school. I remember writing a column about the County Fair and covering all of the high school's sporting events. Phil Kotts had a Rexall drug store. There was another one — Kroll's, I think — right across from the movie theater. Later, there was a drive-in. The first movie I ever saw was Commandoes Strike at Dawn. My father took me.

Marvin Sundin was a friend. Dennis Strand, the Schirber girls. Mari was in my class. I dated Roberta. My first girlfriend. They were Catholics. My mother objected.

and the paper published it along with his contact information. As a result, Paul received calls from old friends he hadn't spoken with in over fifty years.

In order to receive his Social Security payments, Paul also needed to establish a bank account, something he hadn't had since the Eighties—but that also required identification. "Finally," Feltes says, "I got someone who knew me at Amalgamated to okay the account for Paul. I think she said something like, 'Well, every so often we should do something for the Sixties.' Here was non-druggie Paul playing the poster boy for the Sixties drug culture."

(3)

I remember driving to the big towns. Grand Forks, Crookston and Thief River Falls. Fargo, a hundred miles away, and Winnipeg, about the same. Much bigger, though. I was ~~very lucky~~. lucky — I could always borrow a car from the used car lot. What else do I remember? Kelly Peterson, my mother's brother. He was some kind of an inventor. He made some kind of a metal submarine and sat in it for about an hour under the Snake River. I remember winning some kind of a golf tournament while in high school. We had sand greens. Shirley Johnson, I remember. And Betty. Their father worked for the post office, I think. The ~~name~~ name of the basketball team was the Warren Ponies. Orange and black. But. I'll stop boring you. It's been nice to remember.

All the best,
Paul Nelson
c/o Evergreen Video
37 Carmine St.
New York, N.Y. 10012
P.S. I'm still a Minnesotan.
The phone number of Evergreen Video is (212) 691-7362
I'm there from 6 to 10 every night but Monday.

P.S. #2
I don't know what the fee is. Enclosed is $15.00. If you need more, let me know.

CAMBRIDGE

Even though Paul's middle name was Clifford, he set up the account under the name of Paul K. Nelson.

William MacAdams believes he knows why: "When his life started to go bad, around the time of the Eastwood article and the Young book, Paul's financial difficulties also began. He did not pay back any of the advance money on the book and, at some point, Paul told me the publisher had taken legal action and was able to confiscate the contents of his bank account—around $600, I think. After that he was afraid to open another account. So my guess is that, continuing to fear he was legally liable and could once again lose whatever money he put in a bank, he changed the *C* to a *K* to avoid detection. As well, for years he was afraid to have a phone in his name so the publisher couldn't locate him."

Once Paul's Social Security was activated in 2005, he began receiving $1,232 towards the end of each month. In addition, he retroactively received $10,951 for what he hadn't been paid since 2001.

"It was almost like he couldn't deal with the good news," Feltes says, "because as soon as he got the money, he really mentally fell apart. Starting right with the 24th of August when he got his deposit put in the bank, he started really having problems."

"The irony," Michael Seidenberg says, "that the moment Paul went on his Social Security pay and had more money than ever, he could not grasp it. For his lifestyle, he all of a sudden had twice as much money as he needed. But he couldn't accept it."

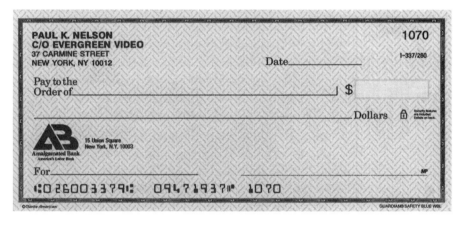

The month before, Steve Feltes reached the difficult decision to let Paul go. "Paul had ceased to become a contributing member of Evergreen Video. He was very grouchy. People would ask for the 'wrong' films, he would vocally protest their choices." He had also become disoriented, uncharacteristically forgetful, and was showing up at work at the wrong times.

Michael Seidenberg: "Steve would be the first to say he was carrying Paul there for the last two years he was working, and I'm sure that's not an exaggeration. I know Paul's feeling about the video shop and the customers in the last years. I used to think to myself constantly, What must he say to people? Because he was so obsessed when he'd get here. It really was the only time in all the years I knew him when I didn't enjoy talking to him. I'd heard him on rants before—I don't have a problem with rants—but it was just too negative. It was an anger at the general public wanting to see *Police Academy 5*. You start to think the whole world is like that. I think it worked him up after a whole week of it. Society disappointed him in a big way then."

"This was when he started doing things like leaving his house or leaving Evergreen and not making it home," Reggie Lewis says, "forgetting his keys in different locations. People said they would start seeing him outside the store at weird times."

Matthew Yeager: "His concept of what day it was, even what season it was, seemed to be slipping." It was not unlike the time warp that Paul had started experiencing around the time of his mother's cancer treatments.

Earlier in the year, Jay Cocks and Verna Bloom had dropped into the video store to say hello. "You could tell he was not on top of things," Cocks says. "One of the first things he said to us when we walked into the video store that last time was, 'Not a new thing in here worth watching.'"

"He was done with movies," Seidenberg says. "You just weren't telling him anything anymore. He already saw too many of the directors he liked go bad. Everything got too big. He couldn't stand later Scorsese films. I think it just comes down to Leonardo DiCaprio. It was like the end of life to him that Scorsese had chosen a new alter ego that was so unsuitable for Paul." Andrew Leigh recalls that Paul summed up the state of cinema this way: "Movies used to be eighty-nine minutes long, and by the end you knew a dozen characters as if they were your best friends. Now they're two hours-twenty, and you know even less about the characters at the end than you did at the beginning."

But life is only habit, and habit holds you as long as life holds you.
—PIERRE EUGÈNE DRIEU LA ROCHELLE,
The Fire Within

Without Evergreen there was a hole in Paul's life that he didn't know how to fill. "That definitely precipitated his downfall," Michael Seidenberg says, "but his downfall was coming. It coincided with him not working there, but was not caused by it. Maybe the thread of going to the video shop was helping him cling, but what was it helping him cling to? He couldn't communicate with people when he got there. In terms of his mental problems, it was a particularly bad time. That was the height of it. He got paranoid. He thought I was doing something behind his back to kick him out of his apartment.

With Michael Seidenberg on East 80th Street circa 1996.
Photo by Nicky Roe.

"When he came to me and explained to me that he was fired, he was in a full paranoid state," Seidenberg says. "'How could Steve do this to him?' He'd 'given his life to the video shop.' He didn't give his life to the video shop. I didn't even know Steve then, but I knew Steve didn't betray him, just like I knew I didn't betray him the week before."

Paul continued showing up at Evergreen several times a week—to help out at the cash register, take out the trash, or have a smoke in front of the shop. Finally, Steve Feltes asked him to please stay away for a while. Paul began going to Seidenberg's apartment instead. "It was probably better that way," Seidenberg says. "The world was smaller here, there were just a few people, and all my friends knew how to deal with him. This was probably a quieter place for him to wind it out."

I t was an immediate sign that something was wrong when Paul arrived at the video shop at ten o'clock one morning. Everybody at Evergreen knew that Paul stayed up all night and slept most of the day. And he seemed especially disoriented. Steve Feltes was away in Philadelphia, but his staff got him on the phone with Paul who said that he'd locked himself out of his apartment three days before and had been spending his nights on a park bench. He said not to worry, that he'd get the keys from Seidenberg when he returned from France. "So I had one of my employees take $400 out of the cash register," Feltes says, "and go up to Paul's and get a locksmith to get into his place. Turns out that Michael was four blocks away in his apartment all the time, had never gone to France, no plans to go to France."

Feltes asked Matthew Yeager to take Paul to Bellevue for a checkup, but Paul was released later that afternoon because there wasn't anything they could do for him. "He clearly didn't want the help," Yeager says, "and he was able to answer enough of the questions on their checklist that he could've appeared capable of taking care of himself, I suppose."

A month later, Martin Scorsese's Bob Dylan documentary *No Direction Home* premiered on PBS. Wesley Strick, who'd written the screenplay for Scorsese's *Cape Fear* remake, couldn't believe it when Dylan introduced Paul Nelson:

> Paul was a folk-music scholar. He didn't play at all. He had
> a whole lot of records which probably couldn't be found

anywhere else in the Midwest except at Paul's house, and he lived there with somebody else. I was listening to records at his house once and I knew they'd be away for the weekend. So I went over there and helped myself to a bunch more records.[51]

"And then my jaw dropped," Strick says, "because he had never once given any indication that he knew Dylan personally. I was just amazed to realize that he was present at the creation and in some way involved in Dylan's development in those early years. I was saying to my wife, 'That's the guy who gave me my big break.'"

From No Direction Home, *November 13, 1995.*
© 2005 Grey Water Park Productions.

Across the country, many of Paul's old friends were similarly surprised—and relieved by how well he looked. In truth, Paul's interview footage had been shot in New York almost ten years earlier.

Paul wasn't in any shape to appreciate his movie debut. He had become his own unreliable narrator. Steve Feltes says, "When Paul started really having Alzheimer's or a close associate of it, he was quite convinced that we had known each other in Minneapolis. He said, 'I remember us walking down Lake Street

51 Bob Dylan from *No Direction Home.* © 2005 Grey Water Park Productions. Used by permission. All rights reserved.

together, talking,' and I said, 'No, we never met, Paul.'" He also believed, because of an old black-and-white photo of himself and Jon Pankake back in their Minnesota days that appears in the film, that his interview had taken place in Minneapolis, not New York. Feltes couldn't convince him otherwise.

Paul wanted to speak with Jon Pankake. He asked Dave Lightbourne, who was working on a book about *The Little Sandy Review*, to let Pankake know that he'd like to hear from him. Lightbourne presumed it was to explain that, because of how Paul's interview was edited, *No Direction Home* gives the impression that the records Dylan appropriated belonged to Paul. Lightbourne, who never relayed the message, sensed that Paul felt uncomfortable taking credit for a story that was only fifty percent his.

Paul had indeed explained to Jeff Rosen, who conducted the interview, that the recordings were Pankake's, but that detail ended up on the cutting room floor. Adding to the confusion, in the film Dylan, referring to Pankake only as "somebody else," flat-out says that the records were Paul's. On the other side of the same coin, Dylan didn't mention Paul Nelson once in his autobiography *Chronicles: Volume One*, which was published the year before the documentary aired, and unequivocally stated that the rare Ramblin' Jack Elliott and Woody Guthrie records belonged to Pankake, whom he painted as a formidable figure who "breathed fire through his nose."

Jon Pankake: "Well, they were Paul's records. We both had the same records. We had these records from England that we had ordered. We both had them."

But that wasn't how Paul always told the story: "It soured my friend completely on Dylan, but it didn't sour me because I sort of saw the humor in the situation. I guess maybe if he'd stolen my records it would've, but he happened to steal a friend's."

Paula Farmer, a filmmaker who worked part-time at Evergreen, had proposed making a documentary about Paul after she read his online interview with Steven Ward. Initially uncomfortable with the idea, he changed his mind. In February of 2006, Farmer arranged to have Paul sit down and reminisce with two of his acolytes, Kurt Loder and *Rolling Stone* senior editor David Fricke, and she and her co-producer Michael Goldberg videotaped the reunion. "What was really sad," Farmer says, "as much as he loved meeting them and going down memory lane, I saw him maybe a week later at the store and he said,

'Who were those people I talked to?'" Another time, because Fricke had given him a ride home the night of the taping, Paul lingered at Evergreen. Farmer says, "He said he was waiting for David to come pick him up."

Bobbi London hadn't seen Paul for two years when she approached him on the street. She'd tried to find him, but didn't know the name of the video store where he worked. She told him how good it was to see him, but he returned a blank stare. "I suddenly realized he didn't know who I was. So I said, 'Hey, it's Bobbi.' He said, 'Oh, I don't have my glasses on. I don't know what I did with my glasses.'" It sounded plausible—more than once over the years she'd paid to have his glasses repaired when all that was holding them together was Scotch tape, just as she'd bought him new running shoes whenever the ones he was wearing were falling off his feet—but this time she sensed it was something more. "Then he started talking about this screenplay he was writing, and that was all he talked about. He said not in his lifetime would he ever see it produced. So I said, 'Yeah, but you never really worried about stuff like that when you started writing. I'm glad you're writing.'"

Paul asked Michael Seidenberg to manage his money for him. He'd pay all of Paul's bills and give him a small, set amount of money each week. "He didn't want more than that amount at a time. But at the end of each week, he would get nervous, like 'I have no money. How am I going to live?' He'd try to bring me things. I'd say, 'No, Paul, this is your money. You can have it all now, if you want it. You don't have to worry. You have food to eat every single day of your life.' But he just couldn't relax, unfortunately."

Nicky Roe: "He didn't even realize it was his money that was being given to him. He'd say, 'I'll give you a book.'"

"He had an intensely bad time and then got better," Seidenberg says. "That's why I was worried again when the intense heat was beginning because I thought it was bound to happen again."

Steve Feltes: "In the spring, Paul would say, 'It's going to be summer and I hate the summer.' I'd say, 'Paul, get an air conditioner.' 'Where would I get the money for an air conditioner?' I'd say, 'Paul, you have $9,000 in the bank.

It only costs $150 to get an air conditioner.' 'Where would I put it?' 'Do you have a window in the living room?' 'It's too crowded in the living room …'"

Feltes noticed that Paul, already slippery thin, appeared to be losing weight. Paul said that he was only eating once daily. "I said, 'Why are you only eating once a day?' He said, 'I can't afford to eat more than once a day.'

"About fifty percent of the time," Feltes says, "he was mentally reasonably okay. He could carry on a conversation, he knew what he was doing. About thirty-five percent of the time he was not remembering things. About ten or fifteen percent of the time he was delusionary."

Manny lived in one of the big new apartment buildings on the hill. The windows of his front room overlooked the UCLA campus. It was the room of a man who loved art and not much besides. Dozens of books had overflowed from the bookshelves onto the furniture, including the closed top of the baby grand piano. The walls were literally paneled with nineteenth-century reproductions and contemporary originals. Entering the room was like stepping into the interior of Manny's head.

—ROSS MACDONALD,
The Zebra-Striped Hearse

Paul was especially disheveled and distracted the last time Reggie Lewis saw him at the video store. He was unshaven, his running shoes were three sizes too large, and he was wearing the same taped and tattered clothing he'd worn when he still worked at Evergreen the year before. "He was swimming in those clothes," Lewis says. "He had this vacant thing going on in his eyes." When he took Paul home to make sure he got there safely, it was the first time he'd been inside the apartment. "It was almost like those apartments of a reclusive guy who hasn't had company in thirty years. It was fascinating, it was frightening, it was something that I had never seen in my life."

In the summertime the apartment must've been stifling at best, suffocating at worst. Paul had arranged portable electric fans to move the stale air from room to room to room. Always more concerned with keeping the light out than letting the fresh air in, he'd hidden every window behind bookcases and old movie posters. Every wall was lined with shelves—some of them fashioned from two-by-fours and bricks—that sagged beneath the weight of thousands of CDs, books, and videotapes. Several disposable Styrofoam shipping containers—one with FAIRLY EARLY MAYBE marked on the side, another with NEWEST—contained thousands of handwritten pages of a screenplay forever unfinished. Where there weren't stacks of arcane music magazines and film journals, and more stacks of CDs, the wood floor was scarred with cigarette burns. A desk lay hidden beneath layers of years-old notes, grocery lists, Nat Sherman inserts, newspaper clippings with the game schedules for the Knicks, Nets, Yankees, and Rangers, and Turner Classic Movies monthly listings. A particularly imposing bookcase, thick with dust, stood directly in front of the stove and the refrigerator. When he was hungry, he went out. There was an ice chest for his Coke. The bathroom was outside the apartment, down the hallway.

After Linda Barna received word that Paul was having health problems, she invited him more than once to stay with her and her family in Pennsylvania. Years before, he frequently came to see them via the ShortLine bus. "He liked to come here and sit on the deck. We have sixty acres here and he'd walk around the land. We'd always have a couple of dogs and a couple of cats, and then he'd play with the kids."

Linda says Paul left a message on their answering machine. "He said, 'I don't think I'm going to come now. I'm feeling better and I'm getting a lot of writing done. But I'd be delighted to come at another time.' I thought it was kind of funny that he said *delighted* because that didn't sound like him really. And that's the last I heard from him."

Occasionally he thumbed through his complete set of *Little Sandy Reviews* and reread what he'd written many years before. "I like that guy," Paul said, "but he's not me anymore."

In April, Paul received a visitor. "They got new management," Michael Seidenberg says, "and the guy talked Paul into bringing him up to his apartment." Thinking he'd been visiting with the new owner, Paul made a note to himself afterwards:

> He actually lowered the rent. New rent is 553.53, if I'm reading this right. I met him when he was trying to get into his new building, so I let him in. Seemed like a nice guy. He actually wants people to stay.

A week and a half later, the eviction notice appeared beneath his door.

Though the rent had crept up to $665 over the years, he couldn't afford to live anywhere else in the city for that price. He'd long ago settled into a lifestyle that he described more than a quarter century earlier when writing about Jackson Browne's *The Pretender*: "plenty of past, a severely pinched present, and no future. *Everything* is an afterthought."

The summer heat rising and his legs hurting more and more, one day Paul arrived at Michael Seidenberg's apartment and gave him printouts someone had made of the RockCritics.com interview and the Warren Zevon article, and a copy of *The Little Sandy Review*. "He told me, about a week before he brought that stuff by, that he'd had this night where he went through everything in his life. His mind was taking him there, so he just went—through every important thing of his life. Hours and hours and hours. When I saw him right after that he was very nostalgic, telling me all kinds of stories and things. More than he would normally talk about himself."

I want to do the most original, most contemporary film, most filmic film possible, reflecting all of our influences from movies, novels, music, and life in these times. Music will play a most important part in the movie (as it often does in Godard), sometimes being as important as the visuals.[52]

---

[52] "Some Extremely Random Notes on a Projected Film Script; or Jac Saves a Life; or Stefanie Powers Meets Belmondo and Bogey on the Road as *High Sierra* Gets Welded to *Breathless* in a Sort of Truffautian-Godardian-Holzmanesque-Wellesian-Hawksian-Chaplinesque-Nelsonian Tragi-Romp Guaranteed to Whet the Appetites and Pop the Eyes of Auteur Film Fans, French Critics, 42nd-Street Rummies, and Anyone Who in His Heart of Hearts Loves Monogram Pictures, the Glories of Gilbert Roland, J.P. Donleavy, Nathanael West, and the Indescribable Magnificence of the Great Maligned 'B'" by Paul Nelson.‡

"I thought there was just one *Look Homeward, Angel*-sized screenplay," Jay Cocks says.

While there'd been talk of different screenplays through the years— including a detective one and a "*Breathless* meets *High Sierra*" hybrid that he wrote with Steve McQueen, Sterling Hayden, and Stefanie Powers in mind—in the end there was only one. By the turn of the century, Paul,

```
NOTES

Young hood.  Old hood.  Gal.  Steve McQueen.  Sterling
Hayden.  Stefanie Powers.

Cross HIGH SIERRA with BREATHLESS and CONTEMPT

Gunfight in field (cars) and bouncing ball scene from
dream.  Final gun battle in rural fields, barns, etc.

Card game to get in characterization.

Old hood: use some Izzy.

Use "I Want Candy" for robbery, murder, etc.

Stefanie heroine more than McQueen hero: pull the Hawks
reverse play.  McQueen wants to quit this life, is
afraid for Stefanie.  Stefanie is not afraid.

Theme: need to be a hero in these times.

McQueen is drawn to Hayden as to an old-time Bogey-type
human being.  So is Stefanie.  Hayden-Stefanie-McQueen
have a sort of father-daughter-son camaradie.

Tribute line for Stefanie: "Are you ready for this hair!"

Theme: The need to be criminal: "I don't want to kill in
my profession, but I need the thrill of knowing that
someone may kill me."  The thrill of the pistol, the
chase, etc.  Gentle but philosophical criminals.

Genre: sunglasses, cigarette smoke, silencer pistols.

Junk heap with old cars: crazy reaction from McQueen; it
scares him about Stefanie.

Robbery to Dylan or R&B tune.

"Thirsty Boots" song while Hayden walks to Stefanie's
grave at the end of the film.  VERTIGO

Bunuel shot of lantern moving to the right while camera
zooms in.

Godardian abstract shot of Stefanie, white helmet, hair,
one eye, etc. to open film.  Come from out of focus to
focus a la THE CINCINNATI KID.
```

OLD ACQUA— for HAYDEN ...

Paul's notes from the Sixties about the kind of movie he wanted to make.

having forsaken all other kinds of writing, spent the rest of his life writing a never-ending screenplay whose characters meant more to him than those in real life.

Cocks: "Paul began to, I think, *need* writing in a way that was more therapeutic and less expressive. An exercise in survival as well as an exercise in artistic fulfillment. The last time I saw him, he said to me at Evergreen: 'Don't go to movies anymore—nothing much to see. Don't even listen to music anymore.' He said, 'I listen to a little bluegrass and I go home and write. All night. I love it.'"

Charles M. Young says, "I do remember him saying that what he liked about it was that there wasn't any editor telling him what to do. He could just sit there and write what he wanted. It was like he was just discovering this, you know, kind of late in life."

Jason Ruscio didn't think much of Paul's claim that he was writing a screenplay. "I just thought, You're my crazy old bird friend who wants to write a script—but who doesn't?" Regardless, Ruscio encouraged Paul to write and even convinced him to come over to his apartment and use his old Macintosh computer to transfer his work from yellow legal pads to a disk.

"He'd been writing it for a long time when I met him in '99," Dave Lightbourne said. "He was still working on it six years later. It was a permanently not-yet-finished crossword puzzle that he could work on to his heart's content forever because there was never a deadline and there was never a purpose for it. He was just an artist wanting to perfect something that he had been envious of other people doing his entire life."

Matthew Yeager: "He would come into the store on cloud nine because a flash of a quote spoke to him of what the character would say. He'd come in and write it down on anything from a napkin to a receipt, put it in his pocket, and take it and figure out how to fit it in."

"Sometimes he would come in with pages upon pages and ask me if we could read a scene or two," Reggie Lewis says.

He said he was writing it for himself and took pride in telling people that Hollywood wouldn't want to go anywhere near it.

"There was some talk in the beginning," Michael Seidenberg says, "when he first started writing the screenplay, that Jeff Rosen would take it to Dylan and they would talk about it. In the beginning. Then he stopped talking about that, so I assumed he realized that it wasn't really a going thing."

Andy Zwerling was eighteen or nineteen years old when he first met Paul. He and his sister Leslie, who was still in junior high, had auditioned for him at Mercury and stayed in touch ever since. "A few years ago, it became very clear that he didn't want to let go of the screenplay. Let's say it was noncommercial. Who cares? Maybe Martin Scorsese would've said, 'You know, Paul, no one's going to put up money for this, but this is really good.' What would be so bad about that?"

Jay Cocks questions whether Paul truly abandoned all hope of seeing the screenplay produced. "He loved movies, and I think if a fairy godfather had come along and said, 'I can make this real,' Paul would've been delighted. You know, as long as it wasn't Mark Rydell or somebody."

Zwerling thinks that Paul and Lew Archer walked the same streets: "He always knew the world was corrupt, but he got very excited if he thought something good could sneak through. The trouble was, I don't think he ever accepted that the good that could sneak through could be his stuff. He reached a point where he didn't care. He just wanted to do it because he wanted to do it."

Paul played the film that would never be over and over in his mind with a pre-car accident Montgomery Clift in the lead. "I don't think he would've settled for anyone else to play it," Yeager says. Paul had even assembled a bluegrass soundtrack for his movie, which David Aaron burned to CD for him one night after work.

Jonathan Lethem: "The most enthusiasm that I would hear from him was in descriptions of the screenplay that he would sometimes offer. My impression was that it was in the mode of something like *Days of Heaven*, that it was a historical Western romance. He also had a kind of obsession with *Heaven's Gate* and I think that it might've also had a resemblance to that had he put it together."

"In the beginning, he used to talk about it *a lot*," Seidenberg says. "In fact, he told me the same scene a few times. It was a scene with a little character of a young girl, I think about nine years old, who falls in love with a soldier in wartime. It was in Europe and he was an American soldier. And it's a pure love, it's not physical. But it would've been physical if there hadn't been that kind of age difference. He had this scene where they dance, where the soldier puts the girl on his shoes and they have a little dance. He loved that scene."

Sometimes it seemed as if Paul were describing two disparate screenplays: one a Western, the other an off-beat WWII romance. They were in fact the same work.

Cocks: "He told me that he was trying to combine Lubitsch and *Bonnie and Clyde*. I read parts of it, and some of it is very, very beautiful. Very lyrical. Funny. Highly idiosyncratic. But it's the work of someone who can't put the pieces together. I remember seeing in it much of Paul's struggle and need, a kind of real romantic yearning, a sort of a darkness and a willful reaching for some kind of light. You're reading the wrestling rather than the result of the struggle. You're looking at the struggle. And that's what happened to Paul."

"He was so alone," Seidenberg says. "He didn't really have people he would talk to about all of his really inner feelings. This was the way he put it out."

The girl in Paul's screenplay, Sophie, was inspired by one of Evergreen's customers. The woman was much younger than Paul and her name was Sophie Malleret. Reggie Lewis remembers the effect she had on Paul. "A small, very petite French woman who had a childlike quality, she was an actress. Paul was just smitten by her. She would come by and he would lose all track of time. However he could help her. She would talk in one- or two-word sentences and he was just aglow."

> For when I first saw her, I had been lonely for so long that I was no longer lonely, if you know what I mean. I had accepted it, even made it thrive. I was somewhat productive, happiness sometimes reared its often unseen head over a book or a song or a movie that had shared its art and emotion with an overly receptive and appreciative soul, no longer chained to a longing for that which has rarely worked, or at least for long. I will not do this again, I often told myself during these halcyon days of aloneness, *this* meaning attempt a romance when lightning does not strike, when I do not feel there is an actual, a real, chance, for the real thing and not a substitute for my newfound friend, loneliness. No, it must be love, at least the hope of it, or nothing. Well, Sophie walked in and it was love. And a loneliness and tumult of hope beyond compare. In short, I grew smarter in brain but dumber at heart, or the other way around.
>
> When I partook of her shy and artless ways, I knew that this was going to be a long and possibly ridiculous trip, and that the seat beside me would quite likely remain unsat in, numbingly empty, except for the imaginary trace of her sweet perfume.[53]

Paul attended her one-woman show and, when she walked through the audience and tapped him on his cap, the fourth wall was broken. "He'd say it was like ecstasy for him," Lewis says. "He would say, 'She touched my head.' For the longest time his only wish was, 'I just want her to go out with me and have a cup of coffee.' I don't think she had any clue what impact she had on him. I guess she never got around to having the cup of coffee with him, but he kept her alive with the screenplay.

"He became the character known as Billy. He was a serviceman and I guess the backdrop was World War II. He had met this little girl named Sophie, who tagged along with him after he got separated from his platoon

---

53 Untitled notes by Paul Nelson, late 1990s to 2006.‡

A small portion of Paul's "Look Homeward, Angel-*sized screenplay."*
Photo by Kevin Avery.

or what have you, and they made their way through the countryside. For the most part there were little conversations between Billy and Sophie, and it was exactly how she would express herself—you know, the real Sophie."

Matthew Yeager: "He knew that it would never be kosher to make a film with a young girl as basically the female lead and all that that might imply. She and Billy would have a very intimate relationship—not sexual. There was always something sort of innocent about Paul and his view of the world. It wasn't sullied by prurient things."

"He just compiled something that was so massive," Lewis says. "People at first were like, 'Oh great, we hear that you're working on a project,' but as years went on they stopped asking about it because they understood this was just like a pacemaker or something. It was just going to keep him alive."

As Paul's memory began to betray him, he'd discuss his characters with Michael Seidenberg. He was desperate to understand who the little girl represented. Was it Bobbi? Doris perhaps? "He said, 'I have trouble writing the soldier, but I have no trouble writing the kid.'" He'd not only forgotten who Sophie was but also that he was Billy.

Voiceover

(a woman's voice, French accent)

Someone once suggested that the story of America could be summed up in the tale of two sets of James Brothers— Henry and William, Frank and Jesse. That's probably true, but I believe there should be two more names added.[54]

When I was a young girl, I knew a man whose father had given him a coin he claimed came from the hand of Billy the Kid less than an hour before the Kid was shot and killed by Sheriff Pat Garrett on a hot and rainy night, July, 1888, in old New Mexico. Billy had given the coin to the man's father, then a wild and adventurous youth going on thirteen, because the boy had fetched some tequila for the Kid and his woman. Decades later, the father presented the coin to his youngest, not his oldest, son. "For luck," he had said, somewhat sternly. "Because you'll need it."

The woman, of course, is Sophie ("She has an offbeat, idiosyncratic beauty that suggests intelligence, determination, character") and the keeper of the coin is Billy ("He has a similar offbeat look, both handsome and haunted"). Paul's screenplay spans the Twentieth Century with a dizzying timeline that in the end doesn't add up, following Billy and his older brother Pat from childhood in Thief River Falls, Kansas (not Minnesota), where their father, "one of the last Western sheriffs," is killed in a bank robbery, to adulthood, where Billy searches for—and is ultimately reunited with—Sophie, almost twenty years his junior.

What's significant about the screenplay that Paul couldn't stop writing, that played over and over in his mind, isn't so much the complex plot, which Paul summarized in twenty-two handwritten pages, but the stories within.

> Billy, shaken by his father's death and believing he has found something like true love with his high school sweetheart, marries Dee.... It isn't as passionate and exciting as he expects, but he figures it will grow. It doesn't and he realizes he has made a mistake.... Without knowing it, he has ... done what is expected in small-town America: marry your high school

---

54 The James Brothers reference, which Paul quoted verbatim in "Warren Zevon: How He Saved Himself from a Coward's Death," comes from *Consenting Adults; or The Duchess Will Be Furious* by Peter De Vries.

sweetheart, both of you dumb as fence posts and neither knowing themselves well enough to know who they were or what they wanted....

World War II breaks out. Pat and Billy enlist. For Billy, it is adventure and an escape from Dee and Kansas.... In 1945, Billy is wounded in a small French village. During a retreat, he kills eighteen German soldiers while defending a wounded French couple and their daughter Sophie in a bombed-out house. The couple and Sophie follow him to the field hospital, other hospitals. He teaches Sophie some English, she him some French. It is clear that they mean a great deal to each other. He is about twenty-five, she is six.

When Billy and Pat return from the war:

After a few weeks back in Kansas and with Dee, Billy decides to go to New York—for a short visit, he tells Dee.... Billy enrolls in NYU. When is Dee coming? Pat asks. She's not, Billy says....

Billy goes to school, enjoys the city, begins to write short stories and articles. It is a tough go, but he gets a few of them printed. He works in a bookstore just down the street from his apartment. He meets Bobbi, a kindred spirit who is everything he ever dreamed of and desired in Kansas. She feels the same about him.... Bobbi is an artist without an art. She works as a receptionist at one of the magazines to which Billy sells articles. When he first sees her, it is—at least on Billy's part—love at first sight....

Thus begins both Billy's and Bobbi's first real romance, first true love. It lasts for three-some years. It is so passionate and pure, so guilt-ridden with baggage from the past, that perhaps it fails for those reasons. And perhaps it succeeds as long as it does for those reasons, too....

They continue to live and love each other to the fullest, but just when Billy begins to gain some recognition as a writer and they no longer have to live on love alone, Billy feels Bobbi drifting away. He doesn't know why or how to stop it. She doesn't seem to know why either. Bobbi leaves, saying it's only for a while and she must leave now to save their love....

Billy is thirty years old. Emotionally desolate. He had had everything he dreamed about in Kansas and he lost it....

Over the years, and there are many, Billy seeks consolation in a few women ..., but realizes that they are, in one way or another, substitutes for Sophie and sometimes Bobbi. He loves them, in his way, and some of the relationships are intense, but they all fail. Nothing lasts, Billy thinks, except Sophie....

He begins to write again. He's never fully stopped writing his articles, which are usually about other people—writers, artists, musicians—whom he admires.

When Billy encounters Sophie, now fourteen, at a Long Island Halloween party held in a *Gatsby*-like mansion, he gives her the coin that his father gave to him when he was a boy. After she runs away, she writes him a letter saying, "I am not ready for you and I do not think you are ready for me.... Please do not try to find me now, though I think you'll try. I will find you, I swear it, when it is the right time and we will be in love then always." Soon after, Billy receives a phone call from a woman who identifies herself as "a friend of Sophie's. She asked me to call you, to help you through this." He tells the woman to tell Sophie that he still loves her. "I'll wait for her." Through the years, the phone calls continue. They are his only means for getting messages to Sophie, to whom he dedicates his first book.

Billy meets the "bawdy, sensitive" Sheree, who reveals herself as the woman behind the phone calls. She brings him up to date with what's happened to Sophie, his lost love:

SHEREE

Then some bastard mugged her, knocked her down and kicked the shit out of her. Broke three ribs. She hit her head on the sidewalk, got a concussion.... In the hospital, the doctors taped her ribs, treated the concussion. They found a small lump in her neck. Lymphoma. Over a year of chemotherapy. Which knocks the shit out of you, honey. She recovered, waited. The doctors said it may come back. It did.... Anyway, more treatment, more recovery, more time lost. But the doctors are 99.9 percent sure it won't come back. Sophie's got most of her strength back. She looks great. A little older but more beautiful than ever. You should see her within six months. About time, huh?

In the meantime, Billy and Pat receive word that their mother has had a heart attack.

> They go back to Kansas. Scene at mother's bedside. Some reconciliation, understanding is reached between mother and sons. And daughter Linda, much younger than Pat and Billy and who I've left out of this summary completely.... The mother dies.

Later, back in New York, Billy is catching a cab to Grand Central Station when a woman wearing a hat and dark glasses asks if she can share the taxi with him. It turns out that they're taking the same train. Once onboard, she saves the seat next to her for Billy. After some small talk, she reaches into her purse and drops into his hand the coin that he gave to her so many years before. "Sophie?" he asks, his voice trembling badly.

The screenplay's final scene is a flashback/dream of Billy and Sophie walking together through his childhood in the Kansas town where he and Pat grew up.

> Billy and Sophie reach the bandstand in the town square, where Billy's father and mother once danced. The lights are on, but there is no one there. They dance. They stop, look at each other. Closeup on their faces. They kiss—(hopefully) one of the most romantic, tender, loving kisses in screen history.[55]

By the last week of June, neither Steve Feltes nor Michael Seidenberg had seen Paul in more than two weeks. Feltes called Seidenberg and introduced himself. They checked with Dallas BBQ, but he hadn't been in there either. They decided to pay Paul a visit.

Feltes: "We didn't say anything, but we were absolutely convinced we were going to find a body. We knocked on his door. We literally both of us smelled around for a bit. It was that old primitive thing: if you don't mention death, it won't happen. Well, we didn't and it didn't."

Seidenberg finally used his key, but there was a chain across the door. He and Feltes were about to lend their shoulders to the cause when Paul's face suddenly appeared in the crack. He removed the chain and let them in. Feltes was stunned by how much Paul had deteriorated since he last saw him. But as bad as Paul looked, Seidenberg says, "He had a calm about him"—and an

---

55 *Phone Messages to Sophie* plot summary by Paul Nelson, late 1990s to 2006.‡

indifference. "Steve and I didn't even know each other, and Paul wasn't surprised that we were together at his door."

> Michael = need some
> money. I got $15 00 . Hungry .

> Michael – I need some
> money. I got $15 00
> total, I need some
> meals.

> Michael = I need some
> money. I got $[illegible] 2.
> I'm hungry. Thirsty . Paul

Paul insisted that he wasn't hungry and that he'd been eating at a new restaurant. They asked him how much money he had. After he showed them thirty dollars, they dug into their pockets and left him with an additional hundred.

Downstairs in the street, standing at the intersection outside the apartment building, Feltes and Seidenberg discussed their next move.

"At this point," Feltes says, "Paul couldn't really afford to live in New York. Where he really should have been was in a nursing home, but the idea of Paul being woken at eight in the morning and eating oatmeal just struck both Michael and me as completely ludicrous. Maybe what would work was if his sister could get him a room or someplace near her in Pennsylvania. We just couldn't figure an option that was going to work. What we should've done, we should've grabbed him and taken him downstairs."

Jay Cocks: "Okay, he's on your shoulder, now what are you going to do? Where are you going to take him? Are you going to take him to your house? He's not going to stay there. He's not going to be happy there. Are you going to lock him up in Bellevue, again on public assistance?"

Feltes couldn't help but be reminded of a scene from one of Paul's favorite films, *Touch of Evil*, when Orson Welles asks Marlene Dietrich to read his future. "You haven't got any," she says. "Your future's all used up."

On the Fourth of July, a police officer called Michael Seidenberg to say that his brother's body had been found in his apartment at 400 East Seventy-Fourth Street. "I immediately figured out what was going on and I went there. That's when the problems started with the non-identification of the body." Seidenberg was willing to go upstairs and identify it, but they wouldn't let him into the apartment. The body had apparently been there for a week. Heat and decomposition had taken their toll, as had the rats.

On July 13, 2006, three days after running Paul's obituary, *The New York Times* issued a correction:

> An obituary on Monday about Paul Nelson, a pioneering rock critic, misstated the cause of death in some copies. While his friend Steven Feltes initially said he had apparently died of starvation, he said later that a cause had not been determined. The New York City medical examiner's office said yesterday that the cause was heart disease.

"When they say he died of starvation, it wasn't that he didn't have food," Seidenberg says, "it's that he chose not to. He had already given up too much. He wasn't giving any more up."

Paul had apparently returned to bed and died a day or two after Feltes and Seidenberg's last visit.

When Mark Nelson flew to New York, the police accompanied him and Michael Seidenberg into Paul's still-sealed apartment to retrieve something from which the medical examiner could derive DNA for the necessary testing.

Seidenberg spied the stack of *Little Sandy Reviews*. When the police weren't looking, he slipped them into a bag and later passed them on to Mark. Something on one of the shelves, where $130 still sat, caught Seidenberg's

On Carmine Street, December 2005.
Photos by Paula Farmer.

eye. "I said, 'His cap. There's nothing that's going to have more DNA than that cap.'" He was right—but afterwards the ME would forever misplace it.

Mark entered the bedroom and looked around. On a shelf by Paul's bedside, near an open copy of Tom Nolan's *Ross Macdonald: A Biography*, he immediately recognized his own red toddler shoes. Despite the countless moves around the city, and so many possessions lost or sold or left behind, Paul had kept them through the years. "The shoes triggered lots of memories and thoughts," Mark says, "both of my childhood and my son—Paul's grandson, a grandson that he did not know he had."

Opened a door to a life little known
Books, movies, stale cigarettes—skeletal remains
Of a journey now ended, the soul having flown.

Shoes on a shelf, so old and so small
Explode conscious with fantasies of what could not be
A father, his father, and a baby son
Three generations spontaneously one.

Speaking in silence words never said
They rest on a shelf near the bed all alone
A message through time to a heart that has grown.

—MARK NELSON,
"Shoes"

Photo by Paula Farmer

He remained Billy.

- BOOK TWO -

GOOD CRITIC PAUL:
THE WRITINGS OF PAUL NELSON

The first thing when you get an agent, if you're known primarily as a rock & roll writer, they tell you, "Don't try to sell a collection of your work, there's absolutely no money in it."
—PAUL NELSON to Leonard Cohen

- BOB DYLAN -

deare irwin. moe. an whole staff.(is ethel still there?) an her
too. good critic paul. an hi t all new shepards. it's me, bob.
me bob writin from the bonny doons of good woodstock.

—BOB DYLAN in a letter to
Irwin Silber at *Sing Out!*, June 1964

Paul's essay about Bob Dylan for 1976's The Rolling Stone Illustrated History
of Rock & Roll *was the closest he ever came to writing the detective novel he
so often talked about in the Seventies. It is also the finest example we have
of the fiction writer he could've become. By expanding on his 1975* Rolling
Stone *review of Dylan and the Band's* The Basement Tapes *and introducing
a decade's worth of previously published writings as "reports" and occasional
dialogue into a framework that demonstrated his love of, and debt to, the
books of Ross Macdonald, Raymond Chandler, and Dashiell Hammett, he
ingeniously dealt with Dylan as a case to be cracked. Or not.*

*Unfortunately, that's not what editor Jim Miller was looking for. "The
essay came in late, as I recall, and was so idiosyncratic that it posed problems
within the book's overall context: of trying to retell a real history. That is why
his essay was pulled in the second edition."*

*Simply getting Paul to surrender the piece (and the other three essays he
was writing for the book) was a formidable challenge. After the deadline*

came and went, Miller and his silent editor, Greil Marcus, resorted to paying him visits, laying on his buzzer, shouting up from the street. According to Marcus:"We had no idea if he was in the apartment or not. We fantasized— it's a commonplace, banal fantasy, everyone's had it—that he was in there dead, not to be found until the neighbors couldn't ignore the smell." And Miller left message after message on Paul's prehistoric answering machine (in between other messages about other missed opportunities and deadlines, including writing the liner notes for the Modern Lovers' debut album):

"Hi, Paul, this is Jim Miller. Are you still alive?" Click.

"Hello, Nelson, this is the old man. Get on the case, or we'll blow you outta the water." Click.

"Mr. Marlowe? This is the Bob Dylan piece. I'm in terrible trouble, I have to get written! I need help! Please!" Click.

"Ned Beaumont? We've got Ross Macdonald. If you ever want to see him again, you have a week to deliver what you owe us. You won't be hearing from us again." Click.

"Paul, this is Ross Macdonald. I'm just calling to ask that you please *do what they ask as soon as you can and everything will work out all right. I'm an old man and I really can't take—" Click.*

And finally, imitating Bob Dylan breaking into song. "Hi, Paul, this is Bob Dylan. 'How does it feel? To be on your own? Like a rolling stone?'" Click.

Marcus was pleased when Paul finally delivered. "I liked the piece enormously. I thought it was worth all of the difficulty that Jim and I went through trying to pry it out of Paul. I was expecting something unpredictable, and that's what we got."

K.A.

BOB DYLAN*

Pleasure? I never seek pleasure. There was a time years ago when I sought a lot of pleasure because I'd had a lot of pain. But I found there was a subtle relationship between pleasure and pain. So now I do what I have to do without looking for pleasure in it.

—BOB DYLAN

It was a diamond all right, shining in the grass half a dozen feet from the blue brick wall. It was small ... and unmounted. I put it in my pocket and began searching the lawn as closely as I could without going at it on all fours.

I had covered a couple of square yards of sod when the Leggetts' front door opened.

A woman came out on the broad stone top step and looked down at me with good-humored curiosity....

I stopped poking at the grass and went up to her, asking: "Is Mr. Leggett in?"

"Yes." Her voice was as placid as her face. "You wish to see him?"

I said I did.

She smiled at me and at the lawn.

"You're another detective, aren't you?"

I admitted that.

—DASHIELL HAMMETT,
The Dain Curse

By Paul Nelson from *The Rolling Stone Illustrated History of Rock & Roll*. © Rolling Stone Press 1976. All rights reserved. Reprinted by permission.

° Reprinted from the original manuscript, which first appeared in *The Rolling Stone Illustrated History of Rock & Roll* as an edited version.

I.

There was a desert wind blowing that night, and the hot breeze that sighed through the open window had just enough muscle to swirl the smoke from the unhappy ghosts of a hundred cigarettes a single time around the solitary desk lamp before giving it up as a bad job.

I knew the feeling.

I had been sitting in the office for days, thinking and rethinking the case, but thoughts about Miranda Abaloni's bright eyes and blue-black hair kept swimming into my mind like the dreams of a kid who's just been told that Christmas is tomorrow, not next week.

Actually it was Cadwallader who had hired me, but I didn't give a damn about him. Somehow the Cadwalladers of this world, though smart enough, all think that life is a debate and if the other guy is human and doesn't talk too well, that kind of makes them his hanging judge.

I didn't know how Miranda felt.

But I meant to find out.

I kept telling myself the case wasn't a big mistake. It added up all right—hell, it had added up from the very beginning—but I just couldn't figure out why. The more I tried to analyze it, the more it resisted my efforts. I got that nervous feeling on the back of my neck that someone very close was telling me to lay off, that to get too involved with a bogus quest for the white-hot center would be to miss the whole point.

Logic is a funny thing to a private detective. It has nothing to do with facts but rather with intuition—a kind of mathematics without damage. After a few lean years, you learned to trust your hunches and, better yet, to draw occasionally to that inside straight no matter what the book said. Especially if the artist you were investigating—in this case, Bob Dylan—made up new rules each time out in the only worthwhile game in town.

What got to me was that I knew what he was doing but I couldn't explain it, not in words anyway. Arguably I'd had some luck with Dylan before, was not unfamiliar with his circuitous, sporadic manner. He wasn't a classicist and he didn't run with the pack. Instead he played spontaneously, from the heart, stringing together such disparate cards that only the force of his will held his ideas together and kept pretentiousness from breaking down the door. The results he got were amazing, often magical. He'd had some bad years in the late Sixties and early Seventies when he'd tried to run some more or less conventional bluffs, but then who hasn't?

Cadwallader probably.

II.

The office was in the Arbogast Building on Embryo Street off Perelman Square, half a block from the Coma Noodle Corporation, right next to the Ambergris Diner and the Dead Souls Church and Motel.

Miranda Abaloni had first walked into it last Monday afternoon. Since then I hadn't been sleeping too well. She had blue-black hair the color of Sheaffer's Skrip ink, a *Mona Lisa* mouth as wide as the barrel of a .357 Magnum, and wore dark brown corduroy jeans and a khaki Boy Scout shirt which made an instant liar out of its insignia. Her girlish face was round as a bottle, and she looked very healthy.

"Hello," I said.

She asked: "This is the Watchtower Detective Agency, isn't it? You specialize in Bob Dylan?"

I said it was and we did.

When she smiled she was exactly what every adolescent or aging romantic asks for in his letters to Santa. If you wanted to prove there were no God, you would have to find some way to overlook Miranda Abaloni.

Unfortunately there was no way to overlook Gideon Cadwallader, the xanthous young man standing next to her. His stainless-steel eyes vacuumed the room for any trace of class and, finding none, caromed off what I hoped was a savage enough display of my own ocular firepower. The molecules in the office seemed to be bouncing.

"Sit down," I said. "What can I do for you?"

After what passed for the amenities, he told me. Curling back a carnassial upper lip which revealed a grayish-green fang no longer than my little finger, he said: "This young woman whom I am sure you have noticed is Ms. Miranda Abaloni—"

I gave her my best smile.

He didn't like it at all. He acted like a sulky child. I apologized and asked him to continue.

"My name is Gideon Cadwallader," he said. "I am a member of the Manhattan Institute of Critical Enterprise, the Majorities Enter the War League, the March Against Repression, and the Committee to Ruin University Debutantes—for their own good, of course. We—"

It may not be easy to laugh and stare at the same time, but I managed it.

He shot me a superior look.

"I'm sorry," I said. "I can see you're serious. But my, ah, initial reaction was to laugh."

He appeared slightly mollified. "I don't think it's funny," he said.

"Some people never do," I said. I looked at Ms. Abaloni. "Malcolm Lowry once wrote in a letter: 'Cheerfulness keeps breaking in.'"

"Let us get down to business," said Gideon Cadwallader, and I knew I wasn't going to like what he was about to say. "At the behest of Miranda, that is, Ms. Abaloni, the organizations to which we belong are—I'm not quite sure how to phrase this—'looking for a hero,' a public figure in which to believe and one who can set the proper sociopolitical standards and yet remain an artist worthy of aesthetic consideration.[1] I am not talking about mere topical songs and their ilk. Ms. Abaloni has suggested, of all people, Bob Dylan, and while I do believe I have driven the wedge of contentious doubt firmly into her underlying perceptions, she insisted we come to you for what she believes may be a valuable report. I concurred. I admire Mr. Dylan—but only to a point. However, I understand that your devotion is steadfast and that your operatives are experts on the man."

"Yes and no," I said. "The Agency's motto isn't 'Mine Eyes Have Seen the Glory of the Coming of the Lord.' I don't like deification because none of us deserves it. I'd put Dylan, the Rolling Stones, and Jackson Browne at the top because they've changed my life the most. I couldn't live without their music. But it's subjective. And there are others, dozens of others. Why pick out one poor sucker and make an example out of him? Dylan certainly makes no claims to perfection—he's got his own demons. He probably doesn't give a damn what we think."

Cadwallader looked immediately pleased. He did a little dance with his feet and actually clapped his hands. It sounded like the love song of two dead fish. "Exactly," he said. "Exactly. Worthy as he is, he is not worthy. No one is." His estimation of me had gone up. I liked it better when he hated me.

Miranda Abaloni looked soulfully at the floor.

"On the other hand," I said.

She moved her lovely head.

"If you're determined to proceed with this."

She rolled an elegiac eyeball in my direction. I picked it up and rolled one back.

"There's probably no one better."

She shook her blue-black hair in agreement.

Cadwallader adjusted quickly. He seemed to be smiling. Then he looked right at me for a very long time.

I looked at Miranda Abaloni.

I was about to make a fool of myself, and Gideon Cadwallader knew it.

---

1 The same year Paul wrote this essay, Elliott Murphy, inspired by his many conversations with Paul about heroism—in literature, movies, and life—wrote and recorded "Lookin' for a Hero," a song that Paul, when he reviewed it, deemed "heavy-handed and confusing."

III.

"**B**ob Dylan. Born Robert Allen Zimmerman on May 24, 1941, in Duluth, Minnesota. Moved to Hibbing when he was six. Played rock & roll in high school but folk music at the University of Minnesota and in New York City where he also wrote topical songs. Bit of a liar about his background—"

"We know all that," said Cadwallader. "It's dull, except for the part about his being a liar. History should be interpretative."

"When the actor James Byron Dean died at twenty-four in an automobile crash in 1955, American movies surrendered the mantle of the archetypal sensitive-but-confused teenager to rock & roll. In the early Sixties Dylan claimed the title by emulating Dean and later certified the transferal by naming his firstborn son Jesse Byron Dylan. What Marshall McLuhan would call a hot connection."

"What Gideon Cadwallader would call frivolous pop sociology. Neither James Dean nor Marshall McLuhan are significant here."

I lit a cigarette and tried to think. At least Miranda Abaloni didn't look bored. She didn't look happy but she didn't look bored.

I said: "In the mid-Sixties Dylan's talent evoked such an intense degree of personal participation from both his admirers and detractors that he could not be permitted so much as a random action. Hungry for a sign, the world used to follow him around, just waiting for him to drop a cigarette butt. When he did they'd sift through the remains, looking for significance. But that's not the scary part. The scary part is they'd find it—and it really would be significant."

"Mystical mumbo jumbo. Undoubtedly the world would be better off were it less enamored of nicotine. Let's have something more specific."

"Cigarette?" I asked.

He just sat there.

"All right," I said. "Interpretive history. Dylan started out as the champ. In the early Sixties, on *Bob Dylan, The Freewheelin' Bob Dylan*, and 1964's *The Times They Are A-Changin'* he knocked out Woody Guthrie, Pete Seeger, the New Lost City Ramblers, Phil Ochs, and quite a few others. Later that year, *Another Side of Bob Dylan* parlayed some highly personal songs into left-right combinations of revolution-evolution that both looked back at folk and protest music and ahead toward rock & roll. He managed at least a draw or a TKO over the Beatles and the Rolling Stones in 1965 with *Bringing It All Back Home, Highway 61 Revisited,* and in 1966 with *Blonde on Blonde*—"

Cadwallader held up his hands in dismay. "I'm sure this is all very interesting," he said. "Do you think we could have it translated from pugilistic to at least pidgin English?"

I handed him a piece of paper that Ellen Willis had written.

> As composer, interpreter, most of all as lyricist, Dylan has made
> a revolution. He expanded folk idiom into a rich, figurative
> language, grafted literary and philosophical subtleties onto
> the protest song, revitalized folk vision by rejecting proletarian
> and ethnic sentimentality, then all but destroyed pure folk as
> a contemporary form by merging it with pop. Since then rock-
> and-roll, which was already in the midst of a creative flowering
> dominated by British rock and Motown, has been transformed.

After he'd read it he handed it to Miranda Abaloni. She read it and handed
it to me.

Cadwallader said: "Perhaps we're getting someplace. I could understand
that. Does Ms. Willis work with you?"

I shook my head. "I wish she did. The agency usually does its own reports."

"Yes," he said, making it sound like one of the longest words I'd ever heard.
Then: "Perhaps we could see one?"

I reached into the files and pulled out some prose about *Highway 61
Revisited, Blonde on Blonde,* and *John Wesley Harding.* I could see the paper
had browned to the color of the pages in the Tower editions of *Red Wind,
Spanish Blood, Blood Money,* and *The Adventures of Sam Spade and Other
Stories.* It looked the same as Miranda Abaloni's Boy Scout shirt. Almost
the same.

"Here," I said.

> On *Highway 61 Revisited,* Dylan's unyielding and poetic point
> of view represents a total commitment to the subjective over
> the objective, the microcosm over the macrocosm, man rather
> than mankind, problems not Problems. To put it as simply
> as possible, Dylan's tradition is that of all great artists—he
> attempts to project, with the highest possible degree of honesty
> and craftsmanship, a personal vision of the world we live in,
> knowing full well that unless the personal is achieved, the
> universal cannot follow.
>
> Not that it's painless. Dylan's concern on *Highway 61
> Revisited* is the classic American Dream—Innocence and
> Experience—a theme that has haunted American writers
> from Melville to Mailer. The music of Bob Dylan is the music
> of illusion and delusion, of men deluded by women, of men
> and women deluded by surface appearances, a music of the

tramp as explorer and the clown as happy victim, where the greatest crimes are lifelessness and the inability to see oneself as a circus performer in the show of life. Thus, in "Ballad of a Thin Man," Dylan will choose the life of emotion rather than the life of reason: "You have many contacts / Among the lumberjacks / To get you facts / When someone attacks your imagination." And again, in "Tombstone Blues," the outcry against "useless and pointless knowledge."

In "Desolation Row," we find ourselves in a dark, Felliniesque world of clowns and grotesques, but Dylan makes it clear that the tragic man is not the clown per se, but the clown who thinks he is something better. Accept chaos, he says, and advance from there: "Don't send me no more letters no / Not unless you mail them / From Desolation Row."

"Like a Rolling Stone" is the definitive statement that both personal and artistic fulfillment must come, in the main, by being truly on one's own. Dylan's social adversaries have twisted this to mean something very devious and selfish, but that is not the case at all. Dylan is simply kicking away the props to get to the heart of the matter: self-knowledge. The final

> You're invisible now, you got no secrets to
>   conceal
> How does it feel
> How does it feel
> To be on your own
> With no direction home
> Like a complete unknown
> Like a rolling stone?

is clearly optimistic and triumphant, a soaring of the spirit into a new and more productive present.[2]

2 Being interviewed for *No Direction Home* in 1995, Paul told Jeff Rosen: "When I first heard 'Like a Rolling Stone' the effect was almost entirely emotional. I don't know what I would compare it to. Dylan was a reader and the fact that he read poetry I guess had some effect. Ginsberg probably had some effect. But I don't know really where it came from. You couldn't call it R&B, you couldn't call it blues. It was just like somebody invented something. I hadn't heard anything like it.

  "It just seemed like a startling personal statement that seemed to sum up the times. One of the good things about the Sixties was a communal feeling that everybody was on the same page for a while when a Dylan record and a Stones record and a Beatles record came out. You knew what everybody was listening to that night basically. 'Like a Rolling Stone' just seemed to be an opening statement of what that was all about. I didn't see it as a selfish song at all. The whole take from the *Sing Out!* point was this is an incredibly selfish, solipsistic, evil, mean song—you know, it's against people—and I just saw it not at all that way, that it was a song about personal freedom."

Blonde on Blonde—the very title suggests the singularity and duality we expect from Dylan. His music has always carried within it its own unexplained tensions; optimism and pessimism merge and submerge amid fragmented icebergs of reality, yet both terms become finally meaningless because Dylan in the end truly *understands* situations, and once one truly understands anything, there can no longer be mere anger, no longer be moralizing, but only humor and compassion, only pity. And, ultimately, only a kind of shifting contradiction, a duality of emotion, a blonde on blonde, where all relationships can remain one, or become two, or fluctuate from between one and two.

In a Dylan song—"Visions of Johanna" or "Stuck Inside of Mobile with the Memphis Blues Again," for example—physical objects are no longer merely physical objects but become moral and intellectual properties as well; the whole world is flattened into a plasticity that is cerebral, not physical, and we are free to float with the images in all of their kinetic brilliance.

Released in 1968, *John Wesley Harding*, the first music Dylan presented to the public after his motorcycle accident in mid-1966, superimposes the literary complexity of both *Highway 61 Revisited* and *Blonde on Blonde* onto the alleged straightforwardness of Dylan's "return to folk music" in a manner rather like certain French directors (Jean-Luc Godard especially) who have taken American genre movies and added layers of twentieth-century philosophy to them. It is as if Jean-Paul Sartre were playing the five-string banjo and confining himself to stating all of his theories in words of under four letters. The folk element gains a Kafkaesque chimera and the philosophy a bedrock simplicity which leaves it all but invisible and thus easy to assimilate. While there is no rock & roll here, the warm, inherent mysticism of Southern Mountain music never quite sounded like this before.

Gideon Cadwallader and Miranda Abaloni read for a long time. I just sat and watched them. It was getting dark outside. My teeth were clenched.

Finally Cadwallader said: "Fragmentation without representation may not be tyranny, but neither is it aesthetically or politically sound. Tell me, do men ever delude women? Do you 'accept chaos'?"

I stared at him.

He said: "We don't exactly want the world 'flattened into a cerebral plasticity,' do we? I should think that you, particularly, wouldn't want that. Do you think of yourself as a 'clown'? A 'happy victim'?"

I didn't know what to say.

"Do you think of Ms. Abaloni as a clown? No, certainly not. One should always try to be 'something better,' don't you agree? Perhaps you prefer 'pity.' To be both emotional *and* deluded does not seem wonderful to me. Knowledge is seldom either 'useless' or 'pointless,' and there is a great difference between optimism and pessimism. As a detective you should deal more with facts, less with imagination—they *are*, after all, your business. Is a concern for mankind really that odious? Aren't the sentiments expressed in 'Like a Rolling Stone' a veritable hymn to monomaniacal selfishness? That Dylan can neither maintain nor retain any semblance of a coherent style suggests an identity problem of apocalyptic proportions. The man simply does not know who he is or why he hates both himself and his audience so much. If he does know he is unwilling to tell. I'm afraid I find his fecund fatalism quite appalling. This nonsense about 'duality' sounds like nothing so much as a diagnosis for schizophrenia. Perhaps a chronic inability either to see the world clearly or to come to grips with anything or anyone in it is what Dylan *and* his admirers suffer from."

"That's not what I wrote," I said.

"Isn't it?"

"Those reports are ten years old—"

"When you loved neither wisely nor too well," Gideon Cadwallader said.

I looked at Miranda Abaloni.

"Don't be too sure," I said.

IV.

After they had gone I won't say I wasn't worried. Passion has its potholes, I thought, and I had badly underestimated Cadwallader. No more.

Howard Hawks made a movie once called *The Thing*. The Thing was a manlike vegetable from outer space that went around killing people for sustenance. Robert Cornthwaite wanted to keep it alive for science, but Ken Tobey saw that wasn't possible. Both argued so well I never knew who was right. In the end they killed it.

Who was the Thing in this case?

I swung my feet up on the desk, thumbed a match, set fire to a cigarette, stared at the phonograph, and got ready to face the music. I had always prided myself on being a professional, an eye who looked up and straight into all that

197

heaven allowed. In my life there was always a new case, new clients, a few old ones who never left. Thus far I had managed to satisfy most of them—and myself as well—with the proper explanations at the proper time. This go-round I didn't feel half so lucky.

The Basement Tapes was playing. The music, put down in 1967 with the Band, between Dylan's accident and *John Wesley Harding*, was nine years old but it could have been made nine minutes or nine decades ago; it wouldn't have mattered. It had once been illegal, sold under the counter. Hell, even now, on sale free and clear, it wasn't complete—these things never are. It still *sounded* illegal.

"Goin' to Acapulco" came on. The song was about everything it wasn't about as well as what it was about, if you know what I mean. I thought it was probably about Miranda Abaloni. Beauty does that to me sometimes.

What a case, I thought. On the one hand, randiness, roots, memory, archetypal American music and its obsession with mystery and death. All there and all true. On the other, sweet revenge in the form of Gideon Cadwallader wooing the white-hot center with the blowtorch of reason.

I asked myself if I'd ever touched the white-hot center of anything.

V.

He looked particularly smug the next day. Even his sallowness seemed freshly polished, and he beamed like a pale yellow sun coming out of the pollution just to shine on Miranda Abaloni. Who was walking up the hall toward us.

"We'd like to talk about women," he said.

I said: "Here comes one now."

He made a face.

I hit him with a sheaf of reports.

> Between 1969 and 1975, Dylan's career slumped badly. After *John Wesley Harding*, he ignored the abyss and tried to convince the world he was just another happily married family man. On *Nashville Skyline* (1969) and *Self Portrait* (1970), he challenged such country singers as Elvis Presley, Hank Williams, the Everly Brothers, Johnny Cash, Jerry Lee Lewis, et al., and, for the first time, got routed. *New Morning* (1970) was a mediocre comeback album, the individuality and ambition apparently gone. It wasn't that he made foolish moves, but no moves at all. *Dylan* (1973) scraped the bottom of the barrel—outtakes released without

his consent. Because the expectations for them ran so high, *Planet Waves* and *Before the Flood*, both recorded with the Band in 1974, were the severest disappointments of all. Only 1973's *Pat Garrett & Billy the Kid*, an LP as wrongly underrated as the earlier *Another Side of Bob Dylan*, reinvestigated the old myths, albeit mostly without words. "Knockin' on Heaven's Door" and especially the instrumental, "Final Theme," are songs well suited for either weddings or funerals.

One of the surprising things about the Dylan/Band *Before the Flood* tour was how impersonal and uninteresting it was, how devoid of urgency and emotional credibility. There are those of us who are possessed and those of us not possessed, and with Dylan possession would seem to be nine-tenths of the law. Dispossessed, he apparently had to resort to the delirious pace and pose of a B-movie gangster, sacrificing both stylistic intangibles and the very meaning of the songs for sheer speed in order to create the impression of anger, a handle on which to hang what little real action there was. It sounded fine for a song or two, but the false action soon fostered more effort than effect. Onstage, he seemed absolutely harmless. Did these songs—most of his great ones—no longer mean anything to him or had he simply been away from live performance for too many years? Perhaps he had something else on his mind.

"How easy you make it for me," Cadwallader said. "I need hardly comment on six years of waste. It is odd to equate them with a happy marriage, though. According to you, Dylan would seem better off an aesthetical but antisocial misfit."

"You have a gift for small truths, Cadwallader. But they just won't grow into bigger ones for you because you have no regard for context—and it's that kind of case. Your machine's broken. It's stuck on zero. It subtracts but won't add."

"Tell me, do you think Dylan would consider Ms. Abaloni an 'angel' or a 'bitch'? I believe those are the terms most often used to describe his attitude toward women. Saviors or destroyers—and ne'er the twain shall meet?"

"I think you'd better read the next report," I said.

"Look at her," he said. "Would their union be fire and brimstone, a dark ceremony consummated in some puritanical Midwestern tabernacle, the male cowering in fear and drooling with holiness? Or would he simply send her a postcard from time to time telling her how he wrote 'Sad-Eyed Lady of the Lowlands'?"

"I think their union would probably be lovely," I said.

His marriage rumored troubled, his recent tour and albums treated somewhat indifferently by a less-than-worshipful press, Bob Dylan seems haunted and uncertain again, and that may be very good news. If ironical, such a statement would be both cheap and cruel, but irony has little to do with Dylan's current marital situation, however it may turn out, or with the near-total success of 1975's *Blood on the Tracks*. Ambiguousness seems a word more apt for this romantic rethink. When the adventurer Jay Gatsby finally got his Daisy alone, "He knew that when he kissed this girl and forever wed his unutterable visions to her perishable breath, his mind would never romp again like the mind of God." What to do when ambiguity and the realization of the quest prove inseparable? Either crack up or become a sadder, wiser man. Because he is strong, Bob Dylan has chosen the latter course.

If *Nashville Skyline, New Morning*, and *Planet Waves* were essentially about the stable joys of marriage, family, and a happy home in rich bluegrass country, much of *Blood on the Tracks* emanates from a rented room in the dark, bohemian section of town where one can listen to the trains at night. It is to Dylan's great credit that he condemns neither circumstance: like most of us, he is an outcast who dreams of the possibility of a fusion of the two extremes. He began his career as a loner, reveling in the intangibles and uncertainties of his life, but then dropped out of contact and context into the sheltered opulence of rural Woodstock and began sending back platitudes which were as surprising as they were unbelievable. The nadir of this movement was reached with *Planet Waves*, whereon Dylan seemed almost to turn himself inside out in an agonizing and futile effort to convince both us and himself how incredibly content he was. The unintended effect was far from pleasant.

If subterranean tension won out over an overwrought tenderness on *Planet Waves*, the reverse curiously holds true on *Blood on the Tracks*. There is a great deal of personal pain here, and second thoughts abound ("I can change, I swear"), but everything seems deliberately cushioned by myth, distanced by meditative rumination and an artful overview of the lifetimes of ritual staying, leaving, or being told to go which all of us inevitably experience and reexperience. This is the way it is for me now, Dylan appears to be saying, and this is the way it has been and will be again for both of us: something lost, something gained. "Tangled Up in Blue" seems a more than appropriate phrase for this saddest and most beautiful of myths.

Although *Blood on the Tracks* is aptly named, it is hardly the wasteland of pessimism and self-hatred that some critics have claimed. Far from it. The album is vital and alive, its despair tempered throughout with the joy of being a survivor, all senses intact, whose dreams are still made of iron and steel.

"Egotistical, exploitative, and profoundly sexist," said Cadwallader. "Elegant romantic hogwash. We—"

"We?" I looked at Miranda Abaloni and asked: "Have you ever heard 'Ballad in Plain D,' Miss Abaloni? 'To Ramona'? 'Love Minus Zero/No Limit'? 'If You See Her, Say Hello'? 'Sara'?"

She nodded.

"If you were to fall in love with Bob Dylan, Miss Abaloni, and he lucky enough to be in love with you, how much do you think his politics would disturb whatever was good about the relationship?"

Gideon Cadwallader stared.

As she held up her hand, thumb and forefinger extended.

The space between her fingers was barely wide enough to let through any light at all.

VI.

I was on my fourth carton of cigarettes, and time was running out fast. I knew I had to take a shot at it soon, but no man likes to play the fool. Truths? There were no truths in this case. I had known that for a long time, that and little else. In death and matters of the heart, we are all of us amateurs, someone once said. Maybe it was me.[3]

Gideon Cadwallader and Miranda Abaloni were reading reports.

Nineteen-seventy-five was to be the true beginning of a new era for Bob Dylan, not 1974. All along the watchtower, he had

---

3 "I literally meant that," Paul said, "I didn't know whether it was me or not. I had to check it out with research and say, 'Can you find this in any *Familiar Quotations*, because it sounds like something?' And nobody could find it. Somebody might come and point it out in a book to me and it wouldn't surprise me. I think I made it up, but I don't know."

missed it by one. *Blood on the Tracks* and *Desire* (January, 1976) were the LPs that convinced us once and for all of his love for his wife Sara; the ubiquitous Rolling Thunder Revue, not the *Before the Flood* tour, made us believe he had not thrown it all away as a live performer. After living for two years in Los Angeles, he returned to the streets of New York City, and once again as it had fourteen years earlier, Manhattan's magic took hold of him. He even looked like the Kid again. In *The Go-Between*, L.P. Hartley wrote: "The past is a foreign country: they do things differently there." Sometimes, but not invariably. For Bob Dylan, the postman always rings twice.

Desire may be a very special album, but it's also Part Two of *Blood on the Tracks*. About that LP Greil Marcus wrote: "At once, the tale of an adventurer's war with a woman and with himself, and a shattering attempt to force memory, fantasy, and the terrors of love and death to serve an artist's impulse to redeem disaster by making beauty out of it.... [The] songs are as obvious and as unsettling as the weather; no one can fail to understand them, and no one can get to the bottom of them, either.... The odyssey of a mythical lover possessed by an affair he can never resolve."

More than any other Dylan album, *Desire* hews to the lifeline, is closer to eternity, at times seems to be looking right over the edge. Surely one of its themes has to do with the mythopoeic, *eternal* consequences of a man's actions and/or What Might Have Been. There is *real* death in these songs, and the acknowledgment of it lurks behind them like some strangely benevolent shadow: "Time is an ocean but it ends at the shore / You may not see me / Tomorrow."

"Sex and death, death and sex," Cadwallader said. "Perhaps we are dealing with the *real* Bob Dylan here. A specious—"

"No," I said slowly, rolling the syllable across my tongue like a billiard ball on the table of night. "No." I bit off the end of the word sharply.

"You don't—"

I said it again. Twice.

Nobody said anything for a while. I let a cigarette burn down between my fingers until it made a small red mark. It had been that kind of caper. The end was very near. I could feel it on the back of my neck. Suddenly I felt very sad.

"He *is* guilty, you know," Cadwallader said. "I think that is significant." Somehow it seemed important to him.

"Fine," I said. "He's guilty. But guilty of what, Cadwallader? Of caring enough to want it all—the myth *and* the reality? You want to destroy one under the guise of protecting the other, and that's such a tiny ambition for a man of your intelligence. Even if you manage it, what have you done? Rid the world of romance? Christ, you can find anyone guilty if that's all you want to do, but someday you'll have to take a stand of your own without checking the book first. Then some bright guy will walk into your office and tell you you're full of it, and then what will you do?"

"You haven't exactly solved the case," he said. He acted like a sulky child.

"No," I said thickly. My face was set hard and deeply lined. "I haven't solved the case and I don't intend to. No one will ever figure out Dylan the way you want to—somehow it would be indecent. He's tried to hit the longest home runs in the history of rock & roll, and I respect him for that. I don't know what his values are because they keep moving, but I suspect they're at least as good as mine. That's enough for me."

"You're not serious," he said. "You don't expect me to think—"

"I don't care what you think," I said.

VII.

I nodded toward the inner office to indicate that I was going in there, and went in there. I picked up a piece of paper about the Rolling Thunder Revue benefit for Rubin Carter, then a prisoner in New Jersey. Dylan had raised a lot of money to free him.

When a man's case is in shambles, he's supposed to do something about it, I kept thinking. It doesn't make any difference what you thought of it. It was your case and you're supposed to do something about it. I gave the report to Cadwallader.

> It is 9:57 p.m. Suddenly, Bob Dylan, looking like a cross between a New Mexico gypsy and a glittery New York Doll, is in front of the microphone, lining out "When I Paint My Masterpiece." When Dylan leans triumphantly into a line that isn't even on the recorded version—"It sure has been *one helluva life!*"—I feel a rush of excitement (for him? for me?). On "It Ain't Me, Babe," his Chaplinesque harmonica playing drives the crowd into a frenzy. When the harmonica comes out, it's like the real Dylan has arrived.

"The Lonesome Death of Hattie Carroll" is Dylan's best protest song, and he sings it now with a staccato anger and authority so intense and pure that a later rendering of the similar but inferior "Hurricane" is musically, if not politically, anticlimactic. Dylan avoids sentimentality by fusing fire and ice in "Hattie Carroll," and this mixture of rage and severity, when combined with the near-brutal austerity of his singing, somehow suggests a cosmic system of justice so infinite and implacable that the courts and judges of this world seem worth taking seriously only until the purge comes. I can feel it breathing down my neck right now.[4]

I don't know what to say about the trilogy of songs with which Bob Dylan closes the concert. "Sara," "Just Like a Woman," and "Knockin' on Heaven's Door," in the context offered here, are so clearly about the Dylans' amorphous marital situation that perhaps the only correct response is to cry—which I almost do, which he almost does. From "Sara, oh Sara / Don't ever leave me / Don't ever go" to "Yes, I believe it's time for us to quit" to "Mama, take these tears from my eyes," I feel the story of all of our lives—and it's very complicated. Unforgettable would not be too strong a word. It seems significant enough at the time.

I said: "Listen. This isn't a damned bit of good. You'll never understand me, but I'll try once more and then we'll give it up."

He looked worried. His eyes, the color of unset rhinestones, darkened, lightened, got darker again.

"All right," he said.

"Listen. First, when a man has tried to remain whole and tell the truth against all the odds, you get an idea he might be special. It doesn't matter that he makes mistakes, he's still special. Second, it happens we're both in the detective business. Well, when one of your own gets threatened, it's bad business to stand by and let it happen—bad business all around. Third, the songs of Bob Dylan are the hardest, toughest, sweetest, saddest, funniest, wisest songs I know, but I don't know what they're about. Friendship, sex, death, heroism, learning from others, I guess. History and inevitability are in there too. If there are tests, they've all been passed, and what you're hearing are the results. Serious comedy. Deadpan tragedy. That's—"

4 "That's my favorite," Paul said of "Hattie Carroll" when discussing with Lucinda Williams his disdain for topical songwriting, "because he really makes you feel for that person rather than preaching at you. Those are the best kind, where you feel the person and then you feel the larger picture, as well."

He said: "I think—"

"Wait till I'm through and then you can talk. Fourth, I've no reason in God's world to think I can trust you. If I did I'd have to hate all those men and women who aren't afraid to make fools of themselves. Next, I know we need people like you because a world filled with romantics would be a disaster, but a world without them would be worse. That's five of them. The sixth would be that these are inspired times—I respond to myths and so do you. Even you, Cadwallader. You and Miranda Abaloni. But you'll never win her. Even if she wanted you you'd be terrified to really fall in love with her because she might not be perfect and one day you might have to do a job on her. Seventh, you can't accept a set of values that takes in loss—and myths *need* loss. They thrive on it. Allen Ginsberg said of Dylan: 'Who woulda thought he'd say it, so everybody'd finally know him, same soul crying vulnerable caught in a body we all are?—enough Person revealed to make Whitman's whole nation weep.' And eighth—but that's enough. Maybe some of them are unimportant. I won't argue about that. But look at the number of them. Now on the other side we've got what? All we've got is the fact that you want one hard, clean answer."

"I do," he whispered. "Whether you do or not."

"I don't. I won't play the sap for you. As far as I'm concerned, make him a hero because he's the best failure we've got. I like them like that. You want to solve the case? Get another detective."

"I don't want another detective," said Miranda Abaloni.

I jammed on my hat and we went out into the rain. Together.

SLOW TRAIN COMING

Jann Wenner considers this record a masterpiece, and maybe you should listen to him.[5] Here's what I think: Now that Dylan doesn't have Sara to kick around or to kick him around anymore, he's nailed himself to Christ's cross and is blaming us for not understanding his latest martyrdom. Jesus, Bob, they're really not killing Christians in 1979. Worry about your lyrics instead. I'd be more sympathetic if you didn't sound so damn mean-spirited and close-minded about your newfound faith. Next time, don't use the Aphex Aural Depressor.[6]

5 Wenner reviewed the album himself for *Rolling Stone*. "And he just kept rewriting it and rewriting it," Stephen Holden says, "and rewriting it and rewriting it." And Paul had to edit it.

6 As harsh as this capsule critique might seem, it nowhere near approaches Paul's disgust with Dylan's *Shot of Love* album in 1981. "Truth be known," he wrote, "my initial reaction was just another example of the old and familiar Bob Dylan syndrome: i.e., because the man's past achievements have meant so much to so many of us, we tend to give his newest work the benefit of every doubt. No more. For me, it stops right here."

A good friend of Dylan's happened to be in Jann Wenner's office at *Rolling Stone* and had the opportunity to read the review before it went to print. When he heard what Paul had written, Dylan, incredibly angry and hurt, sent word to Wenner that he'd better not run the piece. To his credit, Wenner insisted that he'd never pull a review—but the incident undoubtedly contributed to his decision, later that same year, to issue a decree as to how all future records were to be reviewed in *Rolling Stone*.

BOB DYLAN AT BUDOKAN

What, besides God, has happened to this man?

UNDER THE RED SKY

Like a lot of good Bob Dylan records, *Under the Red Sky* deliberately raises more questions than it intends to answer, yet I can't think of another Dylan album that's ever done so in quite this way or been as difficult to pin down. Many of the songs here seem both innocent and apocalyptic, comic and sad, at the same time. The lyrics often strike a somewhat bizarre but genuinely haunting balance between children's tales and biblical fables, most sounding childlike fresh and as ancient as eternity. More than anything else, *Under the Red Sky* seems to revel in its own mysteriousness, to celebrate the twang of the weird and just how fantastically strange and unbelievable everything we see and know and do is.

Musically, Dylan gathers up a sort of farm-team Traveling Wilburys (George Harrison, Elton John, Randy Jackson, David Crosby, Al Kooper, Slash, Stevie Ray Vaughan, David Lindley, Waddy Wachtel, Bruce Hornsby and others all pitch in on various tracks) who sound anonymously exultant and not supersession stiff. When Kooper kicks off the title tune and "Handy Dandy" with some catchy, *Highway 61 Revisited*-style organ playing and Dylan launches into a goofy talking song ("TV Song") reminiscent of those on his early albums, we think we know where we are, and it's a comfortable place for both Dylan and us. Then the words make us wonder.

"Wiggle Wiggle" starts like a classic double-entendre rock & roll song but soon pushes into scary, disturbing territory ("Wiggle 'til it bites, wiggle 'til it cuts... / Wiggle 'til you vomit fire"). Everything seems pastoral for the little boy and girl in "Under the Red Sky" until they're "baked in a pie" and Dylan sings, "This is the key to the kingdom and this is the town / This is the blind horse that leads you around." "Born in Time" is a torchy love song, timelessly happy and unhappy, while "God Knows" suggests that lovers—and people—can get through anything with belief and perseverance. "It's Unbelievable" and "Cat's in the Well" indicate that there's a lot to get through, with more on the horizon.

So far, my favorite songs on *Under the Red Sky* are "10,000 Men" and "2 X 2," a pair of biblical-sounding stunners that are as wonderfully impossible to summarize and grasp as they are to forget, and "Handy Dandy," which takes off on a "Like a Rolling Stone" riff and just doesn't quit. All this is subject to revision, though, because further listenings—and there'll be plenty—could well lead to new alleys, and who knows for sure what's here, except mystery and a casual mixture of major and minor that sounds like a deliberately throwaway masterpiece?[7]

---

7 This was Paul's last published piece about one of Dylan's albums. "It was a very tough one to write about," he told Bruce Hornsby. "I didn't say this in the review—and I didn't think of it till now—but it has some of the sort of goofiness of *The Basement Tapes*, I guess. That sort of mystery, maybe a little bit more comic than that. I thought he just sort of winged it, and it happened to come off pretty great."

- ELLIOTT MURPHY -

Elliott Murphy was Paul Nelson's rock & roll dream incarnate. The singer-songwriter's music was rooted as much in literary traditions—F. Scott Fitzgerald, Hemingway, and detective fiction—and films as it was Bo Diddley and Bob Dylan. The two men met in Paul's office at Mercury in January of 1973.

"He was the exact opposite of what I thought a record company guy was going to be like," Murphy remembers, "not a jive bone in his body." As his demo tape played, he thought he saw a subtle reaction behind the dark glasses. "He just gave some kind of grunt that was more emphatic than his negative grunt. When he really loved something he'd take an extra puff on his Sherman and that was about it."

Paul's professional courtship of the twenty-three-year-old Murphy extended beyond the two-Coke lunches at La Strada. Paul supplied him with early Dylan bootlegs and, with special import, presented him with the just released debut album by another East Coast troubadour. Paul told him to listen carefully. Bruce Springsteen's Greetings from Asbury Park, N.J. *immediately influenced Murphy. "Not so much in my own approach to music, but it gave me so much confidence." Paul soon took Murphy to see Springsteen play Max's Kansas City and, after the show, introduced them.*

At Paul's spartan apartment, where the myriad of books and LPs created an orbit around the bed, TV, stereo, and the IBM Selectric typewriter situated

213

on a board suspended between two sawhorse legs, Murphy noticed footprints low on the wall where Paul planted his feet and did one hundred sit-ups every day. Paul pulled open a drawer and took out two handguns, a .357 Magnum and a snub-nosed .38. Paul said he wanted to write a detective novel and, if he were going to write about guns, he needed to know how they felt in his hand.[1]

Despite Paul's enthusiasm, the Mercury hierarchy remained lukewarm about Murphy, offering only a conservative $5,000 advance with a minimal royalty. Underwhelmed, Murphy said he'd think about it. By the next day, he and his brother/bandmate Matthew secured a $10,000 offer from Polydor. Murphy took the counterbid back to Paul, whose boss Charlie Fach refused to go higher than $7,500.

Murphy asked Paul what to do. "I felt some kind of allegiance to him because he had really discovered me, so to speak. He became my mentor." Paul told him to accept the Polydor deal. If things didn't work out for the New York Dolls, who hadn't yet signed with Mercury (they would the following week), then Paul's days were numbered. "He said that if he wasn't there, then nothing would happen with me and it would just be a contract I'd be trying to get out of."

Murphy signed with Polydor and recorded his debut album, Aquashow. *Paul dropped in on several of the sessions on the tenth floor of Record Plant East, where, down on the first floor, the Dolls were recording their first LP.* Aquashow *was released in November and Paul wrote about it a couple of months later. A budding singer-songwriter (from Long Island or anywhere else) couldn't have hoped for a better coming out: Paul's eloquent rave landed on the opening spread of the record-review section, right beside a critique of Springsteen's sophomore effort,* The Wild, the Innocent & the E Street Shuffle. *And while Paul went out of his way to downplay any easy comparisons to Bob Dylan, a careless pull quote subverted his efforts: his line, "Aquashow is easily the best Dylan LP since* John Wesley Harding," *was turned into the title "He's the Best Dylan Since 1968," thereby sealing Murphy's fate as the next "new Dylan." Nevertheless, what Paul wrote about* Aquashow *was as personal and heartfelt as Murphy's creation of it. When the singer sang that he was "Waiting for some dream lover like a Great Gatsby," it might as well have been Paul behind the microphone.*

---

1 Citing the same rationale in a 1972 journal entry, Paul had written that he bought the guns for a new screenplay he was writing. William MacAdams believes there was a more immediate reason for purchasing them: "Movies, of course. He got them when he was living on East Fifty-Eighth, a direct result of *Dirty Harry.*" According to MacAdams, Paul knew someone from Connecticut who acquired the guns for him: "Considering how Paul sold off everything he had that could be turned to cash, he was afraid to sell the guns, even if he could find a buyer, lest he get his friend in trouble." Though he never fired them, for many years Paul kept both handguns, along with a third (a .22) and ammunition for each, in his bedroom in a disposable Styrofoam container.

Eighteen months of wrestling with creative and corporate demons passed before Murphy's next album came out, 1975's Lost Generation. *Paul, whose own professional wrestling match had ended when he left Mercury in January and returned to freelancing, stayed in touch throughout. At one point he approached Murphy about serving as his manager. "It would have been pretty strange, Bruce Springsteen managed by Jon Landau and me managed by Paul Nelson. I just don't think at that point I could imagine Paul doing the business."*

If Paul had, in writing about Aquashow, *confessed his rock & roll ideal, his review of* Lost Generation *identified the desires and devils at the heart of the artist—all artists, not just Murphy—and at the same time embraced them as his own. One of Paul's most obliquely confessional, academic, and, with its miasmic array of references and quotations, challenging works, it's all about "the dangers that can befall those who are hung up on heroes."*

"I have often been accused of being the critic most friendly to Elliott Murphy's work," Paul's review of Elliott Murphy's third LP, 1976's Night Lights, *began, "a charge to which I happily plead guilty...."*[2] *Murphy: "I also think there were forces around him saying, 'Okay, Paul, this is Elliott's third album and he still hasn't broken. So maybe you need to use a little more of an objective eye or an objective ear with him.'" Over at* Rolling Stone, *Dave Marsh wrote:*

> In 1973 and 1974 it seemed to many of us in New York that it was a tossup whether Bruce Springsteen, the native poet of the mean streets, or Elliott Murphy, the slumming suburbanite with the ironic eye, would become a national hero first. Well, we all know how that turned out ...[3]

Paul's 1977 review of Just a Story from America *was short and not so sweet. Whereas his expansive notices for the first three albums had each clocked in at over 1,200 words, this time around he said what he had to say in a fourth of that. Straining to call the record one of the year's best and ending with a lovely coda, his sense of disappointment and regret was palpable.*

Chris Connelly: "Part of how you be a good critic is you're willing to be touched, you're willing for the magic to strike you. What was so poignant about Paul was that he kept his heart open like that. If it means that an artist

---

2 Never shy about borrowing from his own work, six years earlier he'd written: "For the past several years, this writer has often been accused of being overly partial to the works of Bob Dylan. It is a charge to which I happily plead guilty."
3 "Elliott Murphy—*Night Lights*" by Dave Marsh from *Rolling Stone*, April 8, 1975. © Rolling Stone LLC. All rights reserved. Reprinted by permission.

who didn't fulfill his promise got to him, well, that's the way it goes. That's cool. That speaks to his openness."

Murphy: "I never thought Paul would write just a glowing review about everything I did. I knew his integrity was completely solid. If he didn't like something he would tell me and he would write about it, if he wanted to."

Regarding Paul's relationship between himself and the artists with whom he became friends, Fred Schruers says, "He wanted their respect and he didn't want them to disappoint him, that's for sure. Likewise, he didn't want to disappoint them. So he would write the piece. If he had to damn somebody who strayed into something he felt was artistically unproductive, he would write that story, but it was painful for him."

When Paul interviewed Murphy for the article "Elliott Murphy's Career: This Side of Paradox," his review of Just a Story from America hadn't yet run. "I was aware that Paul had reservations about the album and probably about what was happening to me personally, as well. I was addicted to cocaine, stopped touring, broke up my marriage, gave all my money to the IRS, left my management, and generally did everything I could to fuck up my career."

Though Paul never wrote about Elliott Murphy again, they remained in touch. Murphy fondly recalls one time in Paul's office in 1980 when the two friends cocked their heads and strained their ears to decipher the lyrics of Joy Division's newest single, "Love Will Tear Us Apart." Paul thought the song was "magic." "His taste was so much more eclectic than you would imagine for the founder of The Little Sandy Review, and his office was so much messier than you could imagine for a writer who wrote such architecturally perfect paragraphs."

The Eighties proved difficult for both men. After Paul resigned from Rolling Stone, he occasionally met Murphy for lunch at Jackson Hole. He still ordered two Cokes but, in place of the veal piccata that he'd enjoyed during better times at La Strada, now he ordered a hamburger.

"It was hard to reach out to Paul. You knew he was in trouble, but he was never needy in that way. When he needed money, he just asked me if I wanted to buy his F. Scott Fitzgerald first editions; he didn't ask if I could loan him money." He still has Paul's copy of The Great Gatsby. "I didn't want him to sell it to somebody else because he's the one who connected Gatsby to rock & roll for me."

One October evening in 1985, Paul met up with William MacAdams at Tramps on West Twenty-First Street to see Murphy perform. Both men arrived with heavy hearts. Earlier that day their hero Orson Welles had died. It was a bad night for Murphy, too, and having Paul there to witness it in an audience of only twenty-five or so made it even worse.

After the concert, Paul and Murphy lingered and danced around their goodbyes. They talked about Bruce Springsteen, but not about how huge a success he'd become. They reminisced about their old days together when Paul had reviewed Aquashow *and* Lost Generation, *and Murphy "thought it was all going to be okay."*

Pausing at the door, looking just as he had when Murphy first set eyes on him a dozen years earlier—same glasses, hat, moustache, a smoldering Nat Sherman stuck between his lips—Paul looked back at Murphy and said, "Well, it could have gone either way." It was a farewell scene worthy of Raymond Chandler.

After Murphy moved to Paris in 1990, he paid tribute to Paul in the liner notes of a CD reissue of Aquashow. *"I sent him a CD, but I don't know if he ever saw it."[4]*

"In some way, I always felt that I let Paul down, that I didn't keep my eye on the prize, that I became victim to my own image, that my lifestyle became more important than my music, that I surrounded myself with the wrong people, that I betrayed his belief in me. And that if I had not made the selfish mistakes I did, then somehow I would have saved Paul. I know it's a fantasy, but it haunts me to this day. I feel somehow responsible for what happened to him—even if that makes no sense to anyone but me."

K.A.

---

4 Paul indeed kept the *Aquashow* CD, as well as a poster from the album's original release.

HE'S THE BEST DYLAN
SINCE 1968

These days, some of us are beginning to realize we have spent far too much time stuck in the middle of some glorious and familiar Sixties boomtown, and that, while the area still has its attractions, a lot of the real action now takes place up the street. Re contemporary music, perhaps a majority of our overcivilized band of Dylan-Beatles-Stones despairados have long championed the belief that, while there are some interesting newcomers, there are no new heroes (nothing, really nothing, to turn off); with the possible exceptions of Rod Stewart and the Who, no one has entered the white rock & roll pantheon since the aforementioned golden triumvirate—and, so the argument goes, no one ever will again.

Unfortunately, in a generalized Nixonian state of the union, this safe, dead-end frame of mind, whether right or wrong, has managed somehow to pass for realism; under such circumstances, perhaps only reunion, nostalgia, and endless intermarriages are possible: Once-young Billy the Kid has evolved himself into Pat Garrett who, threatened by a darkening vision, too quickly shoots down the new Billys because they are not the old Billys.

Well, it's 1974, and a brace of fully qualified William Bonneys has arrived. If rock & roll is to grow, prevalent myths may be overthrown (or at least damaged a little), and the new set of upstarts must be allowed the respectful and necessary dual ritual function of slaying the founding fathers while simultaneously carrying on the old traditions. An auteur theory of popular music should not and does not preclude new heroes, and the best of these— Elliott Murphy, Jackson Browne, the New York Dolls, Bruce Springsteen, Jonathan Richman from the Modern Lovers—have learned, rejected, relearned, and now pay homage to their respective influencers by working peripherally in their genres in mathematics-without-damage fashion. Murphy, Springsteen, Lou Reed, and Mott the Hoople mine the Dylan genre much as Dylan himself once mined Woody Guthrie's and Jack Elliott's; all of these people are murderers and creators, but they are not imitators. If you persist in that folly, then Richman is Reed without tears, the Dolls are the Stones with youthful fangs, Murphy's *Aquashow* is easily the best Dylan LP since *John Wesley Harding* (definitely including those by the master), and Browne's *For Everyman* is quite possibly the finest Byrds-Beach Boys-California album ever.

"The quiet lights in the houses were humming out into the darkness and there was a stir and bustle among the stars. Out of the corner of his eye Gatsby saw that the blocks of the sidewalks really formed a ladder and mounted to a secret place above the trees—he could climb to it, if he climbed alone, and once there he could suck on the pap of life, gulp down the incomparable milk of wonder." Although F. Scott Fitzgerald wrote those lines on Long Island in the Twenties about a different kind of romantic hero, he could have been talking about a spiritual descendant who also chose to be photographed in the Plaza:[5] Elliott James Murphy, twenty-four, and also in quest of myths, born of once-rich and internationally famous show-business parents (father now dead), high-school surfer king, world traveler (a trip to Key West to see what Hemingway found there, down and out in Europe and Hollywood), pragmatic idyllist (he once helped his girl escape from a private school in Switzerland, then rowed to freedom at night across a lake as in *A Farewell to Arms*), movie hopeful (a part in *Fellini's Roma* and a real desperation to play Jesse James), et cetera, ad infinitum.

For someone who sounds as if he invented his life from film fantasies and his favorite Twenties novels, Murphy in person is a likable, totally believable, extraordinarily intelligent young man who sometimes seems caught in the shadow world of the potential teenage tragic hero (James Dean's crushed idealism, astonishing good looks, and some classic AM-radio songs: "Last of the Rock Stars," "Hangin' Out") and the gates-of-Eden, strawberry-fields, no-expectations-land of the true gods of rock & roll. It's nice work, if you can get it.

Musically, *Aquashow* acknowledges its debt to *Highway 61 Revisited* and *Blonde on Blonde* (the organ and harmonica, the full, anthem-like sound of the band), but I'm inclined to believe that any Dylan-Murphy comparison is meaningful only because it isn't completely meaningless. Murphy may sound like what people *think* Dylan sounded like in the mid-Sixties, but a careful replay of the records in question should prove the resemblance superficial at best. Vocally, although both are great rock & roll singers, the two are miles

---

5 Paul is referring to *Aquashow*'s front cover shot. Murphy had requested that photographer Jack Mitchell shoot in the Palm Court of the Plaza Hotel. "That's where part of *The Great Gatsby* took place, and I also wanted a blurry circular frame to the photo like Bob Dylan's *Bringing It All Back Home*."

apart. Murphy's lyrics are solid, direct, and at times less magical and less naïve than many of Dylan's, but they get the job done with equal artistry; Elliott writes about himself and those he knows in specific situations and is far more concerned with the actual past, present, and future Seventies myths and archetypes of a Long Island super-punk with too much brains and too many heroes than he is about creating an alternative science-fiction world filled with people totally transformed from their own reality by a more visionary point of view. Murphy pins his hometowners, suburban teenagers, and families to the wall as if they were characters in some modern-day Walker Evans FSA photo, and not a stream-of-consciousness allegory.

Dylan's major and most credible theme in the Sixties was one of being rootlessly on your own ("Like a Rolling Stone"); in the Seventies, Jackson Browne, who writes about the costs of staying or leaving, gave us a new anthem, "For Everyman," in many ways a complete reversal of Dylan's earlier stand. Murphy, escape in his heart, tries to understand his roots both realistically ("How's the Family," "Hometown," "White Middle Class Blues," "Graveyard Scrapbook") and symbolically ("Like a Great Gatsby" unites two idols: Dylan and Fitzgerald), but no matter where he goes (to the alleged high spots of the world in "Hangin' Out"), he finds himself in the same place ("I won't be there like some dead fly caught in your lampshade"), desperation setting in:

> And don't tell me you don't hear that hometown
>   calling you
> 'Cause you know what, baby, you're still doing all the
>   same things
> You used to do
> Whoa, whoa, darling, you never used to wait till
>   tomorrow
> And now you can't wait at all.

He seems to want something better ("I got two thousand years of the Christian blues"), something with the glories of F. Scott and Ernest's Paris ("Do you ride on ancient ships under Doctor Eckleburg's eyes to heaven / Ticket 1927"), but the hoped-for conversion never takes place: "Waiting for some dream lover like a Great Gatsby / And then I look into the mirror and it's only me."

But Murphy's magic should be enjoyed, not analyzed; his songs are complex, but not difficult: They are always about something that touches us all. Any one of us can understand the agonized mythic ecstasy of the "boy who knows he's gotta play" rock & roll guitar and be a star ("Last of the Rock Stars"—and Elliott is as good a guitar player as he is a songwriter), the decline of Fitzgerald's West Eggers into creatures from Dylan's Desolation Row and Peter Townshend's teenage wasteland ("Hometown"), the lack of communication within families ("How's the Family" "White Middle Class Blues") and between men and women ("Graveyard Scrapbook," "Like a Great Gatsby" and even "Marilyn," a song in which male moviegoers misunderstand the late Marilyn Monroe). There is a lot of pessimism and real terror here ("But now your world begins with never"), but some hope, too ("And if you love the thought of love / Your birth will never end"), because the artist never loses his great compassion or his ability to look at personal relationships.

Aquashow, well produced by Peter K. Siegel, ends with a love song, "Don't Go Away," one of the most beautiful in popular music.[6] Since Elliott Murphy and his work will be with us as long as we have rock & roll, I suggest we play it now.

> Who'd mind
> While we're out
> Anyway?

---

6 Paul had written about Siegel's old group, the Even Dozen Jug Band, a decade earlier in *Sing Out!* and had contributed the liner notes to the band's one and only album.

LOST GENERATION*

It's not so teenage anymore.

—"Lookin' Back"

Elliott Murphy's first album, *Aquashow*, released eighteen months ago, showed exceptional promise and intelligence, prompting many, myself included, to ready a place in the higher echelons of rock & roll for the talented Long Islander. Now, after a lengthy season of hard times—new label, new manager, new producer—Murphy returns to stand, deliver, and collect. On *Lost Generation*, a brilliant but extraordinarily difficult LP, the artist is hurt, angry, and confused by the shifting role of the hero in modern times and the growing division between intoxicating myth and sobering reality in his personal and public lives.

If we are all, to some extent, a compilation of those whom we most admire, Murphy takes it a huge step further; he *needs* heroes, desires dreams, for personal and artistic sustenance. He wears his idols—most of them, significantly, dead ("The past is all that lasts," he has written elsewhere)—proudly on his sleeve: James Dean, Greta Garbo, Scott Fitzgerald, Ezra Pound, Ernest Hemingway, Lord Byron, Jimi Hendrix, Brian Jones, and Lou Reed are all characters in this album. Haunted by their singular accomplishments and trapped by their collective unrealized expectations, none so different from his own, the artist discovers a common ground in the painful struggle to both answer and retain the romantic's archetypal dilemma: How does one deal with the loss of important illusions when those illusions are clearly the key to one's own survival? For Murphy, a man or a generation are lost only when they can no longer believe in those who have taken the greatest risk in aspiring toward personal mythic heroism.

"The stuff of dreams," Humphrey Bogart once remarked about the object of a similar quest; and Murphy's search for his own Maltese Falcon derives from books, records, and films—a tragicomic "problem" most Americans

° Reprinted from the original manuscript, which first appeared in *Rolling Stone* as an edited version.

surely share.[7] But ofttimes in such cases, the hunter can feel more like the hunted as his obsessions ironically turn the tables ("Hollywood / You shaped my life with a Technicolor carving knife / And now I don't know what to feel") to move in on him ("You know, I just can't find nothing real / And the movies are all outside, baby …") as he tries to understand their meaning. A paranoid moralist not unlike many great rock & rollers (Bob Dylan and Ian Hunter immediately come to mind), Murphy will take the risks a potential hero must, up to and perhaps including "Brian Jones and the final getaway," but his pilgrim's progress through the issues of our time—love, war, the costs of stardom, dreamy art, et al.—seems enormous to him, a matter of life and death ("And just when I thought I'd take a Hemingway shot / The F. Scott in me says, man, you'd better not"), and he cannot accept a generation's lack of concern with the trivialization or worse of beliefs for which he'd die. Perhaps too closely attuned to these times, a "rebel with too many causes," he screams in agony: "But who's gonna tell those kids / About all the things we did? / You tell me who's gonna turn them on / To the secrets born with the bomb?" But do they really care? At times, Murphy admits, "I just want to know when it's over."

If it is a long way from the sad suburban epitaphs of *Aquashow* to the gloomier philosophical complexities of *Lost Generation* ("Last of the Rock Stars" on the former LP seems a good transitional song), both albums share an acute epigrammatic sensitivity, a penchant for unhappy endings, and the artist's sense of perennial displacement. In the 1970s, everything's gone to hell; and Murphy, like another Elliott's Philip Marlowe in Robert Altman's film of Raymond Chandler's *The Long Goodbye*, wanders through the big-city debris, muttering, "But that's all right … / That's okay," while he tries to find solace in sex ("History," "Bittersweet," "Visions of the Night," "Lookin' Back"), music ("Manhattan Rock"), and the legends of the past (almost all of the songs).[8] "Hollywood," the LP's opening cut, offers one symbolic explanation of how he (we?) got that way; "History" another:

> Summer in suburbia we'd catch fireflies
> Put them in a jar and watch them die
> You and me, baby, we could have gone so far

"Visions of the Night" and "Lookin' Back" are both corrosive "love" songs, the latter railing vengefully against an early lover's misuse of the myth, the former even more vicious. While the missed opportunities for romance in

---

7 The correct quote by Bogart in *The Maltese Falcon* is "The stuff that dreams are made of." Paul kept a reproduction of the black bird statuette in his apartment.
8 Elliott Gould's throwaway line, repeated several times throughout the film, is "It's okay with me."

"History" are recalled with heartbreak and poignancy ("And there must have been a thousand times I could have had your hand / I could have been your man, you could have been my life"), only in "Bittersweet" is there any real sense of happiness as the woman who became Murphy's wife teaches him a valuable lesson: "You really gotta do something / If only waiting for a brand new style."

In "Bittersweet," Murphy shows his keen sense of perspective, has the good humor to admit defeat ("And look at me / So blind I thought I could see") and possible error in his fanatical mythopoeic quests. He clearly recognizes the dangers that can befall those who are hung up on heroes, and, in "Eva Braun," chronicles what happened to a poet (Ezra Pound) and a nation (Germany) too dazzled by the charisma of Adolf Hitler; Pound's—and Braun's, for that matter—"excuse" is rooted in erotic aestheticism: "But his eyes at night were chilling / And his words were oh so thrilling." The music business seems more than a little like Nazi Germany in "Manhattan Rock," with its Velvet Underground sound and superb first verse

> Here comes that man
> Dressed in Miami tan
> He's got a head full of charts
> Got numbers in his eyes
> And when he talks to me
> About the industry
> I want to join Buddy Holly
> Write my name in the sky

once again keyed to the artist's survival. "I'm sitting on top / Of Manhattan rock," Murphy sings, "Just hoping this backbeat / Gets me by." But it won't, of course: "I'm feeling so low / I got no cash flow / How's this corporation rock & roll / Gonna get by?" Another heroic vision—rock & roll this time—is being subverted by men who are "jamming plastic pop / On the radio."

Things come to a head in the title song. Half anthem, half lament, "Lost Generation" pinpoints the widening gap between vital, viable myth and rapidly degenerating "reality." On this song and throughout the album, Murphy writes like a man in constant touch with big questions, someone who doesn't look away from ambiguous situations too many are afraid to face: Why it doesn't work, why didn't I love her—she me?, the death of the family, the horror of corporate blandness, the stain upon our country, ad infinitum. As in that saddest of old jokes, everything around the artist seems to be dead or dying, and he doesn't feel so well himself; he's scared and hurt, but he still has a bit of Ahab in him when he demands: "And who divides the oceans / When a generation's lost its place? / And who sets the motion / Of the human race?"

On *Aquashow*, Elliott Murphy had the audacity to merge Fitzgerald's *The Great Gatsby* with Dylan's "Like a Rolling Stone" to create a song called "Like a Great Gatsby"; on *Lost Generation*, he invokes Hemingway's Paris in the Twenties, the magic of Hollywood, and many more gods, then winds up tying Pound, Braun, and even Hitler to a rock & roll stake and setting the whole works on fire. One would think Murphy's future bright indeed. *Lost Generation* is in many ways a better album than *Aquashow*—deeper, more melodic, possibly more mature—although perhaps less accessible, more remote. Paul A. Rothchild handled the production with invention, efficiency, and professionalism, though one might wish that the assisting studio musicians, first-rate all, sounded somewhat less smoothly anonymous.[9] But Murphy has more than enough bite to make up for that. He's not lost in his own castle yet; he's out there with the rest of us. When he's on the street, the sun also rises on one of the best.

---

9 Rothchild also produced *The Even Dozen Jug Band* album.

JUST A STORY FROM AMERICA

With his fourth album, Elliott Murphy continues to impress and depress. Once overrated, now underrated, he has always had to struggle passionately to match his brilliant, top-heavy lyrics to a somewhat limited musical imagination—it's usually metaphysics and metaphors, not melodies, that are best remembered from his work. Like its predecessors, *Just a Story from America* is more heroic tonic than headachy torpor, but there are times when one wishes that Murphy were more of a natural and could breathe some tactility into his theses ("Drive All Night" and "Think Too Hard," for example, are much too stiff).

Despite these not inconsiderable shortcomings, Murphy remains an incorrigible talent, and this record is one of the best of the year. Tenaciously thematic, the singer continues to proffer the magics and moral certitude of romanticism and rock & roll, fallen heroes and the awesomely benevolent nighttime, and when he connects, it's like a Dave Kingman home run—all or nothing, no coasting ("Aristocracy is like a crown of thorns / It takes believers").[10] With its haunting boys-choir backing, "Anastasia," a song about childhood, wintry nights, the Romanovs, and the pull of death in the Russian Revolution, uses the old rock & roll/country music ruse of a telephone call from heaven to explore both a personal and collective loss of innocence that is positively—dare I say it?—cosmic. "Just a Story from America" sounds like Paul Simon adapting Theodore Dreiser's *An American Tragedy* for the Top 40, while "Caught Short in the Long Run" boasts a chorus that makes my heart pound. "Rock Ballad," with Mick Taylor playing guitar, conjures up those indescribably sweet but desperate times when you listened all night to music on the radio with someone you loved, and hoped that it would all last.

Elliott Murphy's *Just a Story from America* is an imperfect album about things that matter. Better that than a perfect LP about nothing, nothing at all.

"Elliott Murphy—*Just a Story from America*" by Paul Nelson from *Rolling Stone*, May 19, 1977. © Rolling Stone LLC 1977. All rights reserved. Reprinted by permission.

10 Paul, a longtime Minnesota Twins fan, seldom used sports metaphors, but this is one of his most (albeit inadvertently) inspired. After this review was published and before 1977 was out, the New York Mets' Dave Kingman, as a result of being traded, waived, and having his contract sold, became the only player to compete in all four major league baseball divisions. Similarly, *Just a Story from America* marked Elliott Murphy's third record label so far in a four-album career.

ELLIOTT MURPHY'S CAREER: THIS SIDE OF PARADOX*

In his stylish living room, Elliott Murphy, appropriately seated under a framed poster of the 1949 movie version of his beloved F. Scott Fitzgerald's *The Great Gatsby*, is talking about *Just a Story from America*—his fourth album, third label—and the general confusion of his career. The conversation is good, but the image is even more striking. Aristocratic classiness, everyday common sense, undeniable talent—Robert Redford before the success. As we talk, I keep thinking that Murphy, with his golden-boy good looks and glowing first notices, once must have appealed to hungry record-company presidents in much the same way that Daisy Buchanan cast a spell on Jay Gatsby. But, although the fires still burn, everyone seems a little worried.

"I'm really baffled at this point," Murphy admits about some recent unkind reviews and his relative lack of sales. "I thought that this record was the most commercial I ever made, and I also didn't feel that I consciously made any big sellouts—certainly not in writing the songs. In my mind, I don't see that much difference between the four albums. It amazes me when I see the same critic review one ecstatically and then the next one horrendously. And my own favorite songs—'Caught Short in the Long Run,' 'Isadora's Dancers,' 'Eva Braun'—are always the ones that get zero.

"This whole success thing, this youth-and-money-in-America—it's so unavoidable. It's got to be bad for you as an artist. I'm still living on these false premises. All these record companies [Polydor, RCA Victor, currently Columbia] are signing me because they hope someday 'He's either going to happen *tremendously* or he's not going to happen at all.' And they're betting on the long shot. I love the chance to make these albums, and I've made a profit for every company I've ever been with—they just sell me to the next one. Even though I've never sold a lot of records for any of these companies, they've never wanted to let me go. I've always had to pay my way out."

By Paul Nelson from *Rolling Stone*, June 17, 1977. © Rolling Stone LLC 1977. All rights reserved. Reprinted by permission.
* Reprinted from the original manuscript, which first appeared in *Rolling Stone* as an edited version.

At this point, Murphy is too much a philosophical romantic to be a downright pessimist, but more than intelligent enough not to be overly optimistic about making a permanent mark on something as metamorphic to him as the music business. Oh, he *understands* the business all right—that's part of the problem. He understands it like Ahab understood Moby Dick when, after the initial shock of recognition, both man and abyss stayed rooted in place, staring at one another with love, hatred, and mortal wonder.

"There are the weirdest pressures," he says. "I've had managers and record companies tell me that before you're a success, you shouldn't do things that you have to take too much responsibility for. That it's better to use a producer at this point than not to, because then if the album doesn't happen, you can blame it on the producer. But I don't want to be a success at something that is not what I meant originally to be a success about. I don't want to lose that initial thing that I wanted to do."

Fortunately, Murphy has the kind of sharp, self-deprecating sense of humor that can always let the angst out of the omnipresent introspection on which he seems to thrive. There is constant give-and-take. "I'm doing better than ever, but I'm feeling worse than ever," he acknowledges with a smile, as if that predicament were the story of all our lives. About a set of values—not dissimilar to Ernest Hemingway's famous Code—which he concedes is inherent in his songs, he says: "They're easier to put into the songs than they are to live by, though. That's the problem. That *is* the problem."

Problems obviously intrigue Murphy. He continues: "I've always thought that my biggest problem was that I didn't write love songs—at least a certain type of love song. There must be a million people with broken hearts in this country who are riding around in cars and who want to hear songs about other people with broken hearts, but I don't write that type of love song. I tend to feel sorry for women in general. I think I usually put the man more in terms of just the passive viewer to the whole thing. He's the journalist, he's just recording it. She's the one it happens to."

He laughs when asked about Columbia's "He Could Write a Book" ad campaign, allows that it might have been a mistake, and says: "I told them to say, 'He *Couldn't* Write a Book.' I don't even know if there's room for writing in rock & roll anymore. Sometimes I get the feeling that all those people I'm writing for—those people caught in the middle somewhere between Kiss and Frank Sinatra singing 'My Way'—may just be so disillusioned that they're not even buying records anymore."

Murphy is often accused of being too captivated by the legend of Fitzgerald, of cultivating the reflexes of a novelist instead of those of a rock & roller. He defends his concomitant interest in the Twenties and Thirties, literature ("Raymond Chandler is now my number-two writer"), and rock & roll: "What the Fitzgeralds and Hemingways were to that time has to be what rock & roll stars are to this time. When Scott and Zelda were on the cover of *The Saturday Evening Post*, it was the same as Mick and Bianca being on the cover of *People*. It's pop culture. I think that Jagger is aware of that. I don't think the Stones ever wrote teenage lyrics. I try to write songs about being married and having to pay bills. I try to be somewhat of a journalist about these years and this time."

After the completion of a tour which began in America in February and doesn't end until late June in France (where the artist's "Diamonds By the Yard" has achieved cult status), Murphy will record his fifth album, almost none of which is written yet.

"I don't carry a notebook," he says. "I sort of feel like an athlete who's trying to keep his amateur status—if I were a professional I would carry the notebook." Elliott Murphy stands up and grins. "I'm trying to keep my amateur status—and so far I'm doing damn well at it."

- LEONARD COHEN -

Paul had been obsessed with the songs of Leonard Cohen ever since he first saw him perform in Central Park in 1967. He especially adored Cohen's song "Joan of Arc." "He was mad about it and played it for months over and over again," Bobbi London says. "It's the single most perfect song I've ever heard," Paul told Cohen when he finally had the opportunity. "I don't think I've ever gotten over that song."

In his notes about Cohen's Songs of Love and Hate *LP, he'd written back in 1971:*

> Leonard Cohen's career has reached the point where people are avoiding him for his virtues as well as his vices. A common complaint from those casually interested is that even the "happy" songs are so doom-ridden they can spoil an entire day. It's true, of course, but for those who know his words well, those who cannot be casual about him—a mixed blessing, surely—it's the nighttime that's crucial, and nighttime is seldom the right time for Cohen.
>
> To come right out with it, Cohen, when he's in top form as a lyric writer, is simply the best.

Three years later, Paul wrote about Cohen's New Skin for the Old Ceremony *twice. He was still employed at Mercury when the first one appeared in* The

233

Village Voice; *by the time the second one appeared, in* Rolling Stone, *he was gone—like Cohen's Joan of Arc, "tired of the war / I want the kind of work I had before"—back to writing full-time.*

> "Myself," claims Leonard Cohen, "I long for love and light / But must it come so cruel and oh so bright?" In Cohen's monochromatic, endgame world, where Scott Fitzgerald's famous "In a real dark night of the soul, it is always three o'clock in the morning …" could pass for one of the rules of the game, the answer is almost always yes, the truth almost always yes, the truth almost always cruel and bright. And, not willing to leave it at that, the singer rarely forgets Scott's terrifying last phrases "… day after day."
>
> … Some of the songs are deeply pessimistic—one would not be as haunted by the figures in Bob Dylan's, Randy Newman's, Jackson Browne's mirror—but many are not, and in the rooms of today, Cohen's predicaments seem both real and reasonable, albeit frightening. All victories, all relationships, may be transitory, but there are many beginnings and many endings to almost everything of importance in a life, and Cohen's art is more cognizant of this than most.…
>
> There comes a time in all of our lives when we realize we cannot be to others all that they and we expect us to be, and that moment is often tragic if there is love involved. For me, the art of Leonard Cohen is about that moment, repeated into infinity.[1]

In the end, Paul arguably identified more closely with Cohen than any of the other artists he idolized, calling him "the world's most fatalistic introvert." It was at once a compliment and a challenge to the title.

K.A.

---

1 "Loners and Other Strangers" by Paul Nelson from *Rolling Stone*, February 27, 1975. © Rolling Stone LLC 1975. All rights reserved. Reprinted by permission.

LEONARD COHEN'S
CREATIVE BLOODSHED

"**S**o long as you use a knife, there's some love left," Norman Mailer once wrote in a poem, and the imagery of love and death, holy murderer and holy victim, tenderness and violence, and the ritual of complex connections strongly suggests the precise, magically lonely world of Leonard Cohen. He is like no one else in music; his best songs make Dylan seem like a child, Randy Newman naïve. The most apt analogies come from films, books: Cohen is an aural Ingmar Bergman (similar vision, similar depth: "Story of Isaac," "Joan of Arc"); like Altman's *McCabe and Mrs. Miller*, which uses his songs and matches their mood to perfection, he projects the archetypal lonesome hero caught in a web of betrayal, inertia, good-heartedness, forever unable to take firm hold with a woman, all of it ending in drifting for death. Like Graham Greene, his work is at times rancid with jealousy, yet he can touch the heart with a love song ("Suzanne," "Sisters of Mercy," "Hey, That's No Way to Say Goodbye," "Bird on a Wire") as few others can.

Although his art can be wildly uneven, most of the standard criticisms of it—that the music is shaky, the voice limited, the vision narrow, overly romantic, and too depressing—seem more a matter of taste than a question of talent or the lack of it. Perhaps I am wrong. One can understand someone's reluctance to partake of a world drenched with death and despair, but his awesome openness to mythic heroism, to the spark of love between a man and a woman, carries both the day and the night for me. There have been times when I have been afraid to listen to certain of his songs ("One of Us Cannot Be Wrong," for example), and other times when I've thought he was crazy, but I know that all of the aforementioned songs and the following will be with me forever: "The Stranger Song," "The Partisan" (although he didn't write it), "Seems So Long Ago, Nancy" (an accurate forecast), "Famous Blue Raincoat," "Last Year's Man" (about writing, women, and the wonder of falling in love), "Who by Fire" (a litany of suicide and dying), "Take This Longing," and parts of many others.

The last two songs are from the new Leonard Cohen album (his fifth), *New Skin for the Old Ceremony*, unfortunately not one of his best. Apart from "Fire" and "Longing," only "Chelsea Hotel #2," "There Is a War," and "A Singer Must Die" are even partially realized. John Lissauer's co-production (with the singer, who sings none too well at times here) and generally obtrusive, melodramatic, and quasi-cute arrangements are often more hindrance than help, at odds with the writer's intentions, and seemingly trying for sharp irony in a studio filled with rubber knives. Cohen's bloodshed is too creative for this kind of artificial slaughter; in his room, a lover saying "I need you" or "I don't need you" may strike the recognition of an identical terror.

Maybe I am strange in not finding this artist depressing (I find John Denver and Paul McCartney depressing, but not Cohen). Maybe I believe we are all soldiers in his lonely parade of lovers, forever touching, yet never touching enough ("Yes, many loved before us / I know we are not new"). Or sailors in a mythological sea ("And Jesus was a sailor ... / And when He knew for certain only drowning men could see Him / He said, All men will be sailors ..."—now that's irony, compassion, precision, concept). Perhaps Drieu La Rochelle inadvertently described Leonard Cohen in *The Fire Within*: at night, "a solitary taxi ... rolling along like a ball on a ghostly billiard table." Yet there is hope and triumph in Cohen's courage, just as there is in the final lines of the book: "A revolver is solid, it's made of steel. It's an object. To touch an object at last."[2]

2 Pierre Eugène Drieu La Rochelle's 1931 novel follows the final days of Alain, a drug addict who "always had money, yet never had any. Always a little, never a lot. It was fluid and furtive glamour that perpetually ran between his fingers, but never thickened to any consistency. Where did it come from? Everyone had given it to him: friends, women. Having tried ten different jobs, he had even earned it, but in absurd amounts." Alain, who is married but involved with another woman, ultimately commits suicide.

LEONARD COHEN'S
DOO-WOP NIGHTMARE

When I first met Leonard Cohen, he was telling a good friend of mine that his mother was seriously ill. My friend, whose father had recently died, was so moved by Cohen's mesmerizing familial compassion that she quietly began to cry. Seeing this, Cohen jumped up, left the room, and quickly returned with his famous blue raincoat. "Please cry on this," he said. "It soaks up the tears." And you wonder why I like Leonard Cohen.

Unfortunately, the tales surrounding Cohen's seventh album, *Death of a Ladies' Man*, produced by the once-famous but lately infamous Phil Spector, are neither poetic nor kind, and the LP probably has fewer admirers than buyers. Cohen himself, though he feels the songs are unusually strong, has expressed severe dissatisfaction with the record. Spector, it seems, simply took what the singer felt were tapes still in progress, kept them under lock and key, mixed them like a solitary mad genius, and released the album without bothering to consult with his artist. Not everyone likes a surprise, but Cohen has both dealt out and dealt with enough superromantic irony in his lifetime to walk through it as if it were a fine spring rain.[3]

With such a history, it's fitting that *Death of a Ladies' Man* more than lives up to its notoriety. It's either greatly flawed or great *and* flawed—and I'm betting on the latter.[4] Though too much of the record sounds like the world's most flamboyant extrovert producing and arranging the world's most fatalistic introvert, such assumptions can be deceiving. To me, both men would seem to belong to that select club of lone-wolf poets, Cohen haunted by new skin and old ceremonies and Spector by the reverse. While the latter apparently begs to differ with most of the contemporary world, the former

---

3 The still-infamous-after-all-these-years Spector was convicted in 2009 for the 2003 shooting and killing of actress Lana Clarkson.

4 "I like flawed masterpieces," Paul told Cohen in 1991. "Flawed masterpieces are more human than perfect masterpieces." Borrowing a line from Cohen's then unrecorded song "Anthem," he added: "That little crack is where the light comes in in a flawed masterpiece somehow."

has been known to defer to amatory begging to gain all the experience he possibly can from the sisterly sea around us. Both these guys know what fame and longing are.

But it's silly to take sides about this LP because so much of it is first-rate. Contrary to popular opinion, Leonard Cohen's lyrics, arguably the best in rock & roll, are easily decipherable through the calliopean claustrophobia of Phil Spector's sometimes-padded wall of sound. Actually, except for the very minor "Don't Go Home with Your Hard-On" (a rather pointless wallow in raunch) and "Fingerprints" (wrongheaded country music), Spector displays a good deal of sensitivity toward a type of material (*chansons*, for want of a better word) with which he's never worked. Though his rock & roll hits were often delicate and deliberate mixtures of the simple and the grandiose, it was usually the *music* that was grandiose, not the words. With Cohen, everything's the other way around.

A self-taught singer, Leonard Cohen can get by with six strings and a homemade melody if he has to, but his words are so moody and complex you can't tell up from down, implosion from explosion. Yet Spector's melodies, arrangements, and production generally swim rather than sink, and though he provides an *unusually* dense aural fog (some thirty musicians and seventeen backup singers) for Cohen's inner storms, no one gets run over here because of lack of vision. (Who knows, "Death of a Ladies' Man" might turn up someday on an album of Phil Spector's greatest hits.)

While Spector's contributions to *Death of a Ladies' Man* are anything but lethal ("Memories" is an effective doo-wop nightmare), Cohen's are still the kiss to build the dream on—if you can get to sleep at all after hearing "Iodine" and "Paper-Thin Hotel." The latter is one of his double-edged, liberation-and-revenge songs about infidelity and a cheated lover's claim of lack of jealousy ("A heavy burden lifted from my soul / I learned that love was out of my control"). Then, as the vocal begins to turn murderous ("I felt so good I couldn't feel a thing"), you realize the lover hasn't been telling the truth. Then you realize he *has* been. It's like thinking back to the beginning of one's great failed romance or thinking ahead toward the inevitable finish of what is now sublime: after a while, you don't want to, but what else is there? ("What happened to you, lover?" someone asks the singer on "I Left a Woman Waiting." "What happened to my eyes / Happened to your beauty," he answers. "What happened to your beauty / Happened to me.")

"Death of a Ladies' Man," one of Cohen's finest songs, is a seriocomic marvel that leaves you either anticipating great adventure or wondering if you've just had it. A man and a woman fall in love, and eventually the more realistic woman completely trashes the poor, romantic man, taking *everything*, including his sexual identity. ("The last time that I saw him / He was trying hard to get / A woman's education / But he's not a woman yet.") The song's incredible last verse manages to be terrifying, funny, and philosophically awesome, all at the same time. It's about life and love and could serve as an epitaph for most of us sharing this planet:

> So the great affair is over
> But whoever would have guessed
> It would leave us all so vacant
> And so deeply unimpressed
> It's like our visit to the moon
> Or to that other star
> I guess you go for nothing
> If you really want to go that far.

- NEW YORK DOLLS -

PAUL NELSON LIKES:
Raymond Chandler, Sam Peckinpah, Bob Dylan, Dashiell
Hammett, Nina Holzman, Fellini, the Stones, Mickey Spillane,
Norman Mailer, Harry Smith, dark sunglasses, the Knicks,
John Ford, La Strada (the restaurant), Sherman Cigarettellos,
.357 Magnums, Jack Kerouac, *McCabe and Mrs. Miller*,
making lists, Blue Ash, Jackson Browne, Ross Macdonald,
Coca-Cola, Gotham Book Mart, shooting pool, Boston (before,
during, and after dark), *The Great Gatsby*, Rod Stewart,
poker, color TV, Clint Eastwood, Don Siegel, *Viva Zapata!*,
eating at McDonald's, Sony cassette decks and Sennheiser
phones (especially on airplanes), Hemingway, Scotch tape,
orange writing paper, staying awake, and the New York Dolls.[1]

*Late one August night in 1972, Paul dropped by Bud Scoppa's apartment in
the Village and insisted that Scoppa come with him to the nearby Mercer Art
Center to see this new band he'd found. Scoppa's initial reaction to "this
crazed crowd and this weird cartoon Rolling Stones band" was to return to*

1 By Paul Nelson from *The Festival Songbook*, photographs by David Gahr, text by Paul Nelson and
Tony Glover. © 1973 (renewed) by Amsco Music Publications, a division of Music Sales Corporation.
International copyright secured. All rights reserved. Reprinted by permission.

the relative safety of his apartment. Paul, entranced, stayed. After the show, he called and told Scoppa that he should've stuck around, that they really started making sense to him in the second set.

If all that went wrong in a very short period of time between the New York Dolls and Mercury Records was handled up darkened doorsteps and behind closed doors in a fashion befitting a dysfunctional family, when the band broke up in April of 1975, three months after Paul himself had left the label, he set the record straight in "Valley of the New York Dolls," a lengthy, prominently placed article in The Village Voice. *Flicking on the porch light, he let the bugs fly.*

Robert Christgau: "His brilliance there was in seeing beneath the surface and understanding that David Johansen, in particular, was truly an artist after his own heart. Paul saw that—one of the great lyricists—and he got it immediately. What moved him, the thing that touched him, was that enormously literate—even though it was all faked over with, or covered over with, all kinds of other stuff—heart of that band."

In 1978, Paul wrote about the Dolls again. The occasion was the release of David Johansen's debut solo album. Exercising his recent appointment as Rolling Stone *record-review editor, "David Johansen Goes It Alone" was basically a love letter to the Dolls and what had not come to pass, and a note of encouragement to Johansen that perhaps it still could. In an early draft, Paul even fessed up at the outset: "This will not be your conventional lead review: It's too biased for that. But that doesn't make it wrong."*

Tom Carson: "It wasn't a record review. It was a very personal, very moving piece of writing that was absolutely of no use to the poor consumer trying to find out if this record was worth buying. This was Wenner's self-contradiction: yeah, he wanted straight consumer information, but at the same time he wanted Rolling Stone *to have the prestige of people like Paul or Greil intellectualizing."*

Sixteen years later, Paul was still talking about the Dolls when the band's ex-manager Marty Thau invited him to come over to his Park Slope home in Brooklyn for the weekend. A retrospective CD was in the works and Thau needed liner notes. "He said he hadn't been writing and he kind of begged off very politely." As an alternative, Paul suggested that by recording their discussions it might result in another "Two Jewish Mothers Pose as Rock Critics," a give-and-take between Paul and Lester Bangs—and his favorite chapter—in their Rod Stewart *book. It didn't.*

Paul's hope for the Dolls was a younger, American version of the Rolling Stones. "It was basically as simple as that. There was no reason why they couldn't progress the same way, given time. Maybe they weren't quite as gifted musically, but they got by. I wouldn't know an eighth note in the fourth bar if it bit me. They shoot the arrow, and it hits you in the heart. Basically, that's what they did to me, and I thought they'd be able to do that for millions of people. I thought I wasn't that different from most people and was somewhat representational. If I think that way, there are probably thousands more who think that way, too. It was a responsible business move, but I don't know if it would have made any difference if I had just said flat out, 'I love them. I want to sign them. I don't care what happens.' I just wanted to be around the damn band—it was a simple as that."

K.A.

VALLEY OF
THE NEW YORK DOLLS

The first time I laid eyes on the New York Dolls, they were drunk in a Rolls-Royce Silver Wraith outside the terrace of the Dancers. Lead singer David Johansen had lost the high heel from one of his platform shoes. He said, "I not only accept loss forever, I am made of loss," while, inside the club, the band's record company and managerial brain trust planned the conquest of blue dawns over racetracks and kids from sweet Ioway. The rest of the band—Johnny Thunders, Sylvain Sylvain, Jerry Nolan, Arthur Harold Kane—talked happily about early days spent practicing in a bicycle shop near Central Park. And me? I was a fool for them then just as I am now. My heart goes out to the hopeful sounds.

Though not much of the above is true—my apologies to Raymond Chandler's *The Long Goodbye* and Jack Kerouac's *Visions of Cody*—some of it is, or could be. There was always a sense of American mythology about the Dolls, and those of us who spent three years of our lives working with them had to believe they were more than just another rock & roll group, albeit the most misunderstood of recent times. We learned to measure our nights by Dolls concerts, spent even our holidays going to and from, and Mick Taylor's cryptic putdown—"They're the worst high school band I ever saw"—only further convinced us how right we were. Johansen shot back: "No—we're the *best* high school band you ever saw!" and the point seemed settled. For, after all, the New York Dolls tried to hit the longest home run in American rock & roll: they tried to impose themselves upon a nation's musical and cultural consciousness in a way that hadn't been attempted since the Rolling Stones, the Who, and the Beatles had done it a decade before in England.

Of course, the Dolls failed. Or did they?

Johansen: "In the beginning, we weren't very good musically. That's why we put up with each other. We were all fabulous people…. We're a lot faster than the Stones." Laughter. "At least, younger."

For all their claim to being a band of and for the kids, the Dolls rarely listened to Top 40 music—like them or not, no one could accuse them of creating that music industry euphemism for art, "product"—and their notions of technique mirrored more the tough sparseness of Hammett, the avant-garde fragmentation of Burroughs, and the cruel inward-eye of Nathanael West than the easy flow of media favorites. The fact that AM radio reacted to their songs as if they had dropped from some alien sky was not, in the long run, surprising. Johansen-Thunders did not have the breadth of Jagger-Richard. While the Stones could have written "Bad Girl," the Dolls could never have brought about "Moonlight Mile": they lacked the smoke and duskiness, and their nocturnal sojourn through the desert took them far too close to a deli for the tastes of most of Middle America. Whereas the work of the Stones could encompass the broad human comedy of a Brueghel or a Bosch, the Dolls proved to be subgenre miniaturists. They were unquestionably brilliant, but finally too spare, too restricted, to reach the hidden places in suburban, small-town hearts. In the end, they rode on real rather than symbolic subway trains to specific rather than universal places, played for an audience of intellectuals or kids even farther out than they were; and, when they eventually met the youth of the country, that youth seemed more confused than captivated by them, and could no more imagine itself a New York Doll than it could some exotic palm tree growing in Brooklyn. The Dolls appealed to an audience that had seen the end of the world, had in fact bought tickets for it but probably didn't attend because there was something even funnier on television that night.

Dave Marsh, who loved the group, put it best when he wrote: "The New York Dolls are the dead end of the Sixties approach. They presume a closed community of rock fans, a limited field with common interests closely held. The new kind of rock singers are different. They know how much greater the stakes are, for a rock star who wants to count, but they also know there isn't any way to focus upon them, to make the meaning of having the whole world up for grabs come home."

Nolan: "I suppose everyone will be like the Dolls in a few years. Like a fad. The public and people in general always pick up things from leaders, rock groups especially."

To be the neo-Rolling Stones of the 1970s was to be a not-to-be, and, after two albums and much notoriety, the Dolls broke up in the final weeks of April, the legendary deserts having forever eluded them. If truth be known, the news of their death hardly produced a ripple throughout the nation they sought to win. Their demise was taken as inevitable. The dreams of rock & roll's Dead End Kids burned out like a green light bulb on someone else's marquee, and nobody particularly noticed any loss of illumination. That must have been hard for the band to take, but perhaps no harder than some of the dates they had been forced to accept to remain even nominally solvent in the later stages of their existence. Somehow, everything had gone monstrously wrong; and, like characters in some tragicomic version of *Long Day's Journey into Night*, everyone closely involved was innocent, everyone guilty. The only solution, finally, was to walk away from it, but none of us—musicians, managers (Marty Thau, Steve Leber, David Krebs), myself (the A&R man who signed the group to Mercury Records)—really could.

August 7, 1972: I see Dolls at Mercer Art Center, want to sign them to wary Mercury.

Late August: Dolls ask Merc for $250,000 deal. Merc blanches, sends in more scouts.

September 24: Merc VP Charlie Fach sees Dolls at Mercer. Dolls go on three hours late. Fach stays 15 minutes, says no. I persist.[2]

October 1: Merc VP Lou Simon flies in from Chicago main office, sees Dolls at Mercer. Dolls go on two hours late. Simon loves them, says nothing until he checks the current political climate in Chi, then says no. I persist.

October 8: Merc A&R man Robin McBride flies in from Chi, sees Dolls at Mercer. Dolls go on one hour late. Thunders, wearing platform basketball shoes, kicks hole in stage. Kane's bass comes unplugged; he plays last four songs without making a sound. McBride says no. I persist.

---

2 Paul admitted in 1994: "I don't think I could do this now, twenty years later. I probably sound like Charlie Fach on this, but I don't think I'd stick around anymore, frankly."

Late October: Dolls, turned down by every major label, go to Europe. Merc President I.H. Steinberg and Fach see them in London, say no. I persist. Steinberg becomes enraged, calls Dolls worst band he has ever seen, says I must be crazy. Dolls original drummer Billy Murcia dies in England in a drug-related incident. Nolan replaces him.

Late 1972: I keep trying to convince very leery Merc.

T he Dolls' first performance had been in July at the Diplomat Hotel in the seedy Times Square area ("You all know Times Square," Johansen used to chide his audience. "It's where we all met"), but it was at the Mercer they gained their reputation in a series of concerts that built in momentum until the nights one spent there with 600 similarly delirious people simply were not sane. Those vivacious evenings were like a benign *Clockwork Orange* filmed in a packed-to-the-rafters Hollywood Mutant High wired for massive sound. There was something tremendously heartwarming about the band's all-out assault, fashioned as it was from wit, homage, honesty, self-parody, urban cunning, and the virtuosity of crudeness.

The Dolls and their early following were those kids who used to sneak into the Fillmore East every Saturday night; years later, when their musical time came, they couldn't wait to build their own homemade rocket ship and send it flying toward the moon on a return trip to innocence. If the fuel was more amateur energy than professional talent—well, one had to make do with what was at hand, surely the primary law of the streetwise. And it was a wondrous thing to see the group play rock & roll with the enthusiasm of five people who felt and acted as if they'd just invented it, hadn't quite worked out the kinks yet, but what the hell?—it was raw flash, honest fun, erotically direct, and seemed to define them to, and make them inseparable from, their own kind. While they invented nothing, they did present a peculiar vision—lost youths roaming the nighttime city "looking for a kiss, not a fix," cosmic jet boys "flying around New York City so high," the teenager as group Frankenstein— and carried the music back to simpler times; there were almost no solos, and everybody played and sang as hard as they could until they got tired. Which wasn't often. Although some found their world dangerous and offensive—and not at all the dark side of sentimentality—it never seemed threatening to me. It must have been like this in London when people first heard the Stones, I kept thinking, secretly ruing the day when the Dolls would become stars and go public.

But when the Dolls left their milieu in New York City (the Mercer Art Center, Kenny's Castaways, et al.), something was lost. The many times I saw them in big halls in front of crowds of several thousand, the essence of their particular, insular magic somehow became diluted. Even at the Felt Forum, in their first "legitimate" concert before 5,000 "normal" people (most of whom came to see Mott the Hoople), the band appeared nervous, ineffectual, and—how can one say it?—somewhat lost and harmless. Defanged.[3] They never quite succeeded in finding a way to convey their intimacy and personal charm to a larger audience which ofttimes regarded them as technically inept, emotionally silly freaks—or worse. If there were ever to be a meeting between performer and potential fan, work needed to be done. The Dolls were something special. They required specific, sensitive handling and firm control. Unfortunately, they did not always get it.

January 30, 1973: Merc head of publicity Mike Gormley flies in from Chi, sees Dolls at Kenny's Castaways because he wants to, says yes. I am shocked. Gormley's memo reopens Dolls case.

March 20: Dolls and Merc agree to a deal.

Late June: Dolls finish first album with Todd Rundgren producing. Mixing takes less than six hours. Johansen calls Rundgren "an expert on second-rate rock & roll."

July: Johansen falls asleep in Chi in front of Merc brass at special meeting to discuss Dolls. Steinberg isn't sure whether or not to wake him.

September: Dolls play Whisky and Los Angeles for first time. Five hundred kids line up each night. Thunders falls in love with groupie queen Sable Starr; they become rock & roll punkdom's Romeo and Juliet. Sylvain stays in biggest suite in hotel for week. How? I ask. "It was the room right next to mine," he says, "and it was empty so I just stayed there."

September 23: Johansen arrested in Memphis for stopping Dolls music while the cops beat up a kid. He asks cops what they'd do if he were Elvis. "We'd love to get him!" cops reply.

Late 1973: Dolls named by *Creem* readers as Best New Group and Worst Group of the Year. Despite Rundgren, the first album, *New York Dolls*, sells 100,000 copies.

---

3 "The only time I ever saw Mott was at the Garden with the Dolls," Paul told Ian Hunter, the Hoople's former front man. "You guys completely buried them that night." "Well," Hunter replied, "they were real bad most nights, actually. They came on tour with us. It seemed like they should've been taken away and forcibly taught how to play."

"**T**he Dolls are a vicious kick in the face to all that's careful, passive, and polished about today's popular music. The record companies, most of which have a great investment in exactly the kind of music the Dolls are rallying against, have naturally been turned off …" (Bud Scoppa, *Penthouse*).

Kane, the shyest of the band, after having seen me for at least eight months: "Hi. I'm Arthur."

If the Dolls were difficult to work with at times, it was because they understood nothing of the music business and recording, seemed naïve or unable to learn about either, and were rarely encouraged to exhibit any kind of self-control regarding the bankbook or the clock. To say that their record company thought them a mere critics' hype, did not understand them, and eventually grew to hate them would be an understatement; but, at the beginning, Mercury provided handsomely for the group's every whim. Management started well, too; Thau, the band's Napoleon, and Leber, their legal adviser and financial wizard, showed obvious devotion. As the months passed, trouble set in. The problems with Mercury rarely involved the Dolls personally, but had to do rather with mutual contempt among the men at the top on both sides, opposite viewpoints, management's apparent disdain for necessary budgets and deadlines, the record company's inability to get the group much AM or FM airplay, and—last but not least—money.

The clash between the Dolls and Mercury was finally a classic confrontation between two immovable objects: a company reluctant to spend any more money and a band that did not know how to stop spending it. Thau and Leber's penchant for potentiality required huge sums for bad-boy image-building and Stones-style high living, while Steinberg preferred to drop anchor until the bottom line told him when to raise it. A hot war was being waged. Further, Thau and Leber had begun to quarrel, a situation that proved very damaging at a time when the band needed all the outer stability they could get. The bills were piling up, and the hands at the controls had suddenly become fists.

One can learn much about the trouble among musicians, management, and record company in these excerpts from a confidential report written by Patrick Taton, a Mercury employee in Paris, concerning the group's 1973 French tour:

"November 28: Arrival at Orly. While cameras went into action, Thunders got sick right on the airport floor and had to leave the scene for a minute to pull himself together and make a decent comeback. We spent the afternoon taking pictures at the hotel. The Dolls gave us a hint as to their drinking capacities, which we had to discover at our own expense. In the afternoon, Thunders got sick again and had to be replaced by one of the road managers for photo purposes.

"November 29: Press interviews began with the group, their 'friends,' and managers gulping down champagne and cognac at an incredible speed, while we from Mercury were seated in the other corner of the bar. I was surprised when a not-so-sober Thau came up to us to remark that we weren't really interested in the Dolls because we weren't taking part in the interviews. When the interviews were over, I picked up the bill, which was incredibly high for so short a time. When I told Thau about it, he replied with utmost contempt, 'Peanuts for a band like that!' and continued with some of the most insulting remarks I've ever heard about a record company and its executives.

"Next was a live concert at Radio Luxembourg. Although they had been requested for rehearsals at 17:30, the group were not ready before 19:00 and went to the studio in a frightening state of drunkenness—one of the most nerve-shattering experiences of my 'business' life.

"December 2: Olympia concert. Surprisingly enough, by the time we went to pick them up at their hotel, the Dolls had already set up their gear and rehearsed. The hall was nearly sold out, and the evening ended in a triumph with two encores. The band were then taken to a top restaurant. They invited their friends—over fifty people altogether—all of them lavishly drinking champagne and cognac, making an incredible show of themselves, enraging patrons, and leaving us with a very nice bill.

"December 3: The day started with the news that Thau and Leber had gone back to America. The group were penniless and urgently requested an advance before they would fulfill their commitments: pure blackmail. The Dolls had to go to a TV studio for a very important show. Believe it or not, it took us over three hours to get them out of their rooms, while a frantic and irate producer was calling the hotel every five minutes, threatening to cancel the program and never again work with Mercury. Also, the band's equipment was set up five hours behind schedule. Finally, after a few minor incidents, the show was taped. It was a success from the first minute. The audience reacted very strongly to the storm of noise produced by the group. There was even a fight, a thing that pleased the Dolls very much, although they found French kids not so tough as those from New York.

"December 4: The band were ready to leave, but they had no money with which to pay their bill (rooms, drinks, numerous overseas telephone calls): over $3,500. Stuck again. If I may offer a personal opinion, the New York Dolls are one of the worst examples of untogetherness I have ever seen. Johansen is a very intelligent guy, Sylvain is really clever and nice, the others are quite kind in their own way; but put them together, add their managers (each of them doing his own thing), mix with alcohol, and shake, and you've got a careless, selfish, vicious, and totally disorganized gang of New York hooligans—and I'm really sorry to say so.

"Despite all this, I believe we have managed to do good business."

Sylvain: "I want a Cadillac car. Or a Rolls. I don't care. I'm just dying for a car. I've had three cars, no license. I guess I'm a lucky person."

Johansen: "I used to be lucky. What happened? I grew up. It changed everything."

In 1974, the Dolls released a second LP, *Too Much, Too Soon*, produced by Shadow Morton. It sold about 55,000 copies, and, like the first record, made the charts and appeared on almost every major critic's best-of-the-year list. Not bad for a new band, under the most convivial of circumstances; but the Dolls, unfortunately, were mired in the worst. Thau and Leber split, the group not talking much to either party; and Steinberg, all ire and ice, demanded the repayment of certain loans and a third album to be made only when management and monetary problems were rectified. They never were, of course. The band had no money, and their destructiveness and unpunctuality had alienated many promoters who no longer wanted to book them. Leber valiantly put together a lucrative tour of Europe and Japan, Krebs persuaded Jack Douglas to produce the third album, but the Dolls themselves—disillusioned and no longer trusting anyone—didn't take the offers seriously, and everything eventually fell apart. Legally, the group couldn't break free from any of their contracts. There was not much left to do but go home and die.

The Dolls did make one small comeback, a series of concerts at the Little Hippodrome earlier this year, but even these did little but add to the misconceptions which had always surrounded the band. In the early days, they were constantly referred to as a glitter group, a fag band, five transvestites who played inexpedient rock & roll and who were very offensive onstage. Needless to say, all of these "charges" were false. None of the group is homosexual, nor did the band ever dress as women. The infamous cover for their first LP was conceived as a deliberate eye-catcher—the ultimate satirical statement on makeup and glitter (the group appeared as they naturally look on the back of the jacket)—but somehow all too many people again failed to recognize the Dolls' nihilistic, riffraff sense of humor.[4] At the Little Hippodrome, the band tailored their comeback around the comic conceit of what it would be like to see a rock & roll concert in Red China, and, true to form, were quickly branded as Communists by many in the audience. With that maximum absurdity, perhaps it was indeed time to quit.

T he dreams of so many good people died with the New York Dolls. I can still remember the night we finished the first album. Thau and I raced over to Mercury to have two acetates cut, and later we listened, the ghostly sounds of more than a year's worth of the group's concerts ringing in our ears. I put the dub on the turntable, sheer terror in my heart. Thau, who had discovered the band and had cared enough to spend the very best of himself and all of his money on the project, felt the same. It meant so much to us then. I think both of us suddenly realized that everything had, to some degree, passed out of our hands and into the hands of those kids from sweet Ioway whose legion ultimately said no! in thunder to the hopes of the New York Dolls. As Jean Renoir remarked: "You see, in this world, there is one awful thing, and that is that everyone has his reasons."[5]

I think those kids from sweet Ioway were wrong, or rather perhaps that they never really had a chance to encounter the group on any significant level: on the radio or as part of a major tour. Instead, the band's philosophy of instant stardom and limited, headliner-only bookings proved to be the stuff of dreams. Even a cult favorite must eventually face the nation as a whole, but the Dolls never played by the rules of the game. Neither did the Velvet Underground, and their contributions will last. At times, when I am feeling particularly perverse, I can't blame either of them.

The New York Dolls sang and played terrific rock & roll—their own and other people's—and, in a better world, "Personality Crisis," "Trash," and "Stranded in the Jungle" would have been AM hits. (Perhaps two new songs, "Teenage News" and "Girls," will correct the deficit on some future Johansen LP.[6])

4 When Paul took the record to one of the top FM stations in Philadelphia, the music director refused to play it because of the album cover.
5 One of Paul's favorite quotes, spoken by Renoir in his 1939 classic film *The Rules of the Game*.
6 "Girls" surfaced in 1978 and "Teenage News" in 1979 on, respectively, Johansen's and Sylvain's eponymous debut solo albums.

Individually, each of the group will be heard from again—Thunders and Nolan have already formed a band called the Heartbreakers, Johansen and Sylvain have several plans, Kane is supposedly in California—but no matter. "Live fast, die young, and leave a good-looking corpse," someone once said. The Dolls went out with their high-heeled boots on.

They did it their way and got carried out dead, but with their pride intact. True, they did not grow old with the country, but that's probably the country's loss, not theirs. Corporation rock & roll, wherein musicians like Bachman-Turner Overdrive are more gray-flanneled than the businessmen who kowtow to them, is so formularized, homogenized, and impersonal it must surely cause the death of anything that is at all out-of-bounds, mythopoeic, and rebellious. The Dolls were alive. Perhaps it killed them not to be stars, darkened their personalities and drove some of them into private worlds, but at least they had the courage to become figments of their own imaginations—and those creations were not altogether devoid of nobility. I will cherish always the friendship of each of them. Their last words on record were: "I'm a human being."

"**L**isten, bucko, these are the New York Dolls, the sweethearts of Babylon themselves, the band you're gonna love whether you like it or not ..." (*New Musical Express*).

I do not claim they were the best, but the New York Dolls are still my favorite rock & roll group, although I will understand if you do not like them. I will understand, but deep down, I will not want to know you.

DAVID JOHANSEN
GOES IT ALONE*

There were times when his work came easily
When he could stand up and feel free
He even dreamed of raising a family
Something that now will never be—
Let's rock.

—DAVID JOHANSEN,
"Lonely Tenement"

In the early Seventies, the New York Dolls were the reigning rock & roll band in New York City, the darlings of David Bowie and the avant-garde intelligentsia, Bruce Springsteen and Patti Smith rolled into one, and America's principal purveyors of such newfound concepts as deliberate musical primitivism and the punk rock of futuristic, *haute-couture* street children. A cult band, they were passionately loved or hated, and more than a few critics (myself included) saw in them this country's best chance to develop a homegrown Rolling Stones. The Dolls were talented, and, more importantly, they had *poisonality!* Both of their albums made the charts, but a series of stormy misunderstandings among their record company, their management, and themselves eventually extinguished the green light of hope, and the group disbanded in April 1975 (though David Johansen valiantly continued to front bands bearing the Dolls' banner for the next several months). Like all good romantics, they had destroyed everything they touched.

On *Never Mind the Bollocks, Here's the Sex Pistols*, Johnny Rotten screams a "tribute" to the New York Dolls, and, just after the Pistols' breakup, Rotten was reportedly in New York to talk things over with David Johansen. In my

By Paul Nelson from *Rolling Stone*, May 18, 1978. © Rolling Stone LLC 1978. All rights reserved. Reprinted by permission.
° Reprinted from the original manuscript, which first appeared in *Rolling Stone* as an edited version.

mind, there's a similarity between the two bands (try the Dolls' "Vietnamese Baby" for some social commentary 1973 style), but the real connection may lie in the respective genius of their lead singers. Right now, it seems to me that Rotten is the most important punk rocker to have come out of Britain, while Johansen—with the release of his first solo LP—occupies a similar position in the stateside New Wave. To anyone who really loves rock & roll, what happens to these two men in the very near future is of great concern.

Though it doesn't sound anything like the New York Dolls or the Sex Pistols, *David Johansen* is the first genuine American masterpiece that the counterculture punk-rock/New Wave movement of the Seventies has produced. Obviously, it owes nothing (thank God) to such mundane monstrosities as, say, Peter Frampton's *I'm in You* or Wings' *London Town*, but its roots aren't necessarily Chuck Berry, Muddy Waters, the Rolling Stones, the Who, the MC5, or Iggy and the Stooges either. While *David Johansen* rocks fully as hard as *Never Mind the Bollocks* or *Exile on Main Street* (most of the time, the banks of layered guitars hit like bazookas), surprisingly at least half its songs manage not only to bring up but to bridge the gap between the singer-songwriter rock & rollers—Bob Dylan, Neil Young, Jackson Browne, Warren Zevon, et al.—and jackhammers like the Ramones and the Clash. (Yes, yes, I know that other artists, including some I've already mentioned, also have done it, but it's still astonishing and something of a breakthrough for Johansen's "Donna," "Lonely Tenement," and "Frenchette" to remind you of both the Sex Pistols *and* Dylan's *Blood on the Tracks* or Young's *Zuma*.)

Americans make the poorest nihilists, I guess. Probably because we're too sentimental about the past.

If David Johansen has lost some of his innocence by growing older, it's his experience that makes the new record great. True, there are four leftover Dolls songs (the spunky, R&B-flavored "Funky but Chic," a teenage tribute to "Girls," "Cool Metro," and, incredibly, the elegiac "Frenchette," all of them written with Sylvain Sylvain)—and, on one level, the first three aren't totally dissimilar to the marvelous music described in the preceding paragraphs—but they've all been reworked emotionally so that even the simplest of them rings with more resonance and depth, not to mention professionalism.

"Cool Metro," for instance, a song that once seemed filled with the exuberance of the young Dolls in London ("I went stomping down in Soho / I'm like a walking talking art show / ... you and me we've got to *grow grow grow*"), now sounds as ominous as one of Alfred Hitchcock's murder-in-broad-daylight movies. When Johansen shouts, "Come on!" on "Girls," there's an entire army of galvanizing guitars to lead the charismatic charge, but even this drum-happy anthem has cross references to the darker "I'm a Lover," whose scornful "Yeah yeah yeah" refrain dissects with deadliness the insincerity in *any* claim a would-be lover might aim at his target. To make matters more ironic, the target isn't really listening, and the claims are apparently true. "Not that Much" contains this zinger: "I'm in love with you daddy / But not that much."

It's on the four finest songs that the album's thematic strength comes through. Since 1975, David Johansen has lost both the band that made him famous *and* his wife, so there's real turbulence on "Pain in My Heart." When Johansen sings, "And I *know* / Cause there's a pain in my heart / And it *hurts*," he mixes his voice so low that it takes real determination for him to overcome his romantic predicament and the claustrophobic, Phil Spectorlike wall of guitars that threatens to engulf him.

"Frenchette" is one of those rock & roll love songs ("Remember how we marveled / Darling we were marvelous / And we were marveling at the Marvelettes") that proves the hard way that lost loves make the best art. Like Jackson Browne's "The Pretender," the song is a poignant remembrance of glories that are gone, an exploration of true love and what merely passes for it ("You call that love in French / But it's just Frenchette …") and an understandable but unconvincing reluctance to go through the whole process once again ("… I've been to France / So let's just dance"). Johansen's longing is so palpable that his voice actually cracks during the heartrendingly erotic "I take it down / I'm gonna wash it down / I scrub you on down in any old launderette" verse, and you know that he means it because you can't keep your hands from shaking.

An unlikely but strikingly successful combination of E.L. Doctorow's *Ragtime* and what sounds like a Balkan rock & roll folk dance, "Lonely Tenement" chronicles the long, slow death of the post-1975 ersatz Dolls and the end of a man/woman relationship. The song is a knockout musically, with Scarlet Rivera's evocative gypsy violin-playing riding on top of the ubiquitous gallery of guitars. This is how Johansen must have felt when he was trying to hang on with the ghost of a group:

> In a lonely union hall
> He's waiting for some work to call
> They're waiting for his price to fall
> They've got his ass against the wall
> He's given them his all in all
> They're expecting him to crawl.

And "Donna"—Christ, I could quote every line of it. Like Van Morrison's "The Story of Them," Mott the Hoople's "Ballad of Mott the Hoople," and Neil

Young's "Don't Be Denied," it's about what a rock & roll band means to someone who's been a part of it or loved it and doesn't know what to do now that it's gone ("Hey come on Donna and won't you show us what to do / Hey come on Donna I can't live without you"). It's also a love song—"And when I used to see you / I used to feel like such a man"—and I'm not sure which meaning is more moving. Both of them probably. But when I played "Donna" for three or four Dolls aficionados, there wasn't a dry eye in the place after these lines:

> So won't you just come on back
> And sing for me one more song
> With your guitars playing perfectly
> And your drummer pounding strong....

Sometimes it just gets to you, and there ain't nothing you can do about it.

- PATTI SMITH -

In a perfect world, an artist as evangelical about rock & roll as Patti Smith would have been one of Paul Nelson's heroes. But the world's not perfect, and Paul, in addition to not caring for Smith's music, seemed hard-pressed to mention her name without couching it in some sort of insult. For someone who (to quote Robert Christgau) liked what he liked, Paul could dislike with equal fervor. And though the artists who brought out the worst in him—along with Smith, J.D. Souther, Billy Joel, the Eagles, and Paul McCartney and Wings—were a small but seemingly disparate lot, they did have one thing in common. "Narcissism," Stephen Holden says. "This nasty word was narcissism."

Paul's review of Smith's debut album, Horses, *written in November of 1975 for Boston's* The Real Paper, *finds the critic at odds with the work he's critiquing. As with Bruce Springsteen's* Nebraska *a few years later, Paul wants to like the LP (albeit for completely different reasons). He feels as if it's something he should admire. But doesn't.*

The review is also one of many instances where Paul recycled something he'd written for one publication and sold it to another. Early in 1976, he retooled the piece for Stereo Review. *The resultant article was considerably shorter and less personal, with a few words added or subtracted here and there—but it clearly sprung from the review in* The Real Paper.

As a result, Paul wrote very little for Stereo Review. *Steve Simels, who was the magazine's music editor at the time, says that his "bosses were extremely irked by this. In any case, Paul seemed genuinely not to know that it was uncool to sell the same piece twice."*

Regardless, the review is Paul at his best and, given the prevailing critical mass at the time, his bravest. Reading it for the first time in 2010, Jonathan Lethem says: "Well, that is sobering: how persuasive he can be, even when you have known that is a great record with unshakable certainty for thirty-five years. The power of words, in passionate hands."

K.A.

PATTI SMITH:
A HEROIC MISTAKE

If critics have nightmares, one of the worst would be not liking *Horses*, Patti Smith's ubiquitous debut album. Without missing a beat, the nation's linotypers have shifted from Springsteen to Smith, and there would seem to be no escape from this strange New Jersey Nightingale. Sneakers are out, Rimbaud is in. It's four in the morning, and I'm afraid to sleep. Instead, I stare at the ceiling and reach for my seventy-ninth cigarette. The phonograph has been playing all day and most of the night. Unless they're masochists, the people in the next apartment must be going crazy. My head hurts. I feel so poeticized I could die. The worst has happened. After listening to the record a dozen times, not only do I not like *Horses*, I never want to hear it again—for many reasons, a difficult admission to make.

Difficult personally because I run into Patti—no, I cannot use the journalistic Smith here—all the time in the James M. Cain section of many of Manhattan's best secondhand bookstores. We share something. How could I not like her album? Difficult professionally because being not only a chauvinistic New Yorker but also the erstwhile A&R man who with great difficulty signed the New York Dolls to Phonogram, I feel a loyalty to the primal, near-tribal, deliberately primitive rock & roll of New York City.[1] All those nights spent listening to new bands at the Mercer Art Center and later CBGB were wonderful, even if much of the music was not. Having been through the music business wars, I learned the hard way about the resistance of most record companies toward unformulated acts. In that no-man's-land, the generals all consider Bachman-Turner Overdrive the zenith of creativity. Me, I'd rather be shot. Therefore, I greatly admire Arista's Clive Davis who after a single audition signed Patti Smith, a self-professed avant-garde poet, to a costly contract, then let her alone to make the record she wanted to make.

1 Phonogram's artists were released by Mercury Records in the U.S.

EVERYTHING IS AN AFTERTHOUGHT

Not since the heyday of Frank Capra, a film director whose Thirties and Forties comedies often featured cathartic angels, has such a miracle occurred. That the aforementioned LP is, if I am correct, something of a disaster is almost a moot point—even the mistakes of heroes are heroic. And I may not be correct. *Horses* is so clearly an idiosyncratic first album that perhaps subsequent records will illuminate its not inconsiderable attributes and make it seem much better in years to come than it does now. I doubt it, but I hope so.

Although both inwardly vulnerable and outspokenly naïve, Patti Smith is a half-baked heroine who seems to have accepted her (possible) stardom as if it were a divine right. About her writing, she apparently feels the same way. In several recently published interviews, she reminds me very much of Janis Joplin who, the one time we met, would compulsively answer every possible question, asked or unasked, no matter how foolish it sometimes made her look. Thus Patti can prattle, "That's just an artistic statement. It has nothing to do with me personally. You can't worry about gender when you're doing art on its highest level," and we are expected to delete or swallow whole whatever is sophomoric in this or similar "I was always into art" proclamations. Easy enough to do in a one-to-one situation, to be sure, but on an LP the role of a somewhat unformed and uninformed dictator, however unconscious it may be, sets up repercussions that are harder to ignore.

While *Horses* was being made, Patti Smith and producer John Cale reportedly had long, "totally creative" arguments about how to record almost everything. That Smith won most of the battles but lost the war seems a likely conclusion since much of the LP's production is as minimal as that on a demonstration tape. Granted that none of the band—Richard Sohl, piano; Ivan Kral, bass; Lenny Kaye, guitar; Jay Dee Daugherty, drums—is a virtuoso, Cale in the past has often done fine work with less-than-professional musicians (cf. the Stooges, the Modern Lovers). Here he appears to have been needlessly handcuffed—after all, the man has never been guilty of overproduction—while the artists had their way, neither wisely nor too well, with both the sound (thin, clean, and brittle) and the music (similarly small and uninteresting). Given his due, it seems reasonable that John Cale could have whipped even these musicians into shape (especially since he was a charter member of the group they so slavishly imitate, the Velvet Underground), but ironically he probably never had the chance. The production remains, according to Greil Marcus in *The Village Voice*, "anonymous," and as a result, *Horses* plods far more than it prances.

Patti Smith was a poet who loved rock & roll long before she decided to become a rock & roll singer. Once the equation was made, I suspect, she accepted it as reality and rushed through her first album as if a longer

262

transition period was unnecessary. In *Rolling Stone*, I recently wrote of Paul Simon: "He wouldn't dream of taking the Kierkegaardian leap to faith without first making a reservation at the best hotel on the other side." With Patti, it's more a case of too much faith, (as yet) too little leaping ability. She can talk all she wants about Mick, Keith, and Brian, but where it counts *Horses* sounds less like a Rolling Stones record than it does a poetry reading at the Museum of Modern Art. She may *look*, even *think*, rock & roll, but more often than not her precise recitations still lack the pandemonium and craziness of the real thing for which she is striving. Right now, it's all too serious, not enough fun, more of a drag—and a self-satisfied one at that— than anything else.

(Many Smith aficionados, among them Stephen Holden and Dave Marsh, claim that she must be seen in live performance before a proper judgment can be made. They may be right. Holden, who likes the LP, says that "humor is the glue that holds everything together" for her onstage, and agrees there isn't much of it on the album. "She's like Springsteen or the Tubes in that way," he continues. "Until you've seen them work, you can't fully understand them. Live, she is *very* rock & roll.")

Probably, maybe, I supposed—what is needed here is a phrase that will cover a multitude of sins because I still believe she's running a bluff. Why, when people who know how to play poker assure me that the woman has at least one ace in the hole, do I not change my bet? I don't know. Even with that ace, she doesn't look so tough. Try as I might, I simply can't warm up to *Horses* at all. I respect it, but how much can you respect an LP you wouldn't dream of playing for pleasure? "Patti Smith is nothing if not new" is a familiar line of defense her admirers often bring forth, but to me the record sounds like a morbid, pretentious rehash of the artist's two major influences—Lou Reed and Jim Morrison from the late Sixties. Just that and not much more. Even the album's best song, the brilliant "Land," said to be based on a vision of Jimi Hendrix's last hours, metamorphoses from the Velvet Underground into the Doors for one of its neatest tricks. "Free Money," another of my favorite cuts, cleverly weds love to money, thereby making all double entendres triple, but musically it's again derivative of the late, lamented Underground.

But the Velvets could *play*, and they weren't mixed as if they were recorded in a separate room down the hall from the singer. On most of *Horses*, Patti's voice is so far up front she sounds strident and affected even when she isn't; vocally she's trying to strike sparks off a rubber dinghy. In such isolation, much of her singing is apt to appear arrogant without reason, spoiled, precious—and I think it does. Often she pushes too hard anyway, so there's no need for exaggeration: a mix should be a marriage, not a divorce.

Poetry, I suppose, can be anything that isn't lost in the translation. Patti Smith is a good poet, but even the best of her work seems—I've been trying to think of the phrase for hours—pointlessly pregnant. As an album, *Horses* is too pregnant to be taken seriously, yet it is surely not funny. Pregnant past the point of diminishing returns. So heavy at times it cannot make the simplest movement with grace. A ponderous toddler, it should be protected, but when those huge coils of self-important surrealism unwind aggressively toward me, I find it natural to look for a way out of this place. I've been here before, and the town hasn't aged well. Razorblade Street and Eyeball Lane still look the same, though perhaps a bit more dated, and over there on Arcane Avenue at the Dying Swan Motel and Piano Shop, where only the upper cases hang out, they still measure a man by the width of his donkey and the height of the *A* in his Art. Hard to get a good meal here anymore. In the early Sixties, I had a friend on Philosophers Row who used to play all of his "serious" records in a dark room lighted only by black and purple light bulbs and iridescent art. Incense burned. Nonsense reigned. How sad that he would have loved much of *Horses*.

- JACKSON BROWNE -

Paul Nelson once told someone that Jackson Browne was one of the most brilliant people he'd ever met, "a major artist of this century. He's like Norman Mailer and all those guys. He's in their class. He has this kind of F. Scott Fitzgerald quality—that gorgeousness, but thought as well as gorgeousness."

It's simple enough to talk about lyrics, aims, structure, and all the critical etceteras, but it's very difficult to pinpoint what it is that's actually moved you. It has to do with essences, I think, and all those corny virtues like truth, courage, conviction, kindness, and the rest of them. In other words, as impressed as I am with Jackson Browne's art, I'm even more impressed with the humanity that shines through it. Maybe they're inseparable, but I doubt it.[1]

He used to tell people, "I'm the world's number one Jackson Browne fan" and wrote that Browne's music—"and the man himself as a friend—represents something irredeemably valuable to me. While I'm not exactly sure what, I know I can't afford to lose it."
    But that's exactly what happened.

1 "Jackson Browne: A Ticket to Ride" by Paul Nelson from *Rolling Stone*, March 9, 1978. © Rolling Stone LLC 1978. All rights reserved. Reprinted by permission.

"I was always very grateful that he wrote what he wrote," Browne says. *"I don't want to give it a name or diminish it by encapsulating it in some sort of description of what that was, but it made me feel that I was being received, that I was being heard, by people who really got it."*

Paul found in *"our finest practicing romantic"'s* work a level of understanding and self-awareness that seemed to elude him in his own life.

Looking back, Browne says, *"I feel like I didn't know him very well. Because, while it's one thing to have somebody leaning in to you, intuiting and asking you insightful questions, writing wonderfully about your work, it doesn't really mean that you know anything about that person."*

When Greil Marcus, in 1979, recruited twenty of the best rock & roll writers to contribute to his anthology Stranded—*which album* would *they take to the proverbial desert island?*—Paul didn't have to give it much thought. Jackson Browne's The Pretender *sang not only* to *him, it sang* about *him. Drawing from his expansive 1976* Rolling Stone *cover story* "We Are All on Tour," *Paul delivered a generous analysis of not only* The Pretender *but also his own dreams and desires.*

In 2000, Paul told Steven Ward that "The Pretender is still a great album," but his choice for a desert-island disc had changed. "It would probably be a Ralph Stanley record." When he died, his CD collection contained none of Browne's albums.

K.A.

THE PRETENDER

Doing a piece with a desert-island premise is like writing a suicide note and then sticking around to cry over it. Since the circumstances are both drastic and unignorable, you either lapse into sentimentality ("I not only accept loss forever," Jack Kerouac once wrote, "I am made of loss") or try to Bogart your way through with some wryly stylized stoicism. Either way, you're lost.

Because, though it isn't, being here is too much like real life. On these sands, you've got plenty of past, a severely pinched present, and no future. *Everything* is an afterthought. Or, worse, all that finely honed autobiographical angst you've been saving turns inexplicably into something that's much funnier than if you'd embraced it as a joke in the first place. Even before I was marooned, I'm not at all sure I knew what was funny anymore.

So here I sit, with only my memories, my fondest quotations, a phonograph, and a copy of Jackson Browne's *The Pretender*. Back in the saddle again with *things* instead of people.[2] You find 'em, you lose 'em, you hope to find 'em—a woman, family, friends, ideals—that's what *The Pretender*'s all about. What could be better than that?

Ross Macdonald has a wonderful passage in *The Doomsters*: "Watch it, I said to myself; self-pity is the last refuge of little minds and aging professional hardnoses." Gatsby, the *real* Pretender, had it down cold: he both mourned *and* sought that last, lost golden mote of summer in the second act of his very American life. Probably because Americans make the poorest nihilists, he never quit. Neil Young summed it up best: "It has often been my dream / To live with one who wasn't there." Mine, too.[3]

By Paul Nelson from *Stranded: Rock & Roll for a Desert Island*, 1979. © Mark C. Nelson 1979. All rights reserved. Reprinted by permission.†

2 As if this sentence isn't telling enough in its published form, in the original manuscript Paul crossed out this revealing—and, in the case of the Dylan reference, very funny—digression: "While hardly the most enjoyable ultimate situation, I imagine I've been or could be worse off. (What if I'd grabbed Bob Dylan's *Street-Legal* by mistake?) The old less-is-more theory, I suppose, but then there are those who'll believe anything, who'd prefer a ravishing record to a resplendent redhead. Well, as long as I'm stuck with the former, I do wish I had a book (F. Scott Fitzgerald's *The Great Gatsby*) or a movie (Brian De Palma's *Obsession*) to hold and to look at. At least I've got a good album."

3 The lyrics are from Young's "Will to Love," the same "song about salmon spawning upstream" that Paul played for Lester Bangs.

EVERYTHING IS AN AFTERTHOUGHT

Two of the truest songs I know—i.e., songs that hit me straight in the heart—are Bob Dylan's randy and exhilarating "Spanish Harlem Incident" and Jackson Browne's passionate hymn to romanticism, "Farther On." Though vastly dissimilar (youthful sexual gunfire versus a remembrance of things past), both numbers are built on the bias of hope and an ability to be consumed and transformed by emotion and thought. But if the former exemplifies the jangling pulsebeat of a chance meeting with a pretty girl on the street, then the latter might well refine, reflect upon, and ratify equally volcanic circumstances to represent a (possibly) more mature overall philosophy concerned with the occurrences of a lifetime. "Farther On," like the majority of Jackson's work, has its eye firmly fixed on long distances.

> But the angels are older
> They can see that the sun's setting fast
> They look over my shoulder
> At the vision of paradise contained in the light of the past
> And they lay down behind me
> To sleep beside the road till the morning has come
> Where they know they will find me
> With my maps and my faith in the distance
> Moving farther on.

Back in New York City, I was aware of the profundities in Jean Renoir's credo: "You see, in this world there is one awful thing, and that is that everyone has his reasons." Stranded now on another island, I've got time to think about the specific reasons. While the previously quoted final verse of "Farther On" is the one I'll undoubtedly end my days with, the song's initial stanza once and for all pins to the wall the cosmic haze of growing up. When I first heard it, I was absolutely unable to put any space between myself and someone else's childhood.

> In my early years I hid my tears
> And passed my days alone
> Adrift on an ocean of loneliness
> My dreams like nets were thrown
> To catch the love that I'd heard of
> In books and films and songs
> Now there's a world of illusion and fantasy
> In the place where the real world belongs.

As an adult on this peculiar island, still I look for the beauty in songs.[4] As the sun beats down, I'm reminded that memories are as warm as the climate here, and the loved ones who haunt those memories are warmer still. Though these sands and songs bear traces of mother and father, long-lost wife and child, friends, enemies, lovers, their presences exist once again as works of art—nice to think about, pleasant to listen to, but it gets very cold at night. In a college of soft knocks, some professional pessimist once told me that all of existence could be reduced to a cycle in which false expectations, harsh education, and darkest despair went round and round until it was simply too painful for anyone to make the swing from despair back to expectations again. These days, a lot of optimists would probably relate the same fable, adding only that it's too late to stop now. The reason I picked *The Pretender* was that it seemed to pick me....

Every time I hear *The Pretender*, it makes me feel that it just might be possible to get out of this place.

---

4 In his manuscript, Paul emphatically crossed out this highly confessional passage: "And, from the very beginning, Jackson's *oeuvre* has meant more to me—not only in a critical or analytical sense, but in direct, primal, and probably even tribal ways—than that of almost any other artist. (Perhaps it's a sad admission, perhaps a happy one, but I could piece together a fundamentally accurate depiction of my life in just about all its crucial stages by using only Jackson Browne compositions. As a matter of fact, I *have*—on cassette—and often.) So the work—and the man himself as a friend—represents something irredeemably valuable to me. While I'm not exactly sure what, I know I can't afford to lose it."

WE ARE ALL ON TOUR*

No one ever talks about their feelings anyway
Without dressing them in dreams and laughter
I guess it's just too painful otherwise.
                                    —JACKSON BROWNE,
                                         "The Late Show"

I did not tell them what bound me closest to you. I did not
say … how your willful resolution to wrest the secret of life
gave me heart, and how in your absolute indifference to public
canons … you walked in the light of your inward heroism.
                                    —JAMES JOYCE to Henrik Ibsen

We are sitting in Jackson Browne's hotel room in Boston—his eighth city in nine days—and it is very late, somewhere around five o'clock on a cold October morning. In the next room, Ethan Zane Browne, age three, has just gone to bed after some spirited mock-wrestling with his father, a crisis involving the repair of a toy airplane, and a joyful ride in a makeshift Batmobile which the boy has imaginatively fashioned from one of the hotel's electric shoeshine machines. But now Ethan, who had napped most of the previous day so he could stay up late for two sold-out shows at the Music Hall and the celebration of his daddy's twenty-eighth birthday, is asleep once more; and Jackson's day, which had begun at noon with a long bus ride, is winding down slowly before blurring into the next: up at ten for an even longer bus ride and yet another show.

He is exhausted—the red in his eyes is visible from across the room—but because it has been "a great night," he clearly wants to talk. Perhaps for the first time on this eight-week, forty-five-city tour, everything has come together onstage, and he seems reluctant to surrender that feeling of hard-won satisfaction to something so mundane as a few hours of well-earned rest.

"We Are All on Tour: Are You Prepared for the Pretender—Jackson Browne?" by Paul Nelson from *Rolling Stone*, December 16, 1976. © Rolling Stone LLC 1976. All rights reserved. Reprinted by permission.
* Reprinted from the original manuscript, which first appeared in *Rolling Stone* as an edited version.

Jackson Browne describes himself as a "survivor," and looking at him now, I don't wonder *why?* but *how?* A man blessed with or condemned by a "work ethic" so powerful he finds it "difficult to admit I don't have time to do everything—a trait no doubt inherited from my father," Jackson has accomplished—and survived—much during the past year.

From late October 1975 through February 1976, he worked in Los Angeles producing his friend Warren Zevon's first LP for Asylum, taking only a few weeks off to marry Phyllis Major, the woman with whom he'd been living for over three years. Jackson, Phyllis, and their son Ethan spent most of December in Hawaii. *Warren Zevon* was completed on February 29. On March 1, Jackson began recording *The Pretender*—his fourth and, in my opinion, finest album—with producer Jon Landau. Early on the morning of March 25, Phyllis Major Browne committed suicide by taking an overdose of sleeping pills. All work on the LP was suspended until May 6.

In May, June, and July, Jackson was in the studio five days a week. Throughout most of August and September—except for a camping trip with Ethan—he worked on the album every waking hour, weekends included. *The Pretender* was finished on September 27, and the tour began on October 1 in Cincinnati. Which left only three or four hurried days for rehearsal with a band that, with the exception of David Lindley, knew neither Jackson Browne nor his songs hardly at all save by reputation.

To make matters worse, Jackson started the tour with a sore throat and a bad cold which seriously affected his performance; his voice often cracked, he sometimes forgot lines, and at times his concentration seemed minimal. The band, potentially the best he has ever taken on the road, quite naturally had their own problems with songs they had played less than a week. The overall mood was, in a word, grim.

When Elizabeth Reynolds, Ethan's Bolivian governess, was turned back at the Canadian border because her passport had been lost, Jackson had to spend hours with immigration officials and take full charge of his son for two days in Toronto. A doctor administered antibiotics. Onstage at the Maple Leaf Gardens, the star often seemed invisible: he was there—but very, very oblique. When someone from the audience shouted a request for "Ready or Not," a courtship song manifestly about Phyllis, Jackson spun around, grabbed the microphone, and snapped: "I don't *do* that song anymore. I *know* it but I don't *do* it. What I do instead is that other song, 'The Only Child,' about my son." Back at the hotel, he said, "I'm paying the price now for not taking better care of myself," as he hung out the DO NOT DISTURB sign and shut the door. He was not smiling.

But both concerts in Boston have been glorious. The cold and the sore throat are gone—left somewhere in Buffalo (where Gregg Allman came onstage to join Jackson on "These Days"), Rochester, or Springfield—and the band has achieved precision and potency through persistence and practice. Jackson, shiny-eyed and running on sheer adrenaline, is bone-tired but ecstatic. He wants to talk. If there were people who sold sleep for a living, I find myself thinking, they'd never make more than a few cents off Jackson Browne. And—damaging admission for a journalist to make—I realize how much I like the man.

"I'll tell you a story about Warren Zevon," Jackson says. "We went to this party together. A birthday party for Ethan and J.D. Souther—Ethan was born on J.D.'s birthday. We kept trying to keep it down, but everybody's got to be there, and there are about 200 people. Anyway, it turned out to be a great party because somehow everybody fell into the right spot, and exactly the right people were left at three in the morning. As far as Warren is concerned, it was sort of his coming-out party. Some people knew his tunes, but the society at large did not really know Warren.

"Most of the time at parties, we like to sit around and sing, but there were just too many stellar personalities that night for everybody to do that. I mean, between Joni Mitchell and Carole King and Neil Young and maybe even Jan-Michael Vincent and the Eagles and me, no one's about to start doing a hoot. But Warren starts to sing, and no one's paying any attention, but that's all right with him. Because he's a little drunk and right in that exact moment in time and space when I think he sounds just like Bob Dylan.

"So he sits down at the piano, and I sit down next to him, and there are maybe eighteen people in the room—and they're all motherfuckers. Or *near*-motherfuckers. You know, the motherfuckers and the *near*-motherfuckers. So he sings 'Desperados Under the Eaves,' and, of course, everybody keeps on talking. And that's fine because he winds up having an effect neither of us could have predicted. I mean, maybe that Dylan impression is nothing more than rubbing your finger on the edge of the record and slowing it down just a little. Anyway, he sings a line and then goes: '*HUT!*'

"And eighteen motherfuckers and *near*-motherfuckers turn their heads so fast it makes a wind. *Whooosh!* And Warren was unaware it had happened. I mean, he hadn't played a rank trick to get their attention or anything, he was just singing the song. And he kept right on singing while everybody went: '*Who is that dude?*' It was great because it was his coming-out party, and he really came out, you know."

Jackson shakes his head and smiles.

"You know that song, 'Ready or Not,' about Phyllis? That verse: 'I punched an unemployed actor / Defending her dignity / He stood up and knocked me through that barroom door / And that girl came home with me'? Well, after I'd made the mistake of punching this huge fucker who then stood up and knocked me back about twelve feet, Warren was the guy who walked up to me rather calmly and charmingly with a Waco Bloody Mary in his hand and said: 'You realize, of course, that he is going to kill you.' Something about the honesty of that statement—and the pounding under my eye—made me say, 'You think so, huh?' And Warren sort of gently leaned down to me and nudged me and pushed me through the door. He stood out back with me for a minute, while I figured out what the fuck I had done.

"I mean, he's just been there *forever*, man. I see him as having been there at various times in my life when I actually—and probably unwittingly—made a big change in direction. And he really influenced my thinking. Just look at 'The Pretender.' That line, 'I'm going to be a happy idiot'—it's a little bit raw. That's not exactly the Browne touch, is it?

"I almost took that line out, but J.D. made me put it back. He said: 'Well, you'd be a real fool if you threw that line out because that's what you're talking about and that was what you meant and that was what you said. And if you're going to refine that out of the song, you're going to be out there with the rest of those assholes, trying to make it acceptable.' I thank J.D. for that. And I thank Lowell George for having instigated a whole spirit about feeling a certain responsibility for your friends. And peers.

"Before I produced *Warren Zevon*, I'd been listening to Warren's demos for years. Horrendous. Terrible. But he had a lot of spirit, a lot of soul. Some of my friends would grab me by the scruff of the neck and say: 'Yeah, they're great songs, but has the kid got a career?' I never thought about whether or not the guy was going to have a career. Or whether he'd be, ah, advantageous.

"I mean, when I walked up to my accountants and told them I was going to postpone my album for three months and produce this other guy instead, they looked at me and said: 'Congratulations. You've found a new calling in life. You're going to make records for two percent instead of thirteen.' They were so sarcastic, and that kind of thing never occurred to me.

"The fact is that I've always understood there was a certain thing that Warren was able to do which somehow was not in me, was not part of my nature, but which totally communicated with me. It's that dark humor, man, that *bo-whammo!* He's so kinetic and free, so *naturally* meaningful; I'm more consciously symbolic, *trying* to be meaningful. Maybe I'm a little too structural, a little too careful about how I represent myself. A little too much the ringmaster, the *entrepreneur*, the illusionist. Too cautious about how people see me and what I want them to think about me. Warren's rather raw, you know. Rather uncompromising in his language. I mean, I've never written about the things Warren has written about—but I've lived them. So why aren't they in my songs?"

I bring up the theory that if one were a practicing romantic—almost ludicrously so perhaps—one could see in Jackson Browne's songs an

Arthurian California myth, a contemporary Knights of the Round Table with Jackson as some modern-day Gawain, the young man on the quest, the hero, embodying that myth as opposed to the less consciously fabulous, more realistic persona of an artist like Warren Zevon.

You hit more archetypes than he does simply because you're aiming at them, I suggest. The whole of your work seems to me to be very classically romantic, very consciously mythic.

Pause.

He doesn't say yes and he doesn't say no.

Then: "I love myths, stories—I think about them a lot. I had written 'Rock Me on the Water' about three weeks before I discovered Joseph Campbell's books. He's written a four-volume anthology of myths—*Primitive Mythology, Occidental Mythology, Oriental Mythology, Creative Mythology*—and he says that all myths come down to the same thing: stories born out of imagination, born from within, from the human condition. They're inherited—we know them molecularly. The hero thing is part of our genetic makeup.

"Anyway, after I'd written 'Rock Me on the Water,' I looked through this book, and there were stories about ladies of the lakes, mermaids, sirens, water as a general symbol for rebirth, creation, sexuality, death. And I realized it was really a fantastic book because it was telling me that all these things spring quite naturally from the subconscious, that I had simply and quite naturally written this song about rebirth and the water, and that it was in me to do that. I stopped reading it right there because I knew if I became conscious of these myths, I would start writing the old ones instead of making up my own versions. So when you said 'consciously mythic'—"

Certainly not in a negative way, I explain.

He waves his hand. "Oh, I know that, but I feel it's a good moment to say this thing out loud. This mythology is very natural, it's spontaneous, and it's inherent. It's the same thing that makes a newborn chick maybe an hour old *run from the shadow of a hawk* and *not run* from the shadow of a sparrow. These things are cellular—your memory is cellular. It's eternal and it's magic and it's beautiful. These are things I think about, and I find a great deal of enjoyment and inspiration in them. And when I look at my son—the guy's so intelligent. The guy is so wise and keeps hauling me back to the center. We've all lived before, you know. I rather firmly believe in reincarnation. I have no appetite for the subject—except in purely recreational terms—but it's been absolutely and completely demonstrated to my satisfaction, and I don't feel the need to debate it. It's a belief."

How has it been demonstrated? I ask.

"The first minute I ever saw my son, he ran down eight or ten different little expressions which were so complete and full of character, so remarkable.

275

The cat just ran 'em down, man. It was like Rip Van Winkle waking up after twenty years and sort of stretching and kicking out the old chops—'Let's see, can I still frown? Can I still laugh? Can I still look *rather whimsical*?' The guy just ran 'em down. And as I looked at this little creature who was no more than two hours old, as he yawned and in the space of about thirty seconds went from a blissful, sort of *laissez-faire*, comical *mmmnnn* to an 'Aawww, hey, I'm not sure I like the temperature of the room' kind of expression, it occurred to me that this little dude's been here, man—the guy has lived. I mean, his chops are well developed. The guy's an old soul.

"I don't think my little boy had ever seen anybody smoke a pipe, but his mom gave him a little corncob pipe she bought at the zoo. And I'll tell you, for two weeks that little guy huffed and puffed on that pipe—he knew exactly what it was for. He gestured with it, he sucked on it, and he hung onto it like an old man of eighty or ninety—matter of fact, he looked exactly like somebody who might have lived to a rather ripe old age in another existence, somebody who really never, ever thought about his pipe. I mean, it was not a foreign thing to him, man. The guy grabbed the pipe—he's only three, four months old—wrapped his little paw around it, put it in his mouth, puffed on it, and just hung onto it. And when he'd see something else, he'd sort of wave at it with the pipe or point to it with the pipe.

"So to me, reincarnation is not a question, it's a certainty. I don't need to talk about it. You see, not only do I not give any kind of a shit at all whether anybody else believes in reincarnation, but it doesn't matter to me whether *I* do or not. It's not going to make the slightest bit of difference. The fact is, you're going to be born again. And maybe it's up to you. You can sit there in the ether for a thousand years or three seconds—it's all the same—and then you can put in your application.

"These thoughts are recreational—they don't have the slightest bearing on what I do with my life. If anything, the idea that this subject is fun and interesting—*merely* interesting—is rather a relief, and lets you get down to the basic thing: What are you going to do *now, right now*? Because if you don't want to deal with it, you can check out—people do it all the time. And for that matter, you don't have to come back. But maybe you'll decide that you want to. Maybe you'll look back on your life and decide it was *rather* foolish of you to have taken your life because the problems don't seem to have been *that* insurmountable. And anyway, you still have the same problem—you didn't really quite solve that one in this existence, did you?

"One psychic told me that one of the big considerations for whether or not a soul wants to reenter this mortal plane is that childhood is so horrendous. It's so dangerous and can go so wrong. And that souls reentering this life want to be very careful who they pick as parents. Little Ethan, man—he picked a couple of people who were making such passionate love that I'm sure he was just drawn to that particular thing rather than to a consideration of how it might turn out.

"That's enough of that. Let's go get some breakfast."

Almost every tour story you've ever read is the same: The band hasn't jelled yet, this place is better than that place, yesterday's concert was terrible, things were terrific tonight, but I *still* haven't been able to talk with So-and-so—tomorrow for sure.

This one's no different. You pick up random insights here and there, write them all down in your notebook, then later try to make them seem significant. But the medium of life on the road is its own best message. And its repetitious pattern—that old gray magic—is ultimately more interesting and on target than all of the minor details you keep trying to blow up into major revelations.

In point of fact, being on a tour for two weeks is like going fifteen rounds with one's own romanticism: a glorious endurance test that had best be won—or else. Consider the mythic journey of young men with art, money, talent, idealism, sex and power drives, et cetera, traveling across America in the best—or worst—possible way: by customized bus a few hundred miles a day. "What city are we in?" is the question, but no one usually cares about the answer. Everything's the same, the same, the same, the same—rarely different. Bus ride, soundcheck, concert, hotel, lack of sleep, sleep, bus ride, ad infinitum. Because of the physical closeness and shared sense of purpose, there is a camaraderie—even a language—built almost entirely upon the protective poetics of slapstick humor and the benign recognition of near-constant dislocation: You can be in my dream if I can be in yours, buddy. Every tribe has its rituals—that's why it's a tribe.

After a few days on the tour, you even begin taking notes like this.

October 3/Pittsburgh—Band's third city, my first. Before the soundcheck, Jackson is chasing Ethan from pillar to post in the cavernous basement of the Syria Mosque. "Let's *run*, Daddy," Ethan says when Jackson comes over to say hello. The boy is the center of attention. Everyone tells me the story of Ethan's being introduced to the audience in Columbus last night. Jackson to crowd: "This is my son." Applause. Ethan (shyly): "This is my daddy." Applause. The boy looks out at all of the people, asks: "You know what?" The audience all shouts: "*WHAT?*" Ethan is stunned by the thunderous response. He giggles, then says: "I love you." Bedlam. Wild applause. Jackson to crowd: "Is that too corny for you?"

Jackson and the band are practicing "Sleep's Dark and Silent Gate" in the dressing room. How strange, in a way. A tragic song—which I take to be the singer's reaction to his wife's death—becomes the focal point in a scene of male camaraderie; what first emerged as a deeply personal expression of pain is now public art as well.

On the bus, Jackson seems a little perturbed that everyone is constantly suggesting changes in the order of the songs in the show. Nothing has stayed the same yet, he argues, and as a result, none of us knows what he's doing. "Too much analysis," he says, mock-threatening to sit someplace "where I don't have to listen to this."

Jackson Browne on the art of tuning: "You've got to understand tuning. All you've got to do is take acid and try and tune your guitar, and you figure out that there's no such thing as being in tune."

At the concert, Ethan and his nanny Elizabeth Reynolds sit next to me in the sound booth. After "The Only Child," the boy shouts, "Daddy!" "Is that mine?" Jackson asks. Ethan answers, "Yes!" During "For Everyman," at the precise moment when Jackson is singing "Who'll come along / And hold out that strong but gentle father's hand?" his son's feet slip and he gets stuck in the back of a folding chair. (I swear to God! I wouldn't say it if it weren't true.) After the band plays just three notes of a new song, Ethan begins to sing "Here comes those tears again" very loudly. Jackson invites Ethan onstage, and the two sit together at the piano during "Sleep's Dark and Silent Gate." Jesus! My hands start to shake. "Oh God this is some shape I'm in / When the only thing that makes me cry / Is the kindness in my baby's eye." This certainly outdoes *Blood on the Tracks* for domestic drama, I think to myself. After the song, Ethan does not want to leave. Instead, he sits on the floor and picks at one of David Lindley's extra guitars during "The Pretender." Both Jackson and the audience seem distracted.

After the show, Jackson and I talk for a few minutes. He vows to restrict his son's onstage appearances and is convinced that "Sleep's Dark and Silent Gate" and "The Pretender" were "ruined for those who were hearing them for the first time." I ask him about the "And then we'll put our dark glasses on / And we'll make love until our strength is gone" verse in "The Pretender." "I got that from Phyllis," he says, but he is tired and speaking so softly that I can't hear him. "Who?" I ask. "Phyllis my wife," he says. I feel like a fool.

In the dressing room, the mood is subdued. No one is claiming any triumph. David Landau, Jackson's rhythm guitarist, and I start talking, and then he and Jackson introduce me to the band. They are: David Lindley (various guitars, violin), David Mason (organ), Mark Jordan (piano, acoustic guitar, vocals), Bryan Garofalo (bass, vocals), John Mauceri (drums).

A photographer stops by with some pictures of Jackson. "Pictures of Robin?" Ethan asks. His father smiles. "No, these are pictures of Batman," he says. "*You're* Robin. Remember?" As we get ready to go back to the hotel, Jackson tucks a ragged yellow bath towel under Ethan's coat collar. It hangs down the boy's back until it touches the floor. "What's that?" I ask. "That's my cerp," says Ethan. Jackson laughs and explains: "When I told him about Robin's *cape*, I got my tongue twisted. So he's been wearing his *cerp* ever since. I mean, you've got to get it right the first time with him."

About three in the morning, some of us spend an hour trying to find an all-night restaurant on Fourth Street which is supposed to be "just around the corner" from the hotel. Two teenage girls and a police car are cruising the area. "Which way is Fourth Street?" we ask the girls. They begin an incredibly long discourse which ends with some total confusion about Fifth Street. Jackson just keeps walking and says, "Yeah, and Fourth Street is a block either way." The night is cold, and we run amok aimlessly like high school kids footloose in the big city after an important game. Stories are told about cocaine ("You can kill any disease with it; if you take enough, *nothing* can live in there"), groupies, gang bangs, and other adult indiscretions. Lurid stuff from the collective past—and all interspersed with Jackson's tales about Ethan. Yet an aura of dewy innocence and wonderfully foolish immaturity pervades. It *still* seems like high school. The girls reappear, but nobody pays any attention to them. It's just not their night, I guess.

October 4–5/Toronto—This bus has six bunk beds, five sofas, four rows of seats, a card table, two Sony Trinitron color TVs, a stack of videotape cassettes, two refrigerators, a microwave oven, CB radio, a bathroom, closets, a telephone, and—of all things—a small pipe organ. Hugh Hefner might even consent to spend an hour here, if they put in a swimming pool. But for all its technological wonders, it's still a bus, not the *Queen Mary*. There really isn't very much room. People either watch the *Where's Poppa?* cassette or try to sleep. The hours and cities pass by with dreamy familiarity. Everybody seems sealed in media aspic. No one ever really looks out the window.

Outside a highway cafe, a truck driver asks Ethan if he'd care to inspect his rig. The boy climbs into the huge cab, beeps the horn, pumps the brakes, talks on the CB radio. Out of the corner of my eye, I see Jackson beam like the proud father he is. He looks at me and almost blushes. It is a good moment.

Because of Elizabeth's passport problems, it takes us seven hours just to cross the border into Canada, thirteen to get to Toronto. The immigration officials ask Jackson a lot of questions, many of them ripe with innuendo. "Are you married to this woman? You're *not* married to this woman?" Either way, you can't win. The ribbon of highway gives way to the ribbon of red tape.

Jackson stands up to the pressure very well, giving forceful but polite answers. But I begin to worry about him. He looks like he hasn't slept since 1971.

October 9/Boston—John Logan does Jackson's sound. He is a particularly honest and intelligent man. This is what he said to me after "Late for the Sky" during the first show: "You know, sometimes I think I'm the luckiest man in the world, getting to do Browne." To which I just nod my head in agreement. Tonight was, ah, not bad.

Jon Landau, who produced *The Pretender*, is in town. "I'll tell you," Jackson tells me, "when I see Landau, I have such an overwhelming affection for him. He's really such a great guy. We made all the mistakes together. We've been through so much and shared such an education. Landau taught me everything about drums. He taught me to pay attention to them. If I had been in there by myself, right away I would have told the drummer, 'Hey, man, really lay back there because I'm saying something and I don't want to compete with the drums.' But Landau made me realize that I could sing real soft. And all we'd have to do was to pull the fader up a couple of notches and I'd be louder than shit and the drums would still be blasting. What Landau brought to this whole project was awareness—a special kind of awareness that changed all kinds of things immediately. But he had a great understanding and respect for what I'd done in the past, too. He's really a consummate producer."

I ask Jackson what he thinks about these four lines from "Colors of the Sun" now: "Oh leave me where I am / I am not losing / If I am choosing / Not to plan my life." He laughs. "When I was twenty-one," he says, "I really liked the Bo Diddley line: 'I'm twenty-one—and I don't mind dyin'.' Tonight on my birthday, all I can think about is: 'I'm twenty-eight—and I don't mind tryin'.' These things change, you know."[5]

October 12/Burlington—Jackson Browne on songwriting: "Sometimes you have a word in mind, or you're sitting there playing something and you start to sing—and this *thing* comes out. This little subconscious *blurb*. Something that doesn't mean anything necessarily—but the more you look at it, the more it could mean a whole lot of things. So you begin to try to *make* it mean something. It's cathartic. I have a compulsion to make sense, you know. I delight in making perfect sense, although I rarely do. It's through a process of questions to myself that my songs get written."

Nobody had a clean shirt for last night's concert, and the band talked of "killer sweat." Still almost everyone spends this free day sleeping. Like vampires, most of us get up when the sun goes down, but Jackson and Ethan have been out shopping all day. "I bought more junk today than I ever have in my whole life," Jackson tells his manager, Mark Hammerman. "*Two* nylon

---

5 The correct line from the Bo Diddley song Browne refers to, "Who Do You Love," is: "Just twenty-two and I don't mind dyin'."

jackets, white wristbands—" "Why white? Isn't that carrying this purity thing too far?" Hammerman wonders. "Well, I wanted them to match my headband," Jackson says with a straight face.

October 13/New Haven—It is my opinion that "The Times You've Come," "Ready or Not," "Sing My Songs to Me," "Late for the Sky," and "Fountain of Sorrow" would all fit very well thematically in *The Pretender*. Does Jackson agree? "Oh yeah, probably—sure," he says. "Some of those songs are the same song. By the same song, I mean the next installment of a certain area which I might care to sing about. 'Farther On' is exactly the same song as 'Looking into You.' So's 'Your Bright Baby Blues,' although the structure is different. 'The Only Child' is very much like 'Fountain of Sorrow' and also similar to 'Ready or Not.' And it's obvious that 'Rock Me on the Water,' 'For Everyman,' 'Before the Deluge,' and 'The Pretender' are in the same sequence. 'The Pretender' is merely the latest episode of 'Rock Me on the Water.' I do think that the sequencing of the new album is my most successful, though."

October 14/Binghamton—The concert tonight is great. After a false start on "Before the Deluge," Jackson smiles at the band and mutters to the audience: "They may be sloppy motherfuckers, but they're *my* motherfuckers." When the show ends, he tells the crowd: "Thank you for coming. We came, too."

In the sound booth, Ethan—with his white bibbed overalls, white T-shirt, brown eyes, and blond hair—is stomping his foot while the band plays "The Road and the Sky." At the end of the song, he jumps into the air, looking both pleased and bashful when he sees that Elizabeth and I are smiling at him. He is carrying a *Star Trek* Magna Lite, and is very proud of it. I am reminded of the photograph on the back of *The Pretender*: Ethan emerging naked from the water on some beach in Hawaii, another Browne starting on his mythic journey. Good luck.

J ackson Browne's art works in a wide arc—and never more so than on *The Pretender*, a record of life and death, love and the lack of it, staying or leaving, birth and rebirth. One mood is almost always balanced by another, and the emotions in the songs tend to flow into each other as inevitably as the waves of the sea. It is always darkest— "Linda Paloma," "Here Come Those Tears Again," "Sleep's Dark and Silent Gate," "The Pretender"—just before the dawn—"The Fuse," "The Only Child," "Daddy's Tune"—and, of course, vice versa.

"The Fuse" is the first—and probably the last—song in the circle, if a circle can indeed be said to have a beginning or an end; it sounds very different as a final statement once the rest of the story is known. After a while, at least part of "The Only Child" seems to be as much about Phyllis as it is about Ethan.[6] "Daddy's Tune" is a song that Jackson is singing to his father, but couldn't Ethan just as easily sing all but the last verse to *his* father in twenty years? How many ramifications are there in the last three lines of "Your Bright Baby Blues"—and did you catch the pun in its title? In "The Pretender," what exactly is the hero pretending?

Getting into these songs is not difficult. Getting out of them may be impossible.[7]

The concert in Binghamton is over, and we are riding in the bus to New York City. It is three or four in the morning. Jackson and Howard Burke are sitting across from each other, trying to write lyrics for a song of Howard's called "64 Shows." David Lindley offers to play the cacophone, is politely turned down, and goes to bed. Everyone else is asleep.

"'64 Shows' is a cross between 'Six Days on the Road' and *The Seventh Seal*," Jackson explains. "We're talking about immortality, Howard," he adds. But the words don't come, and we start to talk. In the background, there is the sound of the CB radio.

Jackson tells me about "The People's Violin," a bluegrass song he's writing about a girl in Red China. We talk about Warren Zevon and Jack Tempchin. "I listened to nothing but their demo tapes for two years," Jackson claims. "Phyllis liked them, too." He sings and plays two Tempchin songs I've never heard: "Jazzbird" and "One More Song."[8]

I ask him about "The Fuse."

"It's like 'Rock Me on the Water,'" he says. "It has a long history. I began to write 'The Fuse' during my first album. The first line and the melody— they're from 1971. At one point, I tried to finish the song for the *For Everyman* album, but I didn't. I was going to come out of 'The Fuse' into

6 From an early draft: "In many ways, 'The Only Child' reminds me of Charlie Chaplin's *Limelight*. Both works confront the audience honestly and directly with a lifetime's summation, a final theme, that seems intended to pass right through art and into areas that really matter—those of compassion and personal communication—areas that can change lives. Few artists will ever match the degree of kindness, wisdom, and humanity in these lines to a motherless child who, as the years go by, will surely think back on his tragedy...." "Paul was devoted to Chaplin's *Limelight*," Elliott Murphy says, "and must have seen it a hundred times." A poster advertising the movie was taped over one of the windows in his apartment when he died.
7 Paul: "One of my favorite singers is a traditional balladist from the Southern mountains named Horton Barker. He's dead now but he was an old man of about eighty who sang unaccompanied folk songs. He would always say that 'The problem with these songs isn't getting into them, it's getting out of them.'"
8 Tempchin wrote the Eagles hit "Peaceful Easy Feeling." The year after Paul toured with Browne, he recommended to Rod Stewart that he record "One More Song" (though his advice wasn't heeded).

'Take It Easy.' I had to admit to myself that I didn't know what I was talking about then. Eventually it merged into another song called 'Hello Noah.' I was trying to finish 'Hello Noah' for the *Late for the Sky* album. Then 'Hello Noah' became part of 'The Fuse' again.

"For a long time, I used to consider the song as being rather hopelessly enthusiastic and almost embarrassingly positive. But one of my favorite things about the new album is that you're really ready to hear 'The Fuse' after having heard 'The Pretender.' So 'The Fuse' not only comes before 'The Pretender,' it's a refutation of 'The Pretender.' The overall message at the end of 'The Pretender' is that he's pretending—*he* knows it and *you* know it. He's going to pretend that all he gives a shit about is getting his paycheck, but even then he's saying, 'Say a prayer for the pretender.'

"You can just turn the record over and listen to 'The Fuse,' and it'll start you back in the cycle again."

Would he talk about "Daddy's Tune"?

"When my parents split up, my father moved to Japan and I didn't see him for a long time. But I am my father's son. I kept catching myself looking like him and sounding like him for a long time. Eventually you have to figure out that your differences are rather minimal compared with the things you've been through together. And what that person gave you! It's unfathomable, and there's no way to say thank you.

"On the album, 'Daddy's Tune' was going to be followed by a song called 'Dear Jackson.' I sat down and found this thing in a tin box full of 78s my father had left in a garage. It was an acetate of a recording he had made with Jack Teagarden in the early Fifties. It was a Dear John letter, only it was Dear Jackson. It wasn't written to me—it was just a little song.

> I got a letter today
> From one far away
> Who only wrote to say goodbye
> And though it was written oh so sweetly
> She brushed me off completely—
>
> Dear Jackson
> I'm writing to your old address
> Dear Jackson
> Everything at home's a mess
> The weather is dry
> And so am I
> I just got your Christmas card
> But when you go away

EVERYTHING IS AN AFTERTHOUGHT

Things happen this way
You should have stayed in your backyard

Dear Jackson
I'll be feeling blue tonight
But oh Jackson
That's not what I meant to write
I hope for your sake
That you won't take
The news I must break
Too hard
But your pigeon has flown
And not flown alone
Dear Jackson ...[9]

"Playing this scratchy old 78 was like hearing a voice from the past. Like having this little message from your father saying, uh, there's nothing to say ... this is the way things happen ... so long ... don't worry about it ... 'your pigeon has flown'—my father being my pigeon, you know."

The bus is parked in front of the Summit Hotel on Lexington Avenue now. It is about six o'clock in the morning. Outside, people are going to work. Jackson, David Landau, and I sit looking out the window and talking. It seems better than going into the hotel. Except for us, the bus is empty.

David and I wonder about "Linda Paloma."

"I asked Don Henley to help me with the song," Jackson says. "We spent two or three nights—eight hours at a sitting—working on things like syllables and lines. I'd tell him what I thought I was trying to say, and he'd tell me what he thought I was getting. And after all that time, it would come down to changing a *but* or a *though*. One thing that Henley and I proved was that you could sit down as straight as an arrow, with nothing but a couple hamburgers and a jug of coffee, and get absolutely as confused as you would have if you'd had an ounce of cocaine.

"Van Dyke Parks really helped me with the song, too. He reminded me that Mexican music is very, very simple. 'You don't need to write all those extra words,' he said. 'What we have here is a classic bolero.' He loved it.

"Let me tell you a personal thing. One of my wife's and my favorite songs is this Mexican song called 'Cu Cu Ru Cu Cu Paloma.' When my wife and I first met, we used to hear it quite often because we'd go to this certain restaurant and a certain couple of mariachis would always sing it to us.

9 "Dear Jackson" by Clyde Browne, 1953. © Jack Browne 1953.

"So I sort of set out to rip off this song in 'Linda Paloma.' I think I came closer to ripping off Ry Cooder's version of 'Maria Elena' instead, though. I love Mexican music and wondered how close I could come to sounding authentico. It's a genre I felt comfortable with to write about a particular subject—the classical, ah, *goodbye*. I mean, I don't know whether you focus on whether or not the girl is leaving and whether that is important to you, or whether or not what seems to be wrong is that a person has illusions about *what love should be* rather than *who people are*.

"It was a comfortable place to go with an idea which began with the opening image: 'At the moment the *music* began / And you heard the guitar player starting to sing / You were filled with the beauty that ran / Through what you were imagining.' Now I was singing about Phyllis. It's funny but every time I sang that for her, she never heard 'You were filled with the beauty that ran / Through what you were imagining.' She heard me singing: 'You were filled with the beauty *of the man* / That you were imagining.' Isn't that interesting?

"I nearly changed the line because, coming from her, it seemed more appropriate. But it turns out in the end that it's me singing the song to her. And it says the same thing, so I kept it in.

"At some point, I really feel that I'm going to have to write in some more classical genre because the parts I could write are endless—they occur to me forever. In 'Linda Paloma,' I could have written an entire Mexican song, sung in Spanish, where the mariachis in the background are singing these *rather* cynical and funny lines describing this moony couple at the table with their little problems of love. I hope I got at least some of that *feeling* on the record. In the end, when I sing 'Fly away / Linda Paloma,' the Mexicans in the restaurant were going to say, 'That's right, man, throw the little ones back. Forget it. *Forget it*, man. Let her *go*.'"

It is not without some trepidation that I say: This album is going to be widely taken as the story of you and Phyllis. Is it?

Jackson looks out the window for a minute. John Mauceri has told me earlier that he would like to be a journalist. I wonder how he would like it now.[10]

But Jackson refuses to be as melodramatic as certain writers. "Yeah," he says. "It was like looking at a photograph coming up in a solution, you know.

---

10 Paul rewrote the scene in his *Stranded* essay like this: "For a week now, I've been avoiding an essential question, and I know I'm finally going to ask it. For the first time, I feel like the journalist-as-ghoul."

A subsequent letter to the editor complained about "the evasiveness and apologetic tone of Paul Nelson's article whenever Jackson Browne's wife was mentioned." "Jackson Browne did not want to discuss his wife's death and his bereavement," was the response, "and we respected his privacy." Paul did know, however, the details of the suicide and the stormy relationship that had led up to it, by way of an off-the-record conversation with Mark Hammerman.

When I started to see these songs coming up and I began to see the image, it sort of scared me for a while. It scares me, but in the final analysis, it doesn't bother me. It's all right.

"You've raised a fundamental question, though. I'm not sure how worthwhile my describing such a personal tale is—as a matter of fact, I think it would be more worthwhile if it weren't taken that way—but it's something I simply accept about myself. The nature of my music has to do with dealing with very fundamental things by depicting my own experience. That's the way it is, and I guess it's okay. I mean, the truly personal and private things are not in there—there's nothing that isn't pretty fundamental, you know.

"The album depicts the last couple years of my life, yeah. It picks right up with *Late for the Sky*. However, its coming together was a rather sudden thing. All of these things were sort of like half songs and half ideas—and then at a certain moment, there was really nothing to do but sit down and put them all together.

"One of the most obvious connecting devices on *The Pretender*," he offers, "is in 'Your Bright Baby Blues.' The first line is in the chorus of 'Sleep's Dark and Silent Gate,' and the song is about the same person. It's a chronology: a returning to this person after certain events have transpired and sort of capping her, making a couplet to what one talked about in the first song. It's a capping idea but it's also a concluding idea, you know—concluding a portrait of a person."

Who is Nancy Farnsworth?

"I wrote 'Here Come Those Tears Again' with her. She's my mother-in-law, but if I had met her any other way, she would have been equally fascinating. She's real, you know. She's a friend of mine. Hey, she's somebody I could write a song with—what more can I say? She totally transcends the mother-in-law syndrome. She's more like a kid."

Lexington Avenue is filled with taxis. On the sidewalk, hundreds of people are going to work. They remind me of "The Pretender." I ask Jackson how that song can possibly be autobiographical.

"It is—it's completely about me," he insists. "But what I'm saying is that it's not *merely* about me, it's about a lot of people. I think that I'm talking about people in general when I talk about myself. Now *you* might not see me as a pretender, and *I* don't think of myself as a pretender—*but I have been*. I have an overview of the character. And the thing is cathartic. I mean, I got it out of the way. I'm really describing a whole period of about two years in the songs on the album. By the time I finished the album, the period was concluded. And having said all those things, I'm not a pretender. I don't have to talk about any of this anymore—I mean, talk about it to myself.

"After the Sixties, people began to decide that they would just work in a bookstore or be a plumber or drive a truck—and that would be cosmic, you know. Or—hey, Bob Dylan saying that all he wants is a cabin in Utah and a couple of kids who call him Pa.[11] What an amazing thing for him to say after having been the most rebellious and surly and unhappy and blindingly sarcastic and satirical person. Everything was based on that fundamental attitude he had, you know, and for him to capitulate was wonderful—it was very warming and startling and sad, too.

"Then you come up with this little hope that you're going to find this girl. And right away, you're talking about fulfilling each other's most predictable and mapped-out ideas. It's utterly humorous. It's funny. It's black. 'I'm going to find myself a girl / Who can show me what laughter means'? I could have written that when I was eight—and meant an entirely different thing.

"What is romance? Romance isn't necessarily positive, is it? 'And then we'll put our dark glasses on' is a cynical thing to say because putting your dark glasses on is basically hiding yourself. 'And we'll fill in the missing colors / In each other's paint-by-number dreams'? Remember those little squares with the numbers on them? *This* is supposed to be blue, *this* afternoon is supposed to be lovely, *this* is a picnic. It's prefab, you know. I'd be very unhappy if the 'paint-by-number' line were misread. I mean, I think that's the most cynical thing I've ever said—that your dreams are rather prescribed and determined.[12]

"But you can't escape thinking of life as beautiful. It's the natural thing to do—the one thing we'll *always* do—and *that's* what's positive about 'The Pretender,' not all those vows he makes. That you can actually just laugh at yourself and say, Well, here I am, I'm dreaming about this girl again. She's going to be all these things, we're going to do all these things. And in the middle of that realization, you go, Yeah, well, the truth is that you keep your fucking dark glasses on, you wear your cheaters. We'll probably just keep our shades on and fuck in front of the TV.

"For me, 'The Pretender' is just the right blend of pessimism and endurance. I mean, for some reason, we go on living, you know. That's such a basic thing. For some reason, there's something in us that makes us keep going—'Now the distance leads me farther on / Though the reasons I once had are gone.' The fact is, you probably never even needed a reason to live. What makes these cabdrivers get up every day and to go work? Their lives are probably disgruntled, but they've got this will to live that is really strong. Well, if you weren't like that, you'd just check out. A lot of people

11 Browne is referencing "Sign on the Window" from Dylan's *New Morning* album.
12 To Paul's dismay, he had indeed interpreted the lines in question—"I'm going to find myself a girl / Who can show me what laughter means / And we'll fill in the missing colors / In each other's paint-by-number dreams"—as completely sincere: "That was the verse that just broke my heart," he told Mark Hammerman. "I thought, Jesus, that's what I want. Why can't I find one? In fact, my reaction was, How can he know that?"

do, you know. There are statistics, and they're real high. A lot of people kill themselves. *But I'm not like that. It's just not part of me* to feel that way."

After four sold-out shows at the Palladium in New York, Jackson Browne's sleepless beauties pile into the Batmobile and roll south toward the next Holiday or Ramada Inn. And me, I'm sitting down by the highway, writing just as fast as they can ride. In Binghamton, in the Broome County Arena, there was a huge sign that said SUPPORT THE BROOME DUSTERS, probably a local hockey team, and I realized that in America there are heroes every ten miles or so, with legions of children and adults, assorted sizes, looking up to them. But this Jackson crosses quite a few boundaries, making it possible for those of us who, perhaps like him, just don't want to go home, who want to run once again through the frozen streets of Pittsburgh, a bright baby Browne in hand, his Robin's yellow cerp flying around in the rain.

David Lindley slices off a piece of eternity with his navy blue fiddle during "Cocaine Blues," while Jackson, at four in the morning in front of thousands, confesses that he's been trying to get to Aspen, Colorado, for three years. "But I'm what you call a work junkie," he says, with more than a trace of sorrow in his eyes. In Boston, when he tries to leave the room to fix his son's tiny airplane, the boy pierces hearts with, *"You're not going to the studio, are you?"* At moments like this, perhaps it is possible for Jackson to reject the romantic ideal as a realistic possibility while at the same time accepting the dream of it as a fundamental part of the human condition. There's a train every day, leaving either way.

Onstage, he can snap anthems out of the side of his mouth with the punk elegance of a California Bogart waiting in the fog for some mysterious lady of the lake, her brown hair falling over one eye. I'm not sure what I'm trying to say. Backstage, he was last seen flying like a cannonball, the hero in midair, aimed at one of his roadies who just happened to be looking the other way. "Hey, Eric!" said Jackson Browne at the apex of his arc—"Catch!"

- NEIL YOUNG -

On April 14, 1983, Elliot Roberts, Neil Young's manager, wrote a letter to Paul: "This is to advise you that we will cooperate with you on the Neil Young book." He went on to say that not only would Young be available for interviews and discussions, but that, whenever possible, friends and associates would, too.

The letter was welcome in more ways than one.

"He had that fairly expensive apartment on Lexington Avenue," William MacAdams recalls, "and then he didn't have the Rolling Stone *salary coming in anymore." Paul's agent, Martha Millard, had shopped around his impassioned book proposal and secured him a respectable book deal with Doubleday. He was paid half of his $25,000 advance up front. "That's when he dropped out of sight," Millard says.*

Parke Puterbaugh: "He wasn't able to move forward with it. I remember he would go through the motions of planning. He'd fly out to the West Coast and talk to this person and that person, but it never went much beyond that. I think maybe some people are not meant to write books, you know? I think maybe his medium was shorter, magazine-length features that he could worry over every word. Because if you tackle something as enormous as a book and you have this editorial overview that is so obsessed with every single word and observation, you're never going to get it done."

Two years into the project, in early February of 1985, Paul received an urgent Friday-morning message from Millard on his answering machine telling him that if he didn't speak with the publisher by Monday the contract would be canceled. "All you have to do, Paul, is talk to him. He's willing to help you, he's willing to listen to you. But if he does not hear from you on Monday, we're really up shit's creek and you're going to owe the man $12,500. I don't want to scare you, but you have to deal with this!" While he didn't return her call, he did reach out to the publisher, who gave him an extension until September.

William MacAdams: "That's when I saw Paul—I'm not sure what the verb is—just change. He was always slow in writing pieces, but that's the period when he became unable to finish things. He was fed up with Wenner and Rolling Stone, his mother was dying, he couldn't finish the Eastwood article, and he couldn't write the Neil Young book—that all happened in the same period, and he just really was never the same after that."

K.A.

NEIL YOUNG PAINTS IT BLACK

In the world of the rock star at least, 1975 has been a murderous year for romance. Over and over again, storybook marriages metamorphose into tales from the crypt as the marital bed is replaced by the psychiatrist's couch, the hand on the breast by a finger on the trigger. In *Blood on the Tracks*, *Red Headed Stranger*, and *Still Crazy After All These Years*, Bob Dylan, Willie Nelson, and Paul Simon have told us all about it—endlessly. Listening to these cancerous, often brilliant albums, one feels like a police reporter or a priest hearing a heartbreaking last confession. Now Neil Young takes us on a primal, near-tribal journey from the erogenous to the combat zone, and makes us feel every blow with an intensity that is almost homicidal. Fortunately or unfortunately, his *Zuma* may well be the best example of this depressing new genre. Indeed, it is arguably his finest record.

While *Zuma* is neither as regenerative as *Blood on the Tracks* nor as self-pitying as *Still Crazy*, it naturally partakes of both moods as it rages toward its ambiguous destination. For the most part, Young seems consumed by the failure of his relationship with actress Carrie Snodgress, and this obsession permeates his view of not only his own but even the world's history. "Cortez the Killer," the LP's best song, is ostensibly about Spaniards conquering Aztecs, but its exquisite sexual imagery ("He came dancing across the water / With his galleons and guns / ... On the shore lay Montezuma ..."), its depiction of savaged innocence, and the surprising last verse in which Young and his lost love suddenly and incongruously appear make it finally more personal than panoramic.

If "Cortez" lends to ravaged romance an air of universal sadness and timeless treachery which suggests that even in Eden there is no hope for a satisfactory love affair, much of the rest of the album is the artist's furious reaction to that "reality." Although confused by his situation in several songs, he doesn't whine about it ("Old true love ain't too hard to see / Don't cry no tears around me") but instead invests his pain in what one hopes will be cathartic anger. The seething "Barstool Blues," "Stupid Girl," and "Drive

Back" are never quite balanced by the softer, sometimes "saner" tracks ("Pardon My Heart," the tortured "Danger Bird," others) because Young rips almost the whole of *Zuma* open with some of the most vulnerable, visceral, and evocative electric guitar playing I've ever heard. Dominating and truly agonized, it tears at the soul with even more insistence than the gripping vocals and lyrics—and seems to inspire Crazy Horse to new heights of poignant, violent rock & roll.

The singer paints it somewhat black even on the LP's more hopeful songs. On "Lookin' for a Love," the chorus warns: "But I hope I treat her kind / And don't mess with her mind / When she starts to see the darker side of me." Crosby, Stills, Nash & Young are reunited on "Through My Sails," the beautiful and ominous number which closes the album. It is obvious that some sort of emotional resolution has been reached here, but whether the artist ends with the optimism of a new beginning or suicide is not made clear. Lines like "Still glaring from the city lights / Into paradise I soar" and "Wind blowing through my sails / It feels like I'm gone" can be read either way.

I prefer the former interpretation, and so does Young, I hope. He has come through brilliantly in 1975. *Tonight's the Night* and *Zuma* are powerful, tangible evidence that things can't be all bad, even when they seem to be.

YOUNG'S ONE-STOP
WORLD TOUR

The Boarding House
San Francisco, May 26 and 27, 1978

When Neil Young performed with Crazy Horse at the Palladium in New York City almost two years ago, he made such an impression on me that sometime during the opening show (for which I had a ticket), I knew I had to see them all. For the first time in my life, I patronized the scalpers. Though the tickets cost something like thirty bucks apiece, they were the only way to get in, and I just couldn't let the music stop. Here was rock & roll so primal and unexplainable that I simply wanted to let it wash over me, pulse through me. When Young wandered out and began to play songs like "Cortez the Killer" and "Like a Hurricane" on his black electric guitar, I figured I'd at last found the perfect target for that most overused of adjectives: *mythic*. For once, none of the answers mattered, because the questions themselves formed such complete and satisfying entities—entities that had long crossed the border of Freudian logic and were now headed out toward the farthest of the far countries. *Neil Jung*, I wrote in my notebook. A not-inappropriate pun.

At his recent five-night gig at the Boarding House (a club that seats fewer than 300), Young played four acoustic guitars, harmonica, and piano. There was no backup band. Surprisingly, the lack of electricity diminished neither his rock & roll effectiveness nor his enormous mystique, though it did make clear his folk-music roots. ("Sugar Mountain," in fact, almost sounded like a summary of how, for some, folk music leads naturally into the perhaps-more-lethal art of rock & roll. After he'd sung it, someone in the audience said, "That song's about being twenty." No, I thought to myself, that song's about *not* being twenty.) At any rate, Neil Young's "1978 world tour"—he plans to spend the rest of the year working on his second movie, *Human Highway*, much of which was filmed at these concerts—proved that he doesn't need anybody but himself up there, that he can rule a stage through the sheer force of his will. *Strength*, I wrote in my notebook. Pure strength.

Before the first set, I noticed I'm not the only fanatic who's flown all the way across America just to hear Neil Young. John Rockwell from *The New York Times* is here, and he seems as obsessed as I do. As does Cameron Crowe from *Rolling Stone*'s Los Angeles office. While we're waiting, we trade stories, the best of which are that Young once wrote, recorded, but didn't issue an album made up entirely of songs whose *titles* other people had made famous ("Born to Run," "Sail Away," "Greensleeves," etc.), and that he's got well over 175 songs in releasable form—nearly twenty LPs' worth. There are three large wooden Indians on the dimly lit stage. We sit and stare at them for a while. They seem to say it all.

When Young appears onstage—he doesn't ever seem to walk on: all of a sudden, he's just *there*—he announces, "It's good to be back on the boards again, as Mick Jagger said in 1967." He pauses for a moment, looks down, then fixes the crowd with a benevolent, behind-blue-eyes stare. His eyebrows are so black he looks like a cartoon varmint trying to emulate the barrels of a shotgun. "Just think of me as one you never figure," he says. My God, the guy can read minds, I think. Not only that, but he's his own best critic.[1]

True to his word, Young does a lot of things no one can figure. Technically, he's literally wired for sound with a set of complicated electronics that enable him to move about freely without any visible microphones. (Once, when something goes awry in the control room, he emits static and sputters like the Six Million Dollar Man-gone-bad.) Musically, he plays impeccably—and *in tune*. And with *Comes a Time*, his new record, due out soon, you'd expect him to do quite a few songs from it, right? Wrong. He does three: the title tune, the lovely "Already One" (about his ex-wife, Carrie Snodgress, and his son, Zeke), and "Human Highway." He doesn't sing that many old favorites either, though "Birds," "After the Gold Rush," "Sugar Mountain," "Down by the River," "Cowgirl in the Sand," and a Buffalo Springfield song called "Out of My Mind" invariably bring the house down.

Instead, Young stalks the stage like a slightly seedy James Stewart/Henry Fonda type—moving in arhythmic bobs and weaves, he sometimes seems to be performing a near-tribal dance—and guides us through a raft of new (or at least unreleased) material: "Out of the Blue and into the Black," "Thrasher," "Shots," "Pocahontas," "Powderfinger," "Sail Away," "Ride My Llama" ("an

1 This is also a near verbatim quote from Young's then still unreleased "Powderfinger": "Just think of me as one you never figured / Would fade away so young / With so much left undone...."

extraterrestrial folk song"), "The Ways of Love." Of these, I'd bet *at least* two are masterpieces. "Out of the Blue and into the Black" is about—well, here are some of the words:

> My my, hey hey, rock & roll is here to stay
> It's better to burn out than to fade away ...
> The king is gone but he's not forgotten
> This is the story of Johnny Rotten ...
> Hey hey, my my, rock & roll can never die
> There's more to the picture than meets the eye....²

And "Thrasher"—a complex and incredibly touching song about friendship, duty, work, and death, I'd guess after four listenings—sounded even better, especially on the twelve-string guitar.

In the manner of the best of the traditional blues singers, Neil Young seems totally alone onstage in a way that almost no contemporary performer ever does. But he's not foreboding, and you don't feel shut off. Head down, chin tucked into his shoulders like a boxer, he peers out at you with those all-knowing eyes filled with humor and flashes that beatific, silly grin. Like Muhammad Ali, he may well be the greatest. But we'll never know until we hear those 175 or so unreleased songs, will we? How about it? I'm ready and raring to go.

---

2 When this song was ultimately released the following year as the opening cut on Young's *Rust Never Sleeps* album, it was titled "My My, Hey Hey (Out of the Blue)"; its electric-crunch, LP-closing counterpart was called "Hey Hey, My My (Into the Black)."

- BOOK PROPOSAL -
RUST NEVER SLEEPS:
THE NEIL YOUNG STORY

Since the start of his professional career in early 1967, Neil Young has been praised as a major artist and widely recognized as a rock superstar. Praised and recognized three times over, you might say. First, as a founding member of one of America's great seminal rock & roll bands, the Buffalo Springfield. Second, as a premier—some would say *the* premier—solo rock performer from 1969 to the present (his influence is enormous). Third, as a member of Crosby, Stills, Nash & Young in 1970 and 1971. While it's certainly impressive to have been a part of two such renowned rock & roll groups, it's much more impressive to have retained the reputation of a serious artist while remaining an international star, since the terms are by no means synonymous—especially in rock & roll, especially for fifteen years. Indeed, of all the major rock performers who started in the Sixties (Bob Dylan, the Rolling Stones, the Who, et al.), Neil Young is the only one who is consistently better now than he was then. (Robert Christgau, author of *Christgau's Record Guide*, concurs, having named Young one of his three Artists of the Decade in the December 17, 1979, issue of *The Village Voice*. His two other choices were the lesser-known R&B and soul performers George Clinton and Al Green.)

Young's longstanding critical credibility and commercial clout are sound arguments for a book about him (i.e., the sales will be there), but they're really not my primary reasons for wanting to write it. I suppose that all of those more personal reasons resonate from my claim that Neil Young—instead of losing himself as an artist, lapsing into a nostalgia act, selling out, burning out, or becoming a self-parody—keeps improving. And improving in ways that are invariably surprising, even to veteran Young aficionados. Basically: *after fifteen years, there's still no predicting what he'll do!* (In this respect, he reminds me of Picasso, Nabokov, Jean-Luc Godard.) Other performers I admire—performers who haven't been at it nearly as long (Bruce Springsteen and Jackson Browne, for instance)—generally manage to maintain and often improve upon their high standards. But neither artist really (or rarely) *stuns* you with new approaches, new imagery, new characters, new sounds, etc. With Springsteen and Browne, each album usually moves logically into the next one. With Neil Young, each album, though distinctively his, sounds incredibly *free*.

Needless to say, such a performer does not follow trends, not even those he sets. Indeed, Young's wide-ranging artistry as both a songwriter and instrumentalist seems resolutely wed to instinct, to a need not to be tied down to anything but communication. Though his lyrics are as literate as any in rock & roll, he writes them quickly, stressing spontaneity rather than too much calculation. "If I'm writing right," he says, "I'm in the same place that I am when I'm playing.... There's a line that you just don't cross over." "Pocahantas," from *Rust Never Sleeps*, is a good example of the connections that Neil Young can make with his instinctive approach. This is what I wrote about it in *Rolling Stone*:

> A saga about Indians, "Pocahontas" starts quietly with these lovely lines
>
> > Aurora borealis
> > The icy sky at night
> > Paddles cut the water
> > In a long and hurried flight
>
> and then jumps quickly from colonial Jamestown to cavalry slaughters to urban slums to the tragicomic absurdities of the present day:
>
> > And maybe Marlon Brando
> > Will be there by the fire
> > We'll sit and talk of Hollywood
> > And the good things there for hire
> > And the Astrodome and the first tepee
> > Marlon Brando, Pocahontas and me.
>
> With "Pocahontas," Young sails through time and space like he owns them. In just one line, he moves forward an entire century: "They massacred the buffalo / Kitty corner from the bank." He even fits in a flashback—complete with bawdy

joke—so loony and moving that you don't know whether to laugh or cry:

> I wish I was a trapper
> I would give a thousand pelts
> To sleep with Pocahontas
> And find out how she felt
> In the mornin' on the fields of green
> In the homeland we've never seen.

Try reducing *that* to a single emotion.[3]

Young has written songs as sensitive and beautiful as any by the most fragile and aesthetic singer-songwriter, yet he has played life-and-death rock & roll with the delirious ferociousness of the Rolling Stones and the Sex Pistols at their most sordid and seedy (Johnny Rotten is a big Neil Young fan). His melodies are among the finest in rock (see *Christgau's Record Guide*), while his raw and passionate electric-guitar playing boasts a tactility and uniqueness unmatched by any guitarist since Jimi Hendrix (Greil Marcus, author of *Mystery Train*, agrees with me on this). His singing is as distinctive as Bob Dylan's: once you've heard him, you'll never mistake him for anyone else. I'd rank his live shows with those by Bruce Springsteen, the Clash, or, during their heyday, the Rolling Stones.

I could go on praising this or that facet of Neil Young's talent, but I'm sure the point is made. To me, he's not only rock & roll's most interesting artist but the genre's most interesting *person*. The curiosity about him is legend. He hasn't talked much to the press and has a reputation as a loner, so those who love his work really *want* to know about him. Yet when he has granted interviews, he's come across as being witty, intelligent, and very insightful about his own music and that of others. He seems extremely self-aware and displays none of the insecurity and ego often associated with being a rock star. He certainly doesn't live a rock star's life: instead, he works a ranch in northern California, often dropping out of the music scene for relatively long periods of time.

I've met Young and gotten along with him well. He's agreed to talk to me for this book and has assured me that there'll be no great problems about access, the right to quote song lyrics, etc.[4] He's aware that the book will be

3 "Neil Young: Every Promise Fulfilled" by Paul Nelson from *Rolling Stone*, October 18, 1979. © Rolling Stone LLC 1979. All rights reserved. Reprinted by permission.
4 Paul had already been burned, back in the mid-Sixties, when it came to quoting song lyrics. "I was going to do the first Dylan book," he told Jim DeRogatis, "but Dylan refused permission for his lyrics. That killed that pretty much. That would have been the first rock book."

about his life as well as his work, and he's all for it. So am I, because *Rust Never Sleeps: The Neil Young Story* is a book I am dying to read, let alone write.

- ROD STEWART -

Paul Nelson was just shy of forty-two when, in December of 1977, Rolling Stone *sent him on tour with thirty-two-year-old Rod Stewart. The two men had both spent the first half of the Seventies together at Mercury Records where they became good pals. Stewart especially liked Paul's knowledge of literate rock & roll and often picked his brain.*

"That's why I recorded 'Only a Hobo,'" Stewart says today. "I'd never heard it before until he played it to me. He was such a Dylanologist and he loved Bob Dylan, and he would turn me on to such obscure Bob Dylan songs. He was always pestering me to do one song called 'The Walls of Red Wing,' which was about reform school." Paul also suggested that he record "Mama, You Been on My Mind" (which he did) and "Dusty Old Fairgrounds" (which he didn't, but Blue Ash did). "I think I've got another one from him," Paul told Stewart in 1977, "a ballad called 'London Girl' that nobody's ever heard. I don't think Dylan even knows it exists. It was like from the first years in Minnesota."[1]

In the course of numerous interview sessions for "Rod Stewart Under Siege," Paul tried unsuccessfully to get the rocker to analyze his own seemingly self-referential lyrics. "Rock & roll is not that important, Paul" was Stewart's response. "I really think we're taking it too serious. We shouldn't be talking like this."

---

1 The song was actually called "Liverpool Girl," and Paul had heard Dylan play it at Dave Whitaker's house in Minneapolis in 1963.

Paul listened to Stewart's tales about his folks with a mixture of fascination and envy—it bore little resemblance to his own Minnesota upbringing. At one point, Stewart turned the table on Paul and asked him about his own life.

"I'm divorced and I have a kid. I fell in love with somebody else and left. I walked out on them. I guess I'd probably do it again. I have doubts, you know, that maybe that was the shot. I'm not going to have any more kids, I'm not going to have a family. Was it right? I don't have enough doubts to actually get married and have kids—but I don't know if I'm going to feel that way when I'm fifty."

Stewart understood. "Have you missed out on the best thing you should've had. Getting late in the game."

Conversations like this were not uncommon. Then one day the friendship stopped. Paul told Lester Bangs: "When I saw him after my Rolling Stone article he really brushed me off, although Jann has told me that he loved that article. But he refuses to talk to me on the telephone, so I think he thinks that all rock critics are out to get him. He does respond very, very negatively to criticism. I sure wish he'd talk. He just thinks we're all out to get him" *and* "I don't feel any sense of viciousness about him—I just sort of feel sad."

In 1979, Paul signed a contract with Delilah Communications that stipulated he would turn in a fifty to eighty thousand-word manuscript on or before May 1, 1980. In return, he would be paid $15,000 in three installments.

Bangs had recommended Paul to fledgling editor Karen Moline at Delilah. "I was in complete awe of Lester. If he said, 'Paul Nelson is the guy,' I said to my bosses, 'Paul Nelson is the guy,' and that's how you got the job.

"Now, when it came to Rod Stewart, Paul could not deliver."

Charles M. Young: "Deadlines were like grades for him. I mean, it was just like, 'Well, I don't care if it's in on time. I want it to say what I want it to say. If it takes me six months to say it—if it takes a year and a half to say—then that's how long I'm going to take.'"

Moline has never forgotten Bangs's explanation for Paul's tardiness. "Videos and VCRs had just come out. So Lester told me that the reason Paul couldn't deliver was because he was spending twenty hours a day watching old movies on video that he'd been wanting to see all of his life. I don't know if it's true or not, but it was such a wonderful comment in the worst possible way for somebody on deadline. I still have this image of Paul in his little apartment, sitting there with his hat on in the dark watching old movies."

The publisher was not similarly charmed. "Rod Stewart was a very big deal in those days," *Moline says.* "We had great pictures, and we had no text. Then it got to the point where he wouldn't even answer the phone." *Nick Tosches recalls Moline becoming so desperate that at one point she camped out on Paul's doorstep.*

But Paul wasn't holed up watching videos—not all the time anyway. He was also desperately in love and in the process of moving Laura Fissinger from Minneapolis to New York to marry him. Unable to write, he lifted much of his 1976 essay about Stewart from The Rolling Stone Illustrated History of Rock & Roll *and, virtually in its entirety, "Rod Stewart Under Siege" from* Rolling Stone.

Moline: "We didn't even check. We were grateful to get five paragraphs from him so the book could get published.

"I just think he made a deal and he panicked. Instead of just saying, 'I must withdraw,' he'd probably already spent the money—I mean, this is speculation—and he didn't want to not go through with it. He wanted the book out. There was very little outlet for people of this caliber."

But one or two articles does not a book make, and Paul's heart wasn't in it anyway. "I didn't really want to do it," he told Jim DeRogatis. "I don't think Rod wanted to cooperate at all, because I did this one piece in Rolling Stone *["Rod Stewart Under Siege"] that some people thought was favorable and others thought, 'God, how could you write such a negative piece?' I did it and I just got bogged down. I must have told Lester this, and he just said, 'I'll do it with you!' He just sat down and batted out a hundred pages at a stretch—that Kerouac thing. He must have had five times as much as we used in the book, and I was struggling over my forty pages or whatever.*

"Lester probably wrote seventy percent of the book. Most of the chapters are his, but he still said, 'I want your name to be first.' Then we decided we should do something together for it. Since we didn't write alike, I didn't see how we could write a piece together. I suggested a conversation, that would make sense, and we did it for a few hours. I don't think either one of us thought we did much of anything, but that's one of my favorite things." They called the resultant chapter "Two Jewish Mothers Pose as Rock Critics." "Every time I look at it I'm amazed at how well it came out. We didn't do anything to it—that's what we said—and it didn't seem like anything when we were talking, but somehow it worked magically in print. That's my favorite part of the book, and one of my very favorite things I've ever been involved in."

Bangs wrote in the book's preface that, while what Paul had written may be regarded as the "truth," Bangs made up the rest.

Paul gave Stewart his due when discussing his work with Bangs in their colloquial chapter. "Well, I think he's really a complex guy. Yet the last time I talked to him, or it seems like every time I've seen him, there's been a little less of him that I could relate to. Each time I talked to him he seemed less and less aware of what the whole outer world was, and more and more closed off from it."

Michael Seidenberg: "I don't remember him having any regrets about the book, but he was very clear about his opinion of Rod Stewart. He said that he was a great musician who chose to be a rock star—that he sacrificed his music for fame. I think he had as little regret about the book as Rod Stewart had about his career choices."

"He had a history of breaking your heart and he doesn't do that anymore," Paul said. "With most guys it wouldn't make much difference because they were never good to start with, but with Rod it does make a difference. There was something that we missed. And when it does show up on record and is still there, it makes you even more sad because it's not there all the way through. It's just there occasionally."

Paul, who never would have been so judgmental of the choices Gatsby made, cut his old friend Stewart little slack when he wrote the book's final chapter, "Everyone Has His Reasons."

Six years ago, when I was asked to sum up Rod Stewart's career for *The Rolling Stone Illustrated History of Rock & Roll*, I'm afraid I responded by assigning both the artist and his first six records—*The Rod Stewart Album, Gasoline Alley, Every Picture Tells a Story, Never a Dull Moment, Smiler,* and *Atlantic Crossing*—to a rock & roll heaven so unbelievably pure that even a saint (let alone a good-hearted, semirepentant sinner) might feel unworthy of walking around the place.

Since 1975, there have been four more LPs—*A Night on the Town, Foot Loose & Fancy Free, Blondes Have More Fun,* and *Foolish Behaviour*—not all of them bad by any means. But, from the vantage point of 1981, the Stewart story certainly turned out differently from what most of us expected in 1975. As a young man in his twenties, Rod Stewart seemed to possess an age-old wisdom: some of the things he told us we might have learned from our grandfathers. In his thirties, however, he suddenly metamorphosed into Jayne Mansfield.[2] What's a fan to think? Because of its instantaneous, combustible, and life-affirming/life-threatening nature, rock & roll—not unlike first love—often changes so fast that you don't know what to make of it. Hoping you're not a total fool, you close your eyes, kiss the girl, and she shows you the door. But is it an entrance or an exit? Small wonder we're all scarred and scared.

Smiler and *Atlantic Crossing* should have been the tip-offs, I suppose, yet they didn't sound like such terrible turning

---

2 Hearing this passage today, Stewart says, "I wouldn't mind being Jayne Mansfield," offering a loud chortle as punctuation. He pauses, then says, "No, he was right. I suppose when I first moved to Hollywood I got carried away with everything I read about myself and sort of needed someone like Paul and Lester Bangs to get me back to earth."

points then. Perhaps we were still blinded by the beauty of *Gasoline Alley* and *Every Picture Tells a Story*, or by the singer's genuinely likable personality. (Hard to believe, but Stewart was considered the Bruce Springsteen of his time: our least-affected, most-down-to-earth rock star.)

Calling his essay a "six-year-old valentine"—"a heart, carved in a tree by the side of the road with many forks, several of which I didn't see"—Paul reached for a John Fordian "When the legend becomes fact, print the legend" kind of a resolution. At least a little bit. "Let some of the legend linger, I'd argue, because parts of it are still true. Maybe, with Rod Stewart, the past is all that lasts."

When *Rolling Stone* updated its *Illustrated History of Rock & Roll* in 1980, I didn't have the heart to expand the Stewart chapter. There'd been so little I'd liked of the new work, and I'd changed my mind about some of the old. Each time I saw the man, we seemed to have less and less in common. I really hated his Hollywood, male-tart/starlet image, the manner in which he responded to (and completely misunderstood) punk rock, and the way he blamed the press—instead of himself—for turning his early fans against him.[3]

... So how do the ten LPs rank now? Like this, I'd say:

The Rod Stewart Album	C+
Gasoline Alley	A
Every Picture Tells a Story	A+
Never a Dull Moment	A-
Smiler	D-

3 About Paul's friendship with Stewart, Greil Marcus says: "Jackson Browne and Zevon, these are people he comes to admire as artists or performers and becomes friendly with them, and they become part of each other's lives. With Rod Stewart, his relationship had started when he was at Mercury, and he was working with Rod Stewart in a professional way that had nothing to do with the writer and subject. So the relationship had a different basis."

And about Paul's essay in *The Rolling Stone Illustrated History of Rock & Roll*: "I had been uncomfortable with the Rod Stewart piece because I felt it was softheaded. I felt it was all bound up in Paul's affection for Rod Stewart personally, and so I wanted that piece replaced in the second edition. I was really touched that Paul had taken the piece I had written not as a rebuke to him for having written something not good that had to be replaced but as part of a conversation or an argument between two friends or two fans about this person whom Paul knew and I didn't, though we both knew his music. I think that can tell you a lot about his whole attitude towards music and writing, literature, movies. It was a generosity of spirit where it is not a question of protecting turf, it's not a question of pursuing a reputation or dominance in the field or priority over somebody else. That was never what Paul's goals were. I don't mean that he didn't understand other people working in that way, but he just put it aside. That wasn't interesting to him, it wasn't compelling."

Atlantic Crossing	C
A Night on the Town	B
Foot Loose & Fancy Free	B-
Blondes Have More Fun	D
Foolish Behaviour	C-[4]

While Paul came a little later than most of his critical colleagues in confirming the singer's fall from grace, it still must've been a difficult trigger to pull. Despite the book's highly critical tone, he left in "Rod Stewart Under Siege"'s implied promise to the singer, "I just can't imagine doing a hatchet job on you," perhaps paying penance for one of the few times in his career when he'd mistaken friendship for art.

Sitting in the Astor Court at the St. Regis Hotel, Stewart says, "There's not much I can tell you," placing a finger to his nostril where the cocaine used to go. "So a lot of it's faded—as have most of the Seventies." He's forgotten that Paul worked with him at Mercury when Stewart was the label's biggest act. After being read something that Tom Nolan wrote in 1975, shortly after the release of Atlantic Crossing—

Rod is in a good mood, thoughtful and open. Tonight he is talking about Paul Nelson.

Nelson is a critic whose Sixties folk publication, The Little Sandy Review, *numbered Stewart among its ardent readership.*

Rod has fond memories of Nelson. He says now, "I admire Paul Nelson more than anyone. He's always been the one who's best understood what I've been trying to accomplish. He still does—look at the review he just did of my album in Rolling Stone. *Yeah, I really love Paul. Let's all drink to Paul Nelson tonight," he says, raising his wine glass, and everyone at the table follows suit.[5]*

—Stewart says, "I don't recall it, mate. I'm sorry." Nor does The Little Sandy Review *ring a bell. "If it was before* Sing Out!, *then I don't remember it." Nevertheless, he raises his glass. "Well, we'll still drink to Paul."*

K.A.

4 "Everyone Has His Reasons" from *Rod Stewart*, 1981. © Mark C. Nelson 1981. All rights reserved. Reprinted by permission.
5 "Rod Stewart Faces the American Dream: A Solo Spotlight, a Hollywood Mansion, a Glamorous Girlfriend, and Lower Taxes ... Every Picture Tells a Story, Don't It?" by Tom Nolan from *Rolling Stone*, November 6, 1975. © Rolling Stone LLC 1975. All rights reserved. Reprinted by permission.

ROD STEWART UNDER SIEGE*

That's no' just a game of football played by professionals, that's you on trial for your life. And they wonder why everybody drinks at these games? I'll tell you why, your guts are churning so bad you *need* to be half-bevvied or you'd faint. Please God let us win this year. Please God don't let the team do anything silly. Please God give Scotland a break.
—IAN ARCHER AND TREVOR ROYLE,
We'll Support You Evermore,
a book about Scottish football

Now you ask me if I'm sincere
That's the question that I always fear
Verse seven was never clear …
—ROD STEWART,
"I Was Only Joking"

I. SAN ANTONIO

Rod Stewart's hotel room is one vast pile of dancer's tights, body stockings, and ballet slippers. Not any ordinary tights, stockings, and slippers, mind you, but the finest that finance can finagle: apparel so expensive and expansive that I think for a moment about Daisy weeping over a stack of Gatsby's luxurious shirts. Then I have to laugh out loud.

There seems to have been a firestorm of pastels in here, and the effect is incredible: a veritable montage of money. It's as if Capezio had exploded, spraying every square foot of the suite with shrapnel so chic it could only inflict the so-called "million-dollar wound." Servants sort through the royal rubble looking for Cinderella's slipper. Another trunk is opened, and the air is filled with flying silks and soft pigskin. An aquamarine ballet shoe lands in my lap. "Hot Legs," a song from the recent *Foot Loose & Fancy Free*, pounds away on a huge cassette machine, while Tony Toon, Stewart's personal assistant, calls the star "she." Is this the true story of rock & roll?

In dilettantish disarray, Stewart himself is striding through the debris like some suave, henna-headed Hamlet, soliloquizing about the problem of having two blue slippers for his left foot, none for his right. He's serious, but he's not serious. Somehow, he still looks like a football player, and I'm glad. He seems to be thinking about a dozen things at once, telling me about a Scottish flag he's got hanging out one of his windows, talking about an old Bob Dylan tune he'd like to record, and remembering our days together at Mercury Records. We're good friends, and it feels that way, but we're both more than a little nervous about the formal circumstances of this meeting.

I just can't imagine doing a hatchet job on you, I tell him, praying to myself he hasn't changed much. "You're in My Heart," "You Got a Nerve," and "I Was Only Joking" sound like the same old Rod to me.

He's apparently never heard the phrase *hatchet job* before, and it makes him smile. He repeats it a few times, then tells me about a bad review from Miami. The temperature rises. "I appreciate what you say," he says. Someone hands him a blue slipper. "But, at the same time, I hope you'll write what you see." It's for his right foot.

We seem to have made a separate peace.[6]

In the elevator going down to the lobby, Stewart remembers I once asked him why "Tonight's the Night" was his only happy love song. "I was so surprised," he says. "Then I realized that what you said was *true*."

One of the roadies pipes up: "They all ought to be happy!"

"Nooooooooo," Rod wails, slapping palm to forehead. His face contorts into an expression of ersatz anguish, and he falls straight backward into the wall.

The whole band cracks up laughing.

---

6 Trying to allay Stewart's trepidations toward critics, Paul told him, "There are writers who go out and deliberately know they're going to do a really negative piece. If I don't like the artist or respect the artist, I don't want to do a piece about the artist. Because it's so easy to write snappy, negative, jokey pieces. It's very hard to say why you like something or why something moves you. It's very hard. It's very easy to make cynical jokes about anyone."

On the way to the concert, the limo is ordered to slow down as we all cheer the Scottish flag hanging from the eleventh floor of the Hilton Palacio del Rio.

In the dressing room, we get a chance to talk a bit. An English couple has sent Stewart a bottle of John Courage beer. There's a note tied to a Tartan scarf around the bottle's neck. They've driven several hundred miles and want to come backstage. Rod tries to arrange it.

He says he and the band are getting their second wind now, revving up for the December dates at the Forum in Los Angeles. That this new band—Jim Cregan, Gary Grainger, Billy Peek (guitars), John Jarvis (keyboards), Phil Chen (bass), Carmine Appice (drums)—is one with which he'll "make a last stand, unless we become complacent." It's clear that Stewart regards his final days with his former group, the Faces, as nothing more than "parody."

When he talks about Los Angeles, he often makes that city sound like some youthful prairie town dreamed of and longed for by the aging heroine of a Willa Cather novel. It's not Scotland, he admits, and he misses London, but to him the Forum concerts signify the triumphant return of a "local lad," whereas he always feels "inadequate" and like an "outsider" in the East, especially in New York City. "No matter how many times I've played it," he says, "there's still something about Madison Square Garden that terrifies me."

Stewart would seem to be a man who needs communal roots: the camaraderie of a rock & roll band, a friendly city to call his own. "These fucking people who criticize Hollywood," he says. "They've never even lived there. They're a million miles on the other side of the world, and they think that bloody Garbos and people like that still walk around the streets. Really, I think it's a fine rock & roll city. It's a little bit sleepy—it's not as fast as New York—but it's good enough for me to come back to for three or four months, and I won't have anybody knocking it. I mean, I love the place."

"Hot Legs" blasts from the cassette machine once more as the band tries to tune. I'm starting to think how much fun it is being on a rock & roll tour again.[7] Rod looks at his "boys," many of them unknowns, with a father's pride, and I almost expect him to give me a cigar. Instead, he says: "Tonight may not be so good because the acoustics are terrible here. But wait till Denver. We'll really be hot then."

7 The last one had been with Jackson Browne fourteen months earlier.

After the concert—which was, as predicted, mediocre—fifteen or twenty of Stewart's congregation gather for a big supper in the hotel's swank river-level restaurant. It's like *Monty Python's Flying Circus*, directed by John Ford. Voices are raised in beery, maudlin song, and there's a wonderful scene in which everybody toasts the road manager and his shy young lady by singing "Falling in Love Again" every few minutes or so, with Rod providing a letter-perfect imitation of Marlene Dietrich. He also launches into a very soulful rendition of "I Don't Want to Talk About It," only to have the song punctuated, in mock-military manner, by the whole crew shouting "Sah!" after each repetition of the title line. Everybody tells lots of stories and jokes, most of them corny when taken down verbatim, all of them quite touching in the context of comradeship. The code of the road is at work again. Clearly, this is a group of people with no serious ego problems.

A long procession of prospective groupies wanders in and out. One has braids and a big chest. Stewart signs a blouse, the leather patch on the ass of someone's blue jeans, and a soccer ball. Billy Peek, who is very quiet, is approached by a girl who talks so slowly that it takes her forever to get past the two *l*s in his first name: "Bi*llll* … *llll*y." He doesn't seem interested. Some of us try to think up new dialogue for movies like *The Big Sleep* and *Casablanca*. Sample: "Do you want to fool around?" "We wouldn't be fooling, would we?"[8]

Rod disappears, so I walk over to the Alamo, about five blocks away. It looks just like I thought it would: a white, Spanish-style building, front-lit, under a clear Texas sky, half-moon rising. At three in the morning, there's no traffic. The streets are absolutely empty. The plaque on the door reads:

BE SILENT, FRIEND
HERE HEROES DIED
TO BLAZE A TRAIL
FOR OTHER MEN

I sit for a while on a bench by a phone booth in front of the Alamo. Just thinking. Wishing I knew who to call. Moved once again by heroic history. For some reason, I write down the number of the pay phone: (512) 223-0084.[9]

8 Similarly, when Tom Carson first encountered Paul in 1978, he found him and Dave Marsh both sporting dark glasses and smoking Shermans in Paul's office at *Rolling Stone*. "They started trading lines back and forth from Paul's beloved hardboiled detective novels. Marsh capped things off by delivering *The Maltese Falcon* 'I won't because all of me wants to' speech."
9 Paul told Suzanne Vega: "In a lot of the better articles I've written, somewhere a line comes out of my head that I have not even thought and it just goes on the page. It's always the best line in the article. And it's always the first thing the editors want to take out because it doesn't go with the context." Citing this article in particular, he said, "I was sort of wandering around, not knowing Texas and not knowing

Tonight, San Antonio looks more like Paris or Venice than Texas. It's a place pictured in fine dreams. There's a canal from some romantic film, bordered by tall trees hung with Christmas lights, running through the center of the city. Along the canal are balconies, bridges, bookstores, small cafes, and a lovely River Walk (*Paseo del Rio*), now nearly deserted.

As I near the hotel, I notice a man and a woman seated on a white archway that spans the canal. They're talking intently. The man is wearing light tan pants, sporty tan shoes, and a leather jacket. The woman seems mesmerized. Christ, right out of *The Way We Were, Blume in Love,* or *Obsession,* I remember thinking: Redford and Streisand, Segal and Anspach, Robertson and Bujold. Then I realize it's Stewart and one of the waitresses from the restaurant.

Later, from the lobby, I watch them drive away in a battered pickup with Texas license plates. There are still quite a few fans waiting for autographs and etceteras. One of them asks if I've seen Rod. I shake my head no. Like the song says, "The crowd don't understand."[10]

II. DENVER

Britt Ekland and the Sex Pistols are indeed ubiquitous. If you don't believe me, ask Rod Stewart. He can't even walk into a room these days without being buttonholed by journalists who want his opinion about one or the other, and I sense he's getting sick of it. He wants to talk about the success of his latest album, the ongoing tour, or his new band—cruelly dubbed the Faceless by certain critics—but nobody cares. Instead, he's constantly quizzed about either the wrath of the wraithlike actress/ex-housemate who's suing him because he left her, or the pugnacity of the punks, who see him as the prototype of the rich, empty rock & roll star—as nothing, really nothing, to turn off. Britt wants his money (and, out of court, recently settled for a chunk of it), while the Pistols and their fans don't want his art. To a lot of

anybody, not particularly getting along with Stewart very well, and just feeling sort of lonely. There was this telephone booth by the Alamo and I thought, Jeez, I wish I had somebody to call. Who would I call? I went up and I just wrote the phone number down, and I put the phone number in the story. It just worked for some reason. It had nothing even to do with the story. It's just sort of a mood paragraph stuck in. But that's what everybody remembered about the story, is that strange thing."
10 "I asked him about that line," Paul told Lester Bangs. "He didn't know what it meant, said it seemed right to put in. He doesn't seem able to talk about his songs at all, or won't. Probably it's because he is basically an intuitive writer, and I don't think he really knew why he put that line in. For me it spoils the song."
"Sure it does," agreed Lester.
"Until then it's been great."

people, it's as simple as that. Beauty and the beasts must be driving this man crazy.

In a way, they are. Whenever I mention Ekland, Stewart seems to wish I were someplace else. He rolls his eyes like some sulky Sisyphus contemplating the inevitability of the hill and the rock. He's not pleased with questions about Johnny Rotten either, though he tries hard not to be overly negative about Britain's New Wave musical scene. (His two favorites: the Stranglers and Graham Parker and the Rumour.) But what really galls Rod, I think, is the change in attitude of a number of key critics toward him. Ever since the Sex Pistols cast the first stone, too many boulders have followed.

> • John Rockwell in *The New York Times*: "In person, Mr. Stewart comes close to defining the word 'vulgarity.' He dresses in a manner that can only be called silly, tarting himself up in androgynous glitter and assuming all kinds of transparently artificial melodramatic poses. Mr. Stewart is the sort of rocker who can take on the trappings of Las Vegas and not be suspected of selling out, because a Vegas notion of glamour seems to have been his inner ideal all along.... He remains a lesser artist than the real greats of rock."

> • Joe McEwen in *Rolling Stone*: "There are a lot of kids in England who don't care what kind of fashionably gauche trinkets decorate Rod Stewart's high-class Hollywood home or what the exact terms (if any) of his separation from Britt Ekland will be. They do care that Stewart has lost touch with them, not only musically but culturally as well.... As for *Foot Loose & Fancy Free*, it's sure hard to care much about 'Hot Legs' with Elvis Costello and the Sex Pistols around."

While Stewart has enough confidence to think he's at the apex of his art, he's too smart not to be worried, though he's tight-lipped about it. Ironically, now that he's become somewhat of a workaholic (the band toured or made records nine of the last twelve months) and very serious about his career, he's considered more of a playboy than ever. While it's clear that everyone who's traveling with him loves him because he genuinely seems to be just one of the boys, it's also apparent that much of the world no longer shares that opinion.

Me? I'm still a believer, but then I like the guy. Maybe he's lost a little of his personal self-awareness, yet his songs remain sharp, and I trust the emotions behind those songs. Granted, Rod could never have written either "Anarchy in the U.K." or "God Save the Queen." Is Johnny Rotten capable of the warmth and wisdom of "You're in My Heart"?

The Stewart entourage travels in a Viscount four-engine turbo jet done out in three rooms. In the center room, Rod and a Scottish sound mixer (who's had two double Screwdrivers for breakfast and speaks in an accent so thick it's a good thing we're not flying through it) immediately put on a videocassette of a football match. It's England versus Scotland—Rough and McGrain are two of the Scottish players, I note—and there's lots of beer and shouting on the plane as well as in the stadium. Things get so bleary and rowdy that when Scotland's team scores a goal, everybody misses seeing it, and Stewart has to rewind the tape. "It only happened two years ago," he says, winking in my direction.

Carmine Appice on English football: "If you get bored, the American section's up here."

In the Denver Hilton, Rod Stewart puts his hands and nose into fresh cement for posterity. The local Peaches record store came up with the idea, but since Tony Toon isn't sure he can get Stewart down there, the store brings the sidewalk to Stewart. Two workmen carry it in. Rod performs with his hands first, then improvises the climax. His sense of humor and uncanny knack for making the right remark at precisely the right time have rarely been better. As he puts towel to forehead and presses his infamous beak into the wet cement, he asks, with a great deal of concern: "Are there any people on the floor below?"

Stewart, Toon, Jim Cregan, Doris Tyler, Rita Taggart, and I are driven to a Denver discotheque/steakhouse for a late supper. Tyler (in charge of costumes and makeup) and Taggart (an actress and the tour masseuse) are called, with no accuracy and great respect, the Vibrator Sisters. They're two of the smartest, funniest ladies living, and Rod loves to have them around. "I'm glad you like them," he tells me later. "Everyone else on the tour can get so serious, but they're always like the spirit of rock & roll."

In the restaurant, people constantly ask for the star's autograph. His meal is interrupted several times, but he seems amazingly unconcerned about it. "What price glory?" Rita whispers to me as a blue-haired matron from the next table leans over to introduce her husband—who doesn't really react—to Rod. Stewart just smiles at him and says: "I can see you're not impressed. Can't say that I blame you." While he can be cynical about things like that, somehow he can't help being gracious and generous at the same time.

Rod and Jim start talking about their parents, who still live in England. In a matter of minutes, they're off on a familial marathon, running the gamut from awesome sentiment to awful sentimentality. The stories are wonderful to hear. Stewart thinks so much of his mother and father he even makes recordings of reunions of the clan, claiming he gets most of his best lines that way: "I look to me family for a sense of humor. When I go back to them, they truly make me laugh, though I don't know if I'm laughing at them or with them. Either way, I want to be with them."[11] Though the restaurant is very noisy, I turn on the cassette machine. Rod is saying:

"Me and me dad were going to a football match, and me dad came out in his old coat—and it was *rough*. It was an old black coat and he had outgrown it, and me mum said: '*You* can't go out in that bloody old coat! Your son's a millionaire. You'll disgrace the street.' Funny.

"Then there was this thing about the wine, because no one drinks wine at me house, right? But I brought a bottle of wine in when I was back last time. I opened it up and I said, 'Mum, we have to decanter the wine,' and she said, 'What?' I said: 'We have to decanter. We have to pour it into a decanter.' She said, 'Well, what's that?' I said, 'It's like a big vase,' and she said, 'We'll take the flowers out of the vase on top of the television and put it in there.' I said, 'No, we can't do that,' and she said: 'Oh, there's an empty milk bottle outside. Why don't you put the wine in the milk bottle?' Little things like that really bring you back to square one. Me mum's a classic.

"Three years ago, we had a gathering of the clan. I hired three bagpipers in full regalia for New Year's Eve. Just as the clock struck twelve, they came in and played 'Amazing Grace.' You know how 'Amazing Grace' goes. On the pipes, it's so stirring. Me dad cried his eyes out. I'll never forget it. The only thing that could bring a tear to me dad's eye was the sound of the pipes and when Scotland scored a goal. Especially against England.

"Ron Wood, he talks about his dad like he was a fucking hero. When the Faces started to make a lot of money, he bought his dad a color television. And his dad was so proud of his color television that he had it chained to the wall, in case somebody tried to steal it. To this day ...

---

11 A slightly drunken Cregan added: "I ended up realizing about four year ago—maybe more—five year ago, that I actually was my father's son. You're the same mold. You can't break out of it—"

"Somebody can," Paul disagreed.

"Me and me dad were at a football match at Wembley. It was halftime, and I went downstairs to get a drink. When I came up, me dad was crying. I said, 'What are you crying for?' He said, 'You should have seen it.' The whole of fucking Wembley—80,000 Scots—were all singing 'Sailing.' And me dad thinks, 'Me boy started all that.' That means more to me than anything."

Back at the hotel, Rod and I sit down and tape an interview for about two and a half hours. It doesn't go very well, and we both know it. Stewart invites Cregan to stick around, apparently so we can't delve into anything too deeply. At the same time, he's sympathetic toward the problems of my job. I get the feeling he wants to get this thing out of the way quickly, with as much dignity as possible for both of us. He answers everything honestly— sometimes too honestly, I think—but his heart's just not in it.

Stewart on the new band: "Musically, this band is totally superior. I always feel that what we sound like onstage is what the Faces were always trying to sound like—a tightly knit rhythm section with a piano and a lot of rhythm guitar on top of that. The Faces never had it, but there's something the Faces had that this band will never have. I mean, the thing with me and Woody together."

On being criticized by the British punk bands: "What the fuck! I make records. You don't have to buy them if you don't want them. Shit, leave them alone. What am I supposed to do with the money I earn? Give it back? Give it away?

"As Pete Townshend said on television the other week: 'I've made my mark. I've done the records. It's up to them to come and knock me off the top position.' That's the way it should be, but I wouldn't have had the guts to say that. I love him for doing it. I think that fucking guy's magic. He's done it all. He's served his fucking dues. These cunts haven't.

"They say, Well, fucking Rod's gone to Hollywood with a movie star, right? The cunts! I come from the same background as they do. In England, all rock & roll comes from the working class. That's your only way of getting out of the rabble. I come from nothing. Then, all of a sudden, I'm faced with a lot of glamorous women. What the fuck am I going to do?

"The Sex Pistols have a big album now. A lot of money's being grossed. A couple of million dollars. And they'll get paid for it. Then we'll see what they do. Give it back to the fucking record buyers? That's anarchy, isn't it?

"The whole New Wave has destroyed itself immediately. A second and third wave will come from there. The summer before last, it looked promising.

Then the big fucking record companies came in, the big fucking business moguls. All of a sudden, there were clothes designers and punk fashion shows. That's what killed it for me. It's really dead in England. The first wave's dead.

"In America [with the New York Dolls, et al.], it was a music, period. In England, it's a fashion foremost, an attitude, a stance. Which isn't the way it should be. It's phony bollocks. So let's wait for the second wave. That might bring on something good."

On *Foot Loose & Fancy Free*: "It was supposed to be a double album, but we had to stop because of the tour. There was no concept. A lot of the tracks reflect what I was going through at the time with Britt. In fact, I knew the title of the album before we busted up. It must have been in the back of me mind that it was going to happen. The title is a straightforward statement of independence. I felt I'd been tied down for too long and I wanted to break away. Domesticity—that's death for me."

On "You Got a Nerve": "Sometimes what you're writing about is what you *wouldn't* want to happen to you. I couldn't think of anything worse than that—the woman goes off and she fucks somebody else on the other side of the world and comes back and says, 'Let me in.' I've never been mistreated like that. Perhaps I'm asking for it. It hasn't happened yet, and I wouldn't wish it on my worst enemies. People say to me, 'This must be about Britt. She's done that to you.' And I say, no, she hasn't done that to me. She had no bearing on the song whatsoever."[12]

On "(If Loving You Is Wrong) I Don't Want to Be Right": "That really fit into what was happening. I was seeing Liz Treadwell, but Britt didn't know. The whole track was done live in the studio. Liz was there, and I'm singing, 'If loving you is wrong, I don't want to be right....' You couldn't *help* but sing it with guts. That was the last track we recorded."

On "You're in My Heart (The Final Acclaim)": "It wasn't totally about Britt. The first verse could have been about Liz. It could have been about anybody that I met in that period—and there were a lot of them. It's about three women, two football teams, and a country—Scotland."

On the line, "You'll be my breath should I grow old": "I think that must have been about me mum and dad."[13]

---

12 "It's a very scary song," Paul told Stewart. "Those are very scary lines." Reciting the final verse— "Please, please go away / I loved you once / I don't love you now / Please, please go away"—he said, "It's happened to me" (though he didn't clarify whether he meant the times that he'd been on the sending or receiving end of such sentiments).

13 Paul cited "You'll be my breath should I grow old" as "the line that gets to me the most in that song." He liked the next line, too: "You are my lover, you're my best friend."
"Oh, your lovers are always your best friends," Stewart said.
"Not always," Paul said, "no."
Stewart agreed: "Nah, you're right. Fuck it, you're right. Of course, you're right."

Before the soundcheck the next afternoon, Stewart is sitting on the edge of the stage, playing Woody Guthrie songs on an acoustic guitar. He looks at the myriad of roadies setting up the band's equipment. "Shit, there are people on this tour I don't even know yet," he says sadly.

I like soundchecks. You can sit way in the back of an empty auditorium and think—if I only knew what to think. Something about all that open space just gets the mind rolling, and it's such a contrast to the pandemonium of the show later. During the soundcheck, the band is perfectly relaxed, and the playing always seems to have that something extra—or perhaps *lacks* something extra—that invariably strikes me as being more natural and private and revealing (i.e., better) than the official version. I think someone should start making live soundcheck LPs.

I'm totally schizophrenic about Stewart and his new band in concert. From a distance, everything appears overwrought and impersonal: Rod playing straight through to the audience with the broadest possible star appeal, the meaning of the songs be damned. But up closer, where I can see his face, he looks like a man who's completely sincere. And his interpretations not only make sense, they're very moving.

I can't really figure it out.

III. LOS ANGELES

Jim Cregan seems to have taken Ron Wood's place as Rod Stewart's number-one road buddy. They're together most of the time. Cregan, Rod confides—in a tone so reverent it's ridiculous—is the only reason he doesn't allow tickets to be sold for the seats behind the stage. That way, Jim's bald spot won't show.

In return, Cregan tells a lovely story about how Stewart recorded the highly confessional "I Was Only Joking." The first time any of the musicians heard the lyrics was during the vocal take, since Rod had simply scat sung or hummed in the appropriate places while the instrumental tracks were cut. When he finally sang the words, he did it rather sheepishly, shyly glancing up at the band every few seconds to see if they thought the song was too corny. They didn't.

Stewart and I are sitting in his Holmby Hills house (which he stipulated that I not describe), talking about the old days, watching yet another videocassette of Scottish football, and seeking to discover whether either of us has improved his technique in the art of the formal interview. "So it's come to this," he says, and we both laugh. I ask him how he's suddenly become such a prolific songwriter.

"I think I spoke to Bernie [Taupin] once," he says. "I asked him how he and Elton [John] went about writing songs. And he said: 'Well, I write the lyrics, I give them to Elton, and he just sits down at the piano and makes with the music. It's as easy as that.' I thought, Shit, me and Woody don't work like that. It's really hard work when we do it because we do it the other way around. There's no freedom in doing it our way. You're stuck—you've got to make each word fit the music." He shakes his head in disbelief. "So, after years and years, I suddenly learned how to write songs."

Out of the blue, Rod admits: "I want to see how good the band is. I keep shouting me mouth off about them, but I want to *really* see how good they are. I want to get away from the way we are now. Perhaps I shouldn't say this, but we're not really gaining any new ground. We're doing something now that I love—making good rock & roll—but I think there's a lot more to rock & roll. We're going to try to start taking it away from the Chuck Berry rhythm guitar and the regular chords. I want to see how far we can go."

Does Stewart think he and Britt Ekland will ever get back together?

"Well, it's impossible at the moment. We aren't going to get back together. I look upon it probably as being a big mistake. It might be a mistake on my behalf, it could have been a mistake on her behalf. I know we were good for each other. Very good for each other. Who made the first bad move, whether it was because of what I did or because of her reaction to what I did, I don't know. All I know is what I did was legal."

Legal?

"What I did was not breaking any law whatsoever. There was never a pact between us. I think perhaps in a drunken moment I might have said I'd try to be faithful, but she knew me track record when she met me. And I did me best but I fell short, like many of us do. I'm still a sucker for a pretty face and a pair of long legs, but I'm the only fuck-poor bastard who's ever got sued over it.

"It's difficult to know what to say because everything I say nowadays seems to get completely blown out of proportion and thrown back in me face. Just for the record, I'm totally fucking fed up with reading about meself, especially in the European press. So I'm very reluctant to talk about it. But she's nowhere near as bad as people make out she is. I mean, she's the most dedicated woman

I've ever known when it comes to being with one guy, and I appreciate that. Her biggest problem is there's always been a language barrier there. A lot of people didn't ever understand her. She doesn't speak the Queen's English, and I think that many times when she'd try to be funny, it came across as being cynical and sarcastic.

"But the fucking amount of money [$12.5 million] she's trying to sue me for! There isn't that much money in the world, I'm sure. I make nowhere near that much. But I think when a woman's been hurt like I hurt her—because I completely crushed her world around her—they just become irrational and do the most wicked thing. She always did say she'd cut me balls off, but I didn't know what she meant. Now I know what she meant. She didn't *literally* mean she'd cut me balls off. She'd cut me wallet off."

(In her book, *True Britt*, Ekland remembers it this way: "Once Rod told me that his other women hadn't cared if he slept around. I looked at him straight between the eyes. 'Then that's where I'm very different,' I said. 'I would mind a great deal. In fact, if you screw another woman while you're with me, I'll chop off your balls.' Rod's face puckered with fear. He knew that I meant every word.")

What would Stewart have done if the tables had been turned?

"She knows that. I told her that. I said, 'If you'd have done that to me, you wouldn't have heard anything. That would have been it.' I'd have been off or she'd have been kicked out of me house—there would have been no coming back. It's never happened to me, thank God, as far as I know, and I'm pretty sure I'm shrewd enough that I'd know if it ever did. That would be it. I'd say goodbye. I mean, if I can't give a woman everything, then fuck it."

I find it difficult to believe his claim that he's never been hurt in love.

"Never. I've always been the one to push and shove and say, Sorry, that's it, darlin', it's all over, goodbye. Take twenty Valiums and have a stomach pump and that's the end of it. I've been very lucky, but I know that one day I'm going to get fucking stung something terrible."

I still wonder why he did it.

"Boys will be boys, Paul," he says with a sigh of resignation. He's not smiling.

Stewart and I once played a game of pool in Miami Beach. I beat him, and he's never forgotten it. Of course, I haven't let him. Now he wants his revenge. He builds up a strong early lead, but I distract him by asking questions. (He kept bumping my arm every time I was about to shoot in Florida.) I mention something about "You're in My Heart."

He says: "A few days ago in San Antonio, I woke up with that bird. Woke up, and the old sun was coming through the curtains. She says to me, 'Go and turn the radio on.' Out comes: 'I didn't know what day it was….' There's fucking magic in it! It wasn't the lyrical content. It was just, shit, that's my song that I wrote when I was in bed at home and I had the flu. And here I am in the middle of San Antonio with a strange woman about a million miles from me hotel, and here it comes on the radio. I think it's the most marvelous thing in the world. Your song goes through the channels, it's pressed, it's a bit of plastic, and it comes all the way back to you. And there's your feelings, coming through a radio. Does that sound really silly?"

I tell him I don't think so.

"I mean, there's this fucking thing where no one seems to grow old," he says. "You might get a few wrinkles around your eyes, but the instinct is still there. It's there in front of us all the time. All of these women. And if it's flashed in front of your face, you want to take it. Who wouldn't?

"It's like we're in a time capsule. Without flattering meself, I know I look exactly the same as I did seven years ago. It's not that you're not allowed to grow older, it's just that time goes so quickly that you haven't got time to grow older—in attitude, appearance, or anything. It's almost like we're not growing up at all.

"Sometimes I look at meself and I think, Fuck, you're the same person with the same basic needs as you were five years ago. And that shouldn't be. I'm thirty-two now and I think, Shit, I must be a bit more mature. But I'm not. Still gullible for a long leg and a big tit." He can't help but smile. "I always look upon meself as being very immature."[14]

(Ekland in *True Britt*: "He was still a boy, not a man.")

Rod starts talking about his collection of *objets d'art* while I put together a four-ball run.

"I'm sure everybody must think I spend every day standing on the terrace watching the fucking football matches," he says. "But, of course, I don't. I want to spend the money that I'm earning. I go off to Paris and buy lamps and things like that.

"The first thing I ever bought of any price was a sterling silver picture frame that I bought with the first week's royalties I ever got from Jeff Beck. I just saw it in the store, and it was a beautiful thing. I've still got it.

"No one's ever collected in me family. I suppose I was just trying to improve meself. It might have been that. It might have just been the fact that whatever I started collecting was so interesting, so beautiful. I've always admired beauty

---

14 "So do I," Paul said. "I've debated time after time whether, Jesus Christ, get a regular job and settle down, or should I keep going this crazy way, being broke all the time and have a good time? I finally decided I should keep going this way, being broke all the time and having a good time."

in anything, whether it be a painting, motor cars, the way someone plays football, the way they sing, or whether it's a lamp. I think that's one thing you don't *learn*. You certainly can't learn that."

Is there any one thing he particularly wants?

"Oh, yeah, hundreds. Hundreds. But if there's one thing I'd love to have, it would be a painting by J.M.W. Turner. But no one's got that much money. I don't even know as there's ever been one up for sale. But, more than that, I want Scotland to win the World Cup. There's a book—"

Stewart brings out a copy of *We'll Support You Evermore* and reads aloud the quote that begins this article. When I write it down in my notebook, he's very concerned that I get it right. It clearly means a lot to him.[15]

"That sort of sums it up," he says. Then he decides otherwise. "No, it doesn't. You never sum up anything."

I sink the eight ball into the corner pocket. Rod looks extremely pained. Much as I like the guy, he sure can't shoot pool. But then, there's a lot of things I can't do either.

There's a cab waiting for me outside. Stewart and I say goodbye. Just as I get out the door, he yells: "Hey, Nelson, who's doing the pictures for this article?"

"I don't know," I answer. I mention a woman photographer both of us know.

"Ohhhh, you got to keep in good with her," Rod Stewart says with mock solemnity. Then he flashes that enormous grin. "Would you ask her," he says, "if a fuck is out of the question?"

---

15 The irony is that Paul either copied down the title wrong or, when he typed up his notes, he omitted a word. Both his manuscript and the printed article in *Rolling Stone* refer to the book as *We'll Support Evermore.*

- IAN HUNTER -

Along with "Bob Dylan," "Rod Stewart," and "Folk-Rock," "All the Young Dudes" was the fourth essay Paul penned in 1976 for the first edition of The Rolling Stone Illustrated History of Rock & Roll. *As the man responsible for signing the untameable New York Dolls to their first recording contract, he seemed the natural choice to write a critical assessment of the careers-to-date of three other often conspicuous and daring artists: Lou Reed, David Bowie, and Ian Hunter. He'd even worked with the first two while at Mercury.*

Lou Reed, David Bowie, and Ian Hunter share a similar troubled vision of life and death—an outlook of unblinking fatalism that haunts even their legitimate lighter moments. They are all survivors, natural outsiders by unnatural choice or intuitive chance. Like Bob Dylan—a major influence on Reed and Hunter and for whom Bowie has written a song on *Hunky Dory*—each is a self-conscious mythographer and mythmaker deeply involved in the archetypes of the ultra-urban Seventies. The strain of androgyny runs through both Reed and Bowie, although Hunter seems to flirt with it merely momentarily in the title song on Mott the Hoople's *All the Young Dudes* (an album produced by Bowie, who has also produced Reed). Bowie and Hunter perform songs that Reed has written, while Reed and Bowie are the spiritual fathers of such Seventies rock & rollers as Patti Smith, Elliott Murphy, Jonathan Richman, the Modern Lovers, the New York Dolls, Talking Heads, Television, and a veritable host of glitter- and punk-rock bands too numerous to mention....[1]

With the essay, Paul accomplished the unthinkable for a rock critic: he inspired one of the artists he was critiquing—and whose work so inspired him. In 1979, Ian Hunter told him that his words—specifically, calling Hunter, Reed, and Bowie "natural outsiders"—in tandem with a recurring dream, had resulted in the song "The Outsider" on his new album, You're Never Alone with a Schizophrenic. *"I thought that was a great title for a song. Because it's the observation thing. Because you do feel like an outsider, it's absolutely true. Observation. Noncommittal."*

The interview with the singer-songwriter also revealed to Paul that Toulouse-Lautrec had been correct: "One should never confuse the artist with the art." Hunter in person was a tad contrary to the kindred spirit Paul had found on vinyl and not quite the rock & roll savior he had painted him to be in earlier reviews. He didn't share Paul's adoration of the Dolls ("New York has always had this thing," Hunter said, "they've always looked after their own; hence the legend of the Velvet Underground") and took exception to the rock press's blossoming deification of the Clash. "The singer's beginning to learn how to sing and the bass player is still beginning to learn how to play. It's not all attitude and commitment and excitement."

"Yeah, but it's nice to see that," Paul quietly argued. "You don't see that too much anymore, I don't think. That's what's nice about your record: there's commitment there as well as professionalism. If it were just *professionalism, it wouldn't be that interesting." He cited* McGuinn, Clark & Hillman, *a recent release by the former Byrds: "It's very professional, but they've got nothing to say at all anymore."*

"Well, it gets more difficult. Maybe when these guys," Hunter said of Paul's punks, "have done as many albums as the Byrds have done, they'll be having a problem to think of something to say, too."

"That could be," Paul allowed.

Regardless, he greatly admired You're Never Alone with a Schizophrenic *and ran his almost 2,000-word piece, "Autumn Fire, Spring Fever," as lede review in* Rolling Stone. *In the same article, he wagered on a young singer-songwriter named Steve Forbert and his debut album,* Alive on Arrival.

It was an odd pairing—Hunter, the reluctant godfather of punk, having his work considered alongside Forbert, the wanting/unwanting heir to the throne of "new Dylan" whom Paul seemed to be knighting as an honorary Young Dude—but Paul skillfully hung his review of two such disparate artists on the one thing they had in common: their age difference. While he confirmed Hunter's status as one of rock & roll's senior and most credible practitioners, he heralded Forbert's arrival on the scene. Paul graced the younger man, however, with a decidedly (to borrow from Hunter's title) schizophrenic notice.

Steve Forbert: "I did notice that the review gave and it also took away. The second half is totally dissed, and at the time I saw that as much as anything. I remember it now, at this very moment, that I was like, 'Yes, Mrs. Lincoln, but how was the play?' But I didn't dwell on it. It was the lede review—so what do you want?"

Paul's writings about Ian Hunter and Mott the Hoople are among his best. It's doubtful that any other critic with so large an audience at his nicotine-stained fingertips ever examined and praised Hunter's work in such detail. Hunter doesn't remember the pieces, however. Danny Goldberg, who now manages him, says, "He just doesn't remember Paul, though he appreciates what he wrote in retrospect."

K.A.

AUTUMN FIRE, SPRING FEVER

Neither Ian Hunter's *You're Never Alone with a Schizophrenic* nor Steve Forbert's *Alive on Arrival* boasts any special thematic pretensions, but both records set off reverberations that reach deeper than any particular track on either. Each offers an affecting wholeness, a rare unity of mood, that makes its own statement as much between the lines as in the grooves. Forbert calls one of his songs "Steve Forbert's Midsummer Night's Toast," while Hunter, despite a preference for fast ones rather than ballads here, somehow always manages to sound like a venerable rock & roll King Lear, raging passionately against the elements. Or like Hamlet, sitting in the graveyard, holding his own freshly unearthed skull (instead of Yorick's) in his hands, gazing into its eyeless sockets and prophesying autumnal doom.

None of the lyrics of either LP is as important as the way Forbert and Hunter sing them. Steve Forbert shines like Charlie Chaplin's smile on a sweet summer night, his youthful high spirits disarming all criticism as easily and innocently as a pretty girl's figure breaks hearts. Some of his tunes aren't even that terrific, it's just that once he's got you hooked on his free-flowing enthusiasm, every little vocal wink is irresistible. With great strength, Ian Hunter works the darkness on the edge of town. He's out there, an aging, James Dean desperado under the eaves, bending rock & roll phrases in ways that define both meaning and genre. Like Sam Spade turning Brigid O'Shaughnessy over to the cops, he sings: "It's just another *niiiiight!*"—which tells you right away that it isn't. And in his three near-bardic soliloquies, Hunter elevates certain everyday events from the familiar to the fabled through the sheer force of his I've-seen-it-all conviction. *Alive on Arrival* is about being twenty. *You're Never Alone with a Schizophrenic* is about *not* being twenty.

Steve Forbert's a Mississippi-cum-New York City singer-songwriter with so much honesty and energy that he overwhelms his songs with the punch of a punk rocker without ever sounding like one. Though his feverish folk-rock bears no resemblance to either the Sex Pistols or the Clash, he trashes (without trying to) such exploitative New Wave spinoffs as Joe Jackson, the

Police, and the Boomtown Rats while absolutely annihilating the stilted pseudorockabilly posturings of Dwight Twilley and Robert Gordon. There's little calculation here, simply raw talent (the best kind, really) blasting through the roadblocks and over the finish line. People will tell you that Forbert sounds like the early Bob Dylan, but even if they're right, they should be ignored. In 1979, such an approach is misleading and won't get you to the heart of this or any other matter. Anyway, people will tell you anything.

"I'm glad to be so young / Talking with my tongue … / Glad to be so crazy in my day," Steve Forbert beams just a few seconds into his debut album, and those lines are a perfect summation of what's great about *Alive on Arrival*. Side one practically explodes off the turntable, the tour-de-force singing coming straight at you like a field-of-fire missile with HAVE A NICE DAY painted on its warhead. In "Goin' Down to Laurel," Forbert's so hyperkinetic and positive that he doesn't even *hear* someone who's trying to tell him a hard-luck story. "Yeah, best of luck and all / And try to have some fun," he mouths matter-of-factly before soaring into what he's really interested in: "They tell me this great life can always"—a pause while he dives for cover from a volley of drumbeats—"*END!*," though the vitality of the vocal belies anything but further adventures.

Laurel may be "a dirty, stinking town," but the singer "know[s] *exactly* what [he's] going to find" there. He's got more than enough confidence, in "Steve Forbert's Midsummer Night's Toast," to hoist a triumphant shot glass to the bad things in his life: "Here's to all the shitty jobs that I despise," he grins, and it's catchy. Throughout the record, fierce and funny asides roll off him like eager beads of sweat. The joyous, stop-start, Buddy Holly-hiccupy "What Kinda Guy?" is a snappy series of such sendups as "I'll tell you truly / That I sometimes lie."

One of the best qualities about *Alive on Arrival* is that Forbert, though he's "Sitting and listening with a young man's ear / To all the rainbow dreams," preaches direct action instead of navel-gazing introspection. It's not that he's against the dreams themselves, but he can't stand the idea of just mooning around waiting for them to come true. In "Thinkin'," after the lines, "I look in your eyes / I see shackles and chains," there's a tragicomic, fall-away "*Awwww!*" that gently but succinctly savages someone who's been rendered helpless by analyzing to death all of life's options. This kind of stuff is not for Forbert. In the LP's masterpiece, "It Isn't Gonna Be That Way," he gets very hardheaded about it:

> You've traveled so far
> The wind in your face
> You're thinking you've found

> The one special place
> Where all of your dreams
> Will walk out in line
> And follow the course
> You've made in your mind
> Hey, it isn't gonna be that way …

Totally possessed by the passion of his performance (it's difficult to say which is better, his singing or his harmonica playing), he comes up with an answer that would do Ian Hunter proud: "You'll just have to live / And see what you find."

Of course, *Alive on Arrival* is far from perfect. What's curious about it is that you can skip the whole second half and, with the possible exception of "Big City Cat," not miss a thing. Puffed-up naïveté, archetypal singer-songwriter self-pity, precious sensitivity, and meaningless repetition—in short, all the flaws and philosophies scrupulously avoided on side one—dominate side two and sink it like a stone. But it doesn't matter. Because nothing, nothing in this world, is going to stop Steve Forbert, and on that I'll bet anything you'd care to wager.[2]

Ian Hunter doesn't make many mistakes on *You're Never Alone with a Schizophrenic*. Though he's theoretically old enough to be Steve Forbert's father, he writes and sings more like an especially fatalistic co-conspirator: the deadly but protective William Holden figure, in a rock & roll version of Sam Peckinpah's *The Wild Bunch*, to a gang of younger, more impressionable shootists. Hunter knows all about the promises of life—and, despite their ominous price tags, he's still exhilarated by them—but he knows about death and taxes, too. His ace in the hole is experience, and he uses, with compassionate precision, high cards that only the veteran professional gambler would dare employ: the ironies of success and failure. Through misunderstanding, young Romeo and Juliet will die for love, but Hunter damn well won't. He'd rather go down fighting, holding out for the chance of a last-ditch miracle, because in the end, old hearts take loss harder. They know what it means.

---

2 A little over three years later, having resigned from *Rolling Stone* and freelancing under Jann Wenner's imposed star system, Paul reviewed Forbert's fourth album, *Steve Forbert*, granting it only one and a half stars:

> What's happened to this guy? In the course of four albums, Steve Forbert has metamorphosed from the most incendiary punk-folker on the Greenwich Village scene into a singer-songwriter so listless and unconvincing that he couldn't sell water to a thirsty man in Death Valley. ["Steve Forbert—*Steve Forbert*" by Paul Nelson from *Rolling Stone*, September 16, 1982. © Rolling Stone LLC 1982. All rights reserved. Reprinted by permission.]

Quite simply, *You're Never Alone with a Schizophrenic* is my favorite record so far this year. (Somewhat similar to *Street-Legal*, it makes Bob Dylan sound sick.) Thanks to co-producer/guitarist Mick Ronson plus keyboardist Roy Bittan, bassist Gary Tallent, and drummer Max Weinberg from Bruce Springsteen's E Street Band, Ian Hunter's lion in winter is given a rock & roll roar commensurate with the combustion of his vocals and vision. Not only do the fast songs here match the great rockers from Hunter's Mott the Hoople days (cf. 1972's *All the Young Dudes*, 1973's *Mott*), in some cases, they're probably better. In "Just Another Night," "Wild East," "Cleveland Rocks," and "When the Daylight Comes," Tallent's driving bass pounds like a sprinter's pulse, Ronson's guitars galvanize gloriously, and Weinberg's drums crack like bullwhips.[3]

"Just Another Night" and "When the Daylight Comes" are classics in the "Sweet Jane"/"Rock & Roll" tradition (Mott the Hoople meets Lou Reed's Velvet Underground): seemingly about nothing, they turn out to be about everything—and it's all in the evocative repetition, not in the raucousness. "When the Daylight Comes," in particular, is a beauty. The ultimate on-the-road composition about women (and writing), it boasts enough braggadocio and bashfulness to more than justify the album's title. While the lyrics lurch from almost primal purity ("Alive shines in your eyes; the hungry years are so nice / Our shadows shake in the lamplight—no writer could explain") toward winsome desperation ("I wanna weave you in words, wanna paint you in verse / Wanna leave you in someone else's dreams"), the song fills up with meaning as you listen to it. "Wild East" is a tribute to East Coast music and mores (as opposed to those of the unWild West), while "Cleveland Rocks" pays witty homage to that fine rock & roll city. "Bastard" is the LP's odd number. It's a love song in the form of a domestic quarrel, with lines like these: "Space cow, I'll chew the bad blood running through yuh / Kiss you as you hit the floor."

Ian Hunter's balladic ambitions have always been based in excessive melodrama, and the record's three slow songs bear this out. Never afraid to shoot for the moon, Hunter generally utilizes the power of the positive cliché for ammunition. More often than not, he hits his target, too. "Ships"—the kind that "pass in the night"—is a lovely tune about the difficulties involved in a father-son relationship. As singer and dad talk by the sea, there seems to be an understanding. But then you think back to Hunter's first words ("I said love's easier when it's far away") and his father's last: "He said it's harder now we're far away / We only read you when you write."

---

3 Paul was so taken with the sound of *You're Never Alone with a Schizophrenic* that he told Hunter: "You could just totally go with the music and not listen at all to the lyrics, which isn't generally what I do."

"Standin' in My Light," a diatribe against someone who's preventing the artist's success (more than likely himself), is *You're Never Alone with a Schizophrenic*'s most moving musical moment. An anthem about getting up off the floor and taking another swing, it starts softly with organ and voice, builds slowly as the band comes in and then just goes through the roof on the choruses. Though Hunter denies it, I think the song's about punk rock—a genre he staunchly supports—and the commercial inroads it's made on his brand of rock & roll. There's real love/hate here: "You take my pictures from your walls / Ain't gonna trade with the pain 'n the New York Dolls."[4]

According to Hunter, "The Outsider" is a recurring dream he's had for years. On the surface, it sounds like yet another outlaw number, but its images are surprisingly delicate and timeless. The first two lines could have come from Falstaff, the third and fourth from Warren Zevon:

> Death be my mistress—guns be my wife
> Breath is my witness—'n the roads are my life
> I just skinned my future as clean as a knife
> In a bar on the way from L.A.

After the "Just killed a man in a town called Night Falls / I'm damned if I can remember it all" verse, Mick Ronson plays some electric guitar worthy of Neil Young. And Hunter finishes up by railing against what "The Outsider" and much of *You're Never Alone with a Schizophrenic* are really about: growing up, growing old, and dying. On an album filled with the word *night*, one thing must be said. This man does not go gently.

If ever two LPs complemented each other, *Alive on Arrival* and *You're Never Alone with a Schizophrenic* do. While Steve Forbert's still reveling in his first embrace with music and women, Ian Hunter's hoping this isn't the last good kiss. For Forbert, it's simply the end of the beginning. For Hunter, fortunately, it's nowhere near the beginning of the end. Who can say which is more wonderful or heartbreaking.

---

4 "I certainly misread that one," Paul told Hunter, having interpreted the song as a "rather sympathetic stance" toward punk rock. To the contrary, Hunter said, "It's written about an individual, and it knows who it is." As well, he corrected Paul's belief that the "New York Dolls" mention was a nod to the band so close to Paul's heart: "It was in reference to puppets. It was in reference to people that are hanging off bits of string in corporate situations."

- BRUCE SPRINGSTEEN -

Pleased and embarrassed, Bruce Springsteen laughs, having just reread the four pieces that Paul Nelson wrote about him between 1975 and 1982. "I was shocked at how much I recalled almost every sentence of every piece. They feel like a part of my history to me. I mean, they're actually in my bones somewhere. Those were big stories for me at the time. They could come out right now and they'd be right on the money."

In the summer of 1972, Paul received a call from Ron Oberman. His old boss at Mercury was now head of publicity at Columbia Records where John Hammond had just signed a new act. Oberman was going to attend a concert showcasing the new discovery and wanted to know if Paul would like to tag along. Which was how, in a small downtown Manhattan theater, Paul Nelson became the first music writer to witness Bruce Springsteen perform as a Columbia artist.

A couple of months later, Springsteen, recording his first LP, was still taking the bus in from New Jersey to open for "whoever happened to be on the second half of the bill that night" at Max's Kansas City. He remembers the night Paul, sporting more facial hair than usual, came up after a set and reintroduced himself. "He had the total certified air of the hipster about him. I don't know how old he was at the time, but he seemed a lot older than me." Paul was thirty-six and Springsteen was just shy of twenty-three. "He had that wispy beard and moustache and he had the spectacles and he had something like a newsboy's hat that he would wear. And he always smoked these little brown cigarettes. He always cut a bit of the loner figure—but alone *doesn't come that strange to other loners."*

Paul kept coming back.

"There were a few people who picked up on me very early, before my first record, when I was playing solo at Max's Kansas City, and he's the one who stands foremost in my mind. He would always have somebody with him—I guess 'tastemakers' or whatever you call them, or just people he liked. He was kind of turning people on to me, and we just struck up a friendship. It was very loose."

Three years passed before Paul wrote anything about his new friend, but those early writings helped establish Springsteen's persona and career. "If you were a fan of mine at the time, they were just essential reading. For an artist to have that out there about yourself, it was very helpful in getting across what you were trying to do and who you were trying to be. That was my job the way that I saw it, and he perceived it. That's quite a connection to make.

"Those words really stood out. Paul's writing meant a lot to me emotionally at the time, enough to just flick that switch so that when you went onstage that night you remembered: Hey, you're working on a promise to keep, not to just yourself but to him. He put his ass on the line for you in that last story, so you better be good."

On the same day that Springsteen's third album was released, The Village Voice *headline wanted to know "Is Bruce Springsteen Worth the Hype?" Just as* Born to Run *took the world by surprise, the singer himself wasn't quite prepared for Paul's expansive article, which avoided hagiography and acknowledged "Springsteen's weaknesses" as honestly as his strengths. Although virtually all of his encounters with Paul had either been at concerts or when he'd drop by Mercury to say hello, Paul's piece allowed Springsteen to truly appreciate Paul's depth of understanding. He still finds great pleasure at how Paul captured (a full two months before Springsteen was simultaneously canonized on the covers of* Time *and* Newsweek) *his ambivalence at being at the epicenter of "a media killing to the nth degree": "'In Asbury Park, New Jersey,'" Springsteen reads aloud, "'the blood of the poet must be running both hot and cold about this.' Well, it certainly was," he chuckles.*

Paul, who refused to surrender something he'd written until it was perfect, also understood Springsteen's belief that "he had to deliver a masterpiece.... After all, it could always be better, couldn't it?"

When Paul wrote about Darkness on the Edge of Town *in 1978, only a few months into his new job as editor at* Rolling Stone, *the table of contents quoted him saying, "Seeing Springsteen play Boston made me fall in love with rock & roll all over again." Whereas "Is Springsteen Worth the Hype?"*

had, in its attention to behind-the-scenes details and privileged information, only hinted at the personal relationship between writer and subject, "Springsteen Fever" put it right on the table.

> Tonight, I'm aware that this friendship gives me an edge— that instead of giving me a formal interview, he'd probably rather just talk—and I'm more than a little uneasy about it. When the tape recorder is turned on, both of us are careful not to cross a certain line. I'm glad to see him, but wish the circumstances were different. He seems to feel the same way.[1]

Paul was as much in love with the idea of a rock star who "seems to have as much loyalty to his fans as they do to him" as he was with the enormous talent that had made it all possible in the first place. Yet, for someone as rooted as Paul was in film noir and hardboiled fiction, he was never comfortable with Springsteen's wanderings down "occasional dark alleys."

> Many of the characters in the songs on Bruce Springsteen's new album appear to be trapped in a state of desperation so intense that they must either break through into something better (or at least into something ambiguous) or break down into madness, murder, and worse. *Darkness on the Edge of Town* seems to be about the high cost of romantic obsession for adults, not teenagers ("Mister, I ain't a boy, no, I'm a man" instead of the wonderful but more sentimental "'Cause tramps like us, baby we were born to run"), and while the LP offers hope, it's also Springsteen's blackest—though probably best—work.[2]

When The River *rolled around in 1980, Paul, coming off his failed romance with Laura Fissinger, yearned for the return of more innocent times. Instead, he was struck by the album's "aura of omnipotent dread."*

Springsteen: "That was a part of coming up post-Vietnam. I began post-Watergate, and immediately post-Vietnam my music came out. It was a time when one of the main feelings people were having was, man, they'd been cheated! If you were interested in your Americaness, I don't think you would live without the dread ever again. And so it had to be a part of your work."

1 "Springsteen Fever" by Paul Nelson from *Rolling Stone*, July 13, 1978. © Rolling Stone LLC 1978. All rights reserved. Reprinted by permission.
2 *Ibid.*

If he'd found parts of The River *dark, Paul was wholly unprepared in 1982 for the unrelentingly grim* Nebraska. *Having just resigned from* Rolling Stone, *his private life and finances in shambles, the prospect of giving Springsteen's newest album a bad review was more than he could bear. After all, a bad review had cost him at least one friend, Jackson Browne, and it hadn't even been one of his albums.*

Crystal Zevon: "He was so conflicted about what to do. He just couldn't quite warm up to it. He felt it was derivative of the last album."

Ken Tucker says, "One of the brave things about Paul was that he could get so involved with an artist and yet still write a bad review when he felt that the work deserved it. How could it not be a strain on those friendships? I think it's probably because he could separate the work from the person and that, with the artists that he admired, he never intended it to be a personal attack but more written in sorrow, perhaps an almost prescriptive kind of thing, pointing out weaknesses with the indication that 'Here's where you've gone wrong' and a quiet wish that the work could be as good as it once was."

"It's one thing to feel bad about it," Fred Schruers says, "another to use that creatively to say you're disappointed. That was a uniqueness he had. If Paul was disappointed in you, you really felt it. Because when he was rooting for you, if you were an artist, it meant a lot. It meant a lot both in terms of prestige, wherever he might have reviewed you, and it meant you were doing it right and you were adhering to a kind of code that the music and the musicians had in those days. So if you strayed from the code, it was probably painful to read. It isn't as if any review that's negative isn't painful to read, but with Paul it counted a bit more because you knew he wasn't ever trying to step on your head to advance his opinions with some other critic. It was really about wanting the music to be all it could be and expecting people's motivations to remain what they'd been when they started, as long as those were good and proper artistic motivations. That's part of that moral voice that was never too far in the background with him."

Ultimately, Paul found a way to both praise Nebraska *and raise his objections. "It was interesting," Springsteen says, "rereading the story, how he kind of wound his way into it." Paul's roundabout appreciation of the album was made possible in no small part by his knowledge and appreciation of folk music—another part of his past that Springsteen knew nothing about.*

The review represented a couple of firsts: it was the first time Paul had written for a magazine other than Rolling Stone *in almost five years; and it was his first work for* Musician *magazine. It was also one of the last things he wrote before he faded from view, not to return in print until 1990.*

Springsteen never forgot him. "He disappeared, and I never heard from him much after that. We just drifted apart. He is somebody who played a very essential part in that creative moment when I was there trying to establish what I was doing and what I wanted our band to be about.

"My recollection is he was pretty eccentric, but a lot of people I was meeting in New York at that time might've fit that particular bill. But he had a hard *intelligence, he had a* frailty—*a physical frailty that I felt even back in those days. He obviously was very sensitive; it was just something you sensed in him. Those were the kinds of people you hooked up with at the time. You felt like: this guy needs* this *thing as much as I do, needs this music or whatever that spirit is you're trying to manifest or need to feel manifested. It's just one of those understandings that runs between people. That probably was the basis of our connection and our relationship and maybe what he felt in my music."*

K.A.

IS SPRINGSTEEN
WORTH THE HYPE?

Two years ago, hardly anyone at Columbia knew how to spell his name, but now his new album, *Born to Run*, due out within the week, is all they can talk about up there. Hope of the future. Big star. Gold record. The works. Across the land, corporate drums are making sure everybody gets the message: a new savior is at hand. The Seventies are being primed for a media killing to the nth degree. Pressing plants work long into the night. The time, as they say in the business, is right.

In Asbury Park, New Jersey, the blood of the poet must be running both hot and cold about this. In the summer of '72, Bruce Springsteen, winless after half a decade of bar-band wars, had just written several long, very unusual songs—yet another new beginning for him—and was reading Anthony Scaduto's biography of Bob Dylan. He'd just finished the part where Dylan goes up to Columbia, auditions for the legendary John Hammond, walks out with a record contract. One day later, Springsteen and guitar were in Hammond's office; and history, sensing the chance to live up to its reputation, did indeed repeat itself.

Two LPs later, Bruce could boast moderate album sales, a small but rabid concert audience, and a critical reputation which was fast snowballing. Earlier incomprehension over his music—he was immediately labeled the new Dylan, the new Van Morrison—gradually gave way to cult pandemonium. When the eminent Jon Landau saw the singer perform in Boston and wrote, "I saw rock and roll's future and its name is Bruce Springsteen," the careers of both men soon became intertwined.

Springsteen was having major problems recording a third LP. He and producer-manager Mike Appel had been working for eight months in a Long Island studio; the results were one completed song, "Born to Run," and such incredible frustration Bruce at times threatened to give up making records altogether. Although *Greetings from Asbury Park, N.J.* and *The Wild, the Innocent & the E Street Shuffle* were highly regarded, almost no one, record company and critics alike, thought they were produced well; and many suspected that it was Springsteen himself who was responsible for the technical agony and ecstasy. Such assumptions were more than partly correct. In the studio, Bruce was astigmatic and shortsighted, a perfectionist who frequently took the long way around simply because he didn't know the short one. That depression had set in would be an understatement.

Landau, who had once produced the MC5 and Livingston Taylor, seemed the perfect solution. He loved the music, understood it, and, equally important, could offer an analytic and pragmatic approach as a logical balance to Springsteen's mercurial naïveté. They liked each other personally. If Landau was somewhat in awe of the kind of instinctual genius who could resolve aesthetic problems by compounding them, Bruce had no less respect for someone who invariably got to ten by counting out nine individual numbers, one at a time. It was the ideal artistic marriage of creative madness and controlling method.

Together they cut "Thunder Road," and when Springsteen discovered he could write a song one night and successfully record it within the next few days, he was so astonished he began writing and rewriting the rest of the album with renewed intensity. Why hadn't someone told him it could be this easy! The word "easy," however, can have pejorative overtones; and with Bruce, one is never talking about an economy of mood. The singer was convinced he had to deliver a masterpiece, and since nothing is ever perfect, especially to someone whose art is based on volatility, it became difficult to decide the exact degree of near-greatness attainable; once he and Landau had started a song off on the right road, Springsteen, out of uncertainty and the increasing pressures of oncoming and perhaps unwanted fame, didn't know when to stop. Or didn't dare. After all, it could always be better, couldn't it? People are going to expect so much. Let's just take a few more weeks because …

"Outside the street's on fire / In a real death waltz / Between what's flesh and what's fantasy / And the poets down here don't write nothing at all / They just stand back and let it all be / And in the quick of the night / They reach for their moment / And try to make an honest stand / But they wind up wounded / Not even dead / Tonight in Jungleland."

At the Bottom Line, Wednesday, Springsteen begins the first show in almost total darkness, a single blue spotlight faintly limning the singer at the piano during the quiet opening minutes of "Thunder Road." It is a magic moment, avoiding pretentiousness only because it works, for Bruce has carefully cultivated the late James Dean's idiosyncratic timing, added a professional street character's sense of the dramatic, a dancer's knack for picaresque tableau, and wrapped the whole package with explosive vulnerability and the practiced pose of a tender hood. Thus the upcoming, split-second move from singular near-silence into vehement, resounding rock & roll as the band comes onstage—a trick picked up from R&B groups and one which Springsteen will repeat all night—is a surprise only to the uninitiated, a delicious treat to the aficionado. The house has gone wild.

The night has an air of expectancy—one may even say privilege; there is an intensity present, a premonition that this is where the best music in America might well be happening in the next few hours, and the hope that it may be true. All ten shows, Wednesday through Sunday, have been sold out for weeks, but at two o'clock this afternoon, a line began to form at Mercer and Fourth. By seven, several hundred kids were milling about in a pouring rain, gambling at long odds on the chance to buy one of the thirty-six standing-room-only tickets. Inside the club, every other person is carrying either a notebook or camera to certify the event. Both Springsteen and the band seem aware of threat and promise, and try too hard. A bunch of South Shore street punks all sharped up for a big night in New York town, they are so charged with energy and good humor they push right past the audience, pointlessly sending the lost wail of barrio serenades all the way up to Eighth Avenue, surely one of Bruce's spiritual homes.

If the street's on fire outside, inside so are we, the singer seems to be saying from the secret heart of those small-town rock & rollers set loose for the first time with booze and cars in Neon City. Hey, man, did you see that! Sexy innocents hang out on corners, soaking up urban vignettes and striving in vain for the obscene loveliness of the true street hustler. From the cheap seats in Jersey, "Thunder Road" is Springsteen's recurrent American dream, yet another incarnation of the runaway and his woman—gimme my girl and let us outa here!—trying for the ultimate escape, no questions asked, no promises given: "Hey, what else can we do now? / ... Well, the night's busting open / ... We got one last chance to make it real."

One last chance to make it real is the way Bruce approaches his concerts, too. Everything must get crammed in, whether it fits or not, the story lines accelerating until both singer and band reach bursting point so often that what is at first exhilarating and climactic later becomes mere hysterical redundancy. Too many times, one twenty-minute song will follow another, their formats so similar the mind begs for brevity or at least a different set of reflexes with which to respond. Happily, Springsteen has dropped completely what appeared to be a creeping narcissism in many of last year's concerts—in comparison, he is naturalness personified now—but he still has not learned that less can be more, that one well-aimed bullet can create just the kind of impact he wants while a dozen random shots may do nothing so much as burn out an audience before their time has come. Granted, he is a master at those small bits of stage business that can suddenly illuminate occasional dark alleys, but why he chooses to walk such mean streets at all remains a mystery.

Actually, Sunday night's initial show makes practically any criticism obsolete. For the first time all week, the singer seems flexible and relaxed—Chaplin's mobile tramp and Valentino's slippery lover playfully filling the air with smoky mise-en-scene from an antic Forties film noir, then delivering a Bogart, brass-knuckled haymaker that puts everyone away. It's *Casablanca* all over again, with a gaucho Groucho in the lead. The pacing is much improved, the set structure faultless. Nothing gets repetitious. From a near-perfect mixture of bright talk (the introduction to "The E Street Shuffle"), fast ones ("Born to Run"), oldies (the Searchers' "When You Walk in the Room"), palpably intimate slow songs (in the middle of the set, "Thunder Road" done strictly solo), and raging rockers (the best "Rosalita" yet), Springsteen fashions the kind of seamless, 150-minute performance that most artists can only dream about, never realize. On my feet, clapping, never wanting it to end, I ask myself when I've ever been so moved by a concert.

Four times: Dylan doing "Like a Rolling Stone" anywhere in '65 or '66, the Rolling Stones at the Garden in '72, Jackson Browne in Toronto in '73, and a few of the New York Dolls' late shows at the Mercer Art Center that same year.

All of the above, of course, indicates that even Springsteen's weaknesses stem from too much talent, not too little. When you can achieve just about anything you want onstage, it's hard not to stay there until you've rung all the bells; and one often gets the feeling that Bruce is having so much fun he'd gladly pay the crowd to let him do just that. Ironically, if he weren't as good as he is—and he is close to being the best we have—no one would be concerned with such minor issues as pace and overreach. In the long run, the stamina and purity of personal vision should be applauded. To be tenaciously naïve is far preferable to following the safe, downhill path that leads straight into the formulaic nowhere of much of today's music business. Small wonder he wants to keep clear of that and case the promised land on his own.

Someone at Sigma Sound in Philadelphia tells this story about Bruce. The singer was in town when David Bowie was recording *Young Americans* there, and the two met briefly. Things went very well. Bowie had just finished doing a song and, during the break, asked an engineer to order lunch for him. Various musicians wandered about, smoking and talking. When the food came, Bowie retired to a side room, ate it, then started recording again. Springsteen was both shaken and amazed. "He didn't even ask his band if they wanted anything," he said. "And when the food came, he didn't eat with them." To a young man from Asbury Park, the power of stardom had been made clear. Not only could he not understand it, he hated it.[3]

Yet there it is, out there like an anxious Jack the Ripper, eagerly awaiting to confer the bloody award. In the East, Springsteen is already a legend—in Washington, D.C., advance orders on his new album already outnumber those for Elton John's—and he has made great inroads in Ohio, Texas, and parts of the Midwest. The South and the Far West remain question marks, but the smart money is betting there'll be a new star in rock & roll heaven when *Born to Run* is released.

I wouldn't doubt it. For me, it's his best record, curbing most of the excess but none of the force of the only artist I know who could combine the sound of Phil Spector with the singing of Roy Orbison. (The names come from Bruce.) *Born to Run* lists three producers—Springsteen, Landau, Appel—but Landau freely acknowledges that "Bruce made every important artistic decision on the LP. The biggest thing I learned from him was the ability to concentrate on the big picture. 'Hey, wait a second!' he would say. 'The release date is just one day, but the record is forever.' Mike's great strength in the studio was his energy, his ability to keep everybody's spirit together. No matter how bad it got, he could always get things going again."

Out front, fame is at the door and knocking loudly. There's too much light out there, and the countdown has begun. In the back, under the haze of a romantic's moon, maybe no one will notice two figures on a fire escape jump down and run hand-in-hand through tenement backstreets toward Spanish Harlem. On Broadway, it's midnight in Manhattan, so walk tall, somebody says. Walk tall or, baby, don't walk at all.

Everything is quiet. Only a whisper.

"Sandy, the aurora is risin' behind us / Those pier lights, our carnival life forever / Oh, love me tonight for I may never see you again / Hey, Sandy girl, my baby."

Quieter. But if we're lucky, Bruce sighs,

"Maybe we could slip away / Maybe we could steal away / Maybe we could slip away... / Just for a second."

3 Whether in deference to Springsteen or Bowie, Paul crossed this entire section out of his final manuscript.

LET US NOW PRAISE FAMOUS MEN*

There's something wrong with beauty—don't you know that? If it could stay inside, if it didn't touch the world, why then it would be fine. But it makes its way into your heart and then you burn. Can you take a live coal into your heart and not burn?

—JONATHAN VALIN,
Final Notice

Economically and aesthetically, the start of the Eighties put a real damper on the music business, and things weren't so hot elsewhere either. Indeed, you could probably say—without too much oversimplification—that 1980's middle months represented the fallout between the opening clamor of the Clash's *London Calling* and the final blast of Bruce Springsteen's *The River*, two double albums with a lot more in common than most people would think. From the stark, homemade look of their predominantly black-and-white packaging to their gritty, straightforward, to-hell-with-the-state-of-the-art sound, *London Calling* and *The River* are passionately political: i.e., deeply, often desperately, concerned with how working-class men and women are getting along in times as troubled as ours. Both Springsteen and the Clash are morally and historically committed to the directness and honesty of rock & roll—and to what this music can mean to those whose hearts are smoldering with anger or shame. In their *Apocalypse Now* manner, the Clash come right out with it, though they're not incapable of dreaming about "Spanish songs in Andalucia / The shooting sites in the days of '39" or recording a tune called "Brand New Cadillac." Next

* Reprinted from the original manuscript, which first appeared in *Rolling Stone* as an edited version.

to Bruce Springsteen, however, they sometimes seem very innocent: they still believe in total victory.[4]

Springsteen doesn't. His protagonists—all veterans of their own foreign wars—may hope for the big win, but they've been through the mill (or factory) enough times to realize that even the smallest success can be tremendously shaky. While lines like

> Once I spent my time playing tough guy scenes
> But I was living in a world of childish dreams
> Someday these childish dreams must end
> To become a man and grow up to dream again
> Now I believe in the end

ring true, such sentiments are usually surrounded by an aura of omnipotent dread that makes them sound more like reveries from the past or wishful thinking than statements about the future. There's nothing apocalyptic or innocent about *The River*. (Try listening to it right after *Born to Run* and you'll understand what I mean.) It's a contemporary, New Jersey version of *The Grapes of Wrath*, with the Tom Joad/Henry Fonda figure—nowadays no longer able to draw upon the solidarity of family—driving a stolen car through a neon Dust Bowl "in fear / That in this darkness I will disappear." Quite often, he does.[5]

Since *The River* is the culmination of a trilogy that began in high gear with *Born to Run* (1975) before shifting down for *Darkness on the Edge of Town* (1978), you might expect it to stand and deliver weighty conclusions, words to live by. Well, they're there, if you want or need them, and they're filled with an uncommon common sense and intelligence that could only have come from an exceptionally warmhearted but wary graduate of the street of hard knocks. Here's one example: "Now you can't break the ties that bind / You can't forsake the ties that bind." Or: "Two hearts are better than one / Two hearts girl get the job done." Or: "Everybody needs a place to rest / Everybody wants to have a home ... / Ain't nobody like to be alone." Or: "Where the dark of night holds back the light of the day / ... you've gotta stand and fight for the price you pay." Quoted out of context, without

4 Springsteen is pleased that Paul picked up on the link between *The River* and the Clash. "I always felt a great affinity for not just the Clash but the punk rock movement. Though I was probably technically outside of it here in the States, I felt a deep connection to those things, and he runs right through it. There was a tremendous feeling of satisfaction. I mean, in the end you do write to be understood, and there just seems to be less of that out there now, you know."

5 "Could've been," Springsteen allows when asked if Paul might've planted the seed for, fifteen years down the road, the songwriter's "The Ghost of Tom Joad." "Those were my influences at the time and they've very much continued to be so.

the evocative musical accompaniment of the E Street Band and Springsteen's unsparingly emotional singing, these lines seem incredibly simple yet sturdy. Not very cosmic but they'll do, I suppose, if you feel the necessity to nail some sort of slogan to the wall. Then you can sit back and stare at it and miss the whole point—not to mention the scope—of the album.

Scope, context, sequencing, and mood are everything here. Bruce Springsteen didn't title his summational record *The River* for nothing, so getting hit with a quick sprinkle of lyrics is no solution when complete immersion is called for. Each song is just a drop in the bucket, and the water in the bucket is drawn from a river that can take you on a fast but invigorating ride ("Sherry Darling," "Out in the Street," "Crush on You," "I'm a Rocker"), smash you in the rapids ("Hungry Heart"), let you float dreamily downstream ("I Wanna Marry You"), or carry you relentlessly across some unknown county line ("Jackson Cage," "Point Blank," "Fade Away," "Stolen Car," "Ramrod," "The River," "Independence Day"). When the surface looks smooth, watch out for dangerous undercurrents. You may believe you're splashing about in a shallow stream and suddenly find yourself in over your head.

Keeping the trilogy in mind, if Springsteen's archetypal journey from innocence (*Born to Run*) to experience (*Darkness on the Edge of Town*) taught him anything, it was that he wasn't even halfway home—that, contrary to what F. Scott Fitzgerald wrote, most American lives *do* have second acts. And that these postexperiential acts are usually the ones in which we either crack up or learn to live with our limitations and betrayals. In a way, Bruce Springsteen's journey started in 1973 with *Greetings from Asbury Park, N.J.*'s "Growin' Up" (in which the singer "found the key to the universe in the engine of an old parked car") and gathered momentum that same year with his "for me, this boardwalk life's through" declaration in *The Wild, the Innocent & the E Street Shuffle*'s "4th of July, Asbury Park (Sandy)" before he saw himself finally "pulling out of here to win" in *Born to Run*'s "Thunder Road." Throughout much of *Darkness on the Edge of Town*, Springsteen discovered the meaning of despair.

What makes *The River* really special is Bruce Springsteen's epic exploration of the second acts of American lives. Because he realizes that most of our todays are the tragicomic sum of a scattered series of yesterdays that had once hoped to become better tomorrows, he can fuse past and present, desire and destiny, laughter and longing, and have death or glory emerge as more than just another story. By utilizing the vast cast of characters he's already established on the earlier LPs—and by putting a spin on the time span—Springsteen forces his heroes and heroines into seeing themselves at different and crucial periods in their lives. The connections are infinite (and, some would say, repetitious).

When an artist ties these kinds of knots around several compositions, it's impressive. But when he also uses jump-cut juxtapositions of mood (the one between "I Wanna Marry You" and "The River" is particularly stunning) and more than a few characters in completely contrasting situations, it's downright brilliant. One labyrinthine example: the randy rocker of "Ramrod," who sings

> Hey, little dolly won't you say you will
> Meet me tonight up on top of the hill
> Well just a few miles cross the county line
> There's a cute little chapel nestled down in the pines
> Say you'll be mine little girl I'll put my foot to the
>   floor
> Give me the word now sugar, we'll go ramroddin'
>   forever more

like he no longer believes a word of it but has to keep pushing anyway or he'll die, is probably the same guy who went racing in the street with his buddy, Sonny, and later sang, in "Darkness on the Edge of Town": "I lost my money and I lost my wife / Them things don't seem to matter much to me now / Tonight I'll be on that hill 'cause I can't stop...." He could easily be the reformed husband in "Drive All Night," too (there's an "on the edge of town" reference).

Though they're separated by eight songs, "Drive All Night" is linked with "I Wanna Marry You" by a set of "my girl" refrains that don't appear on the lyric sheet. Yet the shy, naïve narrator of "I Wanna Marry You" (who sweetly and secretly yearns for someone's estranged wife, whom he watches on the street every day) clearly isn't the fortunate protagonist of "Drive All Night." That man wins his wife back. As the reunited couple get ready for bed, they hear a crowd of kids partying in the street. "Fallen angels" and "calling strangers," the husband says. "Let them go ... do their dances of the dead ... / There's machines and there's fire waiting on the edge of town / They're out there for hire but baby they can't hurt us now." What he's saying, I'm sure, is that those kids are who we *were*, but we've survived and this is who we *are*. (Check *Darkness on the Edge of Town*'s "Racing in the Street" and "Streets of Fire" for the "angels"-"strangers"-"fire" imagery, and *Born to Run*'s title track for "suicide machines.")

Immediately following the fantasy of "I Wanna Marry You" (whose main character gently debunks the "fairytale" of "true love" while, in fact, daydreaming about achieving it with a total stranger) is the grim reality of "The River," one of the record's two Dreiserian American tragedies and the second chapter of "Racing in the Street." In "The River," there are no idle thoughts about how nice true love might be. Instead, fate and the new Depression shoot the working-class hero and his high-school sweetheart (Mary from "Thunder Road"?) straight between the eyes:

> Then I got Mary pregnant
> And, man, that was all she wrote
> And for my nineteenth birthday I got a union card
>   and a wedding coat …
> I got a job working construction for the Johnstown
>   Company
> But lately there ain't been much work on account of
>   the economy
> Now all them things that seemed so important
> Well, mister they vanished right into the air
> Now I just act like I don't remember
> Mary acts like she don't care.

But, of course, he does remember the good times, and it's killing him: "Now those memories come back to haunt me / They haunt me like a curse / Is a dream a lie if it don't come true / Or is it something worse…."

After "Drive All Night," the singer witnesses—or imagines he witnesses ("there was nobody there but me")—the results of a bloody car crash in which a young man has been either badly hurt or killed. Since he feels personally involved, it frightens him. "Wreck on the Highway" is *The River*'s last song, and this is the album's hard-won, semi-happy ending:

> Sometimes I sit up in the darkness
> And I watch my baby as she sleeps
> Then I climb in bed and I hold her tight
> I just lay there awake in the middle of the night
> Thinking 'bout the wreck on the highway.

Obviously, there are other ways to ford *The River* and its twenty tunes (e.g., picking out the imagery picked up in John Ford movies would help), but any approach you take is liable to lead in circles. Cars, work, and love need the gasoline of the heart to avoid smashing. "Independence Day"— more Dreiser—is both a beginning and an end: one of the greatest ever. As is a scary little noir named "Stolen Car" that's wound so tight it practically twitches ("I'm driving a stolen car / Down on Eldridge Avenue / Each night I wait to get caught / But I never do").

Musically, *The River* floats more influences than I'd have thought possible: folk balladry, soul singing and R&B, rockabilly, country music, goofy—or not-so-goofy—teen anthems about cars and death (the terrific "Cadillac Ranch"), Gary "U.S." Bonds, Byrds-like folk-rock with ringing twelve-string guitars, party numbers, lots of rock & roll, David Johansen and the New York Dolls ("Crush on You"), Jackson Browne (lyrically, the first half of "The Price You Pay" sounds like a downbeat rewrite of "Before the Deluge"), Elvis Costello (the vocal in "Fade Away")—the list could go on and on.

Throughout much of the LP, producers Bruce Springsteen, Jon Landau, and Steve Van Zandt lean toward a live sound, meeting the songs head-on, like the aural equivalent of, say, action-movie director Howard Hawks's camera placement. As a result, though it can't be compared with a Springsteen concert, *The River* seems livelier and more loose than *Darkness on the Edge of Town*. Of the trilogy, however, I still prefer the innocent zest and relative openness of *Born to Run*.

While most of *The River* runs wide and deep, there are a few problems. Ever since he started conceptualizing and thinking in terms of trilogies, Springsteen has lost some of his naturalness and seemed more than a bit self-conscious about being an artist. At times, you think he's closed off his casualness altogether, that he can't bear the idea of playing around with a phrase when he could be underlining it instead. Will we never hear the spring and summer of "Wild Billy's Circus Story," "4th of July, Asbury Park (Sandy)," "Thunder Road," and "Born to Run" again? Must even the brightest days now be touched by autumnal tones and winter light? Bruce Springsteen isn't an old man yet. Isn't it odd that he's trying so hard to adapt the visions of one?

Though I consider *The River* a rock & roll milestone, in a way I hope it's also Independence Day.

BRUCE SPRINGSTEEN'S
NEBRASKA

When someone told me that Bruce Springsteen had made a guitar-and-harmonica album—no E Street Band, no *Born to Run*-style rock & roll—I guess I expected a record that would wed the flash and slash of early-Sixties folk-period Bob Dylan to the power-packed pull and thrust of the acoustic numbers on Neil Young's *Rust Never Sleeps*: i.e., high-energy instrumental dynamics, American-traditional melodies, muscular singing, lots of rock & roll excitement without the usual amplification. Boy, was I wrong.

When I first heard *Nebraska*, I was shocked and a little dismayed. Here was an LP I could respect until the day I died—ten tunes, from the working-class point of view, about how it feels to try to stay marginally solvent, nonviolent, and more than half-alive in the soul-shriveling age of Reaganomics—but would I ever really warm up to it? Play it for enjoyment instead of edification? Initially, *Nebraska* sounded so demoralized and demoralizing, so murderously monotonous, so deprived of spark and hope that, in comparison, the gloomy songs from *Darkness on the Edge of Town* and *The River* seemed not altogether unhappy. Springsteen had the courage of his convictions, I decided, and had made an album as bleak and unyielding as next month's rent. Only one problem: I didn't want to hear it. So, day after day, I circled *Nebraska*, attempting to listen, trying to escape. At night, I'd dream about the damned thing. A long weekend of this was enough to make me wish I had both a car and a girl or that Wild Billy's Circus was still in town. Over a time, however, my preconceptions and first impressions metamorphosed into something solid and more sensible, and I finally found a road map that took me to the right places.

To get there, I had to journey past Neil Young (making meaningful stops at *Hawks & Doves* and *re-ac-tor*) and Bob Dylan (revisiting "North Country Blues" from *The Times They Are A-Changin'*) all the way back to Woody Guthrie and to even earlier American singers and musicians whom people like Alan Lomax recorded in the Thirties and Forties for the Library of Congress—traditional (and nonprofessional) singers and musicians you've probably never heard of: poor folks, mostly from the rural South, just sitting at home in front of that inexpensive tape or disc machine and telling their stories, sometimes artfully and sometimes artlessly, undoubtedly amazed that anyone from the urban world would place any value on what they were saying or how they were saying it. Since there was a minimum of technology and a maximum of naturalness involved, Lomax and other collectors were able to capture real one-on-one stuff: such aesthetic and mortal unity that it was impossible to separate style from content. You did the song once, the way you'd been doing it your whole life, and that was it. That was it, all right: the song, your whole life and, every so often, a considerable piece of Americana. Like an aural FSA photo.

Well, *Nebraska*—though it's a brand new Bruce Springsteen album with generally characteristic Springsteen melodies and lyrics—feels, even *sounds*, like those old Library of Congress recordings. A quiet, almost recessive confidence permeates much of the music, the ghostly guitar playing mainly mixed way down to a near-indistinct thrumming on the bass strings while the treble strings echo eerie backwoods hints of mandolins and dulcimers. Springsteen's singing is easy and flexible, wonderfully subtle and unpretentious. At times, the language is reminiscent of folk balladry— "Highway Patrolman" opens with this simple declaration: "My name is Joe Roberts I work for the state"—and certain compositions have a timeless, supernatural quality ("Mansion on the Hill," "My Father's House"). Many numbers are directly addressed to an unnamed "sir," which sets up all sorts of interesting resonances: serfs speaking to lords, poor men to rich men, criminals to lawmen, anyone who's ever been caught by the "meanness in this world" to whomever will listen, me to you, you to me.

Nebraska's stories are, of course, contemporary. You read them in the papers and see them enacted in the streets every day. Ralph, with a mortgage and "debts no honest man could pay," gets laid off at the Ford plant, can't find another job, gets drunk, kills a night clerk, and tells the judge he'd be better off dead than spending ninety-nine years in prison. A highway patrolman, rationalizing "Man turns his back on his family he just ain't no good," lets his black-sheep brother escape into Canada. Ashamed that his father is treated shabbily in a used-car lot, a kid vows: "Now mister the day the lottery I win I ain't ever gonna ride in no used car again." In Atlantic City, a man and a woman, about to become involved in a dangerous deal, are so poor they can't afford a used car so they plan to make a run for it on the bus. A workingman, eyes filled with wonder and hate, stares up at the lights of a rich man's house on a hill. He has stared up at that house ever since he was a child. Someone stands beside a dead dog in a ditch and acts as if he expects the dog to come back to life. A night-shift worker, fried on speed, commutes more than three hours a night to see his woman. Some nights, he's flying and happy, but there are other nights when he's so depressed he knows he'll kill any state trooper who dares to stop him. Charlie Starkweather and his girlfriend go on a murder spree, and Starkweather, in a classic love-hate statement, asks that his girlfriend be seated on his lap while he's being electrocuted.[6] And in the LP's shattering final image (straight from "The River"), a groom stands on the banks of a stream, waiting with a preacher for his bride. On *Nebraska*, of course, she never shows up.

But affirmation does, believe me. Not so much in the tagged-on homilies—"Maybe everything that dies someday comes back" or "At the end of every hard earned day people find some reason to believe"—but because one man, just sitting at home in front of a four-track cassette machine on the night of January 3, 1982, felt he had to tell these stories— and tell them in a particular way: one take per tune—to millions of people very much like him all over America. Real one-on-one stuff. Such unity. I guess it's just inherent: hoping for hope.

A last word: it's entirely possible that the total production cost of Bruce Springsteen's *Nebraska* came to less than ten dollars, the price of a single high-quality cassette. What an argument for home taping.

---

6 An image that finds its origin in Fritz Lang's 1937 nod to Bonnie and Clyde, *You Only Live Once*: Henry Fonda, on his way to the electric chair, says: "You can sit on my lap when they throw the switch."

- WARREN ZEVON -

Published in March of 1981, "Warren Zevon: How He Saved Himself from a Coward's Death," the fourth and final piece that Paul wrote about the California rocker, revealed something that the previous three works hadn't: that, in addition to admiring one another professionally, the two men were close friends. So much so that, whether he wanted to or not, Paul became part of the story.

Charles M. Young: "Paul didn't really believe in conflicts of interest that way. He just thought that if you believed in a particular artist, you should be able to interview them and review them. So maybe Paul loved some artists more than he should because he had some personal friendships on the side; but I don't think that takes much away from his legacy. Paul wasn't right about everything—but when he was right, he was really right."

"The artists that he really liked a lot as artists," John Morthland says, "he was really drawn to also as people. There's a school of journalism that says you shouldn't get friendly with your story subjects, and I think that's basically true. But Paul was one of those people who could do it anyhow. He could do it and maintain his integrity about it at the same time."

Peter Herbst: "It is an odd thing that somebody so principled would be able to write about people he knew and not feel that there was an issue. But, on the other hand, the level of insight that he provided tended to outweigh whatever sort of favoritism there was. It wasn't favoritism because he wanted to reward somebody. That was outside of Paul's way of thinking. He never thought that way. But he would be extraordinarily enthusiastic. And Rolling Stone, you know, it's not The Economist."

Greil Marcus recalls the advice he received as a young writer from music critic Ralph J. Gleason, who cofounded Rolling Stone with Jann Wenner. "One thing he told me was that record companies and performers themselves want to become close to writers who they feel can do them good, and the reason they want to do that is that once you become friendly with somebody it becomes very difficult if not impossible to say anything bad about them. It's a way of disarming a critic and insulating yourself from what that critic might have to say about you. Even if he didn't practice what he preached, I took what he said to heart.

"With Paul, I don't think it was a choice. I don't think it was a moral question. These were people he not only respected and admired, but he felt a deep personal affinity with them and wanted to get to know them better. I think these people—you know, if we're talking about Zevon or Jackson Browne—are people who wanted to get to know him better. I don't think they were using him. I never got that impression."

"Okay, so there you have the Mona Lisa of rock profile writing," Young says. "I think the Zevon cover story in Rolling Stone is worth any 150—any thousand—record reviews by anybody else. That profile was dependent on Paul's getting very close to Zevon and getting his trust, which meant that Zevon opened himself up to Paul in a way that you almost never see in a profile. The two of them had a lot in common. They were both aesthetes. They lived in that world of literature and movies and music, and you could see how they just completely hit it off that way. Paul knew he had the subject of his life in that piece: an artist that he was in a position to understand better than anyone else. It's like, 'Jesus, get the story!' And that's what he did." Young cites Hunter S. Thompson's definition of gonzo journalism as having "intense, demented involvement" with what you're writing about. "Paul was a guy who achieved total, demented involvement with his subject matter in that piece. Paul was the true master of gonzo, if that's a definition of gonzo."

Paul remained holed up in his office for months and months trying to finish the piece. More than a year would pass from start to finish. "My memories of Paul during the Zevon thing was that he really was keeping his own counsel," David McGee says. "My sense of Paul is that it was a deep, deep story and it was a journey he had to take and wanted to take on his own. What he had to say he didn't want to talk about."

Paul Scanlon: "I used to stick my head in his door and say, 'How's the Zevon piece coming?' He'd say, 'Oh, better and better' or something like that. But I wasn't around for the drama that came at the end."

By the time managing editor Terry McDonell published the article, the sixty-seven-page manuscript had been reduced to forty. "All I know is he stayed away while that was going on," Parke Puterbaugh says. "He just didn't want to see it get eviscerated. But to be fair, I thought Susan Murcko did a pretty sensitive job of bringing it down to the required length." Murcko doesn't recall editing the piece: "This is a terrible thing to say, but that could have been something that Terry showed to me to get ideas on general places where to cut, and I just wouldn't remember because of the volume of things very specifically music-related coming through." What she does remember: "Just that it was painful."

Young: "I never saw a writer more angry and more devastated than he was by that edit. Now, what's in the magazine reads well, so you have to give whomever did the edit credit for leaving enough stuff in that we can see how great this piece was. But for Paul it was like taking the Mona Lisa and ripping it in half. His masterpiece was ruined.

"I don't think Paul lived for any other reason than because he wanted to get his words right. He was this aesthete who lived in a world of music, literature, and movies, and his contribution to that was his journalism. And when that was fucked with, it demolished it. I have this very strong, vivid memory of Paul being so angry he couldn't even talk. I think if they'd recognized 'Zevon' for the masterpiece that it was and given it truly the 'Fear and Loathing in Las Vegas' treatment that it probably deserved, I wonder if we might've gotten some more great stuff out of Paul."

In April of 1980, Paul called Crystal Zevon. Sounding completely dejected—recovering from hepatitis and another bout of the sinusitis that regularly plagued him—he said, "I'm back to work on the piece. They were originally going to do it in two parts and then they took that back the next day."

Jann Wenner: "I think that that was a setup. Paul knew from the outset that there was no way that we were going to publish this at that length. But there was no talking to him about it. He was going to write an opus on the subject and that was going to be the end of it. He was really writing for his own purpose. And I suppose at the end—of him writing that perfect piece that he wanted to write about Warren that got it all and explained all where Warren stood in the West Coast literature of the dispossessed or whatever the fuck—that in his mind that was so perfectly clear it should be published as is. It takes that kind of ego and that kind of thought, which Paul had, to think of something that vain."

"He was without ego except in what he believed," Jay Cocks says.

Young: "He was traumatized by that edit. That was the turning point of his life. The fact that he didn't write again about rock & roll for a long time, or wrote about it only in kind of sporadic and fitful ways, it's kind of like

Greek tragedy. There was an inevitability about it. I think Paul expected—and he had a right to expect—that the Zevon article would be given truly special treatment. Instead, it was scrunched down to the size of a normal cover story, maybe a little bit longer. For that article not to be recognized as a masterpiece, I think it demolished him. You look at the direction his life went in after that, I don't see what any other argument could be."

"It wasn't just that piece," Bobbi London says, "it was always anything that he turned in. He poured his heart and soul into it, he spent a lot of time with it, and if someone edited anything out it was like it was almost sacrilegious."

On his copy of the original manuscript for "Warren Zevon: How He Saved Himself from a Coward's Death" (the version included herein), Paul wrote in the upper left-hand corner of page one: Unedited Zevon piece—much better than the edited version in RS 339.

K.A.

WARREN ZEVON
COMES OUT OF THE WOODS

Although the woods are supposed to be full of them, upcoming major artists belong to a species so rare that many of us may go for years without ever being sure we've actually seen one. Is he or she the real thing or just another disappointing imitation whose feathers will molt once the wax has turned to gold and the passion to pampered petulance? Time alone can answer such a question, but who among us can resist an irrational guess based on nothing more than intuition and the need to love? Not me.

After listening to his album, I had planned to hedge my bet with something safe, sensible, and somewhat sententious—"Warren Zevon is the finest singer-songwriter to emerge from California since Jackson Browne and Tom Waits"— and to point out how carefully the artist had chronicled a personal and emotional history of Los Angeles (past to present), how zealous and protective Browne had been in producing his friend's first LP, et cetera. But when Warren Zevon walked onstage at the Bottom Line on Friday night and dominated everything in sight like a hungry rock & roll werewolf who had just been uncaged and told the moon was full, my caution collapsed and I realized that all of my initial preconceptions had been wrong. Tom Waits? California? This guy played piano like Keith Richard plays guitar and with the Magnum force of Neil Young on *Tonight's the Night* and *Zuma*.[1] Defiant, he challenged the Bob Dylan of *Highway 61 Revisited* with "I'll Sleep When I'm Dead" and a section from "Desperados Under the Eaves" and managed a draw, spat out the lines to a dozen songs like a Gatling gun trained on ground zero, and literally shook his fist while boasting, "I was the kid!" in "Mama Couldn't Be Persuaded." Protection? This man needed protection about as much as Jack the Ripper needed another sharp knife.

By Paul Nelson from *The Village Voice*, June 21, 1976. © Mark C. Nelson 1976. All rights reserved. Reprinted by permission.†

1 Throughout much of the Sixties and Seventies, the Rolling Stones guitarist vacillated between calling himself "Keith Richard" and "Keith Richards." His pre-punk progeny, the New York Dolls' Johnny Thunders, early in his career waged a similar battle between the singular and the plural, going from "Thunder" to "Thunders."

While *Warren Zevon*—good and gritty and one of the best records of the year—serves as only partial preparation for the impact of the onstage artist, it does make the listener completely aware of Zevon's considerable compositional and organizational skills. The LP moves cyclically back and forth from the dignified and timeless "Frank and Jesse James," an aural movie about outlaws past and two sets of brothers (one of them Phil and Don Everly, with whom Zevon played for two years), to the most modest of autobiographical similes about outlaws present: "Don't you feel like desperados under the eaves / Heaven help the one who leaves." When the end is at hand ("I was sitting in the Hollywood Hawaiian Hotel / I was listening to the air conditioner hum"), the music takes us "back when the West was young" to tenaciously and triumphantly "Keep on riding, riding, riding" through several elegiacally angry and corrosively funny episodes which take place in a Los Angeles so acutely drawn that we can practically smell the sweat inside the fedoras of Philip Marlowe and Lew Archer.

Zevon enters the album mythically as a gambler's son in "Mama Couldn't Be Persuaded," a song about his parents. In his tragicomic crawl through the City of Angels, he encounters most of the problems of the archetypal musician—booze ("I'll Sleep When I'm Dead"), drugs ("Carmelita"), and women ("Hasten Down the Wind," "Poor Poor Pitiful Me," "The French Inhaler")—but, like Lou Reed, is finally saved by rock & roll (the wonderful "Mohammed's Radio," an anthem if I've ever heard one) and with his wife leaves Los Angeles for a respite in Spain ("Backs Turned Looking Down the Path").

Although such a critical oversimplification hardly does Zevon or the LP justice, it should suggest that he is a talent who can be mentioned in the same sentence with Bob Dylan, Jackson Browne, Randy Newman, Neil Young, Leonard Cohen, and a mere handful of others—no apologies necessary. If it doesn't, I'll come right out and say it: Warren Zevon is a major artist.

WARREN ZEVON: HOW HE SAVED HIMSELF FROM A COWARD'S DEATH*

Between what contact did to you and how tired you got, between the farout things you saw or heard and what you personally lost out of all that got blown away, the war made a place for you that was all yours. Finding it was like listening to esoteric music, you didn't hear it in any essential way through all the repetitions until your own breath had entered it and become another instrument, and by then it wasn't just music anymore, it was experience. Life-as-movie, war-as-(war) movie, war-as-life; a complete process if you got to complete it, a distinct path to travel, but dark and hard, not any easier if you knew that you'd put your own foot on it yourself, deliberately and—most roughly speaking—consciously. Some people took a few steps along it and turned back, wised up, with and without regrets. Many walked on and just got blown off it. A lot went farther than they probably should have and then lay down, falling into a bad sleep of pain and rage, waiting for release, for peace, any kind of peace that wasn't just the absence of war. And some kept on going until they reached the place where an inversion of the expected order happened, a fabulous warp where you took the journey first and then you made your departure.

—MICHAEL HERR,
Dispatches

Alcoholism. That's what this article's supposed to be about. How Warren Zevon, after some heartwarming and colorful misadventures, licked the

Big A and lived happily ever after, his third and fourth Asylum albums, *Bad Luck Streak in Dancing School* and *Stand in the Fire* (both released in 1980), doing quite well on the charts in these economically depressed times. Zevon: a drinking-man's drinking man, someone who can talk about booze the way Pete Townshend talks about rock & roll. Starring Richard Dreyfuss as our wild and crazy hero, Diane Keaton as ex-wife Crystal, Warren Beatty as Jackson Browne, Gregory Peck as private-eye novelist Ross Macdonald (real name: Kenneth Millar), actress-girlfriend Kim Lankford as herself, and with a special guest appearance by Jack Klugman as "The Doc."

You could write it that way, I suppose. Most of it happened, some of it still might. There was even a laugh or two here and there: the protagonist buys a Christmas quart for his father- and mother-in-law, discovers it's the only liquor left in the house, drinks it all himself before they can sample a drop. But you'd write it that way only if you were totally ignorant. If you didn't realize that alcoholism is now an A.M.A.-recognized *disease*, and that your true alcoholic is sick, desperate, deadly as a rattlesnake, completely out of pride, and about as colorful and heartwarming as a pale white body on a concrete slab. Eventually, a dedicated drunk will maim or kill everything he touches, often putting himself at the bottom of the list. Warren Zevon knows this. And, since I was around for a few key incidents, I hope I do, too.

We are sitting up late at night in Warren and Kim Lankford's rented home in the Hollywood Hills. ("This stupid, pretentious, screenwriter's idea of a screenwriter's idea of a screenwriter's house" is how Zevon describes it. He's particularly chagrined by a four-foot-high, bright-red bathtub. "Very California," he smiles, with a certain amount of grim satisfaction.) Lankford, an actress who's currently starring in the CBS television series *Knots Landing*, has gone to bed hours ago.

Since Warren and I are both night people ("Vampires," he jokes), we've decided to do our tapings from one or two in the morning until dawn, then laze around in the backyard and watch the planes, magnificently framed against a faraway mountain range, make their long, slow descent across the San Fernando Valley toward the Burbank airport. It's a beautiful sight, somewhat unreal. I'm reminded of Hitchcock's movies, where the horror happens in broad daylight.

"From what I know about alcoholism," Zevon is saying, "I'd say there's nothing romantic, nothing grand, nothing heroic, nothing brave—nothing like that about drinking. It's a real coward's death.

"The last time I detoxed, I really didn't know if I was going to die. I really thought I was. I had my hand on the phone, I was afraid that I was going to start hallucinating and shooting guns—I didn't know what was going to happen."

(Zevon had a recurring dream: that he'd grabbed his .44 Magnum, stumbled up the driveway to Mulholland, taken dead aim at a passing car and pulled the trigger. Each time he woke up, he'd scramble for the pistol and frantically count the bullets, terrified there'd be one missing.[2])

"There I was, just holding the phone, clutching the phone, and the strongest thought in my mind was, What a chickenshit way to die. I'm dying from having avoided the pain of living—it's as simple as that.

"I said: God, just give me one more shot, man. Just give me one chance. But don't let me die a fucking coward, lying here shaking from hiding from life.

"This time I really felt that way morally about life. I said, Not *this* way! Shit! Anything but *this*! This is suicide the same as the gun barrel in the mouth, except that it's *infinitely* more cowardly. It's just the worst death—a chickenshit, shivering, quaking, whiny death. There's no keel over, make a young and pretty corpse. I was fifty pounds heavier then. I weigh the same as I did in high school now."

Zevon—bright, clear-eyed, looking as sleek and powerful as Sugar Ray Leonard these days—is talking about the last time he fell off the wagon after his voluntary rehabilitation at Pinecrest, a private hospital in Santa Barbara. He spent four weeks in the Chemical Dependency Unit there. Among other things, the doctors removed what had seemed to be a permanent haze in his physical and mental condition. (I remember once when we were having dinner at Musso & Frank, a waiter—not even ours—took one look at him and brought him a cup of steaming black coffee right in the middle of the meal. Needless to say, Warren was mortified.)

The reason for this final binge—not that an alcoholic needs any special reason, Zevon will tell you—was the visit of Montreal Expos pitcher Bill Lee, about whom Warren had written a song. Lee had liked 1978's *Excitable Boy* very much and mentioned Zevon in several interviews. Warren wanted to play a tape of "Bill Lee" (later included on *Bad Luck Streak in Dancing School*) for him. George Gruel, Zevon's live-in aide-de-camp and a warm and wonderfully understanding man, had some doubts as to what might happen. Gruel, who stands six-feet-five and weighs in at around 250 pounds, is so tough

2 Paul was not threatened by the arsenal Zevon maintained ("We could hold off an army here," the singer boasted) and enthusiastically partook in gunplay with Zevon for George Gruel's camera. "The area where I grew up," he'd tell Bruce Hornsby years later, "everybody had a gun. I had rifles and stuff. I didn't go hunting animals, but I went target shooting and shot bottles. It was just sort of second nature to be around guns."

that you can strike a match on his muscles. After you've lit your cigarette, he's so polite he'll go get you an ashtray. In this instance, his premonition of disaster proved correct.

Zevon tells the story: "I said, 'Now look, George, we don't necessarily have to buy *all* this stuff that the hospital tells us. I've been taking drugs since I was *born*. Let's consider that alcohol may be just another drug experience that I had. So let's just see if I can drink moderately.'

"George said, 'Well, we'll *see*.'

"So there was this one occasion—especially unfortunate since I think it left a bad impression on Bill Lee—when George said, 'Okay. You can have a drink when he gets here. Don't drink anything all day, and I'll let you have a drink then.'

"A couple of days later, George said, 'You don't control the amount you drink. You didn't stop yesterday. You didn't stop today. When are you going to stop?'

"I had a bottle and a half of Wild Turkey left. I said, 'When that's gone.'

"He said: '*Enjoy* it.'

"And that's how we did it. I had to detox again. And for a few days, it wasn't bad. Once again I thought, Aw, see, they make more out of it than they should. Then one night I got what was like the flu, only it wasn't the flu. It was much worse. I really didn't know if my brain was frying, I felt so feverish. I got the chills. There was *no* getting warm enough. I was lying there, shaking and praying. *Praying.* I'm not even a religious man, but there comes a time …"

I first met Warren and Crystal Zevon after his initial performance at the Bottom Line in New York City during the aptly named "I'll Sleep When I'm Dead" tour. Asylum had just released *Warren Zevon*, and I'd listened to nothing else for days. Though I loved the record and had, in fact, been familiar with Zevon's music for years (Jackson Browne having sung several of Warren's songs for me once in Toronto), seeing the man onstage was like experiencing— what?—Browne's "For Everyman," the works of F. Scott Fitzgerald, Sam Peckinpah's *The Wild Bunch*, the New York Dolls, Norman Mailer, Clint Eastwood in *Dirty Harry*, and Ross Macdonald/Ken Millar's Lew Archer novels at a very impressionable age. Rightly or wrongly, your life got changed.[3]

3 Paul took Zevon to his first Clint Eastwood movie, *The Outlaw Josey Wales*. "I was totally unaware of Clint Eastwood up till then," Zevon said. "I knew who he was and I liked him in *Rawhide*, I hadn't seen any of his pictures, I hadn't seen any of the *Dirty Harry* pictures or anything, and you suggested we see *Josey Wales*. I figured it was going to be a dumb Western—and I thought it was *fantastic*. I walked out, if you remember, just euphoric. After that I was determined to see all the Eastwood pictures, and I thought they all were great."

The Zevons—Crystal then seven months pregnant—stayed in New York for a few days, and the three of us became fast friends. Mutual interests, et cetera. I guess we'd each spent too much time attempting to ride out our obsessions on the airwaves of Mohammed's Radio. All I wanted to talk about were Zevon's songs, while Warren and Crystal simply brushed aside my questions and kept asking me about Ken Millar, whom I'd recently met and soon was going to interview in Santa Barbara. They'd read all his books and could quote entire passages verbatim. I was impressed. Providing it's all right with Millar, I said, I'll take you with me for a day or two. It was like I'd invited them to meet God. Though I knew Zevon had something of a drinking problem, I had no idea then how deep it went. This was in the spring of 1976.[4] We stayed in constant touch, saw each other often in Los Angeles, Santa Barbara, Boston, and New York. During the next four years, I would learn all that I would ever want to know about alcoholism.

In the late summer of 1978, Warren Zevon and I became "blood brothers." Late one night, Crystal phoned from their new home in Santa Barbara. She sounded very distraught. Warren's drinking had gotten much worse. They'd had a fight, and he was in New York now to talk to friends: Bruce Springsteen, producer Jon Landau, guitarist David Landau, critic Jay Cocks, me.

I know, I said. He just called. I'm on my way down to the Gramercy Park to see him.

"I talked to him this afternoon," she said. "He told me he loved me and was coming home after he'd seen you, Bruce, Jon, and David. 'Warren,' I said, 'you *did* see Bruce, Jon, and David. Last night at the Palladium. You were so drunk that they had to get someone to take you back to the hotel because they were afraid you'd accidentally kill yourself falling over something backstage.' He didn't even remember being at the concert, Paul."

Shit, I thought.

There was a long pause.

"Will you do something for me?" Crystal asked.

Sure, I said. If I can.

"Will you try to talk him into going into a hospital for treatment? I've already found one right here in town."

---

4 The meeting with Millar, at the Coral Casino Beach Club, took place a month and a half later on July 31. Warren's initial meeting with Millar was somewhat disastrous. "When I brought Warren up to see him," Paul said, "Warren first thing blurted out that he'd been to the Copper Coffee Pot and had the Lew Archer special of roast beef. Macdonald just gave him a stony stare. He didn't say a word. Warren was just mortified that he'd said that."

Yes, I said, with a very large gulp. I'll try.

When we hung up, I wondered what to do. How do you introduce this particular topic into a casual conversation? Warren, old buddy, not to change the subject or anything, but have you ever considered committing yourself? Terrific, I thought. Just terrific.

As it turned out, I needn't have worried. Crystal hadn't sent me in cold—I was the backup. About thirty seconds after I'd knocked on his door, Zevon sat me down in a chair and announced: "I want to ask you a serious question. The answer's important." He looked me straight in the eye. "Do you think I'm a drunk?"

Somehow I'd guessed what he was going to say. And in that split second of intuition, luck was with me. My reply wasn't as dumb as I'd expected.

It went like this: By asking the question, you've already answered it. Your answer's yes. So why not try to get some help—a hospital or something? There's probably one in Santa Barbara. You've got nothing to lose, absolutely everything to gain. After all, if you decide you don't like being sober, you can always buy another bottle, can't you?

He seemed to like the logic—or illogic—of that. We both tried on nervous laughs. Warren looked greatly relieved. All he'd really come to New York for was confirmation. He'd known for a long time what had to be done. He just didn't know if he could do it.

We talked for hours that night: our life stories—successes, failures, future plans, the works. Fear was a major theme. Zevon, who'd spent some time with Igor Stravinsky as a teenager, wanted to make his mark in classical music as well as in rock & roll. There was this unfinished symphony, hanging like a stone around his neck. Me, I wanted to write a series of detective novels, be the next Ross Macdonald.[5] About dawn, we agreed we owed it to ourselves to take our separate shots at it. And to give each other all the support we could. Things had gotten pretty corny by then. "Blood brothers," we swore. If there had been a knife, perhaps some blood would have been mingled. Because we meant it.

---

5 Dave Marsh recalls that Paul told him the series of books would each be set ten years apart. "He said, 'They'd all be the same except what would change would be the price of cheeseburgers.'" Paul told Kenneth Millar that he wanted to write a detective novel that went against Millar's belief that the genre should not attempt to mirror the "serious novel" by focusing too much on the detective's private life. "I have three other more traditional ones that I would rather write first, but it seems to me that it would be a legitimate thing to do. It seems to me that no one has ever shown what a person does in the off hours of the case—if the person has an unhappy romance going or if the person plays poker or if the person likes films or whatever—and it wouldn't be wrong to present a complete picture of a man working for half the book on the case and how that interrelates to the other half of his life."

One of the reasons the Zevons moved to Santa Barbara was the hope that clearing out of Los Angeles would curb Warren's drinking. On his own, he'd attempted to stop, but it didn't work. And the calmness of Santa Barbara, which he'd "mistakenly thought was going to be an idyllic existence," was driving him nuts.

In an eight-page bio he wrote especially for me—during our interviews, Zevon became so obsessive in his desire to capture the facts of his life in proper chronological order that he spent whole days at the typewriter trying to summarize each year—Warren remembers the move this way:

> That summer, we buy a spacious house in Montecito. Our initial reason for looking in the Santa Barbara area is simple: Ross Macdonald lives there.
> It's quiet, peaceful, safe, beautiful. The air is fine.
> It makes me nervous.
> The idea that I can't afford the house makes me nervous.
> The idea that I can afford the house makes me nervous.
> I have the guest house professionally soundproofed and build a four-track "writing studio."
> The studio makes me nervous.

What happened in that studio just a short while after our "blood brothers" ceremony in New York was enough to make everyone who knew Zevon nervous.

"I tried not to drink for a few days when I got back to Santa Barbara," Warren says, "but decided to give myself a little rope at our housewarming. By the end of the evening, I was hanging from it, of course."

Let Crystal tell it: "He had a few beers at the housewarming, and I noticed it. But by the end of the evening, he was definitely sober and proud of it. The next day, some friends came over, and he started drinking more beer. After they left, I mentioned it. He got irritated. There was nothing wrong with having a few beers, he claimed. That wasn't drinking. He said he wasn't going into the hospital, that he could quit by himself. We argued. He got mad and went out to the studio. I went to bed, not knowing what to do. I figured I'd talk to the people at Pinecrest the next day and see how to proceed from there.

"About two in the morning, I heard three shots. They woke me up out of a deep sleep. I just sat straight up in my bed, and the sound of those shots was like a bolt of lightning going through me. I didn't know what had happened. My first thought was that he'd shot himself. Then I thought, Well, there were *three* shots. Sometimes he'd just shoot the gun. But I didn't *know*.

"I got up and looked out the window toward the studio, but I couldn't really see what was going on. So I went out and started walking across the yard. And it wasn't until I started walking across the yard that I started to think of the possibility that he might shoot me, that Ariel [the Zevons' two-year-old daughter] was in the house, that if he was drunk and shot me, what would happen to her?

"I found myself sort of sneaking up to the studio door. When I saw him, his back was turned and he was staring at the couch. I opened the door and went in, and he was just standing there with the gun. He was obviously drunk because he was weaving back and forth. Then I saw his album cover—the *Excitable Boy* cover, a portrait of him—and there were three holes right in the middle of the face. The cover was propped up against the couch, and the bullets had just gone into the couch.[6]

"He turned and looked at me. At first, he looked really scared. I just stared at him. I couldn't believe it. Right away, he put the gun down. Then he laughed—a real nervous laugh—and said, 'It's funny, isn't it?'

"I said, 'Warren, it's not funny at all. This time, it's really not funny.'

"I turned around and walked out of the studio, and he just chased after me, saying, 'Wait a minute, wait a minute, it was a joke.' He was like a little boy, kind of pulling at my arm and crying, 'It was all a joke. It's okay.'

"When we finally got to Pinecrest, he held my hands. He was terrified. But he didn't make any attempt to leave that day. After he checked in, he said: 'Call Joe Smith [president of Asylum] and tell him to issue a press release. Call Paul and tell him to put it in *Rolling Stone* right away.' I think he knew that he might change his mind and try to get out. The press release was his way of making sure he stayed. If he left, he'd feel that he'd betrayed everybody, let his fans down."

Intervention. The very word suggests such a cold and exact, sanctioned and yet sinister interference with another person's life that I still get the shakes whenever I say it out loud. *In-ter-ven-tion.* Is it a Nixonian noun for some act of official pornography, a euphemism for gang rape by governmental robots? No. In a way, it's what Pinecrest has instead of God. While an intervention can seem as harsh and fear-provoking as the idea of eternal damnation, it's also kindly and forgiving. Put it this way: an intervention is an execution with a happy ending. I know because I attended one.

In his four days in New York, Warren Zevon had gone from being an outrageous, falling-down drunk at the Palladium to a courtly but inebriated,

---

6 In his review of *Excitable Boy*, published well before this incident, Paul had written that "the new LP blasts the bull's-eye into smithereens."

Tennessee Williams-style "gentleman caller" (Jay Cocks's wife, the actress Verna Bloom, remembers that, despite the obviously terrible shape Warren was in when he visited them on Long Island, "his manners were perfect and he even made his bed in the morning") to a desperately sick man who felt that death was just as close as the corner bar. Zevon recalls that "coming back from the Cocks's, I spent the entire ride wondering if I'd have to vomit. I couldn't swallow. And when an alcoholic reaches the point where he can't drink another drop of alcohol, then he's about at the end of the road. I wasn't even able to hold down a sip of water. After you left the hotel, I called Crystal for help." When Crystal telephoned to tell me that Warren had entered the hospital, she described his condition: "He's dying, Paul. Some days, he can't even dress himself."

I caught a plane to Los Angeles right away. Jackson Browne—one of Zevon's oldest and closest friends, his producer and co-producer for a time, and the man who'd fought many battles to get Warren signed to Asylum—and I drove up to Santa Barbara the next day for the intervention. Several other people were coming, too. Crystal had explained to us what we'd have to do: make a list of all the times we'd seen Warren drunk and tell him—in no uncertain terms— exactly how he'd acted. Under hospital rules, the whole thing would be a complete surprise to Zevon. His therapist would simply lead him into a room, he'd see many of his friends there, and the horror stories would begin.

Both Jackson and I were apprehensive. I remember wondering how this was going to help. Now that Warren had committed himself, wasn't the long recitation of a series of "sins" needlessly cruel? Wouldn't he hate us for subjecting him to it? Wouldn't it shatter whatever confidence he'd built? And who the hell were any of us to sit in almighty judgment of him? Crystal assured us that the results would be positive.

At the hospital, we had what amounted to a rehearsal. Present were Jorge Calderón (cowriter of "Nighttime in the Switching Yard," "Veracruz," and "Jungle Work"), LeRoy Marinell (cowriter of "Excitable Boy" and "Werewolves of London"), graphic artist and photographer Jimmy Wachtel, Crystal and her parents, Browne and myself. Two doctors read what we had written and, in most cases, insisted that we get a lot tougher and more explicit "for the good of the patient." Rewrites were demanded—sometimes more than one.

Finally, we had our trial run, sans Zevon. Crystal's parents led off, and you could feel their rancor slash like a razor blade. Sweet Jesus, I thought, get me out of here. This hospital's crazy. Next in line, I was trembling so badly that I wasn't sure I could speak. Here is part of what—in a very strange voice—I read:

> Warren, I've seen you drunk probably five or six times, maybe more....

I remember once at your house in Los Feliz when we talked the night away, mostly about writing, writer's block, your new record [*Excitable Boy*]. It was very apparent then that the fear of being unable to write another album went incredibly deep—far deeper than I'd imagined. You talked about writing in terms of life and death (but not suicidally): "I hope I can get these songs out before it kills me." You grabbed a book and, standing on the sofa, read the T.S. Eliot poem about "the fire and the rose." You spoke movingly about wanting—with all your heart—both of them.

It was a fine evening, but at about six or so in the morning, when I had to get back to my hotel, you tried to call a cab for me and were too drunk to dial the number. It was a bad moment for both of us. I didn't want to embarrass you by taking the phone away, but it was agonizing to stand there watching you get one wrong number after another—or drop the phone completely—for about fifteen minutes.

In New York, I saw you drunk during a performance at Trax. The set was so painful that I had to leave. Your timing was shot, your remarks to the audience didn't make sense, and *none* of the greatness of your music came through....

"My writing is conflict," you told me a few nights ago in New York, and I'm sure you're worried about losing that essential *aesthetic* conflict if you don't drink.... You said you admired F. Scott Fitzgerald, felt that Ernest Hemingway took the coward's way out.

It took a lot of courage for you to come to Pinecrest, and I admire you for doing it. I think you did the right thing. If you hadn't, there'd have been *The Crack-up*, which we've also talked about. I love you and I'm proud to be your friend.

Since I'd probably known Zevon for the shortest time and seen him the least, my comments were mild compared to what had preceded and what followed. After about an hour, everyone was finished. Drained though we were, there was a collective sigh of relief. Then one of the doctors turned to Crystal and asked: "Where's your list?" Those three words exploded like shots in the night, ricocheting around the room and bloodying us all before they practically knocked Crystal off her feet.

"I didn't *know*," she stammered, looking ashen. "You mean that I have to tell about all the times that I've seen Warren drunk? And what he did?"

"Of course," the doctor said. "Your list should be the best yet."

An hour later, I felt that I'd led a very sheltered life; that I'd just been pulled through every nightmare sequence a spiritual terrorist like Ingmar Bergman could dream up; that *The Lost Weekend* was nothing more than a pleasant little fairy tale for children; that, were it not for his wife, Warren Zevon would have been dead ten times over; that—if there were still saints in this world—I'd just been listening to one.

After a few minutes of shock, tears, and stunned silence, another doctor led Zevon in. It started all over again. It was even worse this time. One by one, we blundered through our speeches, each of us dreading the moment when Crystal's turn would come. Warren looked dazed and pale, like a small animal who'd been struck on the head. It was impossible to tell what he was thinking.

Zevon remembers Pinecrest vividly: "When I went in, I was still protesting fiercely. For a couple of days, I paced constantly. Sometimes I'd listen for traffic—a boulevard or highway nearby. I'd plan escapes. Of course, I could have walked out the front door anytime, but, sobered up, I was too scared to stick my nose out the door.

"Two days after I entered the hospital, there was an intervention. An intervention is a new technique in therapy that's designed to force the alcoholic to face himself and his actions.

"I was led into a conference room by my therapist, Steve Dudash. All of my closest friends were there. One at a time, they related stories of my atrocious conduct when I'd been drunk. They told me, as tenderly as they could, that they valued me and had faith that I could recover.

"I felt resentment and mostly terror at first. After that, utter despair. Then I realized how much all of these people must genuinely care for me to put themselves through such an ordeal. And if I meant that much to people whom I respected, I felt I no longer had the right to pronounce and act out a death sentence on myself."

When it was all over, one of the doctors asked us all to go up to Warren and put our arms around him. We rose hesitantly. During the entire proceedings, Zevon had barely moved. His face was still a blank. God knows, he had no other secrets left—the intervention had taken care of that. As we approached him, I didn't know what to expect. Maybe he'd never talk to any of us again. Or fall to the floor. Or hit someone.

Then, as if in some kind of dream, we were all one body, embracing Warren. Suddenly, the tension broke. Everyone was crying—happily and unashamedly crying. The secrets *were* gone. And what had taken their place was an amazing sense of communal trust and innocence. We were a roomful of defenseless three-year-olds, members of a primal tribe that had ritually cleansed not Zevon but ourselves. No one could ever take that away from us.

"Blood brother," I said as I threw my arms around Warren. We were both bawling like babies. "Blood brother," he said as he hugged me back.

F or once in my life I had nothing and wanted nothing. Then the thought of Sue fell through me like a feather in a vacuum. My mind picked it up and ran with it and took flight. I wondered where she was, what she was doing, whether she'd aged much as she lay in ambush in time, or changed the color of her bright head.

—ROSS MACDONALD,
The Doomsters

If life were a movie, what a fabulous finale that last scene might have made: wife and buddies, smiling tearfully in Technicolor triumph, as they form a blissful circle around the happier and wiser hero. Modern medicine and psychology win out as the drunk repenteth. A director like Frank Capra would have loved it. In the real world, however, the circle didn't stay unbroken long. A little over a year after the intervention, Warren and Crystal Zevon separated. The divorce has now gone through.

Why? Who can really tell. As is the case with most alcoholics who first take the cure, the time came when Warren wanted to see if he could handle "just one drink." The answer was no. As a result, he ran amok in Los Angeles for a month in the winter of 1979 while Crystal was in Ireland, tentatively beginning her career as a writer.[7] (I found him in a seedy but elegant hotel on Sunset Boulevard and managed to get him back to Santa Barbara and into the hospital for a few days. When Crystal returned, things were all right again for a time.) More importantly, after Pinecrest, the core of their relationship changed. For the good of both parties, the roles of the sober, responsible parent-adult looking after the undependable yet creative child-artist naturally had to be jettisoned. New tickets for the promised land were purchased—paid for with past blood and future promises—but somehow the Zevons, try as they did, never survived the trip or found a compatible new language.

For Crystal, booze had a lot to do with it. She remembers the final blowout this way: "We'd just come back from Hawaii. Warren was going to start *Bad Luck Streak in Dancing School*, and we'd rented a house in L.A. At first, everything was terrific, but then he got real upset with Ariel. He said he

---

7 In 2007, she published the bestselling *I'll Sleep When I'm Dead: The Dirty Life and Times of Warren Zevon*.

couldn't work with her there, that she'd have to leave. I could tell that he was real close to wanting to drink again, that he'd been having a hard time. In Hawaii, he just kept saying he wanted drugs, he wanted one thing or another. I didn't know what to do. I went back to Santa Barbara with Ariel. That night, he called me and said, 'I'd just like to be with you. Could you come back alone?'

"I said I wasn't going to do it, but I wound up driving down for the weekend. We had a fight just as soon as I walked in the door—a fight over nothing. Things got crazy. He drove the car and ran red lights until I finally said, 'Warren, I'm not here to get killed. Let me out.'

"He apologized. We went shopping and then had dinner at a French restaurant. It was probably the best night I can ever remember having with him. I mean, we came home and were just like kids, laughing and playing. Later, we got serious. He said—and I think this was the first time he'd ever made a comment quite so strong—he said: 'You know, we've just put so much into this relationship, and it's everything I've ever wanted. I don't know what happens to me when I go off in other directions, but I don't want other women. I don't ever want anyone but you. So let's just make that commitment and not have to worry about it if we have a fight. It doesn't mean we're going to split up.'

"I was shocked. I think I managed to say, 'Yeah, that's great.'

"The next morning, I got up before he did and went out to get some samples of fabric. We'd been talking about new curtains for the bedroom. When I got home, he grabbed them out of my hands and said, 'That's the ugliest stuff I've ever seen.' He had a coffee cup and he threw it through a window. Then he started screaming about how stupid I was and what bad taste I had. I looked at his eyes and I *knew* immediately. There was a rage there that was like when he was drinking, but it might have been a 'dry drunk,' which happens.

"I couldn't believe what had happened. I guess I wandered down to a hamburger stand. Amazingly, there were some women there who were talking about alcoholism. I walked right over to them and said, 'Look, I wasn't trying to eavesdrop, but I just don't know what to do.' We must have talked for an hour or so. One woman said that her husband had gotten drunk three times before he'd been able to stay sober. They told me to tell Warren that I knew what the problem was—that it wasn't our relationship but the fact that he wanted to drink again—and that I had to allow him to make his own decision. 'Be sure to let him know that if he decides not to drink, you'll always be there for him,' the woman said.

"So I took that advice, bought a bag of hamburgers, and went back to the house. When I got there, Warren was on the phone with the pharmacy, renewing all his prescriptions. He came over, and there was liquor on his breath. I made my speech, but he didn't buy it. I left, not realizing that the marriage was over but just thinking that he needed to hit bottom and make a choice.

"Much later, I told him that if he wanted a divorce, he should file for it, because if it were up to me, I wanted to try to make the marriage work. I would have chosen to separate for a while and get our acts together, but I didn't think Warren could exist without someone for that long."

Zevon tried desperately to explain why he felt the marriage wouldn't work in "Empty-Handed Heart," a ballad from *Bad Luck Streak in Dancing School*. "Empty-Handed Heart" is a love letter written directly to Crystal, though its circumstances are certainly universal.

> Heart jinxed condition
> Never sure how I feel
> Trying to separate the real thing
> From the wishful thinking
> Sometimes I wonder
> If I'll make it without you
> I'm determined to
> I'll make my stand
> And if after all is said and done
> You only find one special one
> Then I've thrown down diamonds
> In the sand …

Then this line of advice to his wife: "Leave the fire behind you and start."[8]

Perhaps there's one more reason for the breakup. Often when a man (or woman) decides—in this case, with the most honorable of intentions—to make a major change in his life, he finds himself wiping the slate clean, changing *everything*. He doesn't mean to, but it happens. And when it does, it's like the song says: a rockslide rolling down a hill.

---

8 When Jay Cocks reviewed *Bad Luck Streak in Dancing School*, even though he called "Empty-Handed Heart" the album's "centerpiece" and "a classic," "Something about the way he interpreted the song just really upset me," Crystal Zevon says, "so I wrote this letter of the angry moment off to *Rolling Stone*." Somebody brought it to Paul's attention. "Paul called me and walked me through the hazards of having that published—'Because,' he said, 'they *will* print it'—and finally talked me out of doing it." Today she finds no fault with the review. "But at the time …"

Don't you wanna show me
You really ought ta get to know me

Ooh I can't help myself ah shoot
Ooh I can't help myself ah shoot …

Flipping and a flopping
Straight into your love I'm hopping …
—BONNIE POINTER,
"Ah Shoot"[9]

These days, Warren Zevon is a relatively happy and healthy man caught up in the act of self-discovery. He's also a man who steadfastly refuses to lay to rest "those days." It's not that he's proud of them—far from it—but that he practically *demands* to be held accountable for past atrocities. (One of the things that really rocked me back on my heels at the intervention was the fact that Zevon had been in an alcoholic stupor for so long that he couldn't remember wrecking hotel rooms, punching people out, or waving a pistol in a close friend and fellow songwriter's face.[10] It was news—literally sickening news—to him that he'd done such deeds.)

After having been drunk for a decade, Warren found reentry into reality a strange and difficult journey. The whole world seemed different: *slower*. Minutes could actually be counted, which was something of a mixed blessing. "Normal" like the rest of us, Zevon felt fine physically but was frequently bored silly. He had all this time on his hands—hours, days, weeks of it—that he couldn't speed up or blot out with booze. Alcoholics just aren't used to everyday regularity.

He's used to it now. I can see it in his eyes as we watch another plane glide toward Burbank. Time is no longer an enemy. There are dance classes, lessons in the martial arts, daily exercises, books to read, songs to write, a symphony to finish, and a new interest in acting undoubtedly fostered by Kim Lankford. (The nights that we don't tape, I can hear Kim and Warren rehearsing a *Knots Landing* script. Scared shitless, Zevon nonetheless tries out for the role of a suspected psycho in one of the show's upcoming episodes. He doesn't get the part but makes a good impression. A year ago, I think to myself, he'd never have had the nerve to risk such rejection.)

"Kim is like Clint Eastwood," Warren says, topping off his fifth cup of coffee with this Zevon-esque simile. I pop the lid off my fifth can of Coke.

9 The song was a particular favorite of Zevon and Kim Lankford's.
10 Zevon told Paul about the time that he discovered, after the fact, that he'd pointed a pistol at J.D. Souther. Crystal Zevon says that he also did it to LeRoy Marinell.

Between us, we've built a small mountain of cigarette butts at the center of a huge ashtray. ("No wonder you guys can't *sleep*," laughs Lankford, who, after her and Warren's first night together, was awakened in the morning by the sound of Zevon blowing the bejesus out of the alarm clock with his .44 Magnum. She handled the entire incident with the aplomb of a Howard Hawks heroine.) Cassettes—Warren's and mine—litter the living room. There must be 500 of them all over the rug. Albums line the wall by the fireplace: Shostakovich, Mahler, Stockhausen, Bartók, and Stravinsky next to Eddie Cochran, Jimi Hendrix, the Clash, the Sex Pistols, the Byrds, Dylan Thomas, the soundtrack from *Casablanca*. There are guitars, a piano, a synthesizer, and a bass signed by Bill Lee. Plus plenty of recording equipment. A shoulder holster hangs over the arm of an easy chair. Zevon tosses me a portfolio labeled *Symphony No. 1*, which he works on nearly every night. I don't quite catch it, and the contents slide to the floor: pages and pages of meticulously annotated music and a dog-eared copy of *Soldier of Fortune* magazine. Perfect.

"Kim is like Clint Eastwood." I mull the remark over for a while. Though that might not be my description—spunky, smart, pretty, and absolutely unpretentious, I would say—I know what Warren means: Kim Lankford knows exactly who she is.

Paraphrasing John D. MacDonald's Travis McGee, Zevon says: "Kim's not looking for herself, she *is* herself. She does what she does, without hardly talking about it at all. And she has a lot of skills. My first impression of her was that she couldn't possibly be a professional actress. Not nearly neurotic enough. Too calm, too pleasant, not hyper. I've seen so much franticness in my life that to meet someone as self-contained as Kim …" Warren stops and looks at the lightening sky. He doesn't have to finish the sentence.

By trying not to influence her man's life, it's clear that Lankford has tremendously influenced it. In many ways, this couple are complete opposites. Picture a somber, soul-searching songwriter, inching his way toward either paradise or paralysis, while his understanding but playful lady pinpoints and defuses problems with a logic so cheery and direct that you almost have to laugh because you didn't think of the solutions yourself. (I find myself wishing that Kim had a sister.) Send Lankford into a room filled with suave, self-centered "intellectuals" and she'd be too shy to speak for an hour or two. But when she did, the effect would be like Clint Eastwood splattering the bad guys in a Sergio Leone movie. Sometimes she gets to the heart of the matter so fast and guilelessly that, if you blink, you miss it. Zevon has been quick to pick up on such salvation. ("I'm so fucking *smart* that I spent the last fifteen years medicating myself into a subhuman condition," he says ruefully.) My friend doesn't blink much anymore.

"When Kim and I first met," Warren is saying, "I felt almost like a virgin because I wasn't used to being sober around women. We talked for days and days. We were both determined not to jump into a symbiotic relationship, and we don't try to be like each other. I no longer feel that a woman is supposed to be a reflection of my attitudes, or vice versa. Both of us had been thoroughly indoctrinated with the idea that you're supposed to *work* at a relationship. Hell, we thought, we already work hard enough—at our careers. Anyway, we have a wonderful relationship that doesn't seem to require constant analysis. We certainly don't sit around and evaluate it all the time. Instead of being *dependent* on Kim, I just look forward to seeing her. She's helped me to loosen up. I only hope that I've helped her."

He has, and not only by introducing her to books, classical music, and new ways of thinking about art. "I understand people much better now—myself included," Lankford says. "I'm more confident." She flashes a mock-wicked smile that lights up the room. "Before I met Warren, I had a tendency to feel that my opinions weren't worth voicing. Now, once you get me going, I hardly ever shut up." She looks at the tape recorder and pauses. "But I guess you've already noticed," she says quietly, capping a lovely blush with a delicious wink.

Jim Houghton, one of Kim's costars in *Knots Landing*, drops by, and we spend a night talking about music and movies. And—of all things—doing card tricks. I only know one, but it's a beauty and stumps everybody. Finally, I take Zevon into the kitchen and explain to him how the trick works: by mathematics, not sleight of hand. He's fascinated. It's like a musical score to him. I can see that he's determined to figure out why one particular card should wind up where it does when it does.

Warren does a card trick, too. He splits the deck, holds up about twenty cards—many of them face cards—and asks Houghton to pick one. (Since Zevon has already let me in on the "logic"—and I use the word loosely—behind his trick, I'm eagerly waiting to watch it fail and get in a friendly dig or two.) "Is it the four of hearts?" Warren asks Jim, who nods yes. I groan out loud as Zevon breaks up laughing. "I can see that we've destroyed Paul's sense of the order of the universe," he gloats, twisting the knife.

"I wouldn't have the guts to try that trick," I reply. "Tell them how it works. If you're not too embarrassed."

"Well, sometimes it doesn't work," Warren says. "A doctor told me about it. There's really no trick at all. You just show someone a bunch of cards—pack a few face cards in there—and a lot of people will pick the four of hearts simply because it's so unthreatening. The only rationale is that the four of hearts is a *nice* card."

I throw up my hands in defeat.

Later that night, after Houghton has left and Lankford has gone to bed, Zevon—as I knew he would—questions me about my trick again. I tell him

I don't know how it works, just that it does. "We've got to figure it out," he says. We spend hours on the task, varying the number of cards used and keeping track of their movement. To my amazement, Warren discovers a shortcut to the payoff, improving the trick by one-third. Then our collective obsessiveness really gets rolling. We assign musical notes to each card, hoping for a piece of atonal music that will reach its peak precisely when the right card is revealed. This takes until dawn, but we think we're on to something—a whole new form of composition. Zevon has filled several pages of music paper with our "art."

"What'll we call it?" he asks as he sits down at the piano.

"*The Four of Hearts*," I answer. "Maybe it'll sound nice and unthreatening."

"Maybe we should call it *The Dreaded Past*," he says.

We both laugh nervously. After all, we might have a masterpiece here. I turn on the tape recorder, and Warren begins to play. You wouldn't believe how bad it sounded.

And my mama couldn't be persuaded when they
    pleaded with her
Daughter don't marry that gambling man ...

Gambler tried to be a family man
Though it didn't suit his style
He thought he had him a winning combination
So he took us where the stakes were high
Her parents warned her
Tried to reason with her
Never kept their disappointment hid
They all went to pieces when the bad luck hit
Stuck in the middle
I was the kid.

                    —WARREN ZEVON,
              "Mama Couldn't Be Persuaded"

The past, let it all go fast: Warren William Zevon. Born in Chicago on January 24, 1947. Spent most of his youth in various California cities: Fresno, San Pedro, San Francisco, Los Angeles, et al. Father, William, a Russian-Jewish immigrant, got off the boat in New York, boxed for a number of years, then became a professional gambler. Still makes his living that way in Gardena, California. Mother, Beverly, a Scots-Welsh Mormon, totally unlike William. Zevon describes her as "extraordinarily withdrawn and repressed—you can barely hear her speaking voice. She did encourage my interest in art, though. My mother's relationship with her parents, Elsworth and Helen, was a tremendously destructive factor in the lives of both my father and I. I was told that my birth nearly killed my mother. They treated my father like a vagabond and roustabout. It must have been terribly uncomfortable for him, so he wasn't there a lot of the time. I wouldn't have been either, if I'd had a choice. Nobody ever told me anything, and my parents' marriage has been a mystery to me all my life. They didn't even let me know that they'd gotten a divorce until long after the fact.

"My grandmother is very senatorial—a big lady in every way. She ran the family. I grew up with a painting of an uncle, Warren, who looked just like me. He was a military man, a golden boy, an artist. He'd been killed in action. I remember my mother telling me, 'Your grandmother's really not wrapped altogether tight since that happened.' Uncle Warren was sort of the dead figurehead of the family, and I was brought up to follow in his footsteps. My ideal was supposed to be a dead man—with my name, looks and career intentions. A dead warrior who'd been waylaid by his heroism. I guess that kind of background gave me the idea that destroying myself was the only way to live up to expectations.

"Also, my mother's side of the family could have been the world's greatest champions and spokesmen for the A.M.A. They just believed in drugs. I can recall very vividly that when I had the slightest illness as a child, I was given powerful drugs. I remember being stoned a lot at a very early age."

There are a few good memories—living with his mother and father as a close-knit family in Los Angeles for a time, becoming an avid surfer while staying with his father in San Pedro, meeting Igor Stravinsky—along with the bad ones. "My friends all saw my father as a sort of Jesse James character," Zevon says. "Which was a mixed blessing. It was neat sometimes. Other times, I think I'd have preferred a Robert Young type."

After having attended several high schools, Warren finally called it quits his junior year and headed for New York to be a folksinger.[11] "What happened in school," he says, "was that I was the kid to whom they always said, 'Keep your mouth shut and you'll get an A.' I was indoctrinated with the idea that I was smart when I was a kid. I broke I.Q. records all over the place. Oh shit, I can remember thinking, I believe you do this act with a cross. They kept accelerating me through Gatorade High in Fresno and Motorcycle High in San Pedro, and then I suddenly found myself in Fairfax High in L.A. It was an excellent school, but I was out of my wire. In chemistry class, I was confronted with the inevitability of flunking, which was weird. The only thing I did well

11 Zevon counted the New Lost City Ramblers and Koerner, Ray & Glover among his folk influences. "As a matter of fact, I learned to play guitar from listening to the banjo parts on the folk records."

in was English. And it's funny, because my English grade depended on a long essay I had to write. Afterward, the teacher took me aside and said: 'Here's your composition and here's your A. Who really wrote it?' I did, I said. And she said, 'You're lying.'"

Zevon's days as a New York folkie came to an abrupt end when, during a pass-the-hat performance at a tiny club in Greenwich Village, he dropped one of his finger picks into the sound hole of his guitar and felt too foolish to continue playing. "I was just awful," he recalls. "Except for chasing the romantic, Bob Dylan dream, I didn't know what I was doing. I went to Florida for a while and then back to California. First Los Angeles, then San Francisco. This was in 1964. I was eighteen. In San Francisco, I met a girl named Tule Livingston, and we lived together off and on for the next few years, mostly in L.A. We got married in 1968. Our son, Jordan, was born in 1969. The marriage broke up shortly after that. There was lots of drugs and drinking."[12]

Throughout the late Sixties, Warren supported himself by playing in various groups, penning commercials for Boone's Farm wines, doing session work ("I'm strumming a guitar somewhere way in the background on Phil Ochs's *Pleasures of the Harbor*"), and writing songs for other artists ("Like the Seasons" and "Outside Chance" for the Turtles in 1967). "In 1966," he says, "I was lyme in a duo called lyme and cybelle. We had an extremely small hit, 'Follow Me.' Interestingly, everybody observed the no-caps e.e. cummings-ism very strictly. I met Jackson Browne in 1968, and we started getting to know one another.

"In 1969, Kim Fowley called me up one day and asked very simply, 'Are you prepared to wear black leather and chains, fuck a lot of teenage girls, and get rich?' I said yes. So we started work on *Wanted Dead or Alive* for Imperial. While we were making the record, I had a sudden attack of taste and told Kim that I wanted to finish the album myself. And he very graciously waltzed out of the project. *Wanted Dead or Alive* was released in 1970, to the sound of one hand clapping."[13]

---

12 "The girl and I were *not* married because when we met we were staunch antiestablishment Sixties people," is what Zevon actually told Paul, "but I prefer it to be taken for granted that we *were* married for my son's sake."

13 Paul reviewed *Wanted Dead or Alive* this way:
   Like old wounds, albums such as this seem to plague every artist who's finally hit it big in the marketplace. Be warned. *Wanted Dead or Alive* is Warren Zevon's *first* LP (recorded in 1970 for Imperial), not the new one that's due shortly.
   If *Wanted Dead or Alive* were interesting or any good, we could cheer its reissue. But Zevon fanatics would be hard pressed to find much merit—or, indeed, even to recognize their hero—in songs whose titles promise a lot ("A Bullet for Ramona," "Gorilla," "Wanted Dead or Alive") but deliver very little. Hey, he just wasn't ready then. Simple as that. ["Warren Zevon—*Wanted Dead or Alive*" by Paul Nelson from *Rolling Stone*, January 24, 1980. © Rolling Stone LLC 1980. All rights reserved. Reprinted by permission.]

Zevon spent the early Seventies working with Don and Phil Everly. He was hired to play keyboards, find new musicians (among them, Waddy Wachtel), and "revitalize" the Everly Brothers sound. "The road, booze, and I became an inseparable team," he notes. During this period, Warren wrote "Carmelita," "Hasten Down the Wind," "Poor Poor Pitiful Me," "Join Me in L.A." (with Tule Livingston), "The French Inhaler," and "Desperados Under the Eaves." He met Crystal in late 1971, and they lived together with two foster children she was taking care of. "We were very happy, and I was writing," Zevon says. "I wrote 'Frank and Jesse James' for and about Don and Phil Everly. In 1972, I was under contract to David Geffen as a songwriter. This was at Jackson's suggestion, of course, though I believe that Geffen liked my songs. He let the contract lapse in 1973, however. Not much work that year.

"In 1974, I moved to Berkeley for a while. Pretty soon, I was playing two or three clubs a night—in other words, finally doing what I'd intended to do a decade earlier in New York. The gigs started looking better, but so did Hollywood. I opted for L.A. again.

"Crystal and I decided to get married in 1974. Hunter Thompson-style, we drove all night—with a best man and bridesmaid, recruited at the last minute—across the desert to Nevada after dropping acid, me pouring down vodka the whole way. I can remember drinking Bloody Marys in one of the big casinos at dawn, waiting for a chapel to open. In spite of the dope—which had worn off anyway—we both cried and took the ceremony and our marriage very seriously."

Though Warren continued to write ("Backs Turned Looking Down the Path," "Mohammed's Radio," "I'll Sleep When I'm Dead"), 1975 began badly. Zevon couldn't find a job and got busted for drunk driving one night in front of the Troubadour. "Crystal and I decided we were fed up," he says. "So we sold everything we owned, except for my Martin guitar and a Sony stereo cassette recorder, and headed for Spain. When we got there, we read all the Ross Macdonald novels, and I played the bars for pocket money. While this was going on, Jackson and David Geffen were bluffing each other over my recording contract and advance. Fortunately, Jackson won. We flew back to Los Angeles and started work on *Warren Zevon*."

In Spain, the Zevons had met David Lindell, a fabulous character straight out of *Soldier of Fortune*. From this meeting came "Roland the Headless Thompson Gunner." Back in L.A., Warren wrote "Werewolves of London" and "Excitable Boy." And Crystal discovered that she was pregnant.

Zevon took to the road when his first Asylum LP was released in 1976. Most critics loved the album. Of the tour, he says: "I began to fall apart. Once again I learned what a good place the road can be for a bad husband. Ariel was born. For Christmas, Crystal, I, and the baby flew to Spain to visit Lindell. It was a disaster. The first night there, I got into a fight with some drunken Spaniards over my version of 'Jingle Bells.' My glasses were smashed and my hand slashed by a broken beer mug. Things went downhill from there. Lindell and I spent Christmas getting twisted all over Marbella. Crystal got pneumonia, so she and Ariel flew back to California. I decided to go to Morocco with a bag filled with Valium, vodka, and Fitzgerald. Too much booze and not enough food. I've always figured that in dragging myself to Tangier and back, I squeezed the last drop of 'glamour' out of my rapidly worsening toxic condition.

"Much of 1977 was a nightmare. Crystal and I lived apart for several months, and I was seriously into the noir life—vodka, drugs, sex. Somehow, I got the songs written for *Excitable Boy*. Jackson begged me to get more sleep for my voice's sake. Waddy Wachtel looked like he wanted to tear his hair out for six months. I thought my days were numbered in fractions. But Crystal and I got back together. We finished the record and enjoyed the holidays peacefully.

"Of course, in 1978, I crashed completely. *Excitable Boy* sold well. *People* magazine—with my help—made me into the dangerous Dean Martin of my generation. 'But he's such a good family man,' they said. Oh boy! In Chicago, I fell off the stage and wrecked my leg. For the rest of the tour, I was in a wheelchair, on crutches, or gimping about. 'The Jett Rink Tour,' I called it, in honor of the James Dean character passing out in the middle of a drunken speech in *Giant*. Clearly, I had carried this F. Scott Fitzzevon thing too far."

If we can think of this great country of ours as polarized between two sets of James Brothers, Frank and Jesse at one end and Henry and William at the other, why, we begin to get some sense of the enormous spectrum in between.

—PETER DE VRIES,
Consenting Adults; or,
The Duchess Will Be Furious

Many thousands of words ago, I said that this story was supposed to be about alcoholism (though I hope there's more to it than that). The reason it's about alcoholism is because Warren Zevon wanted it that way. "I've been a walking advertisement for excess and chaos most of my life," he says, "so it's about time I tried to do something for the other side."

Obviously, Zevon's journey hasn't been in easy one. He and I were going to collaborate on this piece in 1979, not long after he was released from Pinecrest the first time. Crystal called me a few days before I was to leave for Santa Barbara. She and Warren, with the hospital's consent, had decided to take separate vacations. He was in Los Angeles, more than likely drunk, she said. She gave me his number, adding that she didn't know if he'd talk to me. He might feel too embarrassed. "I can't help him, Paul," she told me. "I've tried, but now he's got to help himself. Otherwise it's no good. I hope you understand. I'm going to Ireland as I planned."

I said I understood but caught the plane for L.A. anyway. Perhaps I was being overly melodramatic, yet I had a terrible premonition of what I might find there. A critic from Seattle had given me a Neil Young tape that included an acoustic version of "Powderfinger" (*Rust Never Sleeps* didn't come out until the following year). During the flight, I must have listened to that song fifty times. Like the narrator of Billy Wilder's *Sunset Boulevard*, the protagonist of "Powderfinger" is a dead man who tells us how he was killed. I couldn't get the intervention and its horrors out of my mind. And Neil Young's lyrics

> Shelter me from the powder and the finger
> Cover me with the thought that pulled the trigger
> Just think of me as one you never figured
> Would fade away so young
> With so much left undone
> Remember me to my love, I know I'll miss her

sounded like eulogy, something that one friend might read at another's funeral.

Zevon and I met for dinner. He was friendly but shaky. I don't think he knew that I knew he'd started drinking again. He ordered a Coke with his meal. After dinner, we went to his hotel, ostensibly to begin work on the story of how he'd conquered alcoholism. One look at his room blew that. There were empty bottles everywhere. Full ones, too. Neither one of us knew what to say about it, so we didn't say anything. To me, the room reeked of death. I can't really describe it. The closest I can come is Van Gogh's description of his painting, *Night Café at Arles*: "The most violent passions of humanity … blood red … dark yellow … in an atmosphere of pale sulfur, like a furnace … I tried to show a place where a man can ruin himself, go mad, commit a crime."

As the night wore on, Warren began to drink huge tumblers filled with straight vodka. The conversation was bizarre. Zevon became very drunk, yet he kept talking about how he was cured. Then he'd switch things around and admit that he'd lost the battle. But only for now, he'd claim. "I'll stop drinking tomorrow, and we'll drive up to Santa Barbara," he'd say. "I know I can do it."

He made a brave attempt. For three days, he cut down. Yet he had about as much chance to sober up without professional help as I did to grow a new head. I could see that he was suffering, and I knew what I had to do: *not* preach at him (because then he'd feel even more guilty and probably disappear on me) and somehow get him back into Pinecrest with his ego and sense of honor at least semi-intact. Warren was sending out signals for help and I was receiving them, but it was an uneasy truce. War would break out if either of us made a serious mistake.

Once again, I got lucky. An outpatient from the hospital phoned and asked Zevon for assistance. Warren was to meet him at a lake just north of Santa Barbara. They would talk and fish. Though it sounded like a setup to both of us, it provided an honorable reason—i.e., an offer that Zevon couldn't refuse— to go to Santa Barbara.

Since Warren wasn't sober enough to drive and I didn't have a license, we called a limousine service he'd used in the past. Lee Herron, a man I will always be grateful to, was our driver. Zevon was debating with himself whether to pack up everything and check out of the hotel or keep the room and come back to Los Angeles after I'd returned to New York. I was trying to convince him not to come back—if he did, I frankly believed he'd die there—but I was trying too hard, and he was resisting. "It would take us hours to pack this mess," he argued, walking into the bedroom.

I took a big risk. While Warren was out of sight, I whispered to Herron, who was looking totally confused: "My friend is an alcoholic. He's very sick. I need to get him and his stuff out of here. There's a hospital in Santa Barbara. They'll know what to do. Will you help me?" Herron answered immediately. I'll never forget what he said: "Thank you for taking me into your confidence. Of course, I'll help you."

And help he did. As he and I packed suitcases and boxes, Lee Herron smoothly defused all tension and argument. He had Zevon spinning, but in the best way possible. Before Warren knew what was happening, we were on the road to Santa Barbara. When we got there, Herron dropped me off uptown before taking Zevon out to the lake. I phoned the hospital. Arnie Wallace, Warren's therapist, wasn't available, they said. Perhaps he was meeting Zevon. They didn't know. I walked over to Joseph the Provider, a bookstore owned by two close friends of Warren's and mine, Ralph and Carol Sipper. Zevon was supposed to call me there later. Ralph and Carol were very supportive. Get him back to the hospital, they said.

Warren called at five o'clock. He sounded terrible. "My therapist was at the lake," he said. "He thinks I should recommit myself. I don't *want* to. I told him I didn't *need* to." The voice on the phone was almost pleading.

I made myself sound as tough as I could. "But you *do* need to," I said.

"Oh shit, not you, too," he said. He was crying. "Do you *really* think I need to go back to the hospital? They make you sleep on rubber sheets there."

"We'll change the sheets," I said. "You've got to go back. Ask Lee."

I kept the conversation short, figuring that if I played the bad cop, Herron would play the good one. He did. We agreed to meet for dinner, drive out to Zevon's house in Montecito, pack some things, and take Warren to the hospital.

It wasn't that easy. I waited at the restaurant for three hours. Herron and Zevon finally arrived. Warren had changed his mind about a dozen times. He quickly downed three vodkas. We'd talk quietly for a while, then things would flare up. More vodkas. People were staring at us. Lee and I kept switching roles, desperately trying to keep Zevon calm.

At the house, it was more of the same, only worse. One minute, Warren would agree to the hospital. The next minute, he wouldn't. He had a bottle in every room. The evening went like this: Zevon would stagger out of a room, he and I would talk, Herron would find the liquor and pour it down the drain. By three o'clock, we'd run out of rooms. We were all crazy.

"I've got this nice house," Warren said. "Why can't I stay here and enjoy it?"

I could feel myself getting furious and decided to go with it. Nothing else was working anyway.

"*Because*," I said, picking up something and throwing it across the room. "Because you *don't* enjoy it! And you never *will* enjoy it unless you quit drinking! Now stop all this *shit* about the rubber sheets—they're hardly the issue here—and let's get going."

He just looked at me for a long time. Then he shrugged and said, "You're right. I don't enjoy it. Give me a drink and we'll go."

While Lee got Zevon into the car, I suddenly realized that I didn't know exactly where the hospital was. I'd only been there a couple of times—in daylight. It was four in the morning now, and Santa Barbara shuts down about ten at night. But we were rolling, and I knew I could find the general area. From there, it shouldn't be too difficult. I looked at Warren. He had passed out.

What followed was sheer Keystone Kops. Santa Barbara was pitch black and seemingly devoid of cars and people. We found a big hospital that I remembered was within a few blocks of the clinic. They gave us directions. We still couldn't find it. We'd been driving for almost an hour. Everything looked familiar, but where the hell was Pinecrest? We were so close that I knew I could hit the goddamned place with a rock, if I knew which way to toss it. A police car sped by. We chased it and forced it to the curb at fifty miles an hour. The two officers gave us directions. No luck again. What kept confusing us was a little one-way street. "Fuck it," I said. "This street must be the problem. Let's go up it the wrong way." We did. And there was Pinecrest. Right around the corner. After we checked Zevon in, we sat in the car for a while. Numbness had set in.

Herron was the first to stir. "Do you know the way back to the house?" he asked.

"I'm not sure," I said. "Do you?"

"I don't think so," he said. "But I suppose we can find it."

We were both so tired that neither one of us could stop laughing.

Three days later, Warren was released from the hospital. "I guess they figured they'd have to trust me," he said. He seemed badly shaken and slept most of the time. When he was awake, we played records or watched TV. He was in such rough shape he could barely talk. I tried to think of something that would help. Ken Millar was the answer. He and his compassionate creation—private detective Lew Archer, whose specialty was saving mixed-up young men and women—were surrogate fathers, not only to Zevon and me but to an entire generation. Soon Millar was at the front door. With a look of surprise, Warren let him in. I put on my Nikes and went out for a long run.

When I got back, Zevon was much improved. His eyes were alive again. He even cracked a joke. "You know what pisses me off about you?" he said. "You go out running for three hours and when you come back, you're not even sweating." That night, he started playing the piano. I figured we were home free.

To keep my job, I had to fly to New York the next day. "Look," I told Warren, "Crystal will be here in a week. You can make it until then. Put that iron will to work. It's in your songs, so I know you've got it. When you show up sober at the airport to meet Crystal, tell her you went back to Pinecrest. Think of how proud she'll be." Had I known more about alcoholism, I'd never have left. Zevon spent a week in hell.

It's Warren's story: "Each time you detoxify, it's infinitely worse, just incredibly worse—a lesson I hope I've learned by now. Anyhow, after you left, I had these terrible dreams. You've probably had the experience of screaming yourself awake during a bad dream, right? Well, I'd scream and scream and *not* wake up. I'd literally have to throw myself across the room to wake up. And even then, I wasn't *positive* I was awake. In one dream, you were dragging me out of the mire of a construction site, and everybody was laughing at me. I was covered with mud and slime. And these maggoty, medieval hags and horrible-looking faces—it was like Ken Russell's *The Devils*—were laughing at me and trying to kill me.

"I was depressed and riddled with anxiety. Something called *Stars in Stress* was on TV. You can imagine the irony. I sat there looking at Janis Joplin and Judy Garland footage and didn't know whether to laugh or cry. One night, I just started screaming. I went berserk. I flung open the liquor cabinet. There, in front of all the bottles, was Christmas candy. Sugar! Arnie Wallace had told me to grab sugar. I ate all the candy. If it hadn't been there, who knows. I took *every* bottle—and this would break any boozer's heart—and just poured the liquor into the sink. I was screaming, 'It's my *fucking* life! It's *my* life, not yours! It's *my* life, and you can't have it!' I poured all the liquor out. Then I got rid of the tranquilizers. Down the toilet.

"As I was storming around the house, I came to the realization that all that stuff in the media that made me into F. Scott Fitzzevon, the two-fisted drinker, the adventurer—all that stuff was just bullshit. '*They* don't care if you die,' I said. 'It's just next week's issue.' I looked at those pictures of me that used to be in the bathroom, and there was Jackson and Crystal and John Belushi—all these people—and me standing there looking like a fat clown. I said, 'You're not a fucking *boy* and you're not a fucking *werewolf*, you're a fucking *man*, and it's about time you acted like it.'

"They talk about alcoholics living one day at a time, not knowing if they're going to drink tomorrow. It's really true. At that point, I was going minute by minute. Little things would get me through another hour. The note you left. The movie you said Jay Cocks said was good. *The Medusa Touch*, I think. It was on cable TV, and I watched it over and over. It was the best movie I ever saw. It got me through a whole day.

"Then I got a phone call from a *dear* friend. Someone from the old days, not a musician or anything. I kept telling him, 'I'm all right, man. I'm shaking and I'm feeling shitty, but I'm pounding the piano twelve hours a day and singing and writing songs for myself—telling myself a lot of things in songs.' And he kept saying, 'I understand, Warren. I'm your friend. I understand that if you're an artist, you've got to drink. So why don't I come up there with a bunch of cheeseburgers, a bottle, and an ounce of blow?'

"'No, no, you *don't* understand,' I'm trying to tell him. 'Don't come up here. I'm really happy. I'm really working.' Of course, I'm hysterical by now. 'It's cool,' he says. 'A little vodka, a little cocaine, and you'll be fine in no time.'

"I hung up the phone. It was a shattering experience. If ever I believed that there was a God and a Devil—and that they were just *guys*, you know, one with a tail and the other with a long white beard—it was at that moment. It was just a *satanic* temptation. I started writing another song—something for me, not for other people. It wasn't a good song or anything, but, for me, it was important. It was long and involved, and there were tears running down my face while I was writing it.

"Then I sat down and read T.S. Eliot's *Four Quartets*. This part especially:

> We shall not cease from exploration
> And the end of all our exploring

Will be to arrive where we started
And know the place for the first time.
Through the unknown, remembered gate
When the last of earth left to discover
Is that which was the beginning;
At the source of the longest river
The voice of the hidden waterfall
And the children in the apple-tree
Not known, because not looked for
But heard, half-heard, in the stillness
Between two waves of the sea.
Quick now, here, now, always—
A condition of complete simplicity
(Costing not less than everything)
And all shall be well and
All manner of thing shall be well
When the tongues of flame are in-folded
Into the crowned knot of fire
And the fire and the rose are one

By then, it really was a spiritual experience."

Warren Zevon, Kim Lankford and I see a lot of each other in 1980. During the *Bad Luck Streak in Dancing School* tour (a.k.a. "The Dog Ate the Part We Didn't Like"), Warren and Kim spend almost a week in New York. Onstage at the Palladium, he's in fantastic form and gives such a kinetic, physical performance that some critics take him to task for exhibitionism. To me, these charges are small-minded and ridiculous. This is the first tour on which he's been in shape and sober enough to move. There's a celebration going on up there, and Zevon is trying hard to make up for all those drunken debacles in the past. Once you understand that, it's very touching.[14] As lead guitarist David Landau (who played with Warren on the last leg of the disastrous *Excitable Boy* tour) sails into a soaring solo, I'm reminded of what Zevon said when he asked Landau to join his current band: "David, I'd like you to meet Warren Zevon. You've never met him before, you know."

14 Fred Schruers remembers that night at the Palladium for another reason: Zevon dedicated a song to Paul. "I can't say he seemed totally surprised—just a tiny bit embarrassed. If somebody had tried to hit him with a spotlight, he would've vaporized. I think there was a quiet satisfaction."

Perhaps the highlight of Warren and Kim's week in New York is a meeting with Martin Scorsese. Jay Cocks and I tag along. Scorsese has always loved Zevon's music (especially "Accidentally like a Martyr," which helped him get through a particularly troubled time in his life), and the evening is a great success. When Warren's live album, *Stand in the Fire*, comes out, there's this dedication: "For Marty."[15] (*Bad Luck Streak in Dancing School* was "For Ken Millar.")

I fly to L.A. in October. Zevon and Lankford have moved into a new house, this one not cursed with red bathtubs. I'm interviewing Clint Eastwood for a story, and he and Sondra Locke stop by to visit. Eastwood remembers Warren from three years ago ("He did everything but drink vodka from a silver boot then") and is delighted at the change. Later, Zevon previews *Stand in the Fire* for me. He paces back and forth while I listen. "What do you think?" he asks.

"Along with Neil Young's *Live Rust*," I answer, "it's the best live rock & roll LP I've ever heard."

"Well, at least we're not stuck with another *Four of Hearts*," he laughs.

Stand in the Fire was recorded over a five-night period at the Roxy in Los Angeles. I'm curious how Warren felt onstage in front of a delirious hometown crowd that was obviously pulling for him all the way.

"Let's just say that it was like rescuing the little boy who'd fallen through the ice," he says. "Rescuing him while the whole world was watching."

My last night there, we reminisce about Ken Millar. "Jesus, I remember that day well," Zevon says. "I was in such *terrible* shape. I don't think I've ever felt worse. Ken said a lot of things to me that nobody had ever said before. 'We writers are overcompensated in this society,' he told me. 'In this house, at your age, you feel guilty.' We both got a laugh over our religious backgrounds. And I found myself telling him things that I'd never told anybody. I said I was disillusioned because I thought writing had to be *fun*. He just looked at me and smiled. I told him I drank to *force* the fun, to get rid of the anxiety and guilt I'd had all my life. For the first time, everything made a crazy kind of sense to me. Since what I felt guilty about was also destroying me, crime and punishment were taking place simultaneously, so I must have thought I didn't have anything to worry about. If somebody reprimanded me for my conduct, I could tell them, 'Don't fret. I know I'm being bad, but I'm punishing myself for it. I'm taking care of it.'

"The scariest part about alcoholism—about any addiction, for that matter— is that you credit the booze for all your accomplishments. You could be dying from drink and unable to move anything but one finger, yet still be convinced

15 Paul already knew Scorsese through Jay Cocks. "We had many fine Christmas dinners," Cocks says. "Marty Scorsese would come over sometimes." So would Jeff Rosen and Myra Friedman.

that, without another shot, that finger was going to stop, too. Ken Millar made me realize that I wrote my songs *despite* the fact that I was a drunk, not *because* of it."

"What did you think when you opened the door and saw him there?" I ask.

"It was like a dream come true," Warren Zevon says. "At the lowest point in my life, the doorbell rang. And there, quite literally, was Lew Archer, on a compassionate mission, come to save my life."[16]

---

16 What else Zevon told Paul: "When I really needed life-saving—apart from your having saved it in the first place, which, no matter how much I go on about, you'll play down, I suppose—there was Lew Archer standing at the door after all those years of reading about him saving people's lives and hoping a little of that compassion would rub off on me. I said to him, 'This is a real experience for me because to meet someone I'm so much in awe of *and* to be in such a vulnerable condition at the same time is really something.' And he just said, 'Don't be scared of ol' Ken.'"

- ROSS MACDONALD -

Work on the piece progresses and I'm not too far away from finishing it....

Apologies for taking so long with everything, but this story means a lot to me, and I want it to be as right as I can make it.

—PAUL NELSON to Kenneth Millar,
a letter, September 1978

In 1976, having convinced Rolling Stone *that Ross Macdonald/Kenneth Millar would be a worthy interview subject, Paul embarked on what became the most extensive series of interviews ever conducted with the author. The talks began that April in New York City, where one night at ten o'clock Paul called up Millar at the Algonquin and extended an impromptu invitation to visit a recording studio. David Forman was in the midst of recording his debut album. ("I guess it was this Philip Marlowe thing in 'Dream of a Child,' Forman says. "It got me a lot of mileage with the detective writers.")*

When I was a boy I dreamed that Philip Marlowe
He took me as his partner, took me as his friend
Gave me his fedora, give me shotgun fever

Took me as his partner, to the end.
—DAVID FORMAN,
"Dream of a Child"

Millar, anxious to meet "a different kind of artist," jumped at the chance.[1]
Afterwards, Paul walked with Millar and Forman around the city and ate
cheeseburgers at a deli, finally returning Millar to his hotel at four the
next morning.

Paul's relationship with Millar was complex. Though he was forty at the
time, he told Millar that he was thirty-six; though Millar was sixty, he told
Paul he was fifty-five. Millar was a successful writer whose career could serve
as a template for Paul's, especially since he'd gotten his start writing criticism
(he thought his books were "the novels of a critic"). On a personal level, Millar
was the embodiment of Lew Archer, a fictional yet "forgiving father figure"
who was, according to Paul, "what a man should be," and who cared enough
to involve himself in other people's lives. At the same time, it had to cross
Paul's mind that Millar had quite a bit in common with Paul's own son
Mark—Millar's father had deserted the family early on, too.

After Millar returned to Santa Barbara, he became wary that Paul's piece
might divulge more about his life than he felt comfortable having out there. He
had his lawyer help him draft a letter that said he consented to the interview "on
the express conditions that ... any material to be published by 'The Rolling Stone'
will be submitted to me in advance of publication for my approval of all biographical
material pertaining to my family, and that 'The Rolling Stone' will not publish
any such material not approved by me." An early draft of the letter ended:

> I know these precautions must seem cumbersome and perhaps
> vaguely hostile. They are not intended to be either, believe
> me. They will clear the way for the frank talk we should have,
> and which I look forward to, without the danger of sorrow
> and injury to innocent and unoffending people ~~and to all~~
> ~~whom I love~~.[2]

"He called the same day I got the letter," Paul said, "within an hour, in
fact. He said, 'I hope you're not upset about the letter,' and I said, 'I understand

---

1 The older man was receptive, too, when Paul sent him records by, among others, Warren Zevon and the Rolling Stones. Paul told Keith Richards: "I was playing some Stones records for a friend of mine, Ross Macdonald, who writes mystery novels and is not a rock & roller at all, and tried to explain in terms that he would understand what to listen for in the music. And the only way I could put it was, compared to any other rock & roll band, the Stones records sound like the old Humphrey Bogart *Big Sleep* movies as opposed to made-for-TV movies. They've got atmosphere and they've got that smoky, misty whatever."

2 Letter courtesy of Ralph Sipper. Reprinted by permission.

why you did it. I just want to tell you that it's got nothing to do with the story, that you shouldn't have that kind of fear.' I had told him up front that he could have approval of it in the first place."

Bookseller Ralph Sipper was a mutual friend of Paul's and Millar's. "What Ken feared, I believe, is that the circumstances of his daughter's death would become public knowledge."

Not just Linda Millar's death, but the troubled life she'd led from early on. Driving drunk at the age of sixteen, she'd struck three young boys, killing one of them. Three years later, while attending college, she'd disappeared with two men and became the subject of a well-publicized search, finally turning up in Reno, Nevada. While her 1970 death at the age of thirty-one was always explained by Kenneth Millar as "a cerebral incident," in truth it was a drug overdose.

Sipper: "I recall seeing a hospital report to that effect. When I asked my wife about this she, too, remembers seeing it, possibly in Ken's archive. Carol and I think that at the time we felt no need to report that sad fact to the world. Whom would that information have served?"

Paul told Tom Nolan, "This sheet of paper basically said he could get an injunction and stop the presses if there was anything about the daughter in the piece; this was mostly for the sake of the husband and the grandson." Nevertheless, both Paul and Jann Wenner signed the letter from Millar's lawyer.

In July, armed with two new tape recorders, a new typewriter, and copies of his four essays from The Rolling Stone Illustrated History of Rock & Roll *for Millar to read, Paul flew out to Santa Barbara, the place where Daisy and Tom had honeymooned in* The Great Gatsby. *For the better part of a month, Paul stayed with the Sippers and interviewed Millar either at his home in suburban Hope Ranch or his cabana at the Coral Casino Beach Club.*

Although Paul did his best to navigate around the subject of Linda Millar, it was difficult, especially since some of what happened to her had found its way into her father's fiction. "I don't mind you bringing it up," Millar said. "All I'm concerned about is what gets printed." Later, he said, "The less I talk about my daughter the better. The reason why I don't want to talk about it is that I don't want anything in our interview to depend on that, if you know what I mean."

Paul's nervous response hinted at how he planned to circumvent the issue when the time would finally come to write the piece: "If your daughter is in your books, as I believe that she probably is, if that could be talked about in a way where she was not even mentioned …"

Speaking with Noel Young, founder of Capra Press, Paul said, "It's a tough story to write because I can't use anything about the daughter. That's such a central incident to his whole being. I would like to use it in a nonsensational way to explain some of it, but I can't."

Ultimately, the article did *depend on Linda Millar's presence in the story.* "And Paul, straight shooter that he was," says Sipper, "wouldn't do the piece because he felt it was psychologically important."

When Kenneth Millar passed away in 1983, however, Paul did two things: he finally wrote about his friend and mentor for Rolling Stone—certainly not as he'd always envisioned, as "It's All One Case" was an obituary—and he put together a book proposal for Ross Macdonald: An Oral Biography. *Before year's end, Joan Kahn, an editor at St. Martin's Press (and a friend of Millar's), expressed great interest in Paul's project, but nothing ever came of it. "I think he had a tough time mustering up the energy to tackle it,"* Jeff Wong says.

The next year, Ralph Sipper reprinted "It's All One Case" in his tribute anthology, Ross Macdonald's Inward Journey, *where Paul was listed in the table of contents along with Eudora Welty, John D. MacDonald, Reynolds Price, Thomas Berger, William Goldman—and Ross Macdonald himself.*

In 1990, Paul heard from Tom Nolan, whom he'd known from his Circus and Rolling Stone *days. A fellow Ross Macdonald fan, Nolan had long anticipated Paul's article and now was writing his own book,* Ross Macdonald: A Biography. "Paul was still hoping to do something—and not all that encouraging to me and my project. He was wonderfully cooperative and we did a very good and helpful and useful interview. I was able to quote him and draw on his memories. But as far as the book, he was discouraging to the extent that he wondered if I could do a proper job without getting to the heart of Macdonald's family history. It was his feeling that that was gone, you couldn't get it, you could never find out about it, anybody who could've told you was gone, Ken was gone, his parents were dead, and so on. How could you do a proper book if you didn't know about his upbringing because that was the key, of course, to him and to his work and to everything he wrote about and cared about?

"So he had me agreeing with him for about a week. I was getting depressed thinking, Gee, you know, he's right. I mean, how can you do that? You'll never find that, there's no way. After about a week, I said, 'Wait a minute. People write books about Keats and Byron and Chaucer—people who have been dead for centuries. I bet I could write a book about somebody who's been dead for seven years.'

"I think that Paul was slightly discouraging partly perhaps because he felt that he had the key material. He knew what he had and he still hoped to do something with it." The next year, though, Paul sold his interview tapes to the University of California, Irvine, for inclusion in their Kenneth and Margaret Millar Collection, for approximately $3,000.

Sipper: "To be sure, he put a lot of work into the interview—and of himself, too. And I'm sure the money was welcome for him, since he lived so precariously those days in terms of income."

A few years later, Paul told William MacAdams that he was in the midst of rereading all of the Ross Macdonald novels. "I'd asked him, 'Well, are you enjoying them? How do they hold up?' and he didn't think that they actually did hold up all that well. I know he was disappointed that they just weren't nearly as good as he had remembered them to be."

K.A.

.

IT'S ALL ONE CASE*

It could have been for any number of reasons: maybe it was simply a matter of admiration and respect because the detective novels of Kenneth Millar (who wrote most of his books under the pen name Ross Macdonald) had touched and troubled me more deeply than almost any novels I'd read. Those stories of fractured families, reckless runaways, and damaged young people who were haunted by eerie, early memories that *something* had happened—something terrible, but they weren't quite sure what—seemed both janglingly immediate and terrifyingly tribal, daring somehow to fiddle with the fuse of that timeless bomb within us all, planted somewhere in the past and set to go off who knew when.

Close to explosion, in the winter of 1970 I finished the last available Millar book. Perhaps that's why I did what I did: just to try to get the out-of-print ones. More likely, though, it was an act of no small desperation and guilt—of reaching out for at least the shadows of answers from the creator of private investigator Lew Archer who, like Jean Renoir, knew that the real tragedy in life is that everyone has his reasons. My own existence was certainly a mystery in which the psychic murders seemed to keep piling up: a disgruntled mother, a dead father, no money, a drawn-out divorce from a high-school sweetheart, a mixed-up six-year-old son transported halfway across the continent, the loss of a newfound love with whom I'd dreamed the dream of dreams—give or take a detail, probably your story, too. I guess I felt like somebody in one of Millar's novels—those books to which, with hope, I clung—and badly needed a share of the understanding and compassion he'd shown his characters. For whatever reason, one dark night I picked up the phone, got his number from Santa Barbara Information, and called him. We talked of many things—none of them so dramatic as life stories then—and the connection was made. Later, we met, and I spent much of the summer of 1976 with him and his wife, the mystery writer Margaret Millar.

"Ross Macdonald: December 13th, 1915–July 11th, 1983" by Paul Nelson from *Rolling Stone*, September 1, 1983. © Rolling Stone LLC 1983. And "It's All One Case" by Paul Nelson from *Ross Macdonald's Inward Journey*, 1987. © Cordelia Editions 1987. All rights reserved. Reprinted by permission.

* Reprinted from the original manuscripts from more than one source, which first appeared in *Rolling Stone* in a different version.

Of course, in more general terms, the connection between Kenneth Millar—who died of Alzheimer's disease on July 11, 1983, in Santa Barbara—and his hundreds of thousands of readers was always there: i.e., we all have families, and in all families "crimes" are committed. Millar chose to write detective novels, and it was his particular genius to transform these familial "crimes" into murders, the staples of his genre. But "crimes" within a family are so psychologically complex and usually move in such wide generational cycles—think of your parents, their parents, your children, add (or subtract) some literal bloodshed and you've a case for Lew Archer—that attempting to solve them can be the most dangerous, albeit most important, occupation of all, one that surely requires a humane heart, an open mind, an iron will, and gloves of asbestos.

"*Solve* is the wrong word. Let's say *understand*," Millar told me when I asked him about the ramifications of his detective's repeated assertion, "It's all one case," in several books. Before that, the novelist had said: "The major plots and subplots are all related to each other, and you can't solve the main case without solving the others. This reflects my feeling that we're all members of a single body to degrees that we have no idea, except in moments of what might be called revelation. I think it's literally true—we live or die together. And the influences of just one person on another—any two people who know each other—are absolutely staggering if you trace them. It's the essence of our lives, that interrelationship."

For Ken Millar to understand and come to terms with his own life was a task nearly as formidable as any he set for his characters. Born in Los Gatos, California, near San Francisco, on December 13, 1915, he was soon denied both his native country and parents. His mother, a partial invalid, and his father, a sea captain-poet-journalist, separated, and Millar—sometimes with his mother, often without—spent most of his youth living with one relative after another throughout Canada. "I counted the rooms I had lived in during my first sixteen years," he's written, "and got a total of fifty." In one of our talks in 1976, Millar said: "People don't attach the same importance to a fatherless boy as they do to one with a father. Their judgments of children depend a great deal on the children's immediate background. This was particularly true in the earlier generations. Today, we are much more inclined to take children on their own merits. But in those days, I was my father's son. If I were to turn out well, that would have been a miracle. You know what I mean." In an essay called "A Collection of Reviews," the novelist remembered "the last time I saw my father's living eyes. I was a high school boy in southern Ontario. He was a patient in a metropolitan hospital in Toronto. He had entirely lost the power of speech, but he could still write. He wrote me a few lines in a book on his knee. I wish I could tell you what he wrote to me that day. His writing was so shaky that I couldn't make out the words. But I could see that it was written in rhymed couplets." Small wonder that most of Millar's novels reflect the Oedipal theme.

In 1938, Kenneth Millar married Margaret Sturm, whom he'd met years earlier in high school. They wed on June 2, a date that Millar was to commemorate by making it Lew Archer's birthday. Millar received a doctorate in English literature at the University of Michigan, taught school and, following his wife's lead, began writing (she'd already published four highly praised mystery novels when his first, *The Dark Tunnel*, appeared in 1944) before serving in the Navy during World War II. In 1939, the couple's only child, Linda, was born. Ken Millar had a family again.

And in 1946, "it was sheer fate," he told me with a laugh, that returned him to his homeland to stay. "Fate, of course, operates through all kinds of instrumentalities," he added. "For example, the Navy brought me to California, and the movie industry brought my wife to California, and what brought her to Santa Barbara was a train on which she was planning to go north back to Canada. And the final cause was that she looked out the train window, saw Santa Barbara, fell in love with it, got off at the next station and went back. There you have a wave of causality. But the basic fact—now we're making a plot out of this—is that I was born in California and always wanted to come back."

The rest of the story should have been a happy one, and much of it was. Husband and wife kept writing, were active conservationists, helped found a chapter of the National Audubon Society. But Millar's past refused to stay buried. Though he had consciously used Archer ("not the main object of my interest, nor the character with whose fate I am most concerned") as a shield, "like protective lead, between me and the radioactive material," this method didn't always work. In his introduction to *Archer at Large*, Millar wrote: "Ten years and ten novels later [in the mid-Fifties], seismic disturbances occurred in my life. My half-suppressed Canadian years, my whole childhood and youth, rose like a corpse from the bottom of the sea to confront me. Margaret and I moved to the Bay Area for a year, settling not many miles from my birthplace.... There I went through belated mental growing pains, trying to understand the peculiar shape of my life." Psychotherapy helped, and with 1958's *The Doomsters*, 1959's *The Galton Case* (a perfectly plotted detective story and semiautobiographical prince-and-the-pauper tale about a young man returning to California from Canada), and many of the books that followed, Kenneth Millar took his place with Dashiell Hammett and Raymond Chandler as a master of the modern detective novel. There are no worthy successors on the horizon.

Death always has the last word, however. In 1970, at the age of thirty-one, Linda died of a cerebral accident. Margaret stopped writing for a time, then resumed. In 1973, Ken published *Sleeping Beauty*, a novel about a young girl who's disappeared. Lew Archer finds her and returns her to her family. The book ends like this: "Laurel lay asleep on the bed, a pillow under her dark head and an afghan over it. There was a telephone on the bedside table. Before I used it, I bent over Laurel and touched her warm forehead with my mouth. I could hardly believe that she was alive…. She stirred and half awakened, as if my concern for her had reached down palpably into her sleeping mind. She was alive. I picked up the phone and started to make the necessary calls." That's the kind of man Kenneth Millar was.

I remember so many things about him—his compassion, his intellect, his quietness, his sense of humor, his great modesty, his very great inner strength—but one particular vignette stands out. Millar is standing, hands in his pockets, on one of the rails at the train station where his wife first saw Santa Barbara. He's talking to his young grandson, Jimmie Pagnusat (who's taking the train back to his father in Orange County), about "flattening pennies as a kid on this same railroad line, way up north, way past Seattle, in Canada." He looks up and down the tracks and then jumps, hands still in his pockets, gracefully from one rail to the other. Jimmie and I are amazed. He smiles at us. For some reason, I remember thinking: we come to his novels for comfort in the disaster of our lives, knowing that he and Archer have seen us—and worse than us—and will dispense mercy and kindness or, if they turn us over, will at least understand. Ken Millar—a strong, judging, forgiving father figure for us all.[3]

---

3 Jimmie Pagnusat, who was thirteen years old at the time of the interviews and whom Millar described to Paul as "truly innocent," himself died of a drug overdose in 1989.

- BOOK PROPOSAL -
ROSS MACDONALD: AN ORAL
BIOGRAPHY

Whether or not the best detective, mystery, or spy novels can be taken seriously as superior contemporary fiction as well as excellent genre work is pretty much a moot point by now: very few people are going to argue that, say, Graham Greene, John le Carré, or Robert Stone are mere hacks who grind out blood-and-guts potboilers for easy reading at the beach, because the argument is clearly ridiculous. Genres produce about the same percentage of fine writers as does straight fiction (quite a small percentage in both cases), and, if indeed there is any real difference at such a level of excellence, the best "thriller writers" are more than good enough to make you forget all about the alleged distinctions between "high" and "low" literary forms. Any way you want to look at it, John le Carré's *Tinker, Tailor, Soldier, Spy* or Robert Stone's *Dog Soldiers* are better novels than any that, say, Alberto Moravia has ever written.

In the field of detective fiction, only three names stand out as genre masters *and* important American novelists: Dashiell Hammett (who published his first novel, *Red Harvest*, in 1929), Raymond Chandler (who published his first novel, *The Big Sleep*, in 1939), and Ross Macdonald (who published his first detective novel, *The Moving Target*, in 1949 after writing four non-private-eye mysteries under his real name, Kenneth Millar). While it's somewhat surprising that within the relatively short time span of twenty years, all three major figures of the modern American detective novel—each very different—made their entrances, it's truly remarkable that, since 1949, there hasn't been a single writer of detective fiction who has successfully and consistently taken the genre into new territory. After Macdonald, who died of Alzheimer's disease on July 11, 1983, no worthy successor exists.

Why should anyone publish a biography of Ross Macdonald? For one reason, because he was one of the three great American detective novelists.

By Paul Nelson, previously unpublished, 1983. © Mark C. Nelson 1983. All rights reserved. Printed by permission.

For another: because his books have been translated into more than twenty languages and have sold millions of copies. Obviously, readers care about him—and not only readers of detective fiction. Macdonald's books have a huge following among young people, who view his detective, Lew Archer, as an honest, compassionate, and understanding father figure.... When I first met Macdonald in New York in the winter of 1975–1976, almost every rock & roll critic and musician I knew called me up and asked to meet him. (Dave Marsh, author of *Born to Run: The Bruce Springsteen Story* and other bestsellers, and Kit Rachlis, now arts editor of *The Boston Phoenix*, sat in on an early interview.) In Santa Barbara, where I spent much of the summer of 1976 interviewing Macdonald, Warren Zevon—who had literally memorized several long passages of the Archer novels and who later moved to Santa Barbara simply because Macdonald lived there—drove from Los Angeles to talk to him....

Another reason for a biography is that Ross Macdonald's life was so interesting—and tragic. He was sort of an orphan with parents, and also someone without a country. His father and mother separated when he was three (he was born a Californian), and Macdonald spent his entire youth being passed from one relative to another (over fifty in all), many of whom weren't too thrilled to have him. Such a life left scars, some so deep that it took him decades to come to grips with them.... When he tried to write an autobiographical novel—a non-mystery—that dealt directly with his growing up, he found the subject so painful, so "radioactive," that he never published the book. Instead, he started the Archer series—"the finest series of detective novels ever written by an American," according to William Goldman on the front page of *The New York Times Book Review*—and used Archer as a protective "shield" in order to write about his life "at one remove." Many of the fractured families and runaway children in his novels reflect what happened to him, though the details were almost always changed or disguised.

A loner throughout his youth, Macdonald loved books, movies, and music, and listed many influences in all three fields. Jazz was particularly important to him, and he claimed its urban rhythms helped to develop his style. Before entering college, he spent a summer in Germany right before World War II (*The Dark Tunnel*, his first mystery, is concerned with the rise of Nazism). At the University of Michigan, where he later obtained his doctorate in English literature, he studied under W.H. Auden (another important influence—and a man who loved mystery stories). Macdonald served in the Navy during World War II and wrote his second mystery, *Trouble Follows Me* (about the Japanese), aboard a destroyer.... For a man obsessed by the idea of family, trouble did indeed follow him. His only child, Linda, died at the age of thirty-one.

My 1976 interviews with Ross Macdonald—I have approximately forty-seven hours of tape with him; another fifteen or so hours with the people who knew him best, including his wife—were all formal question-and-answer sessions, not just unstructured gab about whatever crossed our minds. Macdonald did not make small talk easily (his past seemed to have cost him dearly in that respect: he was a very *serious* man) and preferred specific questions, so I had to spend five or six hours preparing carefully for each session. Whenever I tried to wing it, there would be silence—a kindly, comfortable silence for him; not so for me—and I knew I'd have to do more homework next time.

Throughout these sessions, both of us were striving to cover almost every aspect of his life and work. His friends held the view that he was determined to get his life down on tape, to tell his story—or as much of it as he was willing to—to someone whom he felt had studied and understood his books. (He had said that he'd never write an autobiography, because too many people would be hurt.) We talked about everything imaginable: Hammett, Chandler, other writers; how Chandler, in his later years, had consciously tried to destroy the careers of up-and-coming mystery writers, particularly Macdonald's; "high" and "low" culture; Macdonald the teacher-scholar and Macdonald the popular novelist; the formation of and changes in his literary style; how and when to use slang; the influence of F. Scott Fitzgerald's *The Great Gatsby*, his favorite book, on his work (e.g., Macdonald consciously used Archer as the narrator but not the most important character in his novels just like Fitzgerald used Nick Carraway in *The Great Gatsby*); Canada; California; all of his novels and how they related to his life; his themes; his beliefs; his relationship to Archer; his thoughts on a final Archer novel—my God, everything. To summarize some forty-seven hours of conversation would be impossible. No one else has unearthed this much material, nothing close to even a tenth of it—and this is material directly from the source. I think I've read practically every interview Macdonald ever gave, and there's really no competition. Though there will, of course, be other biographies. It would be nice to have the first one.

Why an oral biography? Because the man talked as brilliantly and precisely as he wrote, and I'd rather "hear" someone whom I care about tell his story in his own words, if he's capable of it, and if those words would make a valid and unique book. That is surely the case here. I don't envision the entire book to be transcribed and edited conversation, however. I'd write a long introductory piece as well as several transitional chapters that contained both biographical information and literary criticism. I'd also use some of the material from the interviews with his wife and friends. But, in the long run, I'd like it mainly to be *his* book—his last book, I suppose, except for a stray essay or short story or two. Ross Macdonald meant a lot to me, both personally and as a writer, and I'd like other people to be able to hear his voice in the same way I did.

- CLINT EASTWOOD -

Towards the end of 1979, things were looking good for Paul. He'd secured a contract for his book about Rod Stewart, he was about to begin his sprawling Rolling Stone *cover story about Warren Zevon (though it wouldn't see print until 1981), and in October he found himself in Boise, Idaho, on the set of* Bronco Billy, *beginning a series of interviews with one of the biggest actors and directors in the world—and a longtime personal hero.*

"Paul loved Dirty Harry, *he loved Clint," Jay Cocks says. "This was pre-Clint idolatry and he wanted to do a piece on Clint for* Rolling Stone." *He had already written about him in the magazine, in 1972.*

"It was one of things I was proudest that I ever wrote. When I did the Dirty Harry *review, I took a tape recorder to it and just taped the film sound-wise. I saw it about eight times, but I wanted to get the dialogue right when I quoted it. When I played back the tape, I could just close my eyes and play back the whole movie, shot for shot, in my head just from the soundtrack pretty much." In addition to painstakingly considering* Dirty Harry *as a work of art, the article also accurately predicted that Eastwood "promises to be a major force in the films of the next decade, both as an actor and a director."*

405

The review also came to the attention of the movie's director, Don Siegel, who wrote a letter to Paul:

> Of all the reviews I have read on *Dirty Harry*, some of which have been most complimentary, yours seemed to understand more fully what I was trying to say in the picture than any of the others.

The note undoubtedly meant a lot to Paul, who had always believed that the ideal film version of The Great Gatsby *would've been one directed by Siegel with Eastwood in the lead.*

Stephen Holden: "Of course, Clint Eastwood is another one like Chet Baker who has this enigmatic quality, this mystique, this film noir quality that Paul identified with passionately."

"He got me into a bad spot—well, not really so bad—with Clint Eastwood," Cocks says. "This was the first real sign I had that Paul was having serious *problems." Cocks and his wife Verna Bloom had been friends with Eastwood since she acted alongside him in* High Plains Drifter, *and they'd reached out to the actor-director on Paul's behalf. "Clint says, 'Sure.' So Paul goes out and spends days, maybe weeks, with Clint. Clint loves Paul. They can talk about music and they've got a little bit of jazz overlap (I'm sure there was a lot of Chet Baker conversation). He talks to everybody in Clint's life, and it just goes on and on and on, and he comes back with hours', days', perhaps weeks' worth of tape. And he doesn't finish the piece."*

Paul, hardly a name-dropper, couldn't help himself when he admitted to Warren Zevon, "I still can't get over that Eastwood calls me up at home in New York just to talk." When Paul sent him a thriller that he thought might make a good movie, Eastwood seriously considered it. And when the director was thinking about adapting the novels Firefox *and* Honkytonk Man *(which he ultimately did, both in 1982), he asked Paul to read them, saying he'd "love to" have his opinion on them.*

Cocks: "Now, this is a time when Clint would make a movie a year. The piece was supposed to be a cover story pegged to the appearance of one movie, and Paul didn't make it. So some months go by and the piece still hasn't appeared. He's still laboring on it. Clint calls me up and he says, 'Rolling Stone wants to send somebody else out to talk to me, and I've got a new movie coming out here. I want to be loyal to Paul. I mean, he was here first and he's a great guy and he's your friend and all that. What do I do?' I said, 'Let me check with Paul.' So I checked with Paul: 'No, I'm really going to finish it.' I call up Clint, Clint says, 'Okay,' blows off the second Rolling Stone *thing. I think you can fill in the rest: Paul doesn't finish it."*

Early in 1983, over three years after their first interview, Paul called Eastwood in Los Angeles and apologized for failing to deliver the cover story, blaming most of it on the imposed madness he'd gone through at Rolling Stone *the year before. "I remember you saying there's a time where you have to make your move, and my move was just to get out of there. So I sold a lot of my first edition Hammetts and Chandlers and sold some records to get some kind of stake to stay alive, and just quit.*

"Anyway, I'm awfully sorry it didn't appear yet, but they do want it now again and I'm certainly willing to do it."

"Oh, really?" Eastwood chuckled.

In the meantime, Paul said that, since he was now concentrating on writing books, he'd like to take all the interview material he'd amassed and turn it into Conversations with Clint Eastwood. *Eastwood felt such a project was a bit premature at that stage of his career. When Paul persisted, he said, "Let me think about it a little bit" and changed the subject altogether: "But everything else is cool, though, huh?"*

"Yeah, except for money. You don't get a regular check this way. I think I've got a deal for a Neil Young book, which will probably keep me going for six months' worth of paying the rent and everything, and then I hope to get another one on Ross Macdonald. You have to do a lot of them to really make it. You don't get royalties until after the book is published, and my rent is almost a thousand dollars a month here. So it's a little bit sticky. It's exciting," he added, sounding not excited at all.

The call ended with Eastwood agreeing to another round of interviews and Paul assuring that this time around he'd nail the piece. By the fall, the two men were once again talking on tape. During one of the sessions, Paul made the mistake of asking if Eastwood would consider blurbing the movie trivia book that he and William MacAdams were writing. "I'm sort of embarrassed to ask, but I think it would help sell the book."

"Sure."

When Paul mentioned that the plan was for their agent to begin submitting the first hundred pages of the book to publishers within the next month, Eastwood wanted to know when he would be turning in the Rolling Stone *article about him.*

Paul's voice quavered. "By December first." Eastwood, having already apparently checked with someone at the magazine, said that jibed with his understanding that the article was slated to appear in the traditional January double-issue. "I'll send you a copy of it first because they will undoubtedly cut it," was all Paul said. "I don't have final cut."

Well over a year later, Cocks received another call from Eastwood. He had another film ready to come out and, accordingly, another offer from Rolling Stone *for a cover story—written by somebody other than Paul. "I say, 'I understand,' and he said, 'The problem is that I spent all this time with Paul and I don't want it wasted. I don't want somebody else coming out and starting from square one again. What I want to do is let them use Paul's tapes.' I said, 'That's a tough one. I understand, but Paul's not going to want to do that.'"*

Jann Wenner says that the magazine kept trying to get Paul to write the piece, but to no avail. Betsy Volck says, "Paul would never do a Q&A. It was like the lowest of the low." "He was desperate for money," Michael Seidenberg says. "All he had to do was hand that in and they'd be fine with it. They didn't care. But he couldn't." The story, by Tim Cahill, eventually ran in July of 1985 based on his own interviews with Eastwood.

As if the fact that Paul had failed to write about one of his biggest heroes wasn't punishment enough, there was a ripple effect. "After it was obvious he wasn't going to finish the Rolling Stone *piece," MacAdams says, "he got a call one day from Eastwood's office and they told him that he no longer had permission to use the Clint Eastwood blurb for the book."*

Despite the over seventeen and a half hours he had recorded with Eastwood and almost another ten with his friends and associates, Paul was unable to get beyond page four of his article.

MacAdams: "He was thinking that what he'd already written really wasn't very good, but I recall it as being excellent and telling him, 'No, Paul, it really is good. You should finish this.' But he never did."

K.A.

UNTITLED
CLINT EASTWOOD
ARTICLE

"**N**ow how could a man become a popular movie
star without reflecting the average in one way or another?"
—WESLEY ADDY to Jack Palance in
The Big Knife

From the moment you meet him, if you're on the same wavelength at all,
you realize he's "Clint," not "Mr. Eastwood." Indeed, through some subtle
and spontaneous re-racking of moral manners, you're dead certain that
if you slid a "Mr. Eastwood" at him—as elementary etiquette would seem
to indicate—it'd sound strangely uncourteous (like name-dropping) and
might even cause that famous vein in the left side of his forehead to start
pulsing politely, not in anger but in mild disappointment over having been
misread again.

Oh, your first impressions are vivid enough, no doubt about it. One
minute you're standing barefoot in the hallway of a motel, coughing your
head off and comparing running shoes with Warner Bros. publicist Marco
Barla, and the next minute Barla, while handing you his shoe, is saying,
with mock shock, "Well, look who's here!" and who's there are Clint and
actress Sondra Locke, neither of whom you've seen coming. Clint shakes
hands, asks how the flight was, holds up a foot, proclaims "Pumas." Locke,
taking her cue, demurely deadpans it as long as she can. Everybody starts
laughing at once.

Though the empathy is both understood and appreciated—and the
"Clint" connection made (like Elvis and Ali and Dylan: one name, for the
same and perhaps different reasons)—there's still an unmistakable, uh,
sudden impact. While you're talking to him, you're looking into That Face,

familiar from a million movie screens, posters, and magazine covers, and the effect is sporadically disconcerting. Much later, Norman Mailer would write, rather melodramatically but not without some small degree of truth, that Clint's face might be that of "a murderer or a saint ... or a Presidential candidate." Thinking back, you can claim no such thoughts. Though you wouldn't necessarily want to be around him during a day of wrath—murderer, never. Saint, never. And it's immediately apparent that he's far too intelligent and not nearly malleable or dishonest enough ever to be President. A face on, or from, an American coin maybe—in repose, more high-country pioneer than movie-star politician. The eyes are warm instead of wintry, the mouth smiles easily and the features—sometimes so threatening and granitic to the camera—flex naturally into laugh lines that are unmarred by tension, severity, or insincerity. There's too much youthfulness left, too much humor, too much animation, to consider canonization yet. Monuments don't wear Pumas.

But, if it's instantly clear that the man standing in front of you is someone who has no desire to be larger than life or to play the star offscreen ("It kind of embarrasses me a little to have things written about me"), it's also apparent that no one stays nervous around Clint for long because *he* doesn't allow nervousness. This is difficult to explain, since there's nothing dictatorial, intimidating, or even particularly one-sided about such a highly surprising and likable paradox, but it's not just accidental either. Spend a fair amount of time with him and whatever awe you come away with—and it'll probably be considerable—will be for Clint's craftsmanship and common sense, his talent and tenacity: i.e., all the spectacular (or unspectacular) adjectives that pile up in a pleasing collision—smart, soft-spoken, self-made, considerate, controlled, strong-willed, striving, self-effacing—will spectacularly (or unspectacularly) refuse to go near the noun *fame*, which Clint treats as if it were a reluctant dog on his front porch. Spend more time with him and you realize (somewhat enviously) that he's managed to combine the usually contradictory qualities of total organization, power, and rock-ribbed self-control with a loose-jointed sense of ease, a gift of gab, and a natural penchant for "just drifting around," a phrase he uses fondly and often. Spend still more time with him and you say to yourself, even though you're not presumptuous enough to believe you'll ever get to know him that well: *Jeez, Clint Eastwood is a real best-friend type.*

- LOOKING BACK -

In 1995, Paul's old friend Danny Goldberg asked him to contribute a chapter to an anthology he had in mind about the history of Mercury Records. Goldberg was pleased when Paul accepted the assignment—and pleasantly surprised when he actually handed in a first draft within a reasonable period of time. It was as if Paul had been waiting for twenty years for the opportunity to set the record straight about his years at Mercury and, when it arrived, everything just poured out.

Goldberg sensed Paul's disappointment when, due to a corporate merger that effectively put an end to Mercury, the proposed book never came to pass. "If the book had come out, I felt that what Paul had written would have been one of the main highlights of it." It would've also been Paul's longest published piece of writing and his most unabashedly autobiographical.

K.A.

OUT OF THE PAST

Several months ago, I had lunch with an old friend, someone I'd known for nearly three decades. We first met when he was working for Albert Grossman's management company, and, over the years, we'd shared a similar philosophy and an admiration for many of the same artists (Bob Dylan, Jackson Browne, Bruce Springsteen, David Forman, among others). But, except for a few, far-too-short, chance meetings, we hadn't seen much of each other lately.

After an amiable round of mutual catch-up and some serious talk, Danny, with complete offhandedness, dropped an inadvertent bomb. He said: "By the way, I just had a phone call from an old employer of yours. You remember Irwin Steinberg."

The explosion was small, inner-directed. I managed an affirmative nod.

But Danny, unaware of the tremor, was just getting warmed up. "I've always found it fascinating," he said with great enthusiasm, "that you were the only major rock critic who ever worked for a major record company for an extensive period of time. Early Seventies, wasn't it?" (He may have used one less *major.*)

I rummaged up another nod.

"I love stories about the record business," he said. "What were those days really like?"

So I told him.

In as comic a way as I could muster.

Though I didn't use many of the words I'm going to use here.

But I got the gist of it.

I told my friend Danny Goldberg, who is currently the president of Mercury Records, much of what I remembered about my years there. Five good years, five bad years. The same five years: 1970–1975.

"Irwin Steinberg was the president of Mercury Records then," I said in a voice that no doubt wobbled. "And—though you realize, of course, that I'm greatly exaggerating—the mere mention of his name sets off an implosion that brings back what let's call my Mercurial schizophrenia. It's sort of like

Robert Mitchum in *The Night of the Hunter*. He had the letters *L-O-V-E* tattooed on one hand and *H-A-T-E* on the other. When I'm at my most Mercurial, I've got the composites *like/dislike, like/respect, like/disrespect, dislike/respect, dislike/disrespect,* and *respect/disrespect* burning away in my brain. Pick any combination and you'd be right. And wrong."

Danny laughed.

"It's not like I'd trade those years for something else," I said. "But, man, they were intense. And they still haunt me. Tragicomedy, I guess."

"I understand," he said.

I told him some stories.

He said I should write them down.

"For whom?" I asked.

"Well," he said, swearing that this was all pure coincidence, "I'm putting together a book for Mercury's fiftieth anniversary, which is this year. And I'd love to have you tell all of these stories in print."

"I'll try," I said. "Even if I have to break myself in half doing it."

"Good," he said.

"It might even be fun," I added, foolishly.

The scene shifts to what looks like a tiny New York apartment, decorated early noir or late *Blade Runner*. If there is any lighting at all, it's nearly nonexistent, but there appears to be at least one person—perhaps it's two— sitting on the floor in the corner farthest from the door. It's too black to see anything clearly. The brightest light in the room is the ghostly red that comes from the end of a cigarette slowly being smoked in that dark corner.

Soft as the smoke, someone says, "Irwin Steinberg."

GS: Do you want me to start this? Or would you rather do it?

RWAC: You go ahead. You're supposed to be the voice of reason, right? Though there's really no difference, is there?

GS: A slight difference. Your imagination is greater than mine, but you tend to brood more and get angry. For those reasons alone, I could hardly call you my better half. Which is why I agreed to serve as mediator and let you tell the stories.

RWAC: It seemed like a good idea at the time. Danny laughed in all the right places and thought the stories were interesting for other reasons, too.

You're here to weed out the worst of the angst, rein me in if I go over the top, and prod me with questions. That's why I deemed you the Good Senator. Besides, I can tell a joke better than you can.

GS: Let's just say that I'm here in the interest of fairness to all parties. To you and to those you may wish to slander. And I shall call you the Rebel Without a Cause, which, as you know, is merely a cunning way of implying its opposite, the Rebel With a Cause.

RWAC: I don't like that name much.

GS: How do you think I feel about being called the Good Senator? I know just as much about Mercury Records as you do.

RWAC: You surely do. Ask me a question.

GS: How in the world did you, a freelance rock & roll writer of some stature and an editor of at least two music magazines, ever come to work for Mercury Records? Why did they hire you? Why did you accept?

RWAC: It's hard to tell who you're insulting here. Them or me?

I was recruited by Ron Oberman, who was Mercury's director of national publicity. He worked out of their main office, which was in Chicago. But Ron spent a lot of time in New York, and we struck up a real friendship. Same sensibility, interests, the whole bit. We used to shoot a lot of pool together. Ron was very good with writers, probably because he thought like one.

At the same time, which was early 1970, I was freelancing a lot, mostly for *Rolling Stone.* But my main job was editing *Circus* and writing about two-thirds of every issue: most of the articles, all of the record reviews, and even some of the letters section, wherein such literary notables as Nick Adams, Jake Barnes, Frederic Henry, Dick Diver, and Lew Archer often wrote to tell Gerry Rothberg, the publisher of *Circus* and my all-time-favorite music-business employer, what was what. Gerry seemed to get a kick out of all this.

GS: If you liked Rothberg so much, why did you quit?

RWAC: Because—here's a paradox—all that writing was giving me writer's block. One night, I sat down at the typewriter and couldn't touch the keys. I couldn't physically make myself do it. Next day, the same thing. So I called up Ron and accepted the job as Mercury's East Coast director of publicity. Gerry was very understanding, and I worked for him again, editing the record-review section, several years later.

GS: Were you at all worried about taking the Mercury job? After all, you'd never done publicity before. Never worked for a record company.

RWAC: I wasn't that worried. I trusted Ron, he trusted me, and I'd be reporting directly to him. As a writer, I knew every publicity man, woman, and child in New York—all of the good ones and all of the bad ones—plus all sorts of other record company people. So I knew which approach worked with me, and which didn't. And I knew most of the writers. I knew I could never lie to one about whether or not I liked a record.

Ron knew all of this and said that's why he hired me. He wanted to build up Mercury's credibility.

GS: It's nice to be flattered.

RWAC: Yes, isn't it? Ron told me to keep in touch with the writers and editors I knew. And to get to know all the ones I didn't. Don't push Mercury, he said. Chances are, they'll ask you about it. After that, just use your head. Don't lie. As you know, with writers and editors, it doesn't pay off. Burn them once, and they'll never trust you again.

GS: Christ, this reminds me of the story about George Washington chopping down the cherry tree: "I cannot tell a lie."

RWAC: Now who's slandering whom?

GS: You're right. Oberman was everything you say he was. A most enlightened man. He even allowed you your nobility.

RWAC: "You'll have a company credit card," he told me. Then he said the magic words—and I remember them exactly. He said: "Never eat a meal alone. Ever. Always take a writer, an editor, or an artist—or any combination thereof— to lunch or dinner. Always." I couldn't believe my luck.[1] He told me to travel a lot. To get to know the writers in Boston, Philadelphia, and Washington, D.C.

GS: And this approach actually worked. Even you were surprised by the amount of stories and mentions that it generated. Seemingly less was indeed more.

RWAC: It did, and I was somewhat surprised. To me, it wasn't exactly an avalanche of publicity, but, to the people at Mercury, it was about ten times more than they were used to getting out of the New York office. I was a hit. To my amazement, I discovered that there were a handful of people out there who actually wanted to write and publish stories about Buddy Miles, Sir Lord Baltimore, and Uriah Heep, to name a few.

GS: You're such a snob.

RWAC: Artistically, yes. I admit it. I didn't like a lot of the records Mercury issued, but I could almost always find a way to relate to the artists who made them. Ron had told me that I'd be good with artists, and I guess he was right. Nobody ever hit me. Though I was led to believe that Jerry Lee Lewis might. With Doug Sahm, I was always afraid I'd be arrested.

---

1 Lucky for Paul and every terribly underpaid music writer he knew. Richard Meltzer says he "plugged right into this whole setup where publicists would take you to lunch, where basically the bottom line was they couldn't charge their lunch to their expense account unless they took along a writer. So they were all too happy to do this. The nicest of the bunch was Paul. In retrospect, he's the only one I remember having no strings. Just 'Let's have lunch.' After lunch it would be 'Go to the closet and take forty records.' The reason was, he had determined that forty was the maximum that you could actually carry on foot to Sam Goody's. In those days, if it was sealed without any stamping on it, a buck a record. If it had any signs of being cutout or whatever, thirty-five cents. Otherwise, if he gave you more—you could take as many as you wanted—you'd have to take a cab and it would cut into your payday."

GS: What?

RWAC: I hardly know where to begin with Jerry Lee. When it was announced that he'd headline an oldies show at Madison Square Garden, hellfire broke loose. Before I could even compile a list of people to call, representatives from *Time* and *Newsweek* called me. They said that "important" stories were being planned and that their reporters required lengthy interviews with the wild one himself. Dick Cavett wanted Jerry Lee for his TV show. It was a publicist's dream. The telephone wouldn't stop ringing.

When I told Charlie Fach, who was head of the New York office, he gave me a sickly look and said he'd get back to me. I called Ron. He said that it was great that there was such interest, but there was a problem, too. Didn't Jerry Lee want to do interviews? I asked. Wouldn't he have enough time to do some press? It isn't that, Ron said. We'll have a meeting here right away about what to do. Just stall for time until I call you back.

GS: The postman always rings twice.

RWAC: When Ron called me back, he told me that the Cavett show was all set. But no press interviews. We'll buy tickets for anyone of importance who wants to see the show, he said, and for anyone that you think should be there. But that's it. No interviews. No backstage passes.

Why? I asked.

He told me the whole story.

It came down to this: Mercury was afraid that Jerry Lee might physically attack someone from the press. He'd done that before, and no one wanted to risk another incident.

GS: So you did have to tell some lies after all.

RWAC: Yes. But I could understand these.

GS: Go on.

RWAC: Ron said: Charlie will go with you to the airport to pick up Jerry Lee and his whole crew. Charlie knows Jerry Lee. Believe me, it'll be quite an experience. You'll need eight limos. You're to take him directly to the Cavett show, see that he gets inside, watch the show, and go straight back to the office. Stay completely away from Jerry Lee until the oldies concert—which is three days from now, right?—and stick with Charlie at the Garden. Follow his lead. Charlie knows Jerry Lee. Have fun and tell me all about it Monday. You'll be all right.

GS: And were you?

RWAC: Yeah. And it was quite an experience.

GS: Don't stop now.

RWAC: Well, Charlie and I and our eight limos drove out to this little airport in New Jersey to meet Jerry Lee's private plane. Which, when it finally floundered in, seemed distressingly vintage. And out of that plane came the damnedest and most amazing array of humanity that I'd ever seen: grandfathers and grandmothers, fathers and mothers, husbands and wives, ex-husbands and ex-wives, boyfriends and girlfriends, brothers and sisters and cousins, musicians, managers, nubile teenagers, children of all ages, little babies. Many of them looked quite drunk. As they milled aimlessly about, gazing at the New York City skyline in the distance, they seemed to me sort of a collective picture of Dorian Gray, from the cradle to the graveyard. Though I didn't want to be anywhere near them, I think I fell in love with them all.

And then came Jerry Lee—Dorian Gray himself—apparently undissipated and looking half his age. Blond hair flowing, suntan glowing, he was unbelievably handsome, trim and muscular. At second glance, he still seemed an animated advertisement for good health and clean living. Trouble was, he hadn't been sober for years and, should he get angry, could ignite the solar system. He was followed by two huge men who were carrying an enormous Styrofoam cooler filled with ice cubes and booze. We all said something. I don't remember what.

Jerry Lee had a glass in his right hand. It may have been there for years. Whenever the glass was empty, I knew that someone would fill it up. It was an ancient ritual. Earthly nourishment for the god who provideth.

I got into a car with Jerry Lee's manager. His name was Judd, and he was feeling no pain. Five or six Lolitas piled into the backseat. As we were crossing the George Washington Bridge, one of them pointed to the Empire State Building and announced excitedly: "Oh! That's where they killed King Kong! All those airplanes shot him! I would have liked to have been here then." My heart soared briefly—the magic of the movies!—then sank when I realized that she actually believed that a huge gorilla with a woman in one paw had really been killed some forty years ago atop the very building at which we stared. "But he might have landed on me," she said.

At this, Judd lurched awake and, without preamble, launched into a spirited defense of Southern motherhood. He grew angry, he grew sad, he laughed, he cried, and suddenly, in mid-sentence, passed out face-first onto the padded dashboard. His head bounced back six inches, then three, then settled there until we pulled up in front of Cavett's studio. When the car stopped, Judd sat up, smiled at me, and asked: "Is this the bus depot?"

Before the taping, there was an argument. Jerry Lee refused to go on unless the Styrofoam cooler did, too. Finally, a compromise was reached. The cooler was put behind the couch on which the great one would sit. During commercials, he could visit it. Believe it or not, the show went all right.

GS: Sounds like a nightmare.

RWAC: If you were there on a daily basis, year after year, I'm sure it was. But it was more than that, too. To quote from another movie, it was "the stuff that dreams are made of." I loved it. It's the Mercury memory that I remember most vividly. Every single detail.

GS: How about the big night at the Garden?

RWAC: A complete disaster. Charlie and I waited in the garage backstage for Jerry Lee's limo to arrive. Every ten minutes, the show's producer would scream: "Where the hell is he?" "He left the hotel when I did," Charlie would answer. "He should be here any minute." After about an hour of this, it became too late. "I can't hold the crowd any longer," the producer explained. "Tell Lewis he blew it."

Charlie was mortified. In his pocket, he had an expensive wristwatch, an engraved gift from the company for Jerry Lee. Just as the show ended, eight limousines slid to a halt in front of us. The Adonis that was Jerry Lee bounded our way. "The show's over," Charlie snapped. "Go home. Here's a watch from Mercury. Next time, use it."

And that was the last I saw of Jerry Lee, though he continued to make records for us.

GS: You mentioned Doug Sahm and the fear of being arrested.

RWAC: That's literally true. I liked Doug and was a big fan of his music. Had I been just a writer then and not a Mercury publicist, my memories of him would be fonder and not so flinch-inducing.

GS: Why flinch-inducing?

RWAC: Because I was responsible for him for the worst part of a week on a four-city publicity tour. Ron had given me fair and explicit warning. In fact, he sounded as if he were reading from stone tablets. The thing that you must remember about Doug, he said, is that he will not, under any circumstances, leave his hotel room in the morning without first rolling at least thirty king-sized mega-joints filled with the most potent Texas marijuana you could ever imagine. Whatever you do, do not smoke one. If you do, you will not be able to move. Do not let anybody else smoke one. Doug is used to them. They do not faze him. This ritual of rolling, which must not be interrupted, will take at least one hour. No, better make that two. So plan your time accordingly. If you have a noon plane to catch, get him up at nine o'clock. No, make that eight. You get the idea.

Oh, one more thing, Ron said. Doug is liable to light up one of these joints anytime, anyplace, anywhere, even though I have explained to him the merits and necessity of caution. So be careful.

GS: And did he light up anytime, anyplace, anywhere?

RWAC: You bet. We almost got thrown out of the most important radio station in Philadelphia when Doug stoked up in every hallway. In Washington, D.C., I had to talk a cabdriver out of turning us in at the nearest police station. We had many close calls. Four days of this—each one begun with the endless, boring ritual of the rolling—and my nerves were fried. Doug remained cheerfully oblivious throughout, promised to be more careful, rarely was. And we never got anywhere on time. But we didn't get arrested.

GS: You said earlier that you liked Sahm. Why?

RWAC: If I hadn't have been his designated babysitter, I'd have enjoyed hanging out with him. Then, when I got tired of it, I'd have been able to leave. In many ways, he was a fascinating guy, larger than life, and his music was tremendous. He mesmerized writers. They could never understand why I was so jumpy around him.

Later, when I was in A&R and Doug was no longer on Mercury, I was assigned to put together an album comprising material he'd recorded for us that hadn't been issued. I was given dozens of tapes, most of them a mishmash of mislabeled false starts and incomplete takes. Had Doug bothered to finish even half of the songs he'd started, we'd have had several great LPs. Instead, we got one very short, very good album.[2] All the rest was magnificent fragments.

GS: Let me quote some lines from a piece you once wrote about Rod Stewart: "To a lot of people, Rod Stewart onstage in mid-strut—blond hair flying, handy with brandy and partial to the broad smile and easy wink—offers as good a definition of the full flash of rock & roll as we are likely to get.

"Lining out antics and anthems with the soft-shoe strength and near-total accessibility of his talent and personality, Stewart, even in front of tens of thousands, projects an ex-athlete's warmth, sets up towel-snapping camaraderie among the players, and somehow manages to embody both the extrovert, one-of-the-boys hijinks of the macho carouser and the introvert, aw-shucks-she'd-probably-never-notice-me-anyway self-consciousness of the shyest kid on the block. Even as we envy his outgoing, big-winner's style, we revel in the knowledge that he provides via self-mockery that he can lose as often and as badly as we do."[3]

RWAC: Quote the whole piece. Then I don't have to say anything.

GS: Stewart must have been one of your favorites at Mercury.

RWAC: Not "one of." He was my favorite. I was extremely fortunate to be there during his heyday. Let me point out, though, that the piece you quoted was written after the company and I had parted ways. I never wrote about a Mercury artist when I was working there.

GS: Point well taken. Stewart was kind of a special case, wasn't he? Because his band, the Faces, in which he was lead singer, recorded for Warner Bros. Yet Rod did five solo albums for Mercury.

2 *Rough Edges*, released in 1973.
3 What's quoted is an abbreviated version of what Paul wrote in his review of Stewart's *Atlantic Crossing* and his essay about the singer for *The Rolling Stone Illustrated History of Rock & Roll*.

RWAC: He liked it that way, at least for a while. Despite his obvious star quality, he tried to remain just another guy with the Faces and seemed to need the companionship they provided. His solo records were more intimate and private. He was after something else there. But splitting himself between two companies soon became exceedingly difficult. As his sales and popularity grew, he had to make twice as many albums just to keep both Mercury and Warner Bros. even moderately happy. And Rod was a slow, conscientious songwriter. He really cared. Eventually, things reached the send-me-lawyers-guns-and-money stage. And Warner Bros. won. Easily.

GS: Why?

RWAC: I guess they had better lawyers.

GS: What do you remember most about Stewart?

RWAC: A lot of quiet moments. There was very little fast-lane stuff going on. The first time I met Rod, I gave him a tape of unreleased Bob Dylan songs, and he loved that. He even recorded a couple of them. He used to call me his Dylan expert and mock-demand a new tape each time we got together. We were both Ramblin' Jack Elliott fans, so we talked about him. Rod told me that he wouldn't be nervous about meeting Dylan but would be awestruck in front of Elliott. Rod, in his early days, had busked around Europe as a banjo-playing, beatnik street singer, and had often seen Elliott, who was Woody Guthrie's last traveling buddy, perform in clubs. I remember both Rod's and Ronnie Wood's love for their parents. They spoke of them with such reverence. Ronnie had given his parents a TV set, and his father was so proud that he chained it to the wall so no one could steal it. They could tell stories like that for hours.

Once, on a Faces tour of Virginia and the Carolinas, Rod asked me to watch some of the concerts from backstage so I could get a performer's-eye view of what it was like to have all of those people staring at you, coming for you. All of those eyes, taking direct aim. I told him that it was both exciting and worrisome. He nodded and looked troubled. The next day, we wandered out into an empty field on the edge of town. There was a big clump of trees off to one side. We talked, about what I don't remember. He kept glancing nervously at the trees. All of a sudden, he said: We have to get out of here. There could be someone with a rifle over there, and we'd be sitting targets. Come on, let's go. At first, I was stunned. Why would anyone want to shoot us? I started to say. Then I put it all together. Assassination theories—JFK, RFK, Martin Luther King—had been in the news again. American violence, to be continued. And Rod, being the focal point wherever he went, was feeling all of those eyes aimed right at him. It's too dumb to talk about, he said. And I don't really believe, for more than a minute, that anyone would really want to shoot me. But now do you understand why I wanted you to watch some of the shows from backstage? I told him I did.

Much to my amazement, Rod regarded me as something of a problem solver. And much to my amazement, sometimes I was. During the Virginia-Carolinas tour, the Faces were the headliners of a three-tier concert. The opening acts—the Vanilla Fudge and some band I don't remember—were no competition at all. Sonic sludge. Mere cannon fodder. The first night I got there, Rod told me that so far the audiences had seemed a bit flat, listless, and he couldn't understand why. Wait till you see us, he said. We're playing great. But the crowds—well, I don't know. Maybe you can figure it out.

What time does the show start, Rod? I asked.

Seven o'clock, he said.

We were standing in the hotel bar.

What time is it now, Rod?

Ten-thirty.

Shouldn't we be getting over to the auditorium?

Naw, we've got plenty of time.

What time do you usually go on, Rod?

Eleven. A little after maybe.

Rod, I said. You're telling me that you've let two thoroughly worthless heavy-metal bands play very loud, very bad music to audiences for four straight hours and you can't figure out why those audiences aren't exactly perky when you guys go on. I can tell you why right now. Because they're bloody worn out. You should go on no later than nine o'clock. No, make that eight-thirty.

I knew you were good for something, he said. More than a little sheepishly.

GS: It sounds like you were very good friends.

RWAC: We were. He seemed to want me around a lot, and I wanted to be there.[4] Whenever he brought us a new album, he always played it for me the night before the rest of the company heard it. I never told anyone that, though. Don't know how they would have taken it.

GS: Irwin Steinberg seemed to value your relationship with Rod.

RWAC: According to you.

When Rod had his best-of record ready, I met him in Boston, where the Faces were playing that night. Steinberg hit the roof. Told me over the phone that I was to stay the hell away from *Sing It Again, Rod.* We need that album out right away, he said. Don't go meddling in it and slow it up. Have you seen Rod yet?

No, I said. I just got in. I don't even know if he's checked in yet.

Hold on, he said. I've got another call.

---

4 Once, when Stewart was vacationing in Florida, he called Irwin Steinberg and requested that Paul and Mike Gormley, who replaced Ron Oberman as head of publicity, be sent down to join him. Gormley remembers how pleased Paul had been, on the drive down, when "Doctor My Eyes" came on the radio. "He was flabbergasted that Jackson was on the radio and was actually having that kind of success."

I held on.

That was Rod, he said. He specifically requested that you be present in the studio while he cross-mixes some tracks together. He wants your opinion about how it works.[5]

So what do I do? I asked.

Be present in the studio, he said. Tell him how it works.

Thanks, I said.

And call me right after, he said. Try to hurry it up.

I'll call you when it's all done, I said.

Do that, he said.

GS: I think I detect a little snideness there.

RWAC: Who me?

GS: Didn't you find it at least a little touching when Steinberg came to you for help right before Rod was to play *Every Picture Tells a Story* for the entire company? Here was the president of Mercury asking you to meet him in the hallway immediately after everybody had heard the record and tell him—how shall I put this?—three intelligent things to say to Rod about it.

RWAC: I did find it touching. Proof that he was human. And I told him three intelligent things to say. He got them a little mixed up and went into his Rod's-new-album dance, but it went all right.

GS: Sometimes I think you're every bit as cold as you accuse Steinberg of being.

RWAC: To repeat, I did find it touching. Genuinely touching. But I also found it somewhat troubling that the president of a large record company couldn't, when left to his own devices, come up with anything intelligent to say about his most important artist's best album. Wouldn't that worry you a bit? Music not comprehended here?

GS: For Christ's sake, he was a businessman. Facts and figures are what he knew. He tried hard. You expect too much.

RWAC: Let's drop it for now. I'm feeling schizophrenic again. I don't like it when I get this way.

GS: How about some of the other artists you met while you were still in publicity? David Bowie, Ian Matthews, Uriah Heep, Captain Beefheart, Chuck Mangione?

RWAC: David and Ian I took on long publicity tours—Ian even got me to the West Coast for a few days. And both of them spent a lot of time in New York.[6]

---

5 "His opinions were worth their weight in gold," Rod Stewart says today.

6 Matthews (who subsequently changed the spelling of his first name to *Iain*) fondly remembers the press tour. "Paul and I set out on this epic journey, coast to coast and everywhere in between. Talking to virtually anyone who'd listen. Radio, press, rack jobbers, retailers, you name it. I was the Lone Ranger and he was my Tonto."

David wasn't all that famous then. *Space Oddity* had just come out in America and *The Man Who Sold the World* was soon to follow, if I remember correctly. Not many writers knew him here. In England, however, he had been canonized as the next pretty-boy rock star by a teen magazine called *The Face*, and this seemed to traumatize him. All the while he was in New York, he made it a point to look as unkempt as possible, wearing sloppy sweaters and jeans, rarely shaving, and telling everyone he met that he just wanted to sing his songs and play twelve-string guitar in small clubs like Paul Colby's the Bitter End. He impressed a lot of writers—Ed Kelleher especially—and we all hung out together for several weeks.[7]

Then he went to Los Angeles to do publicity there. And metamorphosed from this deliberately drab, troubled-but-serious moth, very reluctant to meet the flame of fame into a veritable flaming creature—all glitter and glam, lipstick and gowns—butterflying his way through some notoriously bright Hollywood nights.

We in New York were stunned. We didn't mind, but none of us had seen it coming. Did we meet the real David Bowie? Ed kept asking me. Or did they? I didn't know what to answer. Maybe he was genuine in both places, I thought. Or maybe he wasn't. Maybe he still had quite a few more personalities to go. Whatever, I still liked him.[8]

GS: I trust that Ian Matthews didn't metamorphose in Los Angeles. Or anywhere else.

RWAC: Not at all. Ian was always there for you. He even put my picture on the inner cover of one of his albums.[9] Indeed, Ian was so steady and uncontroversial that I'm embarrassed to say that I don't have any funny stories to tell about him. We had one gag that we ran whenever our lot at

---

7 In the early Seventies, Kelleher, yet another critic-turned-screenwriter, had written the screenplays for the low-budget horror flicks *Invasion of the Blood Farmers* and *Shriek of the Mutilated*. He passed away in 2005.

8 Bowie liked Paul, too. "He was one of the kindest, most generous men I've met in or outside of the music business." Paul took hotel room-bound Bowie out to dinner and brought him listening materials and a box of Nat Shermans. One of the albums was *Loaded* by the Velvet Underground, who happened to be playing at Electric Circus, a nightclub in the East Village. Paul arranged for Bowie to attend. A day or two later, still aglow from a backstage encounter, Bowie told Paul that he'd gotten to meet his hero, Lou Reed. Paul good-naturedly broke the news that Reed had left the band some months before. Bowie had actually spoken with Doug Yule.

When Paul accompanied Bowie to Boston as part of a radio tour, he invited Bobbi London to come along. "We picked Bowie up on Sixth Street and Eighth Avenue," she remembers. "Bowie was in a terrycloth coat. It was winter, it was freezing, he was in a phone booth." It was one of the last things she and Paul ever did together before they broke up.

9 Paul asked David Gahr, who'd shot the cover of Blue Ash's first album, to photograph Matthews for his second LP, *Tigers Will Survive*. Matthews included, inside the album's gatefold sleeve, a photo of himself with Paul on the New Jersey shore "just to let him know how much I cared about him." He also included a picture of himself that Paul had taken.

Mercury seemed especially dismal. Together, we'd intone a line from one of his songs: "And the mist was of the deepest kind."[10]

While Ian was in New York, he and I talked to Charlie Fach about signing Richard Thompson, whom Ian had met on a Fairport Convention tour.[11] Charlie told us to make a demo tape. We did, and it was sensational. Charlie offered Richard $500 to sign. Richard was enraged, said he'd never been so insulted. After Richard and Ian stormed out, I asked Charlie to consider upping the offer. Richard Thompson is hardly an unknown, I explained. And $500 seems a bit low. Charlie, as unconcerned as ever about such scenes, simply said: "I've signed better acts for nothing." And that became my nickname for him. In the future, I was to hear those words often.

GS: Uriah Heep?

RWAC: Sweet guys, but their music was just awful. I've always felt that Uriah Heep must have been one of the source bands for *This Is Spinal Tap,* the funniest movie ever made about the music business.

GS: Captain Beefheart?

RWAC: Two great memories, both from the same night. Before his concert at Town Hall, the Captain was backstage being introduced to some Chicago-office dignitaries. When Lou Simon, Steinberg's mock-menacing but mightily imposing second-in-command, stepped forward to shake his hand, Beefheart waved it off. "I've been admiring your necktie," he said. Not missing a beat, Lou answered, "It's yours." Then, drawing a huge pair of scissors from his pocket, the Captain advanced toward Simon's throat, snipped off the tie right below its knot, smiled and said: "Thanks a lot, buddy." To his credit, Lou laughed.

Beefheart did something even better after the concert, something I've never seen any artist do. He invited the entire audience to stay for an extra hour to talk with him, ask him questions. Then he just sat on the edge of the stage, ordered the house lights turned up, and held an informal gabfest with his fans, who were amazed and appreciative. It was really quite wonderful.

GS: Chuck Mangione?

RWAC: This is from a diary entry that I found:

"2-23-72. In Washington, D.C., today for Chuck Mangione at Blues Alley. Turns out to be a disaster, in a funny, disgusting way. All the omens were there: the cabdriver from the airport gets totally lost, a blizzard starts, I get soaking wet, a writer I'm supposed to meet never shows up.

"Supper with Mike Oberman [Ron's brother] and Dawn, his girlfriend. The snow has turned into heavy rain. We walk over to the club to see Chuck.

10 The song was "The Road to Ronderlin." "I think Paul used it first as a kind of secret code. When things would get a little tedious or the politics and the bullshit got a little too deep, one of us would sing that line."

11 Thompson and Matthews had actually been in Fairport Convention together.

And the owner won't let us in. Why? I ask, since there's absolutely no audience and I can't imagine what's wrong with us. 'Because you don't have a coat and tie on,' he says and gives us a lecture on how shitty we look, how he doesn't have to put up with people like us in his place. Chuck comes over with a couple of members of his group, and they look worse than we do. 'A musician's audience is liable to look like the musician,' I try out on the owner, but it doesn't work. 'I can put up with *him*,' the owner says, pointing at Chuck, 'because he's a musician and *in uniform*, but I don't have to put up with your kind.' Chuck argues with him to no avail. I start to get furious. Tell him I've never had any trouble getting into Carnegie Hall when I've been dressed like this. I wind up out in the street in the rain, listening to the music through the window."

That was one of my last days in publicity.

GS: Then you became an A&R man.

RWAC: Yes, but we should make a slight detour here. In the fall of 1971, Ron resigned from Mercury to manage Wilderness Road, a rock & roll band that he really loved. Also, I think he was just fed up with the company, especially the Chicago office. Both of these reasons made perfect sense to me. That's well and good, he told me, but Steinberg is going to offer you my job. He wants you to move to Chicago within a week. Everybody in the Chicago office expects you to take the job.

But you know better, I said.

Yes, he said. I told them that I didn't think you wanted to leave New York. But they don't believe that you'd turn them down. Such an opportunity, a big promotion, more money, all that.

Ron, I said. Except for you—with the possible exceptions of Denny Rosencrantz and Lou Simon and maybe some people there that I've barely met—I can't stand the Chicago office. With you gone, I don't want to go anywhere near it. And I don't want to leave New York.[12]

I know, he said. But if you turn them down, they're not going to take it well. Your job may not be secure.

So be it, I said. Please tell them that I'm honored and flattered that they even considered me, that I deeply appreciate the offer, but that I'm happy where I am and feel very attached to New York.

They're not going to like that, he said. Nobody's ever rejected them before.

Tell me another, I said.

We both laughed.

GS: I think that you constantly underestimate Mercury. They didn't fire you. They obviously liked you, since they let you stay in New York and eventually promoted you into A&R.

---

12 Bud Scoppa: "The Chicago home office was *scary*. I don't know how Paul dealt with those guys. They scared the shit out of me."

RWAC: That's true, and I was grateful for it. But things were dicey for a while. There were a lot of brutal phone calls from Chicago. Everyone asked: How could you let everybody down? How stupid can you get? Steinberg made the trip from anger to disappointment and back again frequently. I think that Ron's silver tongue talked them out of anything drastic and that Charlie kind of liked that I wanted to stay in New York and put in a good word for me. Some months later, he started easing me into A&R, giving me tapes to listen to, asking my opinions about acts that Mercury was considering. This was strange—since Charlie hated rock & roll—but I appreciated both the kindness and the attention.[13]

GS: How did you get along with Mike Gormley, the new head of publicity?

RWAC: On a personal level, all right. Mike had been a rock & roll critic for some Detroit paper, so we had that in common.[14] He was a nice guy, but it soon became apparent that he was being buffaloed by the brass in Chicago and was overawed by the vast mass of regimentation. I think he envied me my spot in New York with all those writers, all those artists around. His hours were from the crack of dawn until six. Mine were from noon or early afternoon until the crack of dawn. Charlie understood this, but no one in the Chicago office ever did. It didn't take long before Mike began sounding desperately unhappy. And I must say that his by-the-numbers, trade-story approach to publicity was just not what I had in mind. I gave serious thought to quitting and probably would have if Charlie hadn't been sliding me toward an A&R gig. He even took me to Chicago for an A&R meeting and let me sign an artist, Mike Seeger, while I was still in publicity.

GS: I'd like to hear more about that meeting, but, before we leave publicity completely, you should tell us "the true story of rock & roll." I believe that's how you always referred to it.

RWAC: Yeah, that's right. Jesus, I'd almost forgotten about it. It happened during my first week at Mercury. I'm going to have to change all the names, though, since some of them are still active.

GS: Let's call the big-name manager the BNM, the big-name act the BNA, the BNA's major label the ML, and the no-name band the Sympathetic Dupes.

RWAC: Oh god, the Dupes. My heart still bleeds for them.

GS: Tell the story.

---

13 Fach remembered Paul this way: "He was a very gentle man, as opposed to most people in the record business."

14 The first time Gormley flew in to meet his New York colleagues, he found Paul waiting for him at LaGuardia. "Paul, not knowing me, got a limo just in case I was a record-executive type." Once in Manhattan, they encountered the customary traffic jam. "Truman Capote walked past the limo and got into this rickety old cab right behind us. I turned to Paul and I said, 'You know, he's supposed to be up here, we're supposed to be back there.' I think Paul figured out that I was maybe more a writer than a record executive. At least at that point."

RWAC: Well, I'm brand new at Mercury and still trying to sort through our roster of artists. The receptionist calls to tell me that one of our acts, the Sympathetic Dupes, is waiting in the lobby to see me. They've driven a thousand miles from the Midwest just to be in New York the day their first album is being released, she says. They're real excited.

Who the hell are the Sympathetic Dupes? I ask. I don't have their record, I've never heard of them, and I don't see their name on any of our lists.

I've never heard of them either, she says. They asked for Charlie, but he's not here. You're the only one around, so I called you.

I think a bit, then say: Tell them I'm on an important conference call, will you? Say that I'm sorry and that I'll be glad to see them in an hour. Meanwhile, I'll call Chicago to see if I can find out who these guys are.

Sounds good, she says. They're awfully nice.

I call Ron. He's not there. I try Lou Simon.

Lou, I say, I've got the Sympathetic Dupes coming in to see me in an hour.

Who? he asks.

Well, they're this band from the Midwest and—

Ah, shit! he yells. The cursing goes on for a long time. Then he says: I'm not mad at you. But they're not supposed to be there!

I tell him that they're here because their LP is supposed to be released today. That they've driven a thousand miles—

More cursing. Well, Lou says, at one time, it was. We might send out a few copies. But they're dead. Don't waste your time with them.

Lou, the receptionist says that they asked for some press kits. I don't have any and—

More cursing. Then: Just get rid of them. They don't know it yet, but we've already dropped them. Give them nothing.

Lou, could you at least send me some press kits? And tell me what's going on?

I'll send you five press kits. Charge them five dollars apiece. These things are expensive. Get the story from Charlie or Ron. Meanwhile, ditch the Dupes.

I pieced together the story from a number of people. It went something like this:

A BNM had a BNA whose contract was up for renewal at a ML. Both the BNM and BNA threatened to go elsewhere unless the ML delivered Fort Knox in an orchid-covered plutonium-coated Rolls-Royce. Elsewhere was one of five middle-level labels, including Mercury. The ML was hedging.

So the BNM went to the Midwest and signed the first five bar bands he saw that could play and sing at the same time and not vomit or fall down. He gave them little or no money but guaranteed them a record deal. They were ecstatic. After all, they now had a BNM and heaven was sure to follow.

In step two of this sham, the BNM courted each of the middle-level labels, using the BNA as bait. I'm seriously considering your company for my BNA, he said. I've heard a lot of fine things about you. But I want to see for myself just how good a label you really are. I've got this terrific group from the Midwest, the Sympathetic Dupes, and I'm really high on them. You give me $50,000, I'll give you a great record, and you show me what you can do with it. If you succeed, and I'm sure you will, then my BNA is practically yours.

Step three found the BNM back in the Midwest. Five bar bands churned out five cheaply produced, demo-quality albums within a few days. The cost of all five was probably under $50,000. The Sympathetic Dupes were thrilled with theirs. A few weeks ago, they were nothing but a local joke. Now they had an LP coming out on Mercury as well as a BNM. Soon, they'd be swilling champagne, breaking lobsters, and fucking groupies with the BNM's BNA. So what if they had less than $200 in their pockets. Hey, let's pile into the car and drive to New York. See our album in Sam Goody's. Go visit Mercury.

But before they got here, step four had been completed. There were five very unhappy middle-level labels. Each of them out fifty grand and stuck with a rotten record made by a group that had already died and would never, ever understand what had happened to them. Yesterday, we had a BNM and an LP ready for release, they would say to themselves, over and over. Now we can't get our BNM on the phone and our label wants nothing to do with us. What the hell happened?

What happened was this: The BNM's bluff had worked, as he figured it would. His BNA re-signed with the ML for more money than anyone thought possible. In addition, the BNM pocketed about $200,000 from the five middle-level labels. The biggest losers were the five bar bands, who were marked forever. And one of them was sitting in my office.

GS: Jesus. Now I begin to understand your cynicism. What did you do with them? Did you tell them what happened?

RWAC: I didn't tell them anything. I just didn't have the heart. I said that their album had been delayed for a few days. Trouble at the plant or something. I took them to lunch, and we ate dead meat and drank poison liquids. I tried to look excited as they told me their fabulous success saga. Just wait until you hear our record, they said. You'll love it. I'm sure I will, I said. Can't wait.

The next day, I gave them their press kits. Didn't even charge them the five bucks apiece. Told Lou to take it out of my salary. He said that wouldn't be necessary. I took them over to *Circus*, where Gerry Rothberg, who'd agreed to a meet, spent a few minutes with them, accepted a press kit, listened to their story, and wished them good luck. They were excited. I showed them the building that housed *Rolling Stone*. Everybody's on deadline up there, I said, so we can't go in. Wow, they said. So that's where *Rolling Stone* is. We had dinner with the most dimwitted rock & roll critic I could think of, someone who wrote so badly that he could seldom get published but was always up for a free meal. I tried hard not to listen to anything that was said. They thought he was great.

As the night came on, they thanked me for showing them around. Said they'd had a wonderful time in New York—except for not being able to reach their BNM—but had to head back home because their money had run out. Be sure to listen to our album, they said. See you soon.

Drive safe, I said. And try to forget that all of this ever happened to you, I thought. You'd be a lot better off with no memory at all.

GS: Did you ever listen to their record?

RWAC: Yes.

GS: How was it?

RWAC: Even worse than you can imagine. Heartbreakingly awful. The Sympathetic Dupes.

GS: Do you remember the band's real name?

RWAC: Fortunately, no.

GS: Shall we get on with something more cheerful?

RWAC: Please.

GS: Mike Gormley hired Bud Scoppa, your best friend, to succeed you in publicity. That must have made you happy. Now there were two rock & roll critics working for Mercury in New York.

RWAC: It did. Now we were ganging up on 'em. Two rock & rollers in New York against twenty bookkeepers in Chicago.

GS: Let's go back to your first A&R meeting, which you attended while still a publicist.

RWAC: As I said, I figured that Charlie wanted me in A&R and that he'd pretty well cleared it with Steinberg and Lou, although nobody had said anything to me about it yet.

GS: But you wanted the job?

RWAC: Yes. I thought, foolishly perhaps, that I could have more of an impact on the company in A&R than in publicity. It was a pretty romantic notion.

GS: Haven't I always told you that your romanticism invariably does you in? In A&R, one's head is always on the block. Failure there is highly visible. And you certainly must have known that Mercury, in those days, was hardly the label of choice for any remotely BNA who had a choice. Or for any promising newcomer.

RWAC: I knew all that. But publicity was a dead end. And I liked the idea of signing and developing young and unknown acts.

GS: Did you like the idea of professional suicide, too? You really were a fool.

RWAC: Now who's maligning Mercury?

GS: You're right. I'm sorry. It wasn't quite as bad as that. You had a chance.

RWAC: Anyway, at my first A&R meeting, they let me sign an artist, Mike Seeger, who, to quote someone, was "America's foremost exponent of rural Appalachian folk music."

GS: And who had, at best, barely enough commercial appeal to sell—what?—a few thousand albums? Did you tell them that?

RWAC: As a matter of fact, I did. It was one of four points that I made in the meeting.

GS: I don't believe this.

RWAC: My first point was that Mercury, like Columbia, should sometimes issue prestigious records simply because they were prestigious, providing we made a little money on them right away.

My second point was that such LPs could not fail to create overall good will and increase Mercury's credibility in the music business. Lots of good press, word of mouth, et cetera.

My third point was that prestigious albums sell forever, provided they're left in the catalog. And that slow, steady sales can add up to decent dollars over the years.

My final point was that we could have Mike Seeger and *Music from True Vine* for $2,000.

GS: I must say, that was very smooth. In a crazy way, it makes sense. I hope you told them that you weren't going to make a habit out of such projects.

RWAC: I did. I told them this was a special case.

GS: And they bought it.

RWAC: Enthusiastically. They thought it was a great idea.[15]

GS: You must have figured that you'd found your niche at Mercury.

RWAC: I hoped so, but I wasn't that dumb. There were plenty of things that happened at the A&R meeting that worried me. Overall, though, I was encouraged.

---

15 Mike Seeger had met Paul, along with Jon Pankake, back in Minnesota in 1960 or '61 when he'd played there with the New Lost City Ramblers. "It was intimidating almost because of their knowledge and their writing ability. When the band played, I just remember this feeling of them being close up front and absolutely quiet and almost impassive while they listened."

"Okay, this is a good picture of Paul," Tony Glover says. "He got the Dolls signed to Mercury, he also got a Mike Seeger solo album produced on Mercury. It's a pretty regular Mike Seeger solo album: autoharp, banjo, fiddle, doing old traditional tunes. A complete Folkways kind of record, on Mercury—along with the New York Dolls."

"I had approached a couple of larger record companies," Seeger said, "but I never would have thought of approaching Mercury." Paul ended up co-producing the album with him, and David Gahr provided the photography.

Pankake: "Paul wanted to have a good review of it in *Rolling Stone*, but he couldn't do it himself as the producer. So that was my one appearance in *Rolling Stone*, to review the Mike Seeger album. A rhapsodic review."

"Jesus, I loved that album," Charlie Fach said. "It's one of the great disappointments that we couldn't bring that home for Paul." Fach passed away in 2011.

GS: What worried you?

RWAC: The fact that nobody seemed to remember anything at all that was said at the last A&R meeting, which I hadn't attended. They argued endlessly about stuff that presumably had been decided months ago. That didn't bode well.

GS: What else?

RWAC: Well, everybody seemed incapable of listening to a song all the way through. More than a minute's worth of music made them all squirm. After we'd heard two or three fragments by an artist, Steinberg would say, Shall we give this guy or these guys $20,000 for this? Such an approach didn't make any sense to me. Fortunately, I wasn't even asked to play a Mike Seeger tape. Apparently, my argument had been so convincing that they didn't even want to hear his music.

GS: Now would be a good time to characterize some of the people in the Chicago office.

RWAC: I knew this was coming, and I've tried so hard to avoid it. About Charlie, the head of the New York office, let me add this: he was one of the most reticent men I've ever known. It was as if he'd been allotted only so many words a month and was afraid he'd use them up too quickly if he said more than a sentence at a time. This could be both maddening and endearing.

GS: We're talking about the Chicago office now.

RWAC: Gormley you already know something about.

Lou Simon's name has come up before, but I should say a little more about him. If you're a movie fan, picture Richard Boone in some of his truly-lethal-yet-sympathetic-villain roles. The parts he played in *The Tall T* and *The Kremlin Letter* are good examples. Crude, menacing, and killers at heart, Boone's venomous bad guys paradoxically had souls at least as sensitive as anyone else's in those films. And they were genuinely—even deeply— funny. Lou was like that. He often achieved real vulgarity. I liked him enormously. And even though he wasn't a fan of many of my artists, I think he liked me, too.

GS: What about Robin McBride, whose business card read "Head of Midwest and International A&R"?

RWAC: Well, that about says it all.

GS: What do you mean?

RWAC: Pompous, pretentious, humorless. The Chicago office's scapegoat. When he handed me his card, I said to myself, Now here's a man who *really* doesn't want to be recognized. To paraphrase the Frank Sinatra character's description of the Laurence Harvey character in *The Manchurian Candidate*: "It's not that Robin is difficult to like. He is *impossible* to like."

GS: He must have had some good qualities.

RWAC: He must have.

GS: What were his musical tastes?

RWAC: Horn bands. Nothing but jazz-rock-fusion horn bands. Some of them the size of the crowds in *Ben-Hur*. They were all terrible. One of them, a truly immense group, sold less than ten albums. And there were thirteen people in the band, I think. Even Steinberg was amazed.[16]

GS: Denny Rosencrantz?

RWAC: When I first met him, he was in radio promotion. He and Stan Bly, another promotion man, had this jive-turkey, soft-shoe vaudeville act that they used to amuse Steinberg and Lou at A&R meetings. It left me pretty unmoved. But when I got to know Denny, we became good friends quickly. He was extremely smart and funny. Within a year, he became the label's West Coast A&R man, a compadre in the everlasting battle of trying to sign talent at Mercury. We slit many a wrist together.

GS: Stan Bly?

RWAC: A very nice guy who never met a record of mine for which he could get airplay. I liked him personally, although I never fully trusted him. I suppose that our relationship was the standard A&R-versus-promotion cliché, with each side blaming the other for not doing the job right.

GS: Jack Kramer?

RWAC: I really don't remember him. I think he had a vote at the A&R meetings, but it seems to me that he did something in publicity, too.

GS: What about Irwin Steinberg?

RWAC: Must we? He comes up often enough, doesn't he?

GS: Let's have another go at it.

RWAC: I think he was miscast as a record company president, and—I mean this kindly—I think he knew it. He had neither the size nor the knowledge for such a role and always seemed very uncomfortable about it. Everything he did appeared forced and unnatural, small and insincere. He couldn't inspire anyone. It was like watching Leslie Nielsen trying to play King Lear. Steinberg could be very touching when he attempted a compliment, but he didn't know how to do it, and it always came out wrong. At such moments, he was a walking, talking Hallmark card, and you felt sorry and sad about the whole thing.

GS: Then there was his temper.

RWAC: Yes, there was that. It was sudden and violent. Out of one side of his mouth, he would coo about how much he admired my rock & roll articles and criticism, and out of the other side, he would beat the hell out of me for

---

16 Paul told Marty Thau: "Robin was the guy who signed a thirteen-piece horn band which actually had more records returned than were printed. Everyone sat around at this A&R meeting trying to figure out how we could have possibly gotten thirteen more back. It had never happened before—it had sold minus thirteen because people returned thirteen of the demos as well as all 5,000 of the album."

my rock-critic's taste. Especially when I was in A&R. Where I was usually double- and triple-checked.

GS: Perhaps he had good reasons. I think he was just trying to steer you toward a more moderate, less impassioned course. There was obviously a clash of personalities. I think he wanted peaceful coexistence.

RWAC: Well, so did I. You may find this hard to believe, Senator, but I didn't start many fights at Mercury. I never considered myself a rabble-rousing rebel. Charlie liked me because I was quiet and polite and didn't do drugs. I may have smoldered some, but I rarely erupted. Less so than almost anyone else in the company. Eruptions and bad temper were more Steinberg's style: hard, quick, icy blasts of fire out of all proportion to what was being said. The consensus in the Chicago office was that he was a complete enigma.

GS: So you really disliked him?

RWAC: Obviously, there were times when I didn't like him very much. Mostly, I was afraid of him. He had all that volatility with nowhere to go, and I didn't feel comfortable whenever I was in his sightlines.[17]

GS: Still, you seemed to do well in A&R at first.

RWAC: Yes. Shortly after what let's call the Mike Seeger meeting, they offered me the position. In fact, the news came right in the middle of one of Mike's fiddle tunes. We were in the studio and had nearly finished recording. The whole LP took us two afternoons. When I played it for everybody at the next A&R meeting, though, no one remembered any of the reasons why we were issuing such a strange album. "What's the hit single?" Stan demanded. "There is no hit single," I explained. "Don't you remember what I said at the last meeting?" He grew angry and asked, "What are we doing with this shit if there's no hit single?" In truth, everyone in the room looked puzzled, except Charlie. "Tell them again," he said. So I repeated the whole four-point speech, and they all nodded their heads and said: "Oh, yeah. Great idea. Oh, yeah." What an eerie moment that was.

GS: But you still managed to sign Blue Ash, the New York Dolls, and Reddy Teddy rather quickly.

RWAC: Not so quickly at all. It took more than six months to sign Blue Ash, my Byrds-Beatles-Who-type band from Ohio. And over a year to sign the Dolls, New York City's rock & roll darlings and the precursors of punk, who proved to be my eventual Waterloo within the company and started a corporate war that was all about money. We gave it slowly, the Dolls spent it fast—and vastly. And there was never enough to go around. Reddy Teddy, my Boston-based rock & roll band, took over a year to sign, and their album ended up a total disaster.

---

17 "I liked him," Irwin Steinberg says. "I hope he liked me. I was busy running the company. I knew he was there. While I knew he was around and we enjoyed having him be a part of us, I don't remember my personally having a really intense relationship with him."

I did manage to acquire some in-concert tapes of the Velvet Underground, recorded in Texas shortly before their demise. I was very excited about this—the tapes were great, and there was enough material for a double-album—but when I made my pitch at an A&R meeting, I got almost nothing back but glazed incomprehension. Suddenly, it dawned on me that practically none of these people knew who the Velvet Underground were. When I mentioned Lou Reed, a slight light went on in a few more pairs of eyes. I talked and talked and talked and finally won the day. We got a double-album, *1969 Velvet Underground Live*, for $20,000. It's still in print, as are both Dolls LPs. All three records made many best-albums-of-the-year lists.

GS: Lou Reed really liked *1969 Velvet Underground Live*, didn't he?

RWAC: He did. When I gave him the dubs of the record, he couldn't wait to hear them. I'd never met Reed before, so I was extremely pleased by his response. "I've got to hear 'Ocean,'" he said. "I remember the night we played it. I thought it was one of the best things we'd ever done. What side is it on?" I told him, and we listened to "Ocean" over and over. He was right. It was one of the best things the group had ever done. This is what it's all about, I thought to myself. This makes working for Mercury worthwhile. I was very happy.[18]

Oddly enough, when Steinberg referred to the Velvets' double-album—both before and after it was released—he always called the band Deep Purple. Once, when he was really angry at me for something or other, he shouted, in front of most of the company: "You know, I never would have put out those Deep Purple records if one of our Nashville artists hadn't gotten sick and had his LP delayed!" That really boosted my morale.

GS: I remember that. It really was a pointless remark. Not one of his better moments.

RWAC: I didn't like it much.

GS: These A&R gatherings are rather like *The Twilight Zone*. Let's concentrate on them for a while. I understand that you've found some notes about two rather important meetings.

RWAC: Yes.

GS: Shall we?

RWAC: "5-29/30/31-73 are being written up in a Boca Raton hotel room on Thursday after the first night of our marathon Mercury meetings down here. Tuesday, I spent all night at the Dolls session (yes, all night: went straight to work Wednesday from the Record Plant, then home to sleep for a few

18 Knowing how much Elliott Murphy liked the group, Paul invited him to write the liner notes for *1969 Velvet Underground Live*. Murphy's whimsical yet reverent notes graced the inside of the gatefold cover, while Paul's peculiarly prosaic comments appeared on the back.

Lou Reed liked what Murphy had written and asked Paul for his number; but Paul mistakenly gave him the wrong one. The next time Murphy visited his mother, she told him that "This very nice boy, Louis Reed, called …"

hours). Then back to the Record Plant for another Dolls session, which lasted until 5:30 a.m. Got a couple of hours of sleep, packed a bag, rushed to the office, caught a cab to the airport at 11:30, and arrived in steamy Florida in the late afternoon on Thursday. It felt like a New York subway station in mid-August.

"Our hotel reminds me of Xanadu in *Citizen Kane*: filthy rich, nearly totally empty. You could roll bowling balls in the lobby at night and not wake anyone up. Had a talk with Jack Kramer and Mike Gormley about company problems, etc. For some reason, Mike is all up in arms about Bud Scoppa. Actually said he might fire him if he doesn't shape up on his TV connections, *Time* and *Newsweek*, non-rock stuff. Apparently, Steinberg and Lou are pissed about it, too. Bud showed me Mike's angry memo before I left this morning, and I didn't think it was anything serious, but now I do. No wonder everybody at *Rolling Stone* thinks Gormley's a dunce. Jesus, this company is so blind it's unbelievable! Here we are in Florida for a four-day think tank about company policy, and they're actually considering firing one of their best people! I don't think it will happen, but I can't believe the question even came up: it never should have. I think Charlie will rush to Bud's defense, though.

"Saw Steinberg briefly at supper, and he was real friendly. He's sky-high on the Dolls, said that eight countries want them. He seems to regard it as a real feather in Mercury's cap—and to give me full credit. (This after screaming at me a few months ago that he'd fire me if I ever brought up the Dolls' name again.) Said some nice things about Blue Ash, too: the *Billboard* pick mainly. Blue Ash finished ahead of all our releases there. Later, he was standing by the elevator and humming 'Space Oddity.' Weird.

"6-1-73. Jesus, it's only Friday at 3:30 in the afternoon and already I'm feeling like a character in an Antonioni movie about corporate boredom. And the days start at 7:30 in the morning and go right through supper. At night, there is zero to do: nothing is open around here. Not even a coffee shop or a Coke machine, let alone stores or a town. We're in the middle of nowhere. It's like being embalmed in a hothouse with the same old company jokes, situations. This morning's meeting had a spark of interest when we finally got off the slide show of figures, but, after lunch, the leader of the talks, some New Age business guru called Larry Platitudes, lagged badly. Day and night dragged on until everybody was beyond caring.

"6-2-73. Our A&R finance meeting this morning was mercifully short— only about two hours—and probably very useful. All the A&R guys kept talking about the rising cost of making rock & roll albums, and it came across pretty strongly that $15,000 is rock bottom now. Charlie and Steinberg sat there and took it all in, seeming to agree with it. I just hope they remember this meeting the next time I try to sign a group.

"After supper, an endless meeting (until 11:30) about insurance and pensions. It lasted so long that, after it was over, we all felt we were old enough to retire and start drawing our pie-in-the-sky pensions. After the meeting, I played four Dolls songs from the Record Plant sessions for Gormley and Kramer. Kramer doesn't like rock & roll, but he seemed to like this a little. Gormley didn't even know it was the Dolls until I told him. Good pair of ears, Mike. Two months ago, you heard two live sets by these guys at Kenny's Castaways and couldn't stop raving to Bud and me about how great they were and about how you were going to champion the Dolls within the company. Two days after that, when you were back in the Chicago office, you were lukewarm again. Tonight, you don't remember a thing. Except that you might fire Bud.

"6-3-73. On and on it goes, these damn meetings beginning at sunrise and designed to set you dozing again within minutes. The fourth or fifth or sixth meeting—the one in which Larry Platitudes proved beyond a doubt that he was totally out of it—even peeved Steinberg a little. As we all staggered out into the empty hallway for supper, Steinberg got off a nice line about disposable paper cars. He and I even shared a laugh. I hope it wasn't our last. During the evening's finale, Larry Platitudes and Steinberg were properly optimistic about Mercury, quoting Thoreau and Emerson, et al. All having a lot to do with the record business, of course.

"It's 10:30 p.m. now. Don't know what I'm going to do until midnight. There aren't many choices, since nothing, not even the bar, is open. At midnight, I'm going to watch Otto Preminger's *Angel Face* on TV. Mitchum and Simmons. It'll be the most intelligent thing I've seen here.

"6-4-73. Today was a big day in my life at Mercury: the A&R meeting. To say that I emerged a hero is true, I think. I played the Dolls tape ('Personality Crisis,' 'Subway,' 'Looking for a Kiss' 'Private World'—all of them incomplete, roughly mixed) for everyone, and the whole company went absolutely wild. Steinberg even did his Rod's-new-album jig. After about a minute of the first song ('Personality Crisis'), Stan Bly raced over to me and said, 'The Dolls are my life!' (Of course, he says that about all of our new acts, although not usually after only a minute. Then, a few months later, after he's failed to get any airplay for them, he says he never liked them in the first place.) Jerry Kennedy, our man in Nashville, went on and on about what great musicians the Dolls were: 'They sure can pick!' I loved that from Jerry, because everybody else at Mercury (except Bud) has bad-rapped the Dolls about their musicianship.

"We had a vote about which three acts on our roster the company would try to promote into superstars. Bachman-Turner Overdrive (one of Charlie's acts), the Dolls, and Tom T. Hall won easily. Blue Ash finished fourth or fifth.

"People even liked one of the new tapes I played. They gave me a definite yes on the Dynomiters, if we can get the right deal. Also, I got a second Blue

Ash LP for October 15 and a Reddy Teddy record for November 15, if we can close our deal in time."

GS: You did well in Boca Raton.

RWAC: It seemed so at the time. But we never signed the Dynomiters. There was no second Blue Ash album. And the Reddy Teddy situation turned bad very quickly. My status in Florida didn't last long. In fact, let's jump ahead and see what happened just before and during the next A&R meeting in Chicago.

GS: Should I put on my helmet?

RWAC: You'd better.

"8-27-73. Today was absolutely *the* worst day I've ever spent at Mercury: *the* all-time worst. From 10 in the morning until 6 at night, nothing but frantic, screaming telephone calls re the Dolls' latest money crisis. Steinberg was a son-of-a-bitch all day, yelling and hollering at Steve Leber [one of the Dolls' managers] like a wild man. He wound up hanging up on both of us, then sending me a nasty telex. Also, he refused to pay anything on my trip to Los Angeles [to see the Dolls play at the Whisky]. Charlie thought that was lousy. In fact, he made a face and told me he'd give me some time off when I got back. Steinberg doesn't have to know about it, he said.

"9-2-73. The Dolls were terrific tonight, and L.A. seems to love them. David [Johansen] did both sets in a scant purple bathing suit, gun and holster, and cowboy boots and hat. 'Hey, kids,' he asked, 'it doesn't matter to you whether we're in tune or not, does it?' 'Trash' now has a long, Romeo and Juliet narrative in the middle of it, with Jerry [Nolan] shyly asking for a kiss on the cheek. 'Give Her a Great Big Kiss' was fabulous, with David and Johnny [Thunder] mock-screaming at each other like a couple of New York cabbies. D: 'What the hell do you *mean*, is she a good *dancer*?!' J: 'Well, how the *fuck* does she *dance*?!' At several points, David would practically tackle Johnny. David—smoking the microphone like a cigar as he paced about like Groucho Marx—to a heckler: 'When I'm up here, I rule! I couldn't interest anybody in a used vacuum cleaner, could I?'

"9-5-73. Jesus, I'm back in New York for half a day, and I get killed the first ten minutes I talk to someone from Mercury. Bud told me that he'd had lunch with Charlie and that it seems possible—maybe even likely—that Blue Ash will get dropped before a second LP. I was so shocked and horrified that I couldn't believe it. All I could do was laugh. 'They couldn't be that dumb, could they?' I asked Bud. 'I think they could,' he said.

"When I talked to Charlie about it, he hedged at first. 'Charlie,' I said, 'I got a solid yes at Boca Raton. Almost half the second album is already finished and paid for. What about all those great reviews that *No More, No Less* got?'

"'Well, that was because *you* were involved with the LP,' Charlie said.

"'Charlie,' I said. "Believe me, this is not a rock-&-roll-critics' conspiracy. Even if I wanted to, I couldn't organize such a thing. Writers write what they think. Christ, I don't even know most of the critics who reviewed the record. We're talking about national press here, Charlie. Doesn't that mean anything?'

"Charlie told me that all of the radio people hated *No More, No Less*. He also told me that if it were up to him, he'd drop everybody except Bachman-Turner Overdrive and the Dolls. Everybody!

"What then? I thought. Bring in a whole new bunch and drop them after one album, no matter how highly they're praised?

"I told Charlie that Willie Mays would never have played for Mercury, since he went 0-for-23 when he first came up with the Giants. Charlie laughed and said that the record business was not like baseball.

"I went back to my office and thought: Which acts ever make it with their first LP, with no company support? Where's the building for the future, the shrewd planning, our own assessment of talent? Steinberg is clearly out of his element when it comes to judging music. And Charlie hates rock & roll. Whenever the Dolls pay me a visit, he runs and hides in his office, making sure that the door is closed. God, I wish I could get out of all this![19]

"9-8-73. Today is the one day I have on which to relax a little before tomorrow night's cocktail party and Monday's crucial A&R meeting in Chicago, and I'm very, very nervous. I feel like I'm betting $18,000-a-year-plus-expenses on a pair of deuces, and that I'm the only player at the table who can't afford to lose. Or that I'm in a game of Russian roulette with a six-cylinder pistol. I've already pulled the trigger four times and hit empty chambers, and now they're demanding a fifth try—and perhaps even a surely fatal sixth. In short, things are very scary right now.

"9-9-73. Tomorrow is the big A&R meeting, and, from the tone of tonight's cocktail party, it is going to be a slaughter. I started out by asking Lou what he thought about Paul Smith booking Blue Ash, and he hemmed and hawed about waiting until tomorrow's meeting and the artist-roster vote. Then, a bunch of us got into a discussion with Steinberg about the record business in general and Mercury in specific, and it became very apparent that Mercury would never be more than a second-rate label, at best. Steinberg's new theory seems to be that R&B, country music, and classical music are both safe and long-lasting, and that rock & roll (re Rod's cancelling his 'live' LP, Uriah Heep leaving, the Dolls' financial problems) is just too crazy to bank on. Therefore, concentrate on the safe areas, double these types of artists, cut down on the rock & roll, trim most of the acts. He came right out and said that he didn't think that Blue Ash would make it.

---

19 Paul said Fach "was terrified of running into one—and what would he say to them? Then I sent David in once. I said, 'Why don't you just go and talk to Charlie for ten minutes.' Then Charlie came to me later and said, 'Gee, that David's a charming guy,' and then Charlie got unafraid of them."

"Now I ask you: Does Steinberg's stance make *any* sense? Since rock & roll commands a lion's share of the market, and that share is growing bigger every day, how smart is Mercury's decision to practically eliminate rock & roll from the label? Can't any of our top executives *think*? Don't they want to make money? Neither Columbia nor Warner Bros. got great just by strengthening their R&B, country music, and classical music rosters, that's for sure. 'Punchless Mercury,' *Esquire* recently proclaimed. They had that right.

"And what's my role in a company that seems scared to death of rock & roll and the artists who play it? I don't know. I guess it's take the money for as long as possible, try my best, hope without any real hope, and maybe I'll get lucky before I get fired.

"Jack Kramer told me about some sociological theory involving three recurring stages, ad infinitum: (1) the age of stupidity, (2) the age of naïve reform, (3) the age of despair. For Mercury, the Florida meetings were the age of naïve reform. We are now in the age of despair, and the age of stupidity starts tomorrow. Me? I'm staying in the age of despair.

"9-10-73. 'Dear God, you know I want your pain, but I don't want it now,' wrote Graham Greene in *The End of the Affair*.

"The A&R meeting was everything I expected it to be—or even worse. Blue Ash is as good as gone, relegated to one more single and no more LPs unless the single hits. And with Stan running the promotion on it, the single has no chance of hitting that I can see. He came out foursquare against the group, as did Steinberg, Charlie, and Lou. None of the support promised (Denny, Kramer, Gormley, et al.) materialized, and I felt like a man in front of a firing squad. No matter what I said in the band's defense (good press, etc.), I knew they were going to pull the trigger. And they did. Blue Ash will be handled by the Chicago office, I was told. I got no reaction to my suggestion that we think about signing the Flamin' Groovies and John Cale: none. Everyone made a 180-degree turn on Reddy Teddy, and plans for their first album are now on hold. Instead, I'm to do a 'decent' $1,000 demo.

"When Ian Matthews's country LP was played, Lou pronounced it 'drivel,' and Charlie said that 'every single we've put out is better than that,' referring to the Jimmy Webb song. McGinnis Flint were called 'dreck.' Bachman-Turner Overdrive were favorably compared to the Allman Brothers, and it's clear to me that Steinberg, Charlie, and Lou are pulling for BTO to outsell the Dolls, although no one said anything bad about the Dolls per se. But no one said anything good about them either, and I'm certainly not the hero I was in Florida for signing them. Acts we're now interested in: the Marketts, Atlantis, Creative Funk, Jerry La Croix.

"More important, it became very clear that rock & roll is dead at Mercury. Steinberg gave last night's speech about R&B, country music, and classical music to the whole company. After which, Lou came up to me, smiled, and said: "I worry about you and your rock & roll."

"Two minor high points. Jimmy Brooks [I don't remember him], talking about payola at a recent DJ convention: 'I got a $50 bill, and I ain't even a disc jockey.' And I collected two new nicknames for Steinberg: Cold Starch and the Other. I still like Ire and Ice best, but the Other does have a ring to it.

"The damn meeting went from 8 in the morning until close to 9 at night: nearly thirteen hours. I caught a plane at 9:45 (via Albany) and got home (via Newark) around 3. And I didn't say goodbye to anybody.

"9-11-73. Told Bud the bad news, and we sat around the office in a state of shock, went to eat at La Strada and sat there in a state of shock, then stumbled back to the office. A few weeks ago, Bud had an offer from A&M's publicity department in Los Angeles, but, until today, he didn't think that he'd accept it. Now he's reconsidering. Both of us were in some kind of bad shape today. I must have looked really desperate, because it showed on other people's faces in the office."

GS: We should talk a little about the artists you signed. You've told me in private that this remains something of a sore spot for you. That—to be melodramatic—you still mourn their loss. And that you never play any of the records you made at Mercury.

RWAC: That's pretty much true. It's not that I'm all broken up inside about it or that my life was ruined, but listening to the two Dolls albums or the Blue Ash LP would still hurt, would bring it all back home again. I have no problem playing the two Mike Seeger records, but they were special cases because they had no great commercial expectations hounding them. Seeger himself told me that I'd pulled off not one but two miracles by ever getting a major label to issue them. He was extremely satisfied with his Mercury experience. His second album was very wittily titled *The Second Annual Farewell Reunion*. And, because they were less personal projects, I wouldn't have any problem listening to Steve Grossman's or David Barretto's LPs. But I lent them to an ex-girlfriend, and she never brought them back.[20]

GS: Why were Steve Grossman and David Barretto less personal projects?

RWAC: Because I liked their work very much, but I wasn't passionately in love with it. For a change, I was clearheaded.

GS: You weren't behaving like James Stewart in *Vertigo*?

RWAC: That's right, I wasn't. Although Steve's tape was given to me by another ex-girlfriend, Barbara London, who was the love of my life and with whom I sometimes did behave like James Stewart in *Vertigo*. Bobbi said that Steve lived in the apartment next to hers and that she'd heard the music

---

20 Barretto's self-titled LP and Grossman's *Caravan Tonight* were both released in 1974.

coming through the walls. She asked him for a tape, liked it, and brought it to me. I liked it, too. I said to myself, Why not take a shot at this? After all, Bobbi's always had good taste, except for the time she dumped me.[21]

GS: What was the music like?

RWAC: It was sort of MOR. Steve was a singer-songwriter who wrote love songs. Only instead of writing "I love her very much," he wrote, "I love him very much." Steve was gay.

GS: And this didn't bother you?

RWAC: No, not a bit. I rather liked the idea. To my knowledge, no one had ever made an openly gay record. I wasn't sure how Mercury would take to it, though.

GS: Could I make a very tasteless bad joke and ask if they openly embraced it?

RWAC: Why not? It's good to see that you've got at least one joke in you.

Seriously, no one at Mercury had any problems with either Steve's sexuality or his material. There were no demands that the songs undergo a sex change. In fact, Steve was the only artist I ever signed that Steinberg and Charlie genuinely seemed to like. We got into a bidding war with RCA, though, and when the price reached $30,000 Steinberg began to quake. But Charlie outright demanded that we not lose Grossman. And we didn't. I was just amazed by the whole thing. I asked myself, Why couldn't they get this excited about Blue Ash or the Dolls? I answered myself, Because Blue Ash and the Dolls are rock & rollers.

GS: Did Grossman's album sell?

RWAC: Not a bit. Or at least not enough. Some Roberta Flack-type singer—maybe it even was Roberta Flack—did a cover version of Steve's single, the name of which I've forgotten. Since she was a woman, it became a conventional man-woman love song. But that didn't sell either. So we said goodbye to Steve Grossman, a loss that Steinberg took especially hard. By now, I was getting used to it.

GS: Wasn't the gay press laudatory?

RWAC: I'm not sure there was much gay press then. The only gay writer who ever talked to me about Steve's LP didn't really care for it. It was too soft and romantic for him. The gays who'll listen to this record, he said, are the ones who want true love and long-term relationships, but that side of the life won't interest the other half at all. He wrote a nice, fair piece about the album, though.[22]

---

21 London, who also designed the back cover of Grossman's LP, says, "He was not my neighbor, he was a friend of friends of mine."

22 London says, "Coming from where he came, which was so rigid and judgmental in so many ways, for him to have the attitude that he had, the more I think about it, he was really quite amazing."

GS: David Barretto?

RWAC: In a way, he came on board as a result of Mercury's connection with Shadow Morton, who produced the Dolls' second LP, *Too Much, Too Soon*, and whom everybody at Mercury really liked. Me especially. We made a singles-label deal with him. Shadow was a man who'd seen too many Montgomery Clift, Marlon Brando, and James Dean movies. He was an excellent producer—he taught the Dolls a lot—and an absolute spellbinder with a personal life so secretive and mysterious that it only added to his aura.

GS: Tell us more.

RWAC: I don't know any more. He gave me a David Barretto tape, and I thought that it was very good. When I played it at the next A&R meeting, we decided to do a Barretto album with Shadow producing. It was also very good. I think that Shadow had been listening to a lot of Fats Domino records at the time, since there were at least a couple of Fats's tunes on the LP. All I really remember about it now is that Shadow asked about fifteen rock critics to sing backup on one of the songs.

GS: That sounds like your idea.

RWAC: It wasn't. Though I wouldn't mind taking credit for it.

GS: Did Barretto's album sell?

RWAC: No. He was soon dropped, too.

GS: Reddy Teddy?

RWAC: Jesus, another catastrophe. Their LP didn't even get released. And as produced by Michael Brown—formerly of Left Banke and Stories fame, but, in 1974, a short-term Mercury producer and A&R man—it didn't deserve to. It had taken me about a year to sign Reddy Teddy, a Beantown-based band that wrote and played exciting, intelligent rock & roll. When I took Brown to see the group, I found that he was even less talkative than Charlie. After Reddy Teddy's gig, he said that he kind of liked the band and then just disappeared. I didn't see him again until we were back in New York and Charlie was telling me that Michael would produce the Reddy Teddy record. Fine, I thought. Maybe, because of Brown's name, we'll get a lot of airplay.

GS: But you had some reservations?

RWAC: I did. Brown seemed to me to be on the verge of a nervous breakdown. He didn't look even remotely happy or act the least bit interested. I wondered if he could communicate with the band at all. Later, Ben Gerson,

---

While he doesn't believe it holds up very well today, Stephen Holden wrote "a big incontinent review" of Grossman's album for *Rolling Stone*. "I just thought Paul was extraordinarily brave in getting that through."

"In other words," Robert Christgau says, "at the same time he was chasing the Dolls around, who were fake gays, he found this gay folkie who he thought was poetic. He was very good at conveying his enthusiasm and explaining why he liked it. I would never have reviewed that Steven Grossman album if it wasn't for Paul Nelson. And right, I only gave it a B, but there it is. It's something."

a Boston writer who was an old friend of both Brown and I, filled me in about Michael: the breakdowns, the music-business screwings early on when Brown was only seventeen, the whole sad story.

GS: What happened at the sessions?

RWAC: Well, he couldn't communicate with the band. He turned their rock & roll songs into something that resembled pop-music pablum and made their meanings sound anemic. The group couldn't even play their songs that way, didn't want to, and asked me to talk to Brown after the first session. I did, very delicately and with great respect and courtesy. But Brown was saying even less than usual.

The next day, Charlie called me into his office. He told me that Michael didn't want me at any more sessions. That I was banned from the studio. Okay, I said. I understand that I'm off the project. However unfair and unwise that I think this decision is, I'll cooperate. Please make a note of that. But, Charlie, I'm telling you this right now: Michael Brown doesn't understand a single thing about either Reddy Teddy or their music. He's going to deliver the worst kind of album—one that's neither here nor there, has no reason to exist, and is totally devoid of any personality. Please make a note of that, too.

GS: And the LP was a fiasco?

RWAC: Yes. I didn't really get blamed for it, but my stock wasn't exactly rising within the company. I was sad. I was mad. I felt that the band had been sabotaged, betrayed.

GS: What happened to Michael Brown?

RWAC: I don't know. I never saw him again. I wish that we would have met under different circumstances.

GS: Blue Ash?

RWAC: I've already told you something about them.

GS: A little more, please.

RWAC: They were my first real signing, my first A&R love. I pulled their tape out of the huge slush pile of mail that I had inherited from the A&R man who had preceded me. It was a terrific tape. I played it for Bud, and he was crazy about it, too. You've got to fly out to Youngstown right away, Bud said. This tape's been here for months. So I did. I saw the group live, and they were even better that way. They were the nicest guys. It took about six months to get them signed. Charlie and Steinberg were lukewarm at first, but the fact that Bud and I were so enthusiastic—and that the deal was cheap—finally won them over. We made the record at Peppermint Productions, John Grazier producing. I commuted from New York to Youngstown for about a month. The whole experience was a joy.

As you know, Stan Bly and most of the promotion men hated *No More, No Less* when it came out. For a while, Charlie let me go back to Youngstown to record another song or two for possible singles. I made at least two trips. Then, in Florida, I got the go-ahead for a second album. Three months later, in Chicago, they almost dropped the band and told me that they would handle all future dealings with Blue Ash. About three weeks after that, they sent me to Youngstown to record four more songs. Which they proceeded to dislike intensely. A week after that, I was informed that the group had been dropped. Two weeks after that, Lou called me and said, What's happening with Blue Ash? I was furious.

Jesus Christ, Lou! I yelled. For weeks now, I've been getting killed about Blue Ash. The least you people can do out there is to stay awake while discussing my projects! Don't shoot me down and then forget you even did it! I care enough about my bands to remember what's said about them. Two weeks ago, I was told that Blue Ash had been dropped.

Well, that's not quite right, Lou said. It is, but it isn't. We want you to go back to Youngstown to record two more songs. Have a good time.

Does that mean there'll be a second LP? I asked. We're hitting double figures in songs now, Lou.

It's far too early to decide that, he said. I wouldn't jump to conclusions. Just do it.

There's nothing like paying for an album that we may never put out, is there, Lou?

Nothing like it at all, he said. Nothing at all. Then he laughed out loud. Aren't you glad you're in the record business? he asked. He hung up without waiting for an answer.

I said to myself, There's one rule I should apply about work: Don't get emotionally involved in anything anymore, because it'll break your heart. Despair is the only safe place to be at Mercury.

GS: Naturally, there was no second LP.

RWAC: You already knew that.

GS: Then why all these trips to Youngstown? Why waste all that money if it's not going to add up to a second album?

RWAC: You'll have to ask them. And their memory isn't too good.[23]

GS: The New York Dolls?

RWAC: No. I've said enough about them. I don't really want to relive that whole experience.

GS: You've got to say something.

RWAC: Over the years, I've turned down every interview about the Dolls. I can certainly turn down myself.

---

23 In 2004, Not Lame Recordings issued *Around Again: A Collection of Rarities from the Vault 1972–1979*, a two-CD set containing many tracks from the second LP's recording sessions. Secich tracked Paul down at Evergreen and gave him the good news. "There's this big silence, about five, ten seconds of silence. Paul goes, 'I guess that proves we were right after all.'"

GS: No, you can't.

RWAC: All right. Saw them. Loved them. Make that, really loved them. Tried forever to sign them. Charlie turned them down first. Lou turned them down second. Steinberg and Charlie turned them down third, after seeing them open for Rod Stewart in England. Steinberg said that they were so bad that he'd fire me if I ever mentioned them again. Robin nixed them. Denny Rosencrantz begged Steinberg to let him fly in to see them. Steinberg refused, said the Dolls were a joke. Gormley, in New York on other business, saw them and told Steinberg yes, then soon amended that to maybe, maybe not.

The Dolls' American and international press clippings now form a stack two feet high. John Rockwell of *The New York Times* loves them and makes it public. So do the Los Angeles papers. And the band still doesn't have a record deal. "2-2-73. Lunch with Danny Goldberg. He likes the group." Top music-biz execs seem to find the Dolls both threatening and amateurish. They're definitely not threatening, and they're professional enough to amass a set of press clippings two feet high.

I hear that Steinberg is in New York. I sit in the lobby of his hotel from six in the morning until he comes down for breakfast. He is surprised to see me. Says, "What are you doing here? I ask him to reopen the Dolls case, not knowing whether he's going to fire me or not. I talk to him for a long time. He listens, either dumbstruck by the fool he's hired or somewhat impressed by the fool's argument and persistence. I have seen the Dolls play nearly 200 times, I tell him. I don't go see bad bands that often. They have an international reputation. They've toured Europe twice. Their pile of press clippings is taller than a three-year-old child. What more do you want? They would like to make an album soon, and their price has come way down. We could sign them for about $25,000, I think. One of the reasons that they would sign with Mercury is that I have seen them play nearly 200 times, and they admire loyalty. Their records would sell. Steinberg agrees to reopen the case. He does not fire me. Mercury signs the Dolls. Soon, I am the hero of Boca Raton.

The Dolls make a fine record. It is produced by Todd Rundgren, who is not exactly Mr. Warmth. He is the last to arrive, the first to leave the studio. I don't even know if he likes the Dolls. Mercury asks one of the Dolls' managers, Marty Thau, and lead singer David Johansen to fly to Chicago for a crack-of-dawn meeting in which all of the company's plans will be exposed. David, who has been up all night so as not to miss the flight, falls asleep five minutes into Lou Simon's opening remarks. His head rests soundly on the boardroom table. Steinberg, to his credit, manages a laugh. Marty, who is sort of the Jay Gatsby in the saga of the New York Dolls—he came, he saw, he won for a while and then lost everything he had—gives me a wink. I smile uneasily.

New York Dolls is released and sells 110,000 copies. That is very good for a first album.[24] The Dolls are on national TV shows, performing live. The Dolls start to spend money. The Dolls continue to spend money. It is Mercury's money. Marty says, "Peanuts for a group like this." Is he right? I don't know. My own private Vietnam starts. The battles are fought in Chicago and New York. And I am the poor grunt in the middle, drawing fire from the generals of both sides. Though most of the heavy artillery and all of the napalm come from Mercury. Whose side are you on? snaps Steinberg. I have friends in both camps, I answer. I am trying to make peace and create order. The Dolls themselves remain loyal. The war goes on and on.

The Dolls make *Too Much, Too Soon*, another fine album. It is produced by Shadow Morton. It sells about 85,000 copies. Marty says that this is a result of the expected backlash from all that publicity. Is he right? I don't know. Mercury begins to worry. More money problems. Vietnam II starts. It is even bloodier than Vietnam I. It goes on and on. The center won't hold. Things fall apart. Two of the Dolls, lead guitarist Johnny Thunder (or Thunders, depending on which day you ask him) and drummer Jerry Nolan, invest in heroin habits. After a while, they refuse to tour because leaving New York will take them away from their connection. No tour, no money. Johnny and Jerry can no longer play as well as they once did. Heartbroken, the rest of the group decides to let them go. The New York Dolls, although they stumble on for a short time after this termination, are done. David forms a new band and lands a deal with another record company. Sylvain Sylvain, the Dolls' rhythm guitarist, does the same thing. I don't know what happens to bassist Arthur Kane.[25] Years later, David becomes Buster Poindexter, and there is another record deal. He makes a few movies that no one remembers. Years and years later, Johnny and Jerry die drug-related deaths.

There. Are you satisfied now? Can you figure out why I didn't want to talk about the Dolls at any great length? Why I don't want to play their records?

GS: I'm sorry. But it was necessary for this piece.

RWAC: Said the spider to the fly.

GS: Let's talk about some of the artists that you tried to sign but couldn't. The ones for which Mercury was outbid or just didn't like.

---

24 Paul arranged for Tony Glover, who'd attended many of the LP's recording sessions, to review it in *Rolling Stone*. "The whole rock scene at that point was groups like Yes and ELO and all that art-rock shit, twenty-five-minute cantatas. It was pretty deadly dull. There wasn't much energy or any raunch to it. It was all kind of intellectual psychedelic haze crap. They were like a breath of fresh air. It was like a garage band in New York City."

25 *New York Doll*, a 2005 documentary by Greg Whiteley, tells how Arthur "Killer" Kane moved to Los Angeles and, after surviving a fall out of a second-floor kitchen window, became a Mormon. In 2004, he realized his dream of reuniting with Johansen and Sylvain as the Dolls. Just weeks after their reunion concert, Kane, thinking he had the flu, went to the emergency room, where he was diagnosed with leukemia. He died two hours later.

RWAC: You're really on a roll here, aren't you? Sure, I'd love to talk about some more of my failures. Since when did you become so sadistic?

GS: The same time that you decided to act like such a baby about this.

RWAC: You've been taking lessons from the Other. But here's your answer. The main ones were Richard Thompson (about whom I'm not going to say another word), Novella Nelson, Elliott Murphy, David Forman, and Jonathan Richman and the Modern Lovers. Nelson was a brilliant cabaret singer every night except the night I took Charlie to see her. End of story. She never made a record. David Forman is one of my favorite artists, but the company wasn't interested. He eventually signed with Arista. But one of my Mercury demo tapes—I forget which song—ended up on his Arista album. Naturally, I have no idea how it got there.[26]

Mercury bid $5,000 for Elliott Murphy, another favorite, but Polydor bid $7,500. Take the $2,500 difference out of my paychecks in weekly installments for a year and match Polydor's offer, I told Charlie. Elliott likes me, and if we give him the money, he'll sign with us. Charlie probably thought I was nuts, but I was dead serious. He rejected my plea.[27] Jonathan Richman and the Modern Lovers were one of the great bands of the Seventies. Like the Dolls, they were thought to be amateurish. In Richman's case, it was just innocence more than it was amateurism. He was either an awkward Fabian with brains or a very youthful Lou Reed still gawking around the girls at the high school prom. His song cycle about unrequited young love and a nerd's romance with the modern world was truly a heart crusher. Many of these songs were never released.[28]

I might add that, over twenty years later, Thompson, Murphy, and Richman are still making records. They each have at least a dozen albums to their credit.[29]

GS: Would I be correct in assuming that your last year and a half at Mercury was neither a rewarding nor a particularly happy time?

RWAC: Absolutely. Whatever small power I'd once had was gone. I made a gallant effort to sign David Forman and a good try for a singer-songwriter

---

26 Paul is referring to "Dream of a Child," but, according to Forman, the admittedly superior demo did not find its way onto the album.

27 "In retrospect," Paul said, "it was a dumb thing to do. But if you're not going to do it with some sense of pride—go after what you really like—why do it at all?" Murphy didn't learn of Paul's proposal to Fach until almost thirty-four years later.

28 Asked about Paul today, Richman says, "All I remember is that he was very nice."

29 It's important to note that a good many of the artists whose work Paul championed, as critic or A&R man—including Bob Dylan, Elliott Murphy, Leonard Cohen, Jackson Browne, Neil Young, Rod Stewart, Ian Hunter, Bruce Springsteen, Greg Copeland, Graham Parker, Lou Reed, and Andy Zwerling—are still writing, recording, and performing. Frank Secich and Blue Ash reunited in 2003; since 2007, he and his new band, the Deadbeat Poets, have released two albums.

In 2006, three weeks after Paul's body was discovered, the New York Dolls (with only David Johansen and Sylvain Sylvain surviving the original lineup) released their third studio album, *One Day It Will Please Us to Remember Even This*. A fourth studio album, *'Cause I Sez So*, arrived in 2009 with with Todd Rundgren returning as producer. A fifth album, *Dancing Backward in High Heels*, was released in 2011.

named Tom Pacheco, who wound up with RCA.[30] There were probably a few more, but I've forgotten. During my last year there, I don't think I could have signed the Beatles, the Rolling Stones, and Bob Dylan if they'd all walked in together and said, We're forming a supergroup and we want to be on Mercury. Robin and several others in the company would have had to check them out first.

GS: I take it you were fired.

RWAC: Yes. And it came as somewhat of a relief.[31] Mercury was a record company in which music was a foreign language, incomprehensible but necessary to put bread on the table. I doubt if there were more than three or four people in the entire company who ever took a record home to listen to for pleasure. A lot of artists knew it, felt it. Small wonder that most of them preferred Columbia, Warner Bros., Atlantic, other labels. I know I would have. Those companies were run by men who had the knowledge, ability, understanding, loyalty, and patience to stick with such artists as Randy Newman, Ry Cooder, Leonard Cohen, to name just a few. How long would any of them have lasted at Mercury, provided we would have signed them in the first place?[32]

GS: All that is pure speculation. The grass is always greener, you know.

RWAC: It may be hypothetical, but I think it's true. Columbia had an A&R man, John Hammond, who'd earned respect by signing great artists since the Thirties. In the Sixties, he signed Bob Dylan. In the Seventies, Bruce Springsteen took his tape to Hammond first, because Hammond *had* signed Bob Dylan. At the time, both Dylan and Springsteen were courageous signings, extreme long shots who have since become legends.

GS: I get the point, and it's effective in a rock-writerly way. John Hammond was always your A&R hero, wasn't he?

RWAC: Senator, I knew John Hammond, and, believe me, I was no John Hammond. I think my record—or records—will bear me out there. Yes, he

---

30 Though Pacheco didn't meet Paul until 1974, he'd known of him since high school when he regularly read *The Little Sandy Review*. Throughout the Seventies, Paul was a frequent fixture at Pacheco's apartment on MacDougal Street in the Village. "I'd hear the doorbell ring at two in the morning and I knew it would be Paul.

"He was really the first critic that really loved my stuff, who was behind me and encouraged me. I was at a point where I was thinking, Ah, I think I should get out of this business. I'm just barely hanging on all the time, doing odd jobs here and odd jobs there."

Paul couldn't convince Charlie Fach to sign the singer-songwriter, so he put him in touch with Stephen Holden at RCA, who did. To date, Pacheco has released well over a dozen albums.

31 Charlie Fach didn't think that the Dolls' lack of success had anything to do with Paul's departure: "I hope he didn't have that impression. We gave them a great shot. Not every act you sign makes it." Mike Gormley says: "They eventually couldn't figure out what the hell he was talking about. I suppose somebody made some sort of genius decision that what Paul did for A&R was not what they were looking for. That's an educated guess. No one ever told me why." Irwin Steinberg says he doesn't remember.

32 Betsy Volck: "The artists loved him and he'd want to sign these groups, but he was savvy enough to know that he wouldn't do the artist a tremendous favor by signing them."

was my A&R hero. Lots of artists felt that way about him, too. Artists are often very romantic people, Senator. They like to be with record companies whose leaders speak their language.[33]

GS: Any last thoughts or memories—some of them favorable, I hope— about the label you love to hate? Or hate to love?

RWAC: I'm just telling you my story, Senator. I don't think that I've exaggerated too much. But it all happened over twenty years ago. We were all so much older then. We're younger than that now. If you talked to fifteen people who were at Mercury then, you'd probably get fifteen different versions of the truth. It's all *Rashomon*, you know.

I remember Rod, a couple of the Faces, and me kicking around a soccer ball on a parking lot somewhere in Virginia. Some kid gave Rod a football. Rod waved all of us back about fifty yards. He'll never kick it that far, I thought. Well, he kicked it so high and so far that it must have gone at least seventy yards. And had a hang time of close to ten seconds.

I remember meeting Muhammad Ali. I was sitting on the front steps of a Chicago hotel at 5:30 in the morning. I'd just gotten back from seeing two Wilderness Road sets with Ron, and there was a Mercury meeting starting in an hour and a half. No need to go to bed, I thought. I'll get plenty of sleep once the meeting starts. And down the street, here comes Muhammad Ali, getting in his morning run for the first Joe Frazier fight, I believe. Other than us, there seemed to be no one else awake in Chicago. He saw me, stopped, and we talked a while, just two guys sitting on some steps at dawn. Ali's always been another of my heroes.

I remember some of the goofy people who brought tapes to my office. One kid simply jammed a Rolling Stones cassette into his boom box and shouted out the songs with Mick Jagger. Another didn't even bother with a tape. He just yelled his lyrics at me without accompaniment. A man in his fifties told me that he was going to be the next big thing. He'd sold his restaurant in Brooklyn to finance his album, which he then played for me. It was schmaltzy Italian love songs and standards. Tenth-rate Dean Martin. "Don't you ever listen to the radio?" I asked him. "Yes," he answered, "I certainly do. That's why I know that all the DJs will be dying to play my record. There's nothing even remotely like it on the radio these days. Right now, everybody's playing crap, and it's so popular that nobody wants to hear it anymore." Now that's a

---

33 In 1979, John Hammond convened a commission designed to update, for the Jimmy Carter administration, the official White House Record Library. Boston music critic Bob Blumenthal's charge was to select 200 rock LPs for the Contemporary Popular section. Among his advisors were Paul. "Paul was my editor in the review section of *Rolling Stone* at the time, and he (like my other friends on the list) kept me from making any selections that were too embarrassing." As a result of their efforts, the collection includes the likes of the Ramones' *Rocket to Russia*, *Never Mind the Bollocks, Here's the Sex Pistols*, and *Trout Mask Replica* by Captain Beefheart.

remark worthy of a Samuel Goldwyn or a Yogi Berra, I thought to myself. "Include me out," I told him, borrowing a choice Goldwynism that I felt sure he'd understand.

I remember all of my artists fondly. And some of the people at Mercury: Ron, Bud, Betsy Volck, who took over in publicity when Bud left for A&M. She and I became very close. And Denny, Charlie, and Lou, when he wasn't being an asshole. Somehow Lou and I seemed to share an unspoken something. Look, his eyes kept telling me, I know you're right about Mercury. That it's all a stupid sham. But I'm in on the joke, and you could be, too. Take the money·and laugh. It's the only sensible, humane solution.[34]

I remember Jerry Kennedy at Boca Raton and his "the Dolls sure can pick" exclamation when I played "Personality Crisis" for the whole company. Every fifteen minutes, he'd come up to me and say, "God, that was good!" Such enthusiasm was unheard of at Mercury.

I don't remember who gave me this advice about A&R, but it was probably Robin or Lou, whose nickname was the Animal: All you have to do to keep your job as an A&R man is to say no to everything. Don't ever sign anyone. That way, you won't make any mistakes. But I felt totally the opposite. I always wanted to do something. Otherwise, why be there?

"3-2-73. We finished the Blue Ash album at 5:19 this morning, and Frank Secich [the band's bassist], who ended it symbolically by smashing an $8 guitar against a cinder block, summed up the moment nicely: 'Eight grown men standing around at dawn, staring at wooden shards and an overgrown brick.' And it was strange. The cinder block, standing stolidly on the floor like an inert rock star amidst four microphones, looked like a *2001* monolith. The morning ritual had some sort of tribal magic. We felt that we had all sacrificed something valuable for something even better. Before I left, Frank came up to me and said shyly, 'Thank you for having us on Mercury.'"

And this undated, unedited, incomplete note about the Dolls: "Although they tottered and lurched about on platform shoes like a ragtag band of young Frankensteins thrashing wildly and comically at their instruments, they were never threatening, always inviting, and filled with Chaplinesque good humor and spunk. They were a traveling Fellini movie. You had the feeling that whatever was happening onstage was happening for the very first time, and that it wasn't merely new but probably important and positively addicting. Once heard and seen and understood, they drew you back again and again, and you came away with the thought that there was no finer music and entertainment anywhere else that night in the whole world. They only knew about twenty-five songs, all of which became precious

---

34 Lou Simon passed away in 2006.

to any true Dolls fan. They always believed that kids all over America would em"

GS: What's "em"? The note ends with an incomplete word and no period?

RWAC: Lots of things end that way, Senator.

GS: Not this article, I hope. Any last words?

RWAC: Do you want to take this full circle? All the way back to the beginning?

GS: Sure.

RWAC: Marty Thau called me the other night. Talk naturally got around to the Dolls. He told me that some twenty-year-old kid had given him his first tip about the band. Know who that kid was? I didn't.

GS: No.

RWAC: Danny Goldberg.

GS: Let's stop here.

RWAC: The show is over. Go home.

Publicity photo commemorating signing the New York Dolls to Mercury, March 1973. Left to right: Jerry Nolan, Arthur Kane, Johnny Thunders, Irwin Steinberg, Sylvain Sylvain, Paul Nelson, Marty Thau, Steve Leber, and David Johansen.

- AFTERWORD -

We were all guilty. We had to learn to live with it.
—ROSS MACDONALD,
The Doomsters

Back in 1976, Paul confided in Kenneth Millar: "There was one thing that I did do that I was, I think, pretty totally guilty of—and it's certainly the worst thing I've done in my life—and that was leave a wife and child for someone else. I went straight to a psychiatrist for years, who kept telling me it wasn't my fault, that this is the way it is, and it takes two sides and all that, and I kept saying yes and no. 'You're taking something away from me that you cannot take away from me. It isn't my fault that we grew apart, but it *is* my fault that I left. My wife and child were innocent. There was no way you could make them co-conspirators in this. I will not relinquish that guilt.'

"Looking back, I wouldn't do it differently. It's the only time in my life, I think, where I have deliberately done something that I knew would—not kill somebody—but really possibly destroy somebody or maim them a great deal psychologically. And I still did it."

What other things had Paul done for which he could not forgive himself? As Mikal Gilmore noted about Paul's romantic travails, this kind of stuff accrues.

Millar told Paul, "Well, of course, the thing is not to maim yourself and not to over-suffer over something like that. We have to learn to recognize that we've done wrong and then be able to turn our back on it. Not be trapped by it. Because, God knows, we all do wrong all the time without wanting to."

When Teddy Roosevelt claimed loneliness a quintessential ingredient of our national character, he hit the psychic bull's-eye, ringing up images of pragmatic pioneers, existential outlaws, and a long line of heroes who dreamt of the purity of their youth even as they drew their guns to eliminate it. "There are no second acts in American lives," someone once said, and a cursory glance at our gods—the cowboy/desperado, the gangster/detective, the movie star/rock & roller—whose lifestyles generally suggest either early and unnatural death or obsolescence, easily reinforces such a statement. To the quiet American, violence, like the perpetual but unreal motion of life on the road, seems to serve as solicitous coin in the realm of the solitary survivor, some kind of necessary stopgap and occupation while a man waits in the sanctified state of loneliness for something to happen, someone to come along or return, his vague search to end.

From Pat Garrett and Billy the Kid to Dirty Harry Callahan, the mythic American hero is a man, almost always womanless, who has somehow been trapped in that curious nether world between comic innocence and tragic experience; unable or unwilling to make a choice, he can at best (or worst) embrace either adjective, neither noun. He has known happiness once, lost it, and now nothing will help. For the sentimental there is Christianity, the "official" solace, itself an uncanny mixture of loneliness and violence, sexlessness and death, its hero a lost and forsaken son slain only to rise again with the promise of a glorious but distant new childhood in exchange for a worn-out, hopeless past. It is small wonder that most Americans worship no god except their own lost innocence, have had in fact to rely on popular literature, films, and music to provide a plausible and workable archetypal "religion," more Jungian than

Freudian, based on the sub-art of genres rather than the more civilized high art of England and Europe.

—PAUL NELSON°

"I was surprised at how bad things had become," Mikal Gilmore says, "that there were certain basic needs and functions around him that he didn't have. That surprised me. But his aloneness, or what others might describe as his curmudgeonly behavior, that did not surprise me."

"There's a certain crossover point where your own aloneness settles in and you hoard it," Paul told Warren Zevon, "it becomes your most valuable possession."

"The thing that always struck me," Steve Feltes says, "was that Paul was ready to sacrifice anything to be able to live the way he wanted to live. So I think he accepted the loneliness as the price he had to pay. I mean, look at the streak of loneliness that runs through the film noir films—the myth of the outsider that I think Paul bought into, that that was all part of it. I don't know if 'happy to pay the price' is the right phrase—but he was willing."

Paul said, "I remember there was this movie *Not as a Stranger* with Mitchum. Somebody told him, 'Stop living your life like a Greek tragedy,' and I thought, Jesus, that's exactly it. I've always led my life like it was a work of art and I was in it. And I still do, I guess, but I'm sort of afraid it will run out into an Antonioni stroll for twenty years, which would bore even me."

In the summer of 2007, filmmaker Jason Ruscio returned to New York. His short, *Eclipse*, had done very well. "That's when I moved to L.A. It opened many, many doors, which quickly closed." He and Petra Wright, his wife and the star of his feature film *Laura Smiles*, were in town for the press screening of the movie. They came down to Carmine Street to invite Paul, but Evergreen was no longer there. A sign in the window read:

Paul Nelson
1936–2006

Wright spotted it first and tried to turn Ruscio away, but not before he saw it, too. At first he tried to convince himself it was only a phone number, but then the truth sank in and he ran into a nearby bar. Ruscio was drunk that night when he dedicated the screening to Paul Nelson.

Evergreen Video, June 2007, almost one year after Paul's death. At the end of the month, Steve Feltes closed down the shop and moved back to Minnesota. Photo by Kevin Avery.

Bob Dylan didn't attend Paul Nelson's memorial service, but his presence was felt. That same week, his *Modern Times* (also the name of Paul's never realized pop-culture column) had reached the top of the charts—his first number-one album in thirty years.

Jonathan Lethem interviewed him the month after Paul died. "I mentioned Paul and Dylan acknowledged the memory. He didn't expand on it at all. It didn't make Dylan suddenly want to tell me all about it, for whatever reason, but he was obviously saddened by what he'd heard."

Mikal Gilmore attended a Dylan concert with Paul in 1988 at Jones Beach. "This was during Dylan's low-radar time, when he was playing with that misbegotten G.E. Smith lineup. The electric music that night seemed rushed, haphazard, almost as if Dylan was alienated from it. But when he got to his section of acoustic performances, he was suddenly magic. These songs—not all written by him—were clearly where he invested his heart and soul that night; spectral singing, unmeasurable longing.

"Paul and I later wondered why Dylan didn't simply do an album in this mode, which he later did with *Good As I Been to You* and *World Gone Wrong*. It was clear something was going on during those performances that night that wasn't happening elsewhere in the live show. Maybe it was simply that standing alone, Dylan could rely on his strengths, trust his heart.

"I think that sometimes artists are the best persons they can be in the art that they make—it's where they realize a potential that they can't or don't live elsewhere. I certainly wouldn't presume to say that was altogether true of Paul, though I would say, on the level of a friendship, he may well have been the purest artist I've known. I think about Paul fairly often these days, and about how deepfelt his writing was. Maybe, like Dylan, it was in those moments and places that Paul was best able to find his heart and express it unflinchingly. I can only wonder where all that went after he stopped writing."

In August of 2007, Mark Nelson traveled to Warren to celebrate his mother's seventieth birthday, a bittersweet celebration. It was Paul's final trip to Minnesota. His cremains were laid to rest in the family plot in a personal service attended only by Mark and Doris.

Because people just didn't get divorced in Warren, he would have understood why, when Doris passed away less than two years later, her obituary made no mention of anybody named Paul Nelson.

- ACKNOWLEDGMENTS -

This book never would have been possible without the encouragement and assistance of a great many people, first and foremost my wife and most beautiful editor Deborah Avery.

Mark Nelson kindly included me in his own discovery of his father and granted me access to all of Paul's papers, recordings, and photographs.

Thanks to Michael Seidenberg for making that call.

Mitch Blank, Verna Bloom, Robert Christgau, Jay Cocks, Steve Feltes, David Gahr (1922–2008), Danny Goldberg, George Gruel, Clinton Heylin, William MacAdams, Elliott Murphy, Kit Rachlis, Jeff Rosen, Gerald Rothberg, Ralph Sipper, Marty Thau, Richie Unterberger, Steven Ward, Lawrence White, Scott Woods, and Crystal Zevon all offered valuable insights, materials, permissions, and support.

Thank you, Jann Wenner.

Tony Glover and Neil Strauss both know what they did.

In addition to contributing the cover illustration that graces this book and designing the layout within, Jeff Wong became a good friend and confidant.

In sharing their memories of Paul Nelson, the following individuals consented to interviews and in many cases suffered my follow-up calls and e-mails: David Aaron, Billy Altman, Linda Nelson Barna, Susan Blond, Phillip

Blumberg, David Breithaupt, Jackson Browne, Tom Carson, Debra Rae Cohen, Chris Connelly, Greg Copeland, Anthony DeCurtis, Charlie Fach (1928–2011), Jim Farber, Paula Farmer, Danny Fields, Laura Fissinger, Bill Flanagan, Steve Forbert, David Forman, Myra Friedman (1932–2010), Deborah Frost, Mikal Gilmore, Mike Gormley, Barret Hansen, Jim Henke, Peter Herbst, Stephen Holden, Jac Holzman, Doris Hoper (1937–2009), Bruce Hornsby, Freedy Johnston, George Kalogerakis, Jon Landau, Kim Lankford, Andrew Leigh, Warren Leming, Jonathan Lethem, Dave Lightbourne (1942–2010), Kurt Loder, Barbara "Bobbi" London, Greil Marcus, Dave Marsh, Iain Matthews, Robin McBride, Terry McDonell, David McGee, Richard Meltzer, Jaime Rivman Mitsch, Karen Moline, John Morthland, Susan Murcko, Novella Nelson, Willie Nile, Tom Nolan, Ron Oberman, Tom Pacheco, Jon Pankake, Rob Patterson, Parke Puterbaugh, John Rockwell, Nicky Roe, Denny Rosencrantz, Jason Ruscio, Andrew Sarris, Paul Scanlon, Fred Schruers, Bud Scoppa, Frank Secich, Mike Seeger (1933–2009), Bruce Springsteen, Irwin Steinberg, Rod Stewart, Wesley Strick, Ariel Swartley, Nick Tosches, Ken Tucker, Suzanne Vega, Betsy Volck, Ed Ward, Paul Williams, Charles M. Young, and Andy Zwerling.

Thank you also Bob Blumenthal, Peter Bogdanovich, David Browne, Tim Cahill, Ronald Cohen, PhD, Norman J. Colavincenzo, Jim DeRogatis, Marc Furstenberg, Michael Goldberg, Barney Hoskyns, Maria LaCalle, Sarah Lazin, Julius Lester, Joe Levy, Stephen E. MacLeod, James Mastro, Daisann McLane, Ryan McWilliams, Leith Merrow, Martha Millard, Jim Miller, George Nadara, Laura Peters, Lucy Pfeffa, Jonathan Richman, Howard Roseman, Stephen Scholz, John David Souther, Phyllis Stein, Jack Tempchin, and Heidi Timm.

A nod to Michael Murphy for suggesting the title.

Lastly, on the publishing front, thanks to Adam Parfrey for seeing the potential in this project and to Gary Groth for making it happen.

- SOURCES & CITED WORKS -

Archer, Ian, and Trevor Royle. *We'll Support You Evermore*. 1976. Souvenir Press.

Banks, Homer, and Carl Hampton and Raymond Jackson. "(If Loving You Is Wrong) I Don't Want to Be Right," © 1972 Irving Music, Inc. (BMI).

Big Knife, The. Directed by Robert Aldrich. Adapted for the screen by James Poe (based on the play by Clifford Odets). 1955. United Artists.

Bowen, Jeffrey, and Truman Thomas. "Ah Shoot," © 1978 Stone Diamond Music Corporation (BMI).

Browne, Clyde. "Dear Jackson," © 1953 Clyde Browne.

Browne, Jackson. "Farther On," © 1974 Swallow Turn Music (ASCAP); "For Everyman," © 1973 Swallow Turn Music (ASCAP); "The Late Show," © 1974 Swallow Turn Music (ASCAP); "Linda Paloma," © 1976 Swallow Turn Music (ASCAP); "The Pretender," © 1976 Swallow Turn Music (ASCAP); "Ready or Not," © 1973 Swallow Turn Music (ASCAP); "Sleep's Dark and Silent Gate," © 1976 Swallow Turn Music (ASCAP).

Cohen, Leonard. "Hey That's Not the Way to Say Goodbye," © 1967 Sony/ATV Songs LLC (BMI); "Joan of Arc," © 1971 Sony/ATV Songs LLC (BMI); "Suzanne," © 1967 Sony/ATV Songs LLC (BMI).

Cohen, Leonard, and Phil Spector. "Death of a Ladies' Man," © 1977 ABKCO Music, Inc./Mother Bertha Music, Inc., and Sony/ATV Songs LLC (BMI); "I Left a Woman Waiting," © 1977 ABKCO Music, Inc./Mother Bertha Music, Inc., and Sony/ATV Songs LLC (BMI); "Paper-Thin Hotel," © 1977 ABKCO Music, Inc./Mother Bertha Music, Inc., and Sony/ATV Songs LLC (BMI).

DeRogatis, Jim. "A Conversation with Paul Nelson, April 21, 1997." RockCritics.com. August 2006.

De Vries, Peter. *Consenting Adults; or, The Duchess Will Be Furious*. 1980. Little, Brown and Company.

Drieu La Rochelle, Pierre Eugène. *The Fire Within*. 1965. Alfred A. Knopf.

461

Dylan, Bob. June 1964. Letter.
Dylan, Bob. "Ballad of a Thin Man," © 1965 by Warner Bros. Inc., renewed 1993 by Special Rider Music; "Desolation Row," © 1965 by Warner Bros. Inc., renewed 1993 by Special Rider Music; "It Takes a Lot to Laugh, It Takes a Train to Cry," © 1965 by Warner Bros. Inc., renewed 1993 by Special Rider Music; "Just Like a Woman," © 1966 by Dwarf Music, renewed 1994 by Dwarf Music; "Knockin' on Heaven's Door," © 1973 by Ram's Horn Music, renewed 2001 by Ram's Horn Music; "Like a Rolling Stone," © 1965 by Warner Bros. Inc., renewed 1993 by Special Rider Music; "Sara," © 1975, 1976 by Ram's Horn Music, renewed 2003, 2004 by Ram's Horn Music; "Tombstone Blues," © 1965 by Warner Bros. Inc., renewed 1993 by Special Rider Music; "Under the Red Sky," © 1990 by Special Rider Music; "Wiggle Wiggle," © 1990 by Special Rider Music; "You're a Big Girl Now," © 1974 by Ram's Horn Music, renewed 2002 by Ram's Horn Music.
Dylan, Bob, and Jacques Levy. "Oh, Sister," © 1975 by Ram's Horn Music, renewed 2003 by Ram's Horn Music.
Eliot, T.S. *Four Quartets*. 1943. Harcourt, Brace & Company.
Fitzgerald, F. Scott. *The Great Gatsby*. 1925. Charles Scribner's Sons.
Forbert, Steve. "Goin' Down to Laurel," © 1978 Welk Music (ASCAP); "It Isn't Gonna Be That Way," © 1978 Welk Music (ASCAP); "Steve Forbert's Midsummer Night's Toast," © 1978 Welk Music (ASCAP); "Thinkin'," © 1978 Welk Music (ASCAP); "What Kinda Guy?" © 1978 Colgems EMI Music, Inc./Welk Music (ASCAP).
Forman, David. "Dream of a Child," © 1976 Fool's Music, Inc. (ASCAP).
Ginsberg, Allen. Liner notes. 1975. *Desire*, Bob Dylan. Columbia.
Hammett, Dashiell. *The Dain Curse*. 1929. Alfred A. Knopf.
Herr, Michael. *Dispatches*. 1977. Alfred A. Knopf.
Heylin, Clinton. Interview with Paul Nelson. 1999.
Hunter, Ian. "Bastard," © 1979 EMI April Music, Inc./Ian Hunter Music, Inc. (ASCAP); "The Outsider," © 1979 EMI April Music, Inc./Ian Hunter Music, Inc. (ASCAP); "Ships," © 1979 EMI April Music, Inc./Ian Hunter Music, Inc. (ASCAP); "Standin' in My Light," © 1979 EMI April Music, Inc./Ian Hunter Music, Inc. (ASCAP); "When the Daylight Comes," © 1979 EMI April Music, Inc./Ian Hunter Music, Inc. (ASCAP).
Hunter, Ian, and Mick Ronson. "Just Another Night," © 1979 Colgems EMI Music, Inc./ EMI April Music, Inc./Ian Hunter Music, Inc./Hyde Park Gate Music, Inc. (ASCAP).
Jewish Week, The. September 7, 1988. Letter.
Johansen, David. "Donna," © 1978 Buster Poindexter, Inc. (BMI); "Lonely Tenement," © 1978 Buster Poindexter, Inc. (BMI); "Looking for a Kiss," © 1973 Seldak LLC/WB Music Corp. (ASCAP); "Pain in My Heart," © 1978 Buster Poindexter, Inc. (BMI).
Johansen, David, and Buz Verno. "Not that Much," © 1978 Buster Poindexter, Inc. (BMI).
Johansen, David, and Sylvain Sylvain. "Cool Metro," © 1978 Buster Poindexter, Inc./Subway Rhythm Publishing Music (BMI); "Frenchette," © 1978 Buster Poindexter, Inc./Subway Rhythm Publishing Music (BMI).
Joyce, James. *Selected Letters*. 1975. Faber & Faber.
Kerouac, Jack. *Visions of Cody*. 1973. New Directions.
Macdonald, Ross. *The Doomsters*, 1958, Alfred A. Knopf, Inc.; *The Moving Target*, 1949, Alfred A. Knopf, Inc.; *The Zebra-Striped Hearse*, 1962, Alfred A. Knopf, Inc. Used by permission. Courtesy of the Trustee of the Margaret Millar Charitable Trust and Special Collections and Archives, University of California, Irvine Libraries, Kenneth Millar Papers.
Mailer, Norman. "Rainy Afternoon with the Wife," 1962, from *Deaths for the Ladies (and other disasters)*, Putnam's.
Marcus, Greil. 1975, "An Album of Wounds." *City*. February 5–18; *Psychotic Reactions and Carburetor Dung*, 1987, Anchor Press.

SOURCES & CITED WORKS

Marsh, Dave. 1973. "New York New Wave." *Melody Maker*. October 6.

McDaniel, Elias. "Who Do You Love," © 1956 Arc Music (BMI).

Murphy, Elliott James. "Anastasia," © 1977 Chappell-Co., Inc./Seldak LLC (ASCAP); "Bittersweet," © 1975 Warner-Chappell Music/Elliott Murphy Music; "Deco Dance," © 1975 Warner-Chappell Music/Elliott Murphy Music; "Don't Go Away," © 1973 Eljamur Music/Warner-Tamerlane Publishing Corp (BMI); "Eva Braun," © 1975 Warner-Chappell Music/Elliott Murphy Music; "Graveyard Scrapbook," © 1973 Eljamur Music/Warner-Tamerlane Publishing Corp (BMI); "History," © 1975 Warner-Chappell Music/Elliott Murphy Music; "Hollywood," © 1975 Warner-Chappell Music/Elliott Murphy Music; "Hometown." © 1973 Eljamur Music/Warner-Tamerlane Publishing Corp (BMI); "How's the Family," © 1973 Eljamur Music/Warner-Tamerlane Publishing Corp (BMI); "Like a Great Gatsby," © 1973 Eljamur Music/Warner-Tamerlane Publishing Corp (BMI); "Lookin' Back," © 1975 Warner-Chappell Music/Elliott Murphy Music; "Manhattan Rock," © 1975 Warner-Chappell Music/Elliott Murphy Music; "A Touch of Mercy," © 1975 Warner-Chappell Music/Elliott Murphy Music.

Nelson, Mark C. "Shoes." 2006. Previously unpublished.

Nelson, Paul. Interviews with Verna Bloom, 1979; Jackson Browne, 1976 and 1980; Bob Buziak, 1991; Jay Cocks, 1979; Leonard Cohen, 1991; Jude Cole, 1992; Greg Copeland, 1982; Jim Cregan, 1977; Ray Davies, 1977; Robert Easton, 1976; Clint Eastwood, 1979, 1980, and 1983; Don Everly, 1968; Phil Everly, 1968; William Campbell Gault, 1976; Dennis Hackin, 1979; Mark Hammerman, 1976; Herbert Harker, 1976; Bruce Hornsby, 1990; Ian Hunter, 1979; Garland Jeffreys, 1977; Jon Landau, 1978; Kim Lankford, 1979; David Lindley, 1976; Sondra Locke, 1979, 1980, and 1983; Fritz Manes, 1979; Margaret Millar, 1976; Larry Moskowitz, 1976; Herb Pedersen, 1976; Arthur Penn, 1969; Keith Richards, 1977; Don Siegel, 1983; Carol Sipper, 1976; Ralph Sipper, 1976; Rod Stewart, 1977; Lynne Sweeney, 1980; Townes Van Zandt, circa 1977; Suzanne Vega, 1980; Lucinda Williams, 1991; Noel Young, 1976; Crystal Zevon, 1976 and 1980; and Warren Zevon, 1976, 1979, and 1980.

Nelson, Paul. Interview with Kenneth Millar. Used by permission. Courtesy of the Trustee of the Margaret Millar Charitable Trust and Special Collections and Archives, University of California, Irvine Libraries, Kenneth Millar Papers. 1976.

Nelson, Paul. 1981. "The Politics of Sin." *Rolling Stone*. October 15.

Nelson, Paul, and Lester Bangs. *Rod Stewart*. Delilah Books. 1981.

Nolan, Tom. *Ross Macdonald: A Biography*, 1999. Scribner

Pareles, Jon. 2006. "Paul Nelson, Critic Who Spanned Folk and Rock, Dies at 69." *The New York Times*. July 13.

Reuss, Richard A. *Folk Scene Diary Summer 1965*. 1965. Archives of Traditional Music, Indiana University.

Scoppa, Bud. 1973. "Sounds." *Penthouse*. July.

Souther, John David. "If You Don't Want My Love," © 1979 EMI April Music, Inc. (ASCAP).

Springsteen, Bruce. "4th of July, Asbury Park (Sandy)," © 1973 Bruce Springsteen (ASCAP); "Atlantic City," © 1982 Bruce Springsteen (ASCAP); "Born to Run," © 1975 Bruce Springsteen (ASCAP); "Darkness on the Edge of Town," © 1978 Bruce Springsteen (ASCAP); "Drive All Night," © 1980 Bruce Springsteen (ASCAP); "Growin' Up," © 1973 Bruce Springsteen (ASCAP); "Highway Patrolman," © 1982 Bruce Springsteen (ASCAP); "Hungry Heart," © 1980 Bruce Springsteen (ASCAP); "Johnny 99," © 1982 Bruce Springsteen (ASCAP); "Jungleland," © 1975 Bruce Springsteen (ASCAP); "The Price You Pay," © 1980 Bruce Springsteen (ASCAP); "The Promised Land," © 1978 Bruce Springsteen (ASCAP); "Ramrod," © 1980 Bruce Springsteen (ASCAP); "Reason to Believe," © 1982 Bruce Springsteen (ASCAP); "The River," © 1980 Bruce Springsteen (ASCAP); "Stolen Car," © 1980 Bruce Springsteen (ASCAP); "Thunder Road," © 1975

Bruce Springsteen (ASCAP); "The Ties that Bind," © 1980 Bruce Springsteen (ASCAP); "Two Hearts," © 1980 Bruce Springsteen (ASCAP); "Used Cars," © 1982 Bruce Springsteen (ASCAP); "Wreck on the Highway," © 1980 Bruce Springsteen (ASCAP).

Stewart, Rod. "You're in My Heart (The Final Acclaim)," © 1977 Rod Stewart (ASCAP).

Stewart, Rod, and Gary Grainger. "I Was Only Joking," © 1977 EMI Full Keel Music/Rod Stewart (ASCAP); "You Got a Nerve," © 1977 EMI Full Keel Music/Rod Stewart (ASCAP).

Strummer, Joe, and Mick Jones, Paul Simonon, and Topper Headon. "Spanish Bombs," © Nineden Ltd. (ASCAP).

Thau, Marty. Interview with Paul Nelson. 1994.

Thunders, Johnny, and David Johansen. "Jet Boy," © 1973 Seldak LLC/WB Music Corp. (ASCAP).

Touch of Evil. Directed by Orson Welles. Screenplay by Orson Welles (based on the novel *Badge of Evil* by Whit Masterson). 1958. Universal Studios.

Unterberger, Richie. Interview with Paul Nelson. 2001.

Valin, Jonathan. *Final Notice.* 1980. Dodd, Mead and Company.

Ward, Steven. "What Ever Happened to Rock Critic Paul Nelson?" RockCritics.com. March 2000.

Woods, Scott, and Steven Ward. "Sorry Ma, Forgot to Bring in the Trash … Tom Carson Talks Straight." RockCritics.com. April 2002.

Young, Neil. "Cortez the Killer," © 1975 Silver Fiddle Music (ASCAP); "Don't Cry No Tears," © 1975 Silver Fiddle Music (ASCAP); "Lookin' for a Love," © 1975 Silver Fiddle Music (ASCAP); "Pocahontas," © 1979 Silver Fiddle Music (ASCAP); "Powderfinger," © 1979 Silver Fiddle Music (ASCAP); "Through My Sails," © 1975 Silver Fiddle Music (ASCAP); "Will to Love," © 1977 Silver Fiddle Music (ASCAP).

Young, Neil, and Jeff Blackburn. "My My, Hey Hey (Out of the Blue)," © 1979 Silver Fiddle Music (ASCAP).

Zevon, Warren. "Mama Couldn't Be Persuaded," © 1976 Music of Evergreen/Zevon Music (BMI); "Desperados Under the Eaves," © 1976 Darkroom Music/Warner-Tamerlane Publishing Corp. (BMI); "Empty-Handed Heart," © 1980 Music of Evergreen/Zevon Music (BMI); "Frank and Jesse James," © 1976 Darkroom Music/Warner-Tamerlane Publishing Corp. (BMI).

- INDEX -

INDEX

- ABOUT THE AUTHORS -

Kevin Avery's writing has appeared in publications as diverse as *Mississippi Review*, *Penthouse*, *Weber Studies*, and *Salt Lake* magazine. He lives in Brooklyn, New York, with his wife and stepdaughter. This is his first book.

Paul Nelson was, in the words of Bob Dylan, a "folk-music scholar" who in 1965 went electric and pioneered rock criticism. A legendary editor for *Rolling Stone* magazine, he also discovered the New York Dolls.

Nick Tosches is the author of fifteen books of fiction, nonfiction, and poetry. His most recent novel, *In the Hand of Dante*, was selected as a *New York Times* Notable Book of the Year.

- ABOUT THE TYPE -

Caledonia is a transitional serif typeface designed by William Addison Dwiggins in 1938 for the Mergenthaler Linotype Company. With the exception of the very first Lew Archer novel and two Archer omnibuses, all of Ross Macdonald's Knopf novels (including two under his given name, Kenneth Millar) were set in Caledonia. As a small tribute to Paul's love of Ken Millar's work, this book is set in a digital version called New Caledonia, introduced in 1982.

But the angels are older
They can see that the sun's setting fast
They look over my shoulder
At the vision of paradise contained in the light of the past.
                                        —JACKSON BROWNE,
                                                "Farther On"